MEMOIRS
SH
By William T. Sherman
VOLUME II

CHAPTER XVI.
ATLANTA CAMPAIGN-NASHVILLE AND CHATTANOOGA TO BENEBAW.

MARCH, APRIL, AND MAY, 1864.

On the 18th day of March, 1864, at Nashville, Tennessee, I relieved Lieutenant-General Grant in command of the Military Division of the Mississippi, embracing the Departments of the Ohio, Cumberland, Tennessee, and Arkansas, commanded respectively by Major-Generals Schofield, Thomas, McPherson, and Steele. General Grant was in the act of starting East to assume command of all the armies of the United States, but more particularly to give direction in person to the Armies of the Potomac and James, operating against Richmond; and I accompanied him as far as Cincinnati on his way, to avail myself of the opportunity to discuss privately many little details incident to the contemplated changes, and of preparation for the great events then impending. Among these was the intended assignment to duty of many officers of note and influence, who had, by the force of events, drifted into inactivity and discontent. Among these stood prominent Generals McClellan, Burnside, and Fremont, in, the East; and Generals Buell, McCook, Negley, and Crittenden, at the West. My understanding was that General Grant thought it wise and prudent to give all these officers appropriate commands, that would enable them to regain the influence they had lost; and, as a general reorganization of all the armies was then necessary, he directed me to keep in mind especially the claims of Generals Buell, McCook, and Crittenden, and endeavor to give them commands that would be as near their rank and dates of commission as possible; but I was to do nothing until I heard further from him on the subject, as he explained that he would have to consult the Secretary of War before making final orders. General Buell and his officers had been subjected to a long ordeal by a court of inquiry, touching their conduct of the campaign in Tennessee and Kentucky, that resulted in the battle of Perryville, or Chaplin's Hills, October 8,1862, and they had been substantially acquitted; and, as it was manifest that we were to have some hard fighting, we were anxious to bring into harmony every man and every officer of skill in the profession of arms. Of these, Generals Buell and McClellan were prominent in rank, and also by reason of their fame acquired in Mexico, as well as in the earlier part of the civil war.

After my return to Nashville I addressed myself to the task of organization and preparation, which involved the general security of the vast region of the South which had been already conquered, more especially the several routes of supply and communication with the active armies at the front, and to organize a large army to move into Georgia, coincident with the advance of the Eastern armies against Richmond. I soon received from Colonel J. B. Fry—now of the Adjutant-General's Department, but then at Washington in charge of the Provost-Marshal-General's office—a letter asking me to do something for General Buell. I answered him frankly, telling him of my understanding with General Grant, and that I was still awaiting the expected order of the War Department, assigning General Buell to my command. Colonel Fry, as General Buell's special friend, replied that he was very anxious that I should make specific application for the services of General Buell by name, and inquired what I proposed to offer him. To this I answered that, after the agreement with General Grant that he would notify me from Washington, I could not with propriety press the matter, but if General Buell should be assigned to me specifically I was prepared to assign him to command all the troops on the Mississippi River from Cairo to Natchez, comprising about three divisions, or the equivalent of a corps d'armee. General Grant never afterward communicated to me on the subject at all; and I inferred that Mr. Stanton, who was notoriously vindictive in his prejudices, would not consent to the employment of these high officers. General Buell, toward the close of the war, published a bitter political letter, aimed at General Grant, reflecting on his general management of the war, and stated that both Generals Canby and Sherman had offered him a subordinate command, which he had declined because he had once outranked us. This was not true as to me, or Canby either, I think, for both General Canby and I ranked him at West Point and in the old army, and he (General Buell) was only superior to us in the date of his commission as major-general, for a short period in 1862. This newspaper communication, though aimed at General Grant, reacted on himself, for it closed his military career. General Crittenden afterward obtained authority for service, and I offered him a division, but he declined it for the reason, as I understood it, that he had at one time commanded a corps. He is now in the United States service, commanding the Seventeenth Infantry. General McCook obtained a command under General Canby, in the Department of the Gulf, where he rendered good service, and he is also in the regular service, lieutenant-colonel Tenth Infantry.

I returned to Nashville from Cincinnati about the 25th of March, and started at once, in a special car attached to the regular train, to inspect my command at the front, going to Pulaski, Tennessee, where I found General G. M. Dodge; thence to Huntsville, Alabama, where I had left a part of my personal staff and the records of the department during the time we had been absent at Meridian; and there I found General McPherson, who had arrived from Vicksburg, and had assumed command of the Army of the Tennessee. General McPherson accompanied me, and we proceeded by the cars to Stevenson, Bridgeport, etc., to Chattanooga, where we spent a day or two with General George H. Thomas, and then continued on to Knoxville, where was General Schofield. He returned with us to Chattanooga, stopping by the way a few hours at Loudon, where were the headquarters of the Fourth Corps (Major-General Gordon Granger). General Granger, as usual, was full of complaints at the treatment of his corps since I had left him with General Burnside, at Knoxville, the preceding November; and he stated to me personally that he had a leave of absence in his pocket, of which he intended to take advantage very soon. About the end of March, therefore, the three army commanders and myself were together at Chattanooga. We had nothing like a council of war, but conversed freely and frankly on all matters of interest then in progress or impending. We all knew that, as soon as the spring was fairly open, we should have to move directly against our antagonist, General Jos. E. Johnston, then securely intrenched at Dalton, thirty miles distant; and the purpose of our conference at the time was to ascertain our own resources, and to distribute to each part of the army its appropriate share of work. We discussed every possible contingency likely to arise, and I simply instructed each army commander to make immediate preparations for a hard campaign, regulating the distribution of supplies that were coming up by rail from Nashville as equitably as possible. We also agreed on some subordinate changes in the organization of the three separate armies which were destined to take the field; among which was the consolidation of the Eleventh and Twelfth Corps (Howard and Slocum) into a single corps, to be commanded by General Jos. Hooker. General Howard was to be transferred to the Fourth Corps, vice Gordon Granger to avail himself of his leave of absence; and General Slocum was to be ordered down the Mississippi River, to command the District of Vicksburg. These changes required the consent of the President, and were all in due time approved.

The great question of the campaign was one of supplies. Nashville, our chief depot, was itself partially in a hostile country, and even the routes of supply from Louisville to Nashville by rail, and by way of the Cumberland River, had to be guarded. Chattanooga (our starting-point) was one hundred and thirty-six miles in front of Nashville, and every foot of the way, especially the many bridges, trestles, and culverts, had to be strongly guarded against the acts of a local hostile population and of the enemy's cavalry. Then, of course, as we advanced into Georgia, it was manifest that we should have to repair the railroad, use it, and guard it likewise: General Thomas's army was much the largest of the three, was best provided, and contained the best corps of engineers, railroad managers, and repair parties, as well as the best body of spies and provost-marshals. On him we were therefore compelled in a great measure to rely for these most useful branches of service. He had so long exercised absolute command and control over the railroads in his department, that the other armies were jealous, and these thought the Army of the Cumberland got the lion's share of the supplies and other advantages of the railroads. I found a good deal of feeling in the Army of the Tennessee on this score, and therefore took supreme control of the roads myself, placed all the army commanders on an equal footing, and gave to each the same control, so far as orders of transportation for men and stores were concerned. Thomas's spies brought him frequent and accurate reports of Jos. E. Johnston's army at Dalton, giving its strength anywhere between forty and fifty thousand men, and these were being reenforced by troops from Mississippi, and by the Georgia militia, under General G. W. Smith. General Johnston seemed to be acting purely on the defensive, so that we had time and leisure to take all our measures deliberately and fully. I fixed the date of May 1st, when all things should be in readiness for the grand forward movement, and then returned to Nashville; General Schofield going back to Knoxville, and McPherson to Huntsville, Thomas remaining at Chattanooga.

On the 2d of April, at Nashville, I wrote to General Grant, then at Washington, reporting to him the results of my visit to the several armies, and asked his consent to the several changes proposed, which was promptly given by telegraph. I then addressed myself specially to the troublesome question of transportation and supplies. I found the capacity of the railroads from Nashville forward to Decatur, and to Chattanooga, so small, especially in the number of locomotives and care, that it was clear that they were barely able to supply the daily wants of the armies then dependent on them, with no power of accumulating a surplus in advance. The cars were daily loaded down with men returning from furlough, with cattle, horses, etc.; and, by reason of the previous desolation of the country between Chattanooga and Knoxville, General Thomas had authorized the issue of provisions to the suffering inhabitants.

We could not attempt an advance into Georgia without food, ammunition, etc.; and ordinary prudence dictated that we should have an accumulation at the front, in case of interruption to the railway by the act of the enemy, or by common accident. Accordingly, on the 6th of April, I issued a general order, limiting the use of the railroad-cars to transporting only the essential articles of food, ammunition, and supplies for the army proper, forbidding any further issues to citizens, and cutting off all civil traffic; requiring the commanders of posts within thirty miles of Nashville to haul out their own stores in wagons; requiring all troops destined for the front to march, and all beef-cattle to be driven on their own legs. This was a great help, but of course it naturally raised a howl. Some of the poor Union people of East Tennessee appealed to President Lincoln, whose kind heart responded promptly to their request. He telegraphed me to know if I could not modify or repeal my orders; but I answered him that a great campaign was impending, on which the fate of the nation hung; that our railroads had but a limited capacity, and could not provide for the necessities of the army and of the people too;

that one or the other must quit, and we could not until the army of Jos. Johnston was conquered, etc., etc. Mr. Lincoln seemed to acquiesce, and I advised the people to obtain and drive out cattle from Kentucky, and to haul out their supplies by the wagon-road from the same quarter, by way of Cumberland Gap. By these changes we nearly or quite doubled our daily accumulation of stores at the front, and yet even this was not found enough.

I accordingly called together in Nashville the master of transportation, Colonel Anderson, the chief quartermaster, General J. L. Donaldson, and the chief commissary, General Amos Beckwith, for conference. I assumed the strength of the army to move from Chattanooga into Georgia at one hundred thousand men, and the number of animals to be fed, both for cavalry and draught, at thirty-five thousand; then, allowing for occasional wrecks of trains, which were very common, and for the interruption of the road itself by guerrillas and regular raids, we estimated it would require one hundred and thirty cars, of ten tons each, to reach Chattanooga daily, to be reasonably certain of an adequate supply. Even with this calculation, we could not afford to bring forward hay for the horses and mules, nor more than five pounds of oats or corn per day for each animal. I was willing to risk the question of forage in part, because I expected to find wheat and corn fields, and a good deal of grass, as we advanced into Georgia at that season of the year. The problem then was to deliver at Chattanooga and beyond one hundred and thirty car-loads daily, leaving the beef-cattle to be driven on the hoof, and all the troops in excess of the usual train-guards to march by the ordinary roads. Colonel Anderson promptly explained that he did not possess cars or locomotives enough to do this work. I then instructed and authorized him to hold on to all trains that arrived at Nashville from Louisville, and to allow none to go back until he had secured enough to fill the requirements of our problem. At the time he only had about sixty serviceable locomotives, and about six hundred cars of all kinds, and he represented that to provide for all contingencies he must have at least one hundred locomotives and one thousand cars. As soon as Mr. Guthrie, the President of the Louisville & Nashville Railroad, detected that we were holding on to all his locomotives and cars, he wrote me, earnestly remonstrating against it, saying that he would not be able with diminished stock to bring forward the necessary stores from Louisville to Nashville. I wrote to him, frankly telling him exactly how we were placed, appealed to his patriotism to stand by us, and advised him in like manner to hold on to all trains coming into Jeffersonville, Indiana. He and General Robert Allen, then quartermaster-general at Louisville, arranged a ferry-boat so as to transfer the trains over the Ohio River from Jeffersonville, and in a short time we had cars and locomotives from almost every road at the North; months afterward I was amused to see, away down in Georgia, cars marked "Pittsburg & Fort Wayne," "Delaware & Lackawanna," "Baltimore & Ohio," and indeed with the names of almost every railroad north of the Ohio River. How these railroad companies ever recovered their property, or settled their transportation accounts, I have never heard, but to this fact, as much as to any other single fact, I attribute the perfect success which afterward attended our campaigns; and I have always felt grateful to Mr. Guthrie, of Louisville, who had sense enough and patriotism enough to subordinate the interests of his railroad company to the cause of his country.

About this time, viz., the early part of April, I was much disturbed by a bold raid made by the rebel General Forrest up between the Mississippi and Tennessee Rivers. He reached the Ohio River at Paducah, but was handsomely repulsed by Colonel Hicks. He then swung down toward Memphis, assaulted and carried Fort Pillow, massacring a part of its garrison, composed wholly of negro troops. At first I discredited the story of the massacre, because, in preparing for the Meridian campaign, I had ordered Fort Pillow to be evacuated, but it transpired afterward that General Hurlbut had retained a small garrison at Fort Pillow to encourage the enlistment of the blacks as soldiers, which was a favorite political policy at that day. The massacre at Fort Pillow occurred April 12, 1864, and has been the subject of congressional inquiry. No doubt Forrest's men acted like a set of barbarians, shooting down the helpless negro garrison after the fort was in their possession; but I am told that Forrest personally disclaims any active participation in the assault, and that he stopped the firing as soon as he could. I also take it for granted that Forrest did not lead the assault in person, and consequently that he was to the rear, out of sight if not of hearing at the time, and I was told by hundreds of our men, who were at various times prisoners in Forrest's possession, that he was usually very kind to them. He had a desperate set of fellows under him, and at that very time there is no doubt the feeling of the Southern people was fearfully savage on this very point of our making soldiers out of their late slaves, and Forrest may have shared the feeling.

I also had another serious cause of disturbance about that time. I wanted badly the two divisions of troops which had been loaned to General Banks in the month of March previously, with the express understanding that their absence was to endure only one month, and that during April they were to come out of Red River, and be again within the sphere of my command. I accordingly instructed one of my inspector-generals, John M. Corse, to take a fleet steamboat at Nashville, proceed via Cairo, Memphis, and Vicksburg, to General Banks up the Red River, and to deliver the following letter of April 3d, as also others, of like tenor, to Generals A. J. Smith and Fred Steele, who were supposed to be with him:

HEADQUARTERS MILITARY DIVISION OF THE MISSISSIPPI
NASHVILLE, TENNESSEE, April 3, 1864

Major-General N. P. BANKS, commanding Department of the Gulf, Red River.

3

GENERAL: The thirty days for which I loaned you the command of General A. J. Smith will expire on the 10th instant. I send with this Brigadier-General J. M. Corse, to carry orders to General A. J. Smith, and to give directions for a new movement, which is preliminary to the general campaign. General Corse may see you and explain in full, but, lest he should not find you in person, I will simply state that Forrest, availing himself of the absence of our furloughed men and of the detachment with you, has pushed up between the Mississippi and Tennessee Rivers, even to the Ohio. He attacked Paducah, but got the worst of it, and he still lingers about the place. I hope that he will remain thereabouts till General A. J. Smith can reach his destined point, but this I can hardly expect; yet I want him to reach by the Yazoo a position near Grenada, thence to operate against Forrest, after which to march across to Decatur, Alabama. You will see that he has a big job, and therefore should start at once. From all that I can learn, my troops reached Alexandria, Louisiana, at the time agreed on, viz., March 17th, and I hear of them at Natchitoches, but cannot hear of your troops being above Opelousas.

Steele is also moving. I leave Steele's entire force to cooperate with you and the navy, but, as I before stated, I must have A. T. Smith's troops now as soon as possible.

I beg you will expedite their return to Vicksburg, if they have not already started, and I want them if possible to remain in the same boats they have used up Red River, as it will save the time otherwise consumed in transfer to other boats.

All is well in this quarter, and I hope by the time you turn against Mobile our forces will again act toward the same end, though from distant points. General Grant, now having lawful control, will doubtless see that all minor objects are disregarded, and that all the armies act on a common plan.

Hoping, when this reaches you, that you will be in possession of Shreveport, I am, with great respect, etc.,

W. T. SHERMAN, Major-General commanding.

Rumors were reaching us thick and fast of defeat and disaster in that quarter; and I feared then, what afterward actually happened, that neither General Banks nor Admiral Porter could or would spare those two divisions. On the 23d of April, General Corse returned, bringing full answers to my letters, and I saw that we must go on without them. This was a serious loss to the Army of the Tennessee, which was also short by two other divisions that were on their veteran furlough, and were under orders to rendezvous at Cairo, before embarking for Clifton, on the Tennessee River.

On the 10th of April, 1864, the headquarters of the three Armies of the Cumberland, Tennessee, and Ohio, were at Chattanooga., Huntsville, and Knoxville, and the tables on page 16, et seq., give their exact condition and strength.

The Department of the Arkansas was then subject to my command, but General Fred Steele, its commander, was at Little Rock, remote from me, acting in cooperation with General Banks, and had full employment for every soldier of his command; so that I never depended on him for any men, or for any participation in the Georgia campaign. Soon after, viz., May 8th, that department was transferred to the Military Division of "the Gulf," or "Southwest," Major-General E. R. S. Canby commanding, and General Steele served with him in the subsequent movement against Mobile.

In Generals Thomas, McPherson, and Schofield, I had three generals of education and experience, admirably qualified for the work before us. Each has made a history of his own, and I need not here dwell on their respective merits as men, or as commanders of armies, except that each possessed special qualities of mind and of character which fitted them in the highest degree for the work then in contemplation.

By the returns of April 10, 1864, it will be seen that the Army of the Cumberland had on its muster-rolls—

	Men
Present and absent	171,450
Present for duty	88,883

The Army of the Tennessee

Present and absent	134,763

4

Present for duty   6 4,957

The Army of the Ohio

Present and absent   4 6,052

Present for duty   2 6,242

The department and army commanders had to maintain strong garrisons in their respective departments, and also to guard their respective lines of supply. I therefore, in my mind, aimed to prepare out of these three armies, by the 1st of May, 1864, a compact army for active operations in Georgia, of about the following numbers:

Army of the Cumberland	5 0,000
Army of the Tennessee	3 5,000
Army of the Ohio	1 5,000
Total	1 00,000

and, to make these troops as mobile as possible, I made the strictest possible orders in relation to wagons and all species of incumbrances and impedimenta whatever. Each officer and soldier was required to carry on his horse or person food and clothing enough for five days. To each regiment was allowed but one wagon and one ambulance, and to the officers of each company one pack horse or mule.

Each division and brigade was provided a fair proportion of wagons for a supply train, and these were limited in their loads to carry food, ammunition, and clothing. Tents were forbidden to all save the sick and wounded, and one tent only was allowed to each headquarters for use as an office. These orders were not absolutely enforced, though in person I set the example, and did not have a tent, nor did any officer about me have one; but we had wall tent-flies, without poles, and no tent-furniture of any kind. We usually spread our flies over saplings, or on fence-rails or posts improvised on the spot. Most of the general officers, except Thomas, followed my example strictly; but he had a regular headquarters-camp. I frequently called his attention to the orders on this subject, rather jestingly than seriously. He would break out against his officers for having such luxuries, but, needing a tent himself, and being good-natured and slow to act, he never enforced my orders perfectly. In addition to his regular wagon-train, he had a big wagon which could be converted into an office, and this we used to call "Thomas's circus." Several times during the campaign I found quartermasters hid away in some comfortable nook to the rear, with tents and mess-fixtures which were the envy of the passing soldiers; and I frequently broke them up, and distributed the tents to the surgeons of brigades. Yet my orders actually reduced the transportation, so that I doubt if any army ever went forth to battle with fewer impedimenta, and where the regular and necessary supplies of food, ammunition, and clothing, were issued, as called for, so regularly and so well.

My personal staff was then composed of Captain J. C. McCoy, aide-de-camp; Captain L. M. Dayton, aide-de-camp; Captain J. C. Audenried, aide-de-camp; Brigadier-General J. D. Webster, chief of staff; Major R. M. Sawyer, assistant adjutant-general; Captain Montgomery Rochester, assistant adjutant-general. These last three were left at Nashville in charge of the office, and were empowered to give orders in my name, communication being generally kept up by telegraph.

Subsequently were added to my staff, and accompanied me in the field, Brigadier-General W. F. Barry, chief of artillery; Colonel O. M. Poe, chief of engineers; Colonel L. C. Easton, chief quartermaster; Colonel Amos Beckwith, chief commissary; Captain Thos. G. Baylor, chief of ordnance; Surgeon E. D. Kittoe, medical director; Brigadier-General J. M. Corse, inspector-general; Lieutenant-Colonel C. Ewing, inspector-general; and Lieutenant-Colonel Willard Warner, inspector-general.

These officers constituted my staff proper at the beginning of the campaign, which remained substantially the same till the close of the war, with very few exceptions; viz.: Surgeon John Moore, United States Army, relieved Surgeon Kittoe of the volunteers (about Atlanta) as medical director; Major Henry Hitchcock joined as judge-advocate, and Captain G. Ward Nichols reported as an extra aide-de-camp (after the fall of Atlanta) at Gaylesville, just before we started for Savannah.

During the whole month of April the preparations for active war were going on with extreme vigor, and my letter-book shows an active correspondence with Generals Grant, Halleck, Thomas, McPherson, and Schofield on thousands of matters of detail and arrangement, most of which are embraced in my testimony before the Committee on the Conduct of the War, vol. i., Appendix.

When the time for action approached, viz., May 1,1864, the actual armies prepared to move into Georgia resulted as follows, present for battle:

en

Army of the Cumberland, Major-General THOMAS

Infantry	4,568
Artillery	,377
Cavalry	,828
Aggregate	0,773
Number of field-guns,	30

Army of the Tennessee, Major-General McPHERSON

Infantry	2,437
Artillery	,404
Cavalry	24
Aggregate	4,465
Guns,	6

Army of the Ohio, Major-General SCHOFIELD

Infantry	11,183
Artillery	679
Cavalry	1,697
Aggregate	13,559
Guns,	28

Grand aggregate   **98,797 men and 254 guns**

These figures do not embrace the cavalry divisions which were still incomplete, viz., of General Stoneman, at Lexington, Kentucky, and of General Garrard, at Columbia, Tennessee, who were then rapidly collecting horses, and joined us in the early stage of the campaign. General Stoneman, having a division of about four thousand men and horses, was attached to Schofield's Army of the Ohio. General Garrard's division, of about four thousand five hundred men and horses, was attached to General Thomas's command; and he had another irregular division of cavalry, commanded by Brigadier-General E. McCook. There was also a small brigade of cavalry, belonging to the Army of the Cumberland, attached temporarily to the Army of the Tennessee, which was commanded by Brigadier-General Judson Kilpatrick. These cavalry commands changed constantly in strength and numbers, and were generally used on the extreme flanks, or for some special detached service, as will be herein-after related. The Army of the Tennessee was still short by the two divisions detached with General Banks, up Red River, and two other divisions on furlough in Illinois, Indiana, and Ohio, but which were rendezvousing at Cairo, under Generals Leggett and Crocker, to form a part of the Seventeenth Corps, which corps was to be commanded by Major-General Frank P. Blair, then a member of Congress, in Washington. On the 2d of April I notified him by letter that I wanted him to join and to command these two divisions, which ought to be ready by the 1st of May. General Blair, with these two divisions, constituting the Seventeenth Army Corps, did not actually overtake us until we reached Acworth and Big Shanty, in Georgia, about the 9th of June, 1864.

In my letter of April 4th to General John A. Rawains, chief of staff to General Grant at Washington, I described at length all the preparations that were in progress for the active campaign thus contemplated, and therein estimated Schofield at twelve thousand, Thomas at forty-five thousand, and McPherson at thirty thousand. At first I intended to open the campaign about May 1st, by moving Schofield on Dalton from Cleveland, Thomas on the same objective from Chattanooga, and McPherson on Rome and Kingston from Gunter's Landing. My intention was merely to threaten Dalton in front, and to direct McPherson to act vigorously against the railroad below Resaca, far to the rear of the enemy. But by reason of his being short of his estimated strength by the four divisions before referred to, and thus being reduced to about twenty-four thousand men, I did not feel justified in placing him so far away from the support of the main body of the army, and therefore subsequently changed the plan of campaign, so far as to bring that army up to Chattanooga, and to direct it thence through Ship's Gap against the railroad to Johnston's rear, at or near Resaca, distant from Dalton only eighteen miles, and in full communication with the other armies by roads behind Rocky face Ridge, of about the same length.

On the 10th of April I received General Grant's letter of April 4th from Washington, which formed the basis of all the campaigns of the year 1864, and subsequently received another of April 19th, written from Culpepper, Virginia, both of which are now in my possession, in his own handwriting, and are here given entire. These letters embrace substantially all the orders he ever made on this particular subject, and these, it will be seen, devolved on me the details both as to the plan and execution of the campaign by the armies under my immediate command. These armies were to be directed against the rebel army commanded by General Joseph E. Johnston, then lying on the defensive, strongly intrenched at Dalton, Georgia; and I was required to follow it up closely and persistently, so that in no event could any part be detached to assist General Lee in Virginia; General Grant undertaking in like manner to keep Lee so busy that he could not respond to any calls of help by Johnston. Neither Atlanta, nor Augusta, nor Savannah, was the objective, but the "army of Jos. Johnston," go where it might.

HEADQUARTERS ARMIES OF THE UNITED STATES WASHINGTON D. C., April 4, 1864.

Major-General W. T. SHERMAN, commanding Military Division of the Mississippi.

GENERAL: It is my design, if the enemy keep quiet and allow me to take the initiative in the spring campaign, to work all parts of the army together, and somewhat toward a common centre. For your information I now write you my programme, as at present determined upon.

I have sent orders to Banks, by private messenger, to finish up his present expedition against Shreveport with all dispatch; to turn over the defense of Red River to General Steels and the navy, and to return your troops to you, and his own to New Orleans; to abandon all of Texas, except the Rio Grande, and to hold that with not to exceed four thousand men; to reduce the number of troops on the Mississippi to the lowest number necessary to hold it, and to collect from his command not less than twenty-five thousand men. To this I will add five thousand from Missouri. With this force he is to commence operations against Mobile as soon as he can. It will be impossible for him to commence too early.

Gillmore joins Butler with ten thousand men, and the two operate against Richmond from the south aide of James River. This will give Butler thirty-three thousand men to operate with, W. F. Smith commanding the right wing of his forces, and Gillmore the left wing. I will stay with the Army of the Potomac, increased by Burnside's corps of not less than twenty-five thousand effective men, and operate directly against Lee's army, wherever it may be found.

Sigel collects all his available force in two columns, one, under Ord and Averill, to start from Beverly, Virginia, and the other, under Crook, to start from Charleston, on the Kanawha, to move against the Virginia & Tennessee Railroad.

Crook will have all cavalry, and will endeavor to get in about Saltville, and move east from there to join Ord. His force will be all cavalry, while Ord will have from ten to twelve thousand men of all arms.

You I propose to move against Johnston's army, to break it up, and to get into the interior of the enemy's country as far as you can, inflicting all the damage you can against their war resources.

I do not propose to lay down for you a plan of campaign, but simply to lay down the work it is desirable to have done, and leave you free to execute it in your own way. Submit to me, however, as early as you can, your plan of operations.

As stated, Banks is ordered to commence operations as soon as he can. Gillmore is ordered to report at Fortress Monroe by the 18th inst., or as soon thereafter as practicable. Sigel is concentrating now. None will move from their places of rendezvous until I direct, except Banks. I want to be ready to move by the 25th inst., if possible; but all I can now direct is that you get ready as soon as possible. I know you will have difficulties to encounter in getting through the mountains to where supplies are abundant, but I believe you will accomplish it.

From the expedition from the Department of West Virginia I do not calculate on very great results; but it is the only way I can take troops from there. With the long line of railroad Sigel has to protect, he can spare no troops, except to move directly to his front. In this way he must get through to inflict great damage on the enemy, or the enemy must detach from one of his armies a large force to prevent it. In other words, if Sigel can't skin himself, he can hold a leg while some one else skins.

I am, general, very respectfully, your obedient servant, U. S. GRANT, Lieutenant-General.

HEADQUARTERS MILITARY DIVISION OF THE MISSISSIPPI NASHVILLE, TENNESSEE, April 10, 1864

Lieutenant-General U. S. GRANT, Commander-in-Chief, Washington, D.

DEAR GENERAL: Your two letters of April 4th are now before me, and afford me infinite satisfaction. That we are now all to act on a common plan, converging on a common centre, looks like enlightened war.

Like yourself, you take the biggest load, and from me you shall have thorough and hearty cooperation. I will not let side issues draw me off from your main plans in which I am to knock Jos. Johnston, and to do as much damage to the resources of the enemy as possible. I have heretofore written to General Rawlins and to Colonel Comstock (of your staff) somewhat of the method in which I propose to act. I have seen all my army, corps, and division commanders, and have signified only to the former, viz., Schofield, Thomas, and McPherson, our general plans, which I inferred from the purport of our conversation here and at Cincinnati.

First, I am pushing stores to the front with all possible dispatch, and am completing the army organization according to the orders from Washington, which are ample and perfectly satisfactory.

It will take us all of April to get in our furloughed veterans, to bring up A. J. Smith's command, and to collect provisions and cattle on the line of the Tennessee. Each of the armies will guard, by detachments of its own, its rear communications.

At the signal to be given by you, Schofield, leaving a select garrison at Knoxville and London, with twelve thousand men will drop down to the Hiawassee, and march against Johnston's right by the old Federal road. Stoneman, now in Kentucky, organizing the cavalry forces of the Army of the Ohio, will operate with Schofield on his left front—it may be, pushing a select body of about two thousand cavalry by Ducktown or Elijah toward Athens, Georgia.

Thomas will aim to have forty-five thousand men of all arms, and move straight against Johnston, wherever he may be, fighting him cautiously, persistently, and to the best advantage. He will have two divisions of cavalry, to take advantage of any offering.

McPherson will have nine divisions of the Army of the Tennessee, if A. J. Smith gets here, in which case he will have full thirty thousand of the best men in America. He will cross the Tennessee at Decatur and Whitesburg, march toward Rome, and feel for Thomas. If Johnston falls behind the Coosa, then McPherson will push for Rome; and if Johnston falls behind the Chattahoochee, as I believe he will, then McPherson will cross over and join Thomas.

McPherson has no cavalry, but I have taken one of Thomas's divisions, viz., Garrard's, six thousand strong, which is now at Colombia, mounting, equipping, and preparing. I design this division to operate on McPherson's right, rear, or front, according as the enemy appears. But the moment I detect Johnston falling behind the Chattahoochee, I propose to cast off the effective part of this cavalry division, after crossing the Coosa, straight for Opelika, West Point, Columbus, or Wetumpka, to break up the road between Montgomery and Georgia. If Garrard can do this work well, he can return to the Union army; but should a superior force interpose, then he will seek safety at Pensacola and join Banks, or, after rest, will act against any force that he can find east of Mobile, till such time as he can reach me.

Should Johnston fall behind the Chattahoochee, I will feign to the right, but pass to the left and act against Atlanta or its eastern communications, according to developed facts.

This is about as far ahead as I feel disposed, to look, but I will ever bear in mind that Johnston is at all times to be kept so busy that he cannot in any event send any part of his command against you or Banks.

If Banks can at the same time carry Mobile and open up the Alabama River, he will in a measure solve the most difficult part of my problem, viz., "provisions." But in that I must venture. Georgia has a million of inhabitants. If they can live, we should not starve. If the enemy interrupt our communications, I will be absolved from all obligations to subsist on our own resources, and will feel perfectly justified in taking whatever and wherever we can find. I will inspire my command, if successful, with the feeling that beef and salt are all that is absolutely necessary to life, and that parched corn once fed General Jackson's army on that very ground. As ever, your friend and servant,

W. T. SHERMAN, Major-General.

HEADQUARTERS ARMIES OF THE UNITED STATES CULPEPPER COURT HOUSE, VIRGINIA, April 19, 1864.

Major-General W. T. SHERMAN, commanding Military Division of the Mississippi.

GENERAL: Since my letter to you of April 4th I have seen no reason to change any portion of the general plan of campaign, if the enemy remain still and allow us to take the initiative. Rain has continued so uninterruptedly until the last day or two that it will be impossible to move, however, before the 27th, even if no more should fall in the meantime. I think Saturday, the 30th, will probably be the day for our general move.

Colonel Comstock, who will take this, can spend a day with you, and fill up many little gaps of information not given in any of my letters.

What I now want more particularly to say is, that if the two main attacks, yours and the one from here, should promise great success, the enemy may, in a fit of desperation, abandon one part of their line of defense, and throw their whole strength upon the other, *believing a single defeat without any victory to sustain them better than a defeat all along their line, and hoping too, at the same time, that the army, meeting with no resistance, will rest perfectly satisfied with their laurels, having penetrated to a given point south, thereby enabling them to throw their force first upon one and then on the other.*

With the majority of military commanders they might do this.

But you have had too much experience in traveling light, and subsisting upon the country, to be caught by any such ruse. I hope my experience has not been thrown away. My directions, then, would be, if the enemy in your front show signs of joining Lee, follow him up to the full extent of your ability. I will prevent the concentration of Lee upon your front, if it is in the power of this army to do it.

The Army of the Potomac looks well, and, so far as I can judge, officers and men feel well. Yours truly,

U. S. GRANT, Lieutenant-General.

HEADQUARTERS MILITARY DIVISION OF THE MISSISSIPPI NASHVILLE, TENNESSEE, April 24, 1864

Lieutenant-General U. S. GRANT, Commander-in-Chief, Culpepper, Virginia

GENERAL: I now have, at the hands of Colonel Comstock, of your staff, the letter of April 19th, and am as far prepared to assume the offensive as possible. I only ask as much time as you think proper, to enable me to get up McPherson's two divisions from Cairo. Their furloughs will expire about this time, and some of them should now be in motion for Clifton, whence they will march to Decatur, to join General Dodge.

McPherson is ordered to assemble the Fifteenth Corps near Larkin's, and to get the Sixteenth and Seventeenth Corps (Dodge and Blair) at Decatur at the earliest possible moment. From these two points he will direct his forces on Lebanon, Summerville, and Lafayette, where he will act against Johnston, if he accept battle at Dalton; or move in the direction of Rome, if the enemy give up Dalton, and fall behind the Oostenaula or Etowah. I see that there is some risk in dividing our forces, but Thomas and Schofield will have strength enough to cover all the valleys as far as Dalton; and, should Johnston turn his whole force against McPherson, the latter will have his bridge at Larkin's, and the route to Chattanooga via Willa's Valley and the Chattanooga Creek, open for retreat; and if Johnston attempt to leave Dalton, Thomas will have force enough to push on through Dalton to Kingston, which will checkmate him. My own opinion is that Johnston will be compelled to hang to his railroad, the only possible avenue of supply to his army, estimated at from forty-five to sixty thousand men.

At Lafayette all our armies will be together, and if Johnston stands at Dalton we must attack him in position. Thomas feels certain that he has no material increase of force, and that he has not sent away Hardee, or any part of his army. Supplies are the great question. I have materially increased the number of cars daily. When I got here, the average was from sixty-five to eighty per day. Yesterday the report was one hundred and ninety-three; to-day, one hundred and thirty-four; and my estimate is that one hundred and forty-five cars per day will give us a day's supply and a day's accumulation.

McPherson is ordered to carry in wagons twenty day's rations, and to rely on the depot at Ringgold for the renewal of his bread. Beeves are now being driven on the hoof to the front; and the commissary, Colonel Beckwith, seems fully alive to the importance of the whole matter.

Our weakest point will be from the direction of Decatur, and I will be forced to risk something from that quarter, depending on the fact that the enemy has no force available with which to threaten our communications from that direction.

Colonel Comstock will explain to you personally much that I cannot commit to paper. I am, with great respect,

W. T. SHERMAN, Major-General.

On the 28th of April I removed my headquarters to Chattanooga, and prepared for taking the field in person. General Grant had first indicated the 30th of April as the day for the simultaneous advance, but subsequently changed the day to May 5th. McPhersons troops were brought forward rapidly to Chattanooga, partly by rail and partly by marching. Thomas's troops were already in position (his advance being out as far as Ringgold-eighteen miles), and Schofield was marching down by Cleveland to Red Clay and Catoosa Springs. On the 4th of May, Thomas was in person at Ringgold, his left at Catoosa, and his right at Leet's Tan-yard. Schofield was at Red Clay, closing upon Thomas's left; and McPherson was moving rapidly into Chattanooga, and out toward Gordon's Mill.

On the 5th I rode out to Ringgold, and on the very day appointed by General Grant from his headquarters in Virginia the great campaign was begun. To give all the minute details will involve more than is contemplated, and I will endeavor only to trace the principal events, or rather to record such as weighed heaviest on my own mind at the time, and which now remain best fixed in my memory.

My general headquarters and official records remained back at Nashville, and I had near me only my personal staff and inspectors-general, with about half a dozen wagons, and a single company of Ohio sharp-shooters (commanded by Lieutenant McCrory) as headquarters or camp guard. I also had a small company of irregular Alabama cavalry (commanded by Lieutenant Snelling), used mostly as orderlies and couriers. No wall-tents were allowed, only the flies. Our mess establishment was less in bulk than that of any of the brigade commanders; nor was this from an indifference to the ordinary comforts of life, but because I wanted to set the example, and gradually to convert all parts of that army into a mobile machine, willing and able to start at a minute's notice, and to subsist on the scantiest food. To reap absolute success might involve the necessity even of dropping all wagons, and to subsist on the chance food which the country was known to contain. I had obtained not only the United States census-tables of 1860, but a compilation made by the Controller of the State of Georgia for the purpose of taxation, containing in considerable detail the "population and statistics" of every county in Georgia. One of my aides (Captain Dayton) acted as assistant adjutant general, with an order-book, letter-book, and writing-paper, that filled a small chest not much larger than an ordinary candle-boa. The only reports and returns called for were the ordinary tri-monthly returns of "effective strength." As these accumulated they were sent back to Nashville, and afterward were embraced in the archives of the Military Division of the Mississippi, changed in 1865 to the Military Division of the Missouri, and I suppose they were burned in the Chicago fire of 1870. Still, duplicates remain of all essential papers in the archives of the War Department.

The 6th of May was given to Schofield and McPherson to get into position, and on the 7th General Thomas moved in force against Tunnel Hill, driving off a mere picket-guard of the enemy, and I was agreeably surprised to find that no damage had been done to the tunnel or the railroad. From Tunnel Hill I could look into the gorge by which the railroad passed through a straight and well-defined range of mountains, presenting sharp palisade faces, and known as "Rocky Face." The gorge itself was called the "Buzzard Roost." We could plainly see the enemy in this gorge and behind it, and Mill Creek which formed the gorge, flowing toward Dalton, had been dammed up, making a sort of irregular lake, filling the road, thereby obstructing it, and the enemy's batteries crowned the cliffs on either side. The position was very strong, and I knew that such a general as was my antagonist (Jos. Johnston), who had been there six months, had fortified it to the maximum. Therefore I had no intention to attack the position seriously in front, but depended on McPherson to capture and hold the railroad to its rear, which would force Johnston to detach largely against him, or rather, as I expected, to evacuate his position at Dalton altogether. My orders to Generals Thomas and Schofield were merely to press strongly at all points in front, ready to rush in on the first appearance of "let go," and, if possible, to catch our enemy in the confusion of retreat.

All the movements of the 7th and 8th were made exactly as ordered, and the enemy seemed quiescent, acting purely on the defensive.

I had constant communication with all parts of the army, and on the 9th McPherson's head of column entered and passed through Snake Creek, perfectly undefended, and accomplished a complete surprise to the enemy. At its farther debouche he met a cavalry brigade, easily driven, which retreated hastily north toward Dalton, and doubtless carried to Johnston the first serious intimation that a heavy force of infantry and artillery was to his rear and within a few miles of his railroad. I got a short note from McPherson that day (written at 2 p.m., when he was within a mile and a half of the railroad, above and near Resaca), and we all felt jubilant. I renewed orders to Thomas and Schofield to be ready for the instant pursuit of what I expected to be a broken and disordered army, forced to retreat by roads to the east of Resaca, which were known to be very rough and impracticable.

That night I received further notice from McPherson that he had found Resaca too strong for a surprise; that in consequence he had fallen back three miles to the month of Snake Creek Gap, and was there fortified. I wrote him the next day the following letters, copies of which are in my letter-book; but his to me were mere notes in pencil, not retained.

HEADQUARTERS MILITARY DIVISION OF THE MISSISSIPPI IN THE FIELD, TUNNEL HILL, GEORGIA, May 11, 1864

Major-General McPHERSON, commanding army of the Tennessee, Sugar Valley, Georgia.

GENERAL: I received by courier (in the night) yours of 5 and 8.30 P. M. of yesterday.

You now have your twenty-three thousand men, and General Hooker is in close support, so that you can hold all of Jos. Johnston's army in check should he abandon Dalton. He cannot afford to abandon Dalton, for he has fixed it up on purpose to receive us, and he observes that we are close at hand, waiting for him to quit. He cannot afford a detachment strong enough to fight you, as his army will not admit of it.

Strengthen your position; fight any thing that comes; and threaten the safety of the railroad all the time. But, to tell the truth, I would rather the enemy would stay in Dalton two more days, when he may find in his rear a larger party than he expects in an open field. At all events, we can then choose our own ground, and he will be forced to move out of his works. I do not intend to put a column into Buzzard-Roost Gap at present.

See that you are in easy communication with me and with all head-quarters. After to-day the supplies will be at Ringgold. Yours, W. T. SHERMAN, Major-General commanding.

HEADQUARTERS MILITARY DIVISION OF THE MISSISSIPPI IN THE FIELD, TUNNEL HILL, GEORGIA, May 11, 1864-Evening

Major-General McPHERSON, commanding army of the Tennessee, Sugar Valley, Georgia

GENERAL: The indications are that Johnston is evacuating Dalton. In that event, Howard's corps and the cavalry will pursue; all the rest will follow your route. I will be down early in the morning.

Try to strike him if possible about the forks of the road.

Hooker must be with you now, and you may send General Garrard by Summerville to threaten Rome and that flank. I will cause all the lines to be felt at once.

W. T. SHERMAN, major-general commanding.

McPherson had startled Johnston in his fancied security, but had not done the full measure of his work. He had in hand twenty-three thousand of the best men of the army, and could have walked into Resaca (then held only by a small brigade), or he could have placed his whole force astride the railroad above Resaca, and there have easily withstood the attack of all of Johnston's army, with the knowledge that Thomas and Schofield were on his heels. Had he done so, I am certain that Johnston would not have ventured to attack him in position, but would have retreated eastward by Spring Place, and we should have captured half his army and all his artillery and wagons at the very beginning of the campaign.

Such an opportunity does not occur twice in a single life, but at the critical moment McPherson seems to have been a little cautious. Still, he was perfectly justified by his orders, and fell back and assumed an unassailable defensive position in Sugar Valley, on the Resaca side of Snake-Creek Gap. As soon as informed of this, I determined to pass the whole army through Snake-Creek Gap, and to move on Resaca with the main army.

But during the 10th, the enemy showed no signs of evacuating Dalton, and I was waiting for the arrival of Garrard's and Stoneman's cavalry, known to be near at hand, so as to secure the full advantages of victory, of which I felt certain. Hooker's Twentieth Corps was at once moved down to within easy supporting distance of McPherson; and on the 11th, perceiving signs of evacuation of Dalton, I gave all the orders for the general movement, leaving the Fourth Corps (Howard) and Stoneman's cavalry in observation in front of Buzzard-Roost Gap, and directing all the rest of the army to march through Snake-Creek Gap, straight on Resaca. The roads were only such as the country afforded, mere rough wagon-ways, and these converged to the single narrow track through Snake-Creek Gap; but during the 12th and 13th the bulk of Thomas's and Schofield's armies were got through, and deployed against Resaca, McPherson on the right, Thomas in the centre, and Schofield on the left. Johnston, as I anticipated, had abandoned all his well-prepared defenses at Dalton, and was found inside of Resaca with the bulk of his army, holding his divisions well in hand, acting purely on the defensive, and fighting well at all points of conflict. A complete line of intrenchments was found covering the place, and this was strongly manned at all points. On the 14th we closed in, enveloping the town on its north and west, and during the 15th we had a day of continual battle and skirmish. At the same time I caused two pontoon-bridges to be laid across the Oostenaula River at Lay's Ferry, about three miles below the town, by which we could threaten Calhoun, a station on the railroad seven miles below Resaca. At the same time, May 14th, I dispatched General Garrard, with his cavalry division, down the Oostenaula by the Rome road, with orders to cross over, if possible, and to attack or threaten the railroad at any point below Calhoun and above Kingston.

During the 15th, without attempting to assault the fortified works, we pressed at all points, and the sound of cannon and musketry rose all day to the dignity of a battle. Toward evening McPherson moved his whole line of battle forward, till he had gained a ridge overlooking the town, from which his field-artillery could reach the railroad-bridge across the Oostenaula. The enemy made several attempts to drive him away, repeating the sallies several times, and extending them into the night; but in every instance he was repulsed with bloody loss.

Hooker's corps had also some heavy and handsome fighting that afternoon and night on the left, where the Dalton roan entered the intrenchments, capturing a four-gun intrenched battery, with its men and guns; and generally all our men showed the finest fighting qualities.

Howard's corps had followed Johnston down from Dalton, and was in line; Stoneman's division of cavalry had also got up, and was on the extreme left, beyond the Oostenaula.

On the night of May 15th Johnston got his army across the bridges, set them on fire, and we entered Resaca at daylight. Our loss up to that time was about six hundred dead and thirty-three hundred and seventy-five wounded—mostly light wounds that did not necessitate sending the men to the rear for treatment. That Johnston had deliberately designed in advance to give up such strong positions as Dalton and Resaca, for the purpose of drawing us farther south, is simply absurd. Had he remained in Dalton another hour, it would have been his total defeat, and he only evacuated Resaca because his safety demanded it. The movement by us through Snake-Creek Gap was a total surprise to him. My army about doubled his in size, but he had all the advantages of natural positions, of artificial forts and roads, and of concentrated action. We were compelled to grope our way through forests, across mountains, with a large army, necessarily more or less dispersed. Of course, I was disappointed not to have crippled his army more at that particular stage of the game; but, as it resulted, these rapid successes gave us the initiative, and the usual impulse of a conquering army.

Johnston having retreated in the night of May 15th, immediate pursuit was begun. A division of infantry (Jeff. C. Davis's) was at once dispatched down the valley toward Rome, to support Garrard's cavalry, and the whole army was ordered to pursue, McPherson by Lay's Ferry, on the right, Thomas directly by the railroad, and Schofield by the left, by the old road that crossed the Oostenaula above Echota or Newtown.

We hastily repaired the railroad bridge at Resaca, which had been partially burned, and built a temporary floating bridge out of timber and materials found on the spot; so that Thomas got his advance corps over during the 16th, and marched as far as Calhoun, where he came into communication with McPherson's troops, which had crossed the Oostenaula at Lay's Ferry by our pontoon-bridges, previously laid. Inasmuch as the bridge at Resaca was overtaxed, Hooker's Twentieth Corps was also diverted to cross by the fords and ferries above Resaca, in the neighborhood of Echota.

On the 17th, toward evening, the head of Thomas's column, Newton's division, encountered the rear-guard of Johnston's army near Adairsville. I was near the head of column at the time, trying to get a view of the position of the enemy from an elevation in an open field. My party attracted the fire of a battery; a shell passed through the group of staff-officers and burst just beyond, which scattered us promptly. The next morning the enemy had disappeared, and our pursuit was continued to Kingston, which we reached during Sunday forenoon, the 19th.

From Resaca the railroad runs nearly due south, but at Kingston it makes junction with another railroad from Rome, and changes direction due east. At that time McPherson's head of column was about four miles to the west of Kingston, at a country place called "Woodlawn;" Schofield and Hooker were on the direct roads leading from Newtown to Casaville, diagonal to the route followed by Thomas. Thomas's head of column, which had followed the country roads alongside of the railroad, was about four miles east of Kingston, toward Cassville, when about noon I got a message from him that he had found the enemy, drawn up in line of battle, on some extensive, open ground, about half-way between Kingston and Cassville, and that appearances indicated a willingness and preparation for battle.

Hurriedly sending orders to McPherson to resume the march, to hasten forward by roads leading to the south of Kingston, so as to leave for Thomas's troops and trains the use of the main road, and to come up on his right, I rode forward rapidly, over some rough gravel hills, and about six miles from Kingston found General Thomas, with his troops deployed; but he reported that the enemy had fallen back in echelon of divisions, steadily and in superb order, into Cassville. I knew that the roads by which Generals Hooker and Schofield were approaching would lead them to a seminary near Cassville, and that it was all-important to secure the point of junction of these roads with the main road along which we were marching. Therefore I ordered General Thomas to push forward his deployed lines as rapidly as possible; and, as night was approaching, I ordered two field-batteries to close up at a gallop on some woods which lay between us and the town of Cassville. We could not see the town by reason of these woods, but a high range of hills just back of the town was visible over the tree-tops. On these hills could be seen fresh-made parapets, and the movements of men, against whom I directed the artillery to fire at long range. The stout resistance made by the enemy along our whole front of a couple of miles indicated a purpose to fight at Cassville; and, as the night was closing in, General Thomas and I were together, along with our skirmish-lines near the seminary, on the edge of the town, where musket-bullets from the enemy were cutting the leaves of the trees pretty thickly about us. Either Thomas or I remarked that that was not the place for the two senior officers of a great army, and we personally went back to the battery, where we passed the night on the ground. During the night I had reports from McPherson, Hooker, and Schofield. The former was about five miles to my right rear, near the "nitre-caves;" Schofield was about six miles north, and Hooker between us, within two miles. All were ordered to close down on Cassville at daylight, and to attack the enemy wherever found. Skirmishing was kept up all night, but when day broke the next morning, May 20th, the enemy was gone, and our cavalry was sent in pursuit. These reported him beyond the Etowah River. We were then well in advance of our railroad-trains, on which we depended for supplies; so I determined to pause a few days to repair the railroad, which had been damaged but little, except at the bridge at Resaca, and then to go on.

Nearly all the people of the country seemed to have fled with Johnston's army; yet some few families remained, and from one of them I procured the copy of an order which Johnston had made at Adairsville, in which he recited that he had retreated as far as strategy required, and that his army must be prepared for battle at Cassville. The newspapers of the South, many of which we found, were also loud in denunciation of Johnston's falling back before us without a serious battle, simply resisting by his skirmish-lines and by his rear-guard. But his friends proclaimed that it was all strategic; that he was deliberately drawing us farther and farther into the meshes, farther and farther away from our base of supplies, and that in due season he would not only halt for battle, but assume the bold offensive. Of course it was to my interest to bring him to battle as soon as possible, when our numerical superiority was at the greatest; for he was picking up his detachments as he fell back, whereas I was compelled to make similar and stronger detachments to repair the railroads as we advanced, and to guard them. I found at Cassville many evidences of preparation for a grand battle, among them a long line of fresh intrenchments on the hill beyond the town, extending nearly three miles to the south, embracing the railroad-crossing. I was also convinced that the whole of Polk's corps had joined Johnston from Mississippi, and that he had in hand three full corps, viz., Hood's, Polk's, and Hardee's, numbering about sixty thousand men, and could not then imagine why he had declined battle, and did not learn the real reason till after the war was over, and then from General Johnston himself.

In the autumn of 1865, when in command of the Military Division of the Missouri, I went from St. Louis to Little Rock, Arkansas, and afterward to Memphis. Taking a steamer for Cairo, I found as fellow-passengers Generals Johnston and Frank Blair. We were, of course, on the most friendly terms, and on our way up we talked over our battles again, played cards, and questioned each other as to particular parts of our mutual conduct in the game of war. I told Johnston that I had seen his order of preparation, in the nature of an address to his army, announcing his purpose to retreat no more, but to accept battle at Cassville. He answered that such was his purpose; that he had left Hardee's corps in the open fields to check Thomas, and gain time for his formation on the ridge, just behind Cassville; and it was this corps which General Thomas had seen deployed, and whose handsome movement in retreat he had reported in such complimentary terms. Johnston described how he had placed Hood's corps on the right, Polk's in the centre, and Hardee's on the left. He said he had ridden over the ground, given to each corps commander his position, and orders to throw up parapets during the night; that he was with Hardee on his extreme left as the night closed in, and as Hardee's troops fell back to the position assigned them for the intended battle of the next day; and that, after giving Hardee some general instructions, he and his staff rode back to Cassville. As he entered the town, or village, he met Generals Hood and Polk. Hood inquired of him if he had had any thing to eat, and he said no, that he was both hungry and tired, when Hood invited him to go and share a supper which had been prepared for him at a house close by. At the supper they discussed the chances of the impending battle, when Hood spoke of the ground assigned him as being enfiladed by our (Union) artillery, which Johnston disputed, when General Polk chimed in with the remark that General Hood was right; that the cannon-shots fired by us at nightfall had enfiladed their general line of battle, and that for this reason he feared they could not hold their men. General Johnston was surprised at this, for he understood General Hood to be one of those who professed to criticise his strategy, contending that, instead of retreating, he should have risked a battle. General Johnston said he was provoked, accused them of having been in conference, with being beaten before battle, and added that he was unwilling to engage in a critical battle with an army so superior to his own in numbers, with two of his three corps commanders dissatisfied with the ground and positions assigned them. He then and there made up his mind to retreat still farther south, to put the Etowah River and the Allatoona range between us; and he at once gave orders to resume the retrograde movement.

This was my recollection of the substance of the conversation, of which I made no note at the time; but, at a meeting of the Society of the Army of the Cumberland some years after, at Cleveland, Ohio, about 1868, in a short after-dinner speech, I related this conversation, and it got into print. Subsequently, in the spring of 1870, when I was at New Orleans, on route for Texas, General Hood called to see me at the St. Charles Hotel, explained that he had seen my speech reprinted in the newspapers and gave me his version of the same event, describing the halt at Cassville, the general orders for battle on that ground, and the meeting at supper with Generals Johnston and Polk, when the chances of the battle to be fought the next day were freely and fully discussed; and he stated that he had argued against fighting the battle purely on the defensive, but had asked General Johnston to permit him with his own corps and part of Polk's to quit their lines, and to march rapidly to attack and overwhelm Schofield, who was known to be separated from Thomas by an interval of nearly five miles, claiming that he could have defeated Schofield, and got back to his position in time to meet General Thomas's attack in front. He also stated that he had then contended with Johnston for the "offensive-defensive" game, instead of the "pure defensive," as proposed by General Johnston; and he said that it was at this time that General Johnston had taken offense, and that it was for this reason he had ordered the retreat that night. As subsequent events estranged these two officers, it is very natural they should now differ on this point; but it was sufficient for us that the rebel army did retreat that night, leaving us masters of all the country above the Etowah River.

For the purposes of rest, to give time for the repair of the railroads, and to replenish supplies, we lay by some few days in that quarter—Schofield with Stoneman's cavalry holding the ground at Cassville Depot, Cartersville, and the Etowah Bridge; Thomas holding his ground near Cassville, and McPherson that near Kingston. The officer intrusted with the repair of the railroads was Colonel W. W. Wright, a railroad-engineer, who, with about two thousand men, was so industrious and skillful that the bridge at Resaca was rebuilt in three days, and cars loaded with stores came forward to Kingston on the 24th. The telegraph also brought us the news of the bloody and desperate battles of the Wilderness, in Virginia, and that General Grant was pushing his operations against Lee with terrific energy. I was therefore resolved to give my enemy no rest.

In early days (1844), when a lieutenant of the Third Artillery, I had been sent from Charleston, South Carolina, to Marietta, Georgia, to assist Inspector-General Churchill to take testimony concerning certain losses of horses and accoutrements by the Georgia Volunteers during the Florida War; and after completing the work at Marietta we transferred our party over to Bellefonte, Alabama. I had ridden the distance on horseback, and had noted well the topography of the country, especially that about Kenesaw, Allatoona, and the Etowah River. On that occasion I had stopped some days with a Colonel Tumlin, to see some remarkable Indian mounds on the Etowah River, usually called the "Hightower:" I therefore knew that the Allatoona Pass was very strong, would be hard to force, and resolved not even to attempt it, but to turn the position, by moving from Kingston to Marietta via. Dallas; accordingly I made orders on the 20th to get ready for the march to begin on the 23d. The Army of the Cumberland was ordered to march for Dallas, by Euharlee and Stilesboro; Davis's division, then in Rome, by Van Wert; the Army of the Ohio to keep on the left of Thomas, by a place called Burnt Hickory; and the Army of the Tennessee to march for a position a little to the south, so as to be on the right of the general army, when grouped about Dallas.

The movement contemplated leaving our railroad, and to depend for twenty days on the contents of our wagons; and as the country was very obscure, mostly in a state of nature, densely wooded, and with few roads, our movements were necessarily slow. We crossed the Etowah by several bridges and fords, and took as many roads as possible, keeping up communication by cross-roads, or by couriers through the woods. I personally joined General Thomas, who had the centre, and was consequently the main column, or "column of direction." The several columns followed generally the valley of the Euharlee, a tributary coming into the Etowah from the south, and gradually crossed over a ridge of mountains, parts of which had once been worked over for gold, and were consequently full of paths and unused wagon-roads or tracks. A cavalry picket of the enemy at Burnt Hickory was captured, and had on his person an order from General Johnston, dated at Allatoona, which showed that he had detected my purpose of turning his position, and it accordingly became necessary to use great caution, lest some of the minor columns should fall into ambush, but, luckily the enemy was not much more familiar with that part of the country than we were. On the other side of the Allatoona range, the Pumpkin-Vine Creek, also a tributary of the Etowah, flowed north and west; Dallas, the point aimed at, was a small town on the other or east side of this creek, and was the point of concentration of a great many roads that led in every direction. Its possession would be a threat to Marietta and Atlanta, but I could not then venture to attempt either, till I had regained the use of the railroad, at least as far down as its debouche from the Allatoona range of mountains. Therefore, the movement was chiefly designed to compel Johnston to give up Allatoona.

On the 25th all the columns were moving steadily on Dallas—McPherson and Davis away off to the right, near Van Wert; Thomas on the main road in the centre, with Hooker's Twentieth Corps ahead, toward Dallas; and Schofield to the left rear. For the convenience of march, Hooker had his three divisions on separate roads, all leading toward Dallas, when, in the afternoon, as he approached a bridge across Pumpkin-Vine Creek, he found it held by a cavalry force, which was driven off, but the bridge was on fire. This fire was extinguished, and Hooker's leading division (Geary's) followed the retreating cavalry on a road leading due east toward Marietta, instead of Dallas. This leading division, about four miles out from the bridge, struck a heavy infantry force, which was moving down from Allatoona toward Dallas, and a sharp battle ensued. I came up in person soon after, and as my map showed that we were near an important cross-road called "New Hope," from a Methodist meeting-house there of that name, I ordered General Hooker to secure it if possible that night. He asked for a short delay, till he could bring up his other two divisions, viz., of Butterfield and Williams, but before these divisions had got up and were deployed, the enemy had also gained corresponding strength. The woods were so dense, and the resistance so spirited, that Hooker could not carry the position, though the battle was noisy, and prolonged far into the night. This point, "New Hope," was the accidental intersection of the road leading from Allatoona to Dallas with that from Van Wert to Marietta, was four miles northeast of Dallas, and from the bloody fighting there for the next week was called by the soldiers "Hell-Hole."

The night was pitch-dark, it rained hard, and the convergence of our columns toward Dallas produced much confusion. I am sure similar confusion existed in the army opposed to us, for we were all mixed up. I slept on the ground, without cover, alongside of a log, got little sleep, resolved at daylight to renew the battle, and to make a lodgment on the Dallas and Allatoona road if possible, but the morning revealed a strong line of intrenchments facing us, with a heavy force of infantry and guns. The battle was renewed, and without success. McPherson reached Dallas that morning, viz., the 26th, and deployed his troops to the southeast and east of the town, placing Davis's division of the Fourteenth Corps, which had joined him on the road from Rome, on his left; but this still left a gap of at least three miles between Davis and Hooker. Meantime, also, General Schofield was closing up on Thomas's left.

Satisfied that Johnston in person was at New Hope with all his army, and that it was so much nearer my "objective;" the railroad, than Dallas, I concluded to draw McPherson from Dallas to Hooker's right, and gave orders accordingly; but McPherson also was confronted with a heavy force, and, as he began to withdraw according to his orders, on the morning of the 28th he was fiercely assailed on his right; a bloody battle ensued, in which he repulsed the attack, inflicting heavy loss on his assailants, and it was not until the 1st of June that he was enabled to withdraw from Dallas, and to effect a close junction with Hooker in front of New Hope. Meantime Thomas and Schofield were completing their deployments, gradually overlapping Johnston on his right, and thus extending our left nearer and nearer to the railroad, the nearest point of which was Acworth, about eight miles distant. All this time a continual battle was in progress by strong skirmish-lines, taking advantage of every species of cover, and both parties fortifying each night by rifle-trenches, with head-logs, many of which grew to be as formidable as first-class works of defense. Occasionally one party or the other would make a dash in the nature of a sally, but usually it sustained a repulse with great loss of life. I visited personally all parts of our lines nearly every day, was constantly within musket-range, and though the fire of musketry and cannon resounded day and night along the whole line, varying from six to ten miles, I rarely saw a dozen of the enemy at any one time; and these were always skirmishers dodging from tree to tree, or behind logs on the ground, or who occasionally showed their heads above the hastily-constructed but remarkably strong rifle-trenches. On the occasion of my visit to McPherson on the 30th of May, while standing with a group of officers, among whom were Generals McPherson, Logan, Barry, and Colonel Taylor, my former chief of artillery, a Minie-ball passed through Logan's coat-sleeve, scratching the skin, and struck Colonel Taylor square in the breast; luckily he had in his pocket a famous memorandum-book, in which he kept a sort of diary, about which we used to joke him a good deal; its thickness and size saved his life, breaking the force of the ball, so that after traversing the book it only penetrated the breast to the ribs, but it knocked him down and disabled him for the rest of the campaign. He was a most competent and worthy officer, and now lives in poverty in Chicago, sustained in part by his own labor, and in part by a pitiful pension recently granted.

On the 1st of June General McPherson closed in upon the right, and, without attempting further to carry the enemy's strong position at New Hope Church, I held our general right in close contact with it, gradually, carefully, and steadily working by the left, until our strong infantry-lines had reached and secured possession of all the wagon-roads between New Hope, Allatoona, and Acworth, when I dispatched Generals Garrard's and Stoneman's divisions of cavalry into Allatoona, the first around by the west end of the pass, and the latter by the direct road. Both reached their destination without opposition, and orders were at once given to repair the railroad forward from Kingston to Allatoona, embracing the bridge across the Etowah River. Thus the real object of my move on Dallas was accomplished, and on the 4th of June I was preparing to draw off from New Hope Church, and to take position on the railroad in front of Allatoona, when, General Johnston himself having evacuated his position, we effected the change without further battle, and moved to the railroad, occupying it from Allatoona and Acworth forward to Big Shanty, in sight of the famous Kenesaw Mountain.

Thus, substantially in the month of May, we had steadily driven our antagonist from the strong positions of Dalton, Resaea, Cassville, Allatoona, and Dallas; had advanced our lines in strong, compact order from Chattanooga to Big Shanty, nearly a hundred miles of as difficult country as was ever fought over by civilized armies; and thus stood prepared to go on, anxious to fight, and confident of success as soon as the railroad communications were complete to bring forward the necessary supplies. It is now impossible to state accurately our loss of life and men in any one separate battle; for the fighting was continuous, almost daily, among trees and bushes, on ground where one could rarely see a hundred yards ahead.

The aggregate loss in the several corps for the month of May is reported-as follows in the usual monthly returns sent to the Adjutant-General's office, which are, therefore, official:

Casualties during the Month of May, 1864
(Major-General SHERMAN commanding).

Killed and Missing.	Wounded.	Total.
1,863	7,436	9,299

General Joseph E. Johnston, in his "Narrative of his Military Operations," just published (March 27, 1874), gives the effective strength of his army at and about Dalton on the 1st of May, 1864 (page 302), as follows:

Infantry	37,652
Artillery	2,812
Cavalry	2,392
Total	42,856

During May, and prior to reaching Cassville, he was further reenforced.

Polk's corps of three divisions	12,000
Martin's division of cavalry	3,500
Jackson's division of cavalry	3,900

And at New Hope Church, May 26th

Brigade of Quarles	2,200
Grand-total	64,456

His losses during the month of May are stated by him, as taken from the report of Surgeon Foard.

Killed	Wounded	Total
721	4,672	5,393

These figures include only the killed and wounded, whereas my statement of losses embraces the "missing," which are usually "prisoners," and of these we captured, during the whole campaign of four and a half months, exactly 12,983, whose names, rank, and regiments, were officially reported to the Commissary-General of Prisoners; and assuming a due proportion for the month of May, viz., one-fourth, makes 3,245 to be added to the killed and wounded given above, making an aggregate loss in Johnston's army, from Dalton to New Hope, inclusive, of 8,638, against ours of 9,299.

Therefore General Johnston is greatly in error, in his estimates on page 357, in stating our loss, as compared with his, at six or ten to one.

I always estimated my force at about double his, and could afford to lose two to one without disturbing our relative proportion; but I also reckoned that, in the natural strength of the country, in the abundance of mountains, streams, and forests, he had a fair offset to our numerical superiority, and therefore endeavored to act with reasonable caution while moving on the vigorous "offensive."

With the drawn battle of New Hope Church, and our occupation of the natural fortress of Allatoona, terminated the month of May, and the first stage of the campaign.

CHAPTER XVII.
ATLANTA CAMPAIGN—BATTLES ABOUT KENESAW MOUNTAIN.

JUNE, 1864.

On the 1st of June our three armies were well in hand, in the broken and densely-wooded country fronting the enemy intrenched at New Hope Church, about five miles north of Dallas. General Stoneman's division of cavalry had occupied Allatoona, on the railroad, and General Garrard's division was at the western end of the pass, about Stilesboro. Colonel W. W. Wright, of the Engineers, was busily employed in repairing the railroad and rebuilding the bridge across the Etowah (or High tower) River, which had been destroyed by the enemy on his retreat; and the armies were engaged in a general and constant skirmish along a front of about six miles—McPherson the right, Thomas the centre, and Schofield on the left. By gradually covering our front with parapet, and extending to the left, we approached the railroad toward Acworth and overlapped the enemy's right. By the 4th of June we had made such progress that Johnston evacuated his lines in the night, leaving us masters of the situation, when I deliberately shifted McPherson's army to the extreme left, at and in front of Acworth, with Thomas's about two miles on his right, and Schofield's on his right all facing east. Heavy rains set in about the 1st of June, making the roads infamous; but our marches were short, as we needed time for the repair of the railroad, so as to bring supplies forward to Allatoona Station. On the 6th I rode back to Allatoona, seven miles, found it all that was expected, and gave orders for its fortification and preparation as a "secondary base."

General Blair arrived at Acworth on the 8th with his two divisions of the Seventeenth Corps—the same which had been on veteran furlough—had come up from Cairo by way of Clifton, on the Tennessee River, and had followed our general route to Allatoona, where he had left a garrison of about fifteen hundred men. His effective strength, as reported, was nine thousand. These, with new regiments and furloughed men who had joined early in the month of May, equaled our losses from battle, sickness, and by detachments; so that the three armies still aggregated about one hundred thousand effective men.

On the 10th of June the whole combined army moved forward six miles, to "Big Shanty," a station on the railroad, whence we had a good view of the enemy's position, which embraced three prominent hills known as Kenesaw, Pine Mountain, and Lost Mountain. On each of these hills the enemy had signal-stations and fresh lines of parapets. Heavy masses of infantry could be distinctly seen with the naked eye, and it was manifest that Johnston had chosen his ground well, and with deliberation had prepared for battle; but his line was at least ten miles in extent—too long, in my judgment, to be held successfully by his force, then estimated at sixty thousand. As his position, however, gave him a perfect view over our field, we had to proceed with due caution. McPherson had the left, following the railroad, which curved around the north base of Kenesaw; Thomas the centre, obliqued to the right, deploying below Kenesaw and facing Pine Hill; and Schofield, somewhat refused, was on the general right, looking south, toward Lost Mountain.

On the 11th the Etowah bridge was done; the railroad was repaired up to our very skirmish line, close to the base of Kenesaw, and a loaded train of cars came to Big Shanty. The locomotive, detached, was run forward to a water-tank within the range of the enemy's guns on Kenesaw, whence the enemy opened fire on the locomotive; but the engineer was not afraid, went on to the tank, got water, and returned safely to his train, answering the guns with the screams of his engine, heightened by the cheers and shouts of our men.

The rains continued to pour, and made our developments slow and dilatory, for there were no roads, and these had to be improvised by each division for its own supply train from the depot in Big Shanty to the camps. Meantime each army was deploying carefully before the enemy, intrenching every camp, ready as against a sally. The enemy's cavalry was also busy in our rear, compelling us to detach cavalry all the way back as far as Resaca, and to strengthen all the infantry posts as far as Nashville. Besides, there was great danger, always in my mind, that Forrest would collect a heavy cavalry command in Mississippi, cross the Tennessee River, and break up our railroad below Nashville. In anticipation of this very danger, I had sent General Sturgis to Memphis to take command of all the cavalry in that quarter, to go out toward Pontotoc, engage Forrest and defeat him; but on the 14th of June I learned that General Sturgis had himself been defeated on the 10th of June, and had been driven by Forrest back into Memphis in considerable confusion. I expected that this would soon be followed by a general raid on all our roads in Tennessee. General G. J. Smith, with the two divisions of the Sixteenth and Seventeenth Corps which had been with General Banks up Red River, had returned from that ill-fated expedition, and had been ordered to General Canby at New Orleans, who was making a diversion about Mobile; but, on hearing of General Sturgis's defeat, I ordered General Smith to go out from Memphis and renew the offensive, so as to keep Forrest off our roads. This he did finally, defeating Forrest at Tupelo, on the 13th, 14th, and 15th days of July; and he so stirred up matters in North Mississippi that Forrest could not leave for Tennessee. This, for a time, left me only the task of covering the roads against such minor detachments of cavalry as Johnston could spare from his immediate army, and I proposed to keep these too busy in their own defense to spare detachments. By the 14th the rain slackened, and we occupied a continuous line of ten miles, intrenched, conforming to the irregular position of the enemy, when I reconnoitred, with a view to make a break in their line between Kenesaw and Pine Mountain. When abreast of Pine Mountain I noticed a rebel battery on its crest, with a continuous line of fresh rifle-trench about half-way down the hill. Our skirmishers were at the time engaged in the woods about the base of this hill between the lines, and I estimated the distance to the battery on the crest at about eight hundred yards. Near it, in plain view, stood a group of the enemy, evidently observing us with glasses. General Howard, commanding the Fourth Corps, was near by, and I called his attention to this group, and ordered him to compel it to keep behind its cover. He replied that his orders from General Thomas were to spare artillery-ammunition. This was right, according to the general policy, but I explained to him that we must keep up the morale of a bold offensive, that he must use his artillery, force the enemy to remain on the timid defensive, and ordered him to cause a battery close by to fire three volleys. I continued to ride down our line, and soon heard, in quick succession, the three volleys. The next division in order was Geary's, and I gave him similar orders. General Polk, in my opinion, was killed by the second volley fired from the first battery referred to.

In a conversation with General Johnston, after the war, he explained that on that day he had ridden in person from Marietta to Pine Mountain, held by Bates's division, and was accompanied by Generals Hardee and Polk. When on Pine Mountain, reconnoitring, quite a group of soldiers, belonging to the battery close by, clustered about him. He noticed the preparations of our battery to fire, and cautioned these men to scatter. They did so, and he likewise hurried behind the parapet, from which he had an equally good view of our position but General Polk, who was dignified and corpulent, walked back slowly, not wishing to appear too hurried or cautious in the presence of the men, and was struck across the breast by an unexploded shell, which killed him instantly. This is my memory of the conversation, and it is confirmed by Johnston himself in his "Narrative," page 337, except that he calculated the distance of our battery at six hundred yards, and says that Polk was killed by the third shot; I know that our guns fired by volley, and believe that he was hit by a shot of the second volley. It has been asserted that I fired the gun which killed General Polk, and that I knew it was directed against that general. The fact is, at that distance we could not even tell that the group were officers at all; I was on horseback, a couple of hundred yards off, before my orders to fire were executed, had no idea that our shot had taken effect, and continued my ride down along the line to Schofield's extreme flank, returning late in the evening to my head-quarters at Big Shanty, where I occupied an abandoned house. In a cotton-field back of that house was our signal-station, on the roof of an old gin-house. The signal-officer reported that by studying the enemy's signals he had learned the key, and that he could read their signals. He explained to me that he had translated a signal about noon, from Pine Mountain to Marietta, "Send an ambulance for General Polk's body;" and later in the day another, "Why don't you send an ambulance for General Polk?" From this we inferred that General Polk had been killed, but how or where we knew not; and this inference was confirmed later in the same day by the report of some prisoners who had been captured.

On the 15th we advanced our general lines, intending to attack at any weak point discovered between Kenesaw and Pine Mountain; but Pine Mountain was found to be abandoned, and Johnston had contracted his front somewhat, on a direct line, connecting Kenesaw with Lost Mountain. Thomas and Schofield thereby gained about two miles of most difficult, country, and McPherson's left lapped well around the north end of

Kenesaw. We captured a good many prisoners, among them a whole infantry regiment, the Fourteenth Alabama, three hundred and twenty strong.

On the 16th the general movement was continued, when Lost Mountain was abandoned by the enemy. Our right naturally swung round, so as to threaten the railroad below Marietta, but Johnston had still further contracted and strengthened his lines, covering Marietta and all the roads below.

On the 17th and 18th the rain again fell in torrents, making army movements impossible, but we devoted the time to strengthening our positions, more especially the left and centre, with a view gradually to draw from the left to add to the right; and we had to hold our lines on the left extremely strong, to guard against a sally from Kenesaw against our depot at Big Shanty. Garrard's division of cavalry was kept busy on our left, McPherson had gradually extended to his right, enabling Thomas to do the same still farther; but the enemy's position was so very strong, and everywhere it was covered by intrenchments, that we found it as dangerous to assault as a permanent fort. We in like manner covered our lines of battle by similar works, and even our skirmishers learned to cover their bodies by the simplest and best forms of defensive works, such as rails or logs, piled in the form of a simple lunette, covered on the outside with earth thrown up at night.

The enemy and ourselves used the same form of rifle-trench, varied according to the nature of the ground, viz.: the trees and bushes were cut away for a hundred yards or more in front, serving as an abatis or entanglement; the parapets varied from four to six feet high, the dirt taken from a ditch outside and from a covered way inside, and this parapet was surmounted by a "head-log," composed of the trunk of a tree from twelve to twenty inches at the butt, lying along the interior crest of the parapet and resting in notches cut in other trunks which extended back, forming an inclined plane, in case the head-log should be knocked inward by a cannon-shot. The men of both armies became extremely skillful in the construction of these works, because each man realized their value and importance to himself, so that it required no orders for their construction. As soon as a regiment or brigade gained a position within easy distance for a sally, it would set to work with a will, and would construct such a parapet in a single night; but I endeavored to spare the soldiers this hard labor by authorizing each division commander to organize out of the freedmen who escaped to us a pioneer corps of two hundred men, who were fed out of the regular army supplies, and I promised them ten dollars a month, under an existing act of Congress. These pioneer detachments became very useful to us during the rest of the war, for they could work at night while our men slept; they in turn were not expected to fight, and could therefore sleep by day. Our enemies used their slaves for a similar purpose, but usually kept them out of the range of fire by employing them to fortify and strengthen the position to their rear next to be occupied in their general retrograde. During this campaign hundreds if not thousands of miles of similar intrenchments were built by both armies, and, as a rule, whichever party attacked got the worst of it.

On the 19th of June the rebel army again fell back on its flanks, to such an extent that for a time I supposed it had retreated to the Chattahoochee River, fifteen miles distant; but as we pressed forward we were soon undeceived, for we found it still more concentrated, covering Marietta and the railroad. These successive contractions of the enemy's line encouraged us and discouraged him, but were doubtless justified by sound reasons. On the 20th Johnston's position was unusually strong. Kenesaw Mountain was his salient; his two flanks were refused and covered by parapets and by Noonday and Nose's Creeks. His left flank was his weak point, so long as he acted on the "defensive," whereas, had he designed to contract the extent of his line for the purpose of getting in reserve a force with which to strike "offensively" from his right, he would have done a wise act, and I was compelled to presume that such was his object: We were also so far from Nashville and Chattanooga that we were naturally sensitive for the safety of our railroad and depots, so that the left (McPherson) was held very strong.

About this time came reports that a large cavalry force of the enemy had passed around our left flank, evidently to strike this very railroad somewhere below Chattanooga. I therefore reenforced the cavalry stationed from Resaca to Casaville, and ordered forward from Huntsville, Alabama, the infantry division of General John E. Smith, to hold Kingston securely.

While we were thus engaged about Kenesaw, General Grant had his hands full with Lee, in Virginia. General Halleck was the chief of staff at Washington, and to him I communicated almost daily. I find from my letter-book that on the 21st of June I reported to him tersely and truly the condition of facts on that day: "This is the nineteenth day of rain, and the prospect of fair weather is as far off as ever. The roads are impassable; the fields and woods become quagmire's after a few wagons have crossed over. Yet we are at work all the time. The left flank is across Noonday Creek, and the right is across Nose's Creek. The enemy still holds Kenesaw, a conical mountain, with Marietta behind it, and has his flanks retired, to cover that town and the railroad behind. I am all ready to attack the moment the weather and roads will permit troops and artillery to move with any thing like life."

The weather has a wonderful effect on troops: in action and on the march, rain is favorable; but in the woods, where all is blind and uncertain, it seems almost impossible for an army covering ten miles of front to act in concert during wet and stormy weather. Still I pressed operations with the utmost earnestness, aiming always to keep our fortified lines in absolute contact with the enemy, while with the surplus force we felt forward, from one flank or the other, for his line of communication and retreat. On the 22d of June I rode the whole line, and ordered General Thomas in person to advance his extreme right corps (Hooker's); and instructed General

20

Schofield, by letter, to keep his entire army, viz., the Twenty-third Corps, as a strong right flank in close support of Hooker's deployed line. During this day the sun came out, with some promise of clear weather, and I had got back to my bivouac about dark, when a signal message was received, dated—

KULP HOUSE, 5.30 P.M.

General SHERMAN: We have repulsed two heavy attacks, and feel confident, our only apprehension being from our extreme right flank. Three entire corps are in front of us.

Major-General HOOKER.

Hooker's corps (the Twentieth) belonged to Thomas's army; Thomas's headquarters were two miles nearer to Hooker than mine; and Hooker, being an old army officer, knew that he should have reported this fact to Thomas and not to me; I was, moreover, specially disturbed by the assertion in his report that he was uneasy about his right flank, when Schofield had been specially ordered to protect that. I first inquired of my adjutant, Dayton, if he were certain that General Schofield had received his orders, and he answered that the envelope in which he had sent them was receipted by General Schofield himself. I knew, therefore, that General Schofield must be near by, in close support of Hooker's right flank. General Thomas had before this occasion complained to me of General Hooker's disposition to "switch off," leaving wide gaps in his line, so as to be independent, and to make glory on his own account. I therefore resolved not to overlook this breach of discipline and propriety. The rebel army was only composed of three corps; I had that very day ridden six miles of their lines, found them everywhere strongly occupied, and therefore Hooker could not have encountered "three entire corps." Both McPherson and Schofield had also complained to me of this same tendency of Hooker to widen the gap between his own corps and his proper army (Thomas's), so as to come into closer contact with one or other of the wings, asserting that he was the senior by commission to both McPherson and Schofield, and that in the event of battle he should assume command over them, by virtue of his older commission.

They appealed to me to protect them. I had heard during that day some cannonading and heavy firing down toward the "Kulp House," which was about five miles southeast of where I was, but this was nothing unusual, for at the same moment there was firing along our lines full ten miles in extent. Early the next day (23d) I rode down to the "Kulp House," which was on a road leading from Powder Springs to Marietta, about three miles distant from the latter. On the way I passed through General Butterfield's division of Hooker's corps, which I learned had not been engaged at all in the battle of the day before; then I rode along Geary's and Williams's divisions, which occupied the field of battle, and the men were engaged in burying the dead. I found General Schofield's corps on the Powder Springs road, its head of column abreast of Hooker's right, therefore constituting "a strong right flank," and I met Generale Schofield and Hooker together. As rain was falling at the moment, we passed into a little church standing by the road-side, and I there showed General Schofield Hooker's signal-message of the day before. He was very angry, and pretty sharp words passed between them, Schofield saying that his head of column (Hascall's division) had been, at the time of the battle, actually in advance of Hooker's line; that the attack or sally of the enemy struck his troops before it did Hooker's; that General Hooker knew of it at the time; and he offered to go out and show me that the dead men of his advance division (Hascall's) were lying farther out than any of Hooker's. General Hooker pretended not to have known this fact. I then asked him why he had called on me for help, until he had used all of his own troops; asserting that I had just seen Butterfield's division, and had learned from him that he had not been engaged the day before at all; and I asserted that the enemy's sally must have been made by one corps (Hood's), in place of three, and that it had fallen on Geary's and Williams's divisions, which had repulsed the attack handsomely. As we rode away from that church General Hooker was by my side, and I told him that such a thing must not occur again; in other words, I reproved him more gently than the occasion demanded, and from that time he began to sulk. General Hooker had come from the East with great fame as a "fighter," and at Chattanooga he was glorified by his "battle above the clouds," which I fear turned his head. He seemed jealous of all the army commanders, because in years, former rank, and experience, he thought he was our superior.

On the 23d of June I telegraphed to General Halleck this summary, which I cannot again better state:

We continue to press forward on the principle of an advance against fortified positions. The whole country is one vast fort, and Johnston must have at least fifty miles of connected trenches, with abatis and finished batteries. We gain ground daily, fighting all the time. On the 21st General Stanley gained a position near the south end of Kenesaw, from which the enemy attempted in vain to drive him; and the same day General T. J. Wood's division took a hill, which the enemy assaulted three times at night without success, leaving more than a hundred dead on the ground. Yesterday the extreme right (Hooker and Schofield) advanced on the Powder Springs road to within three miles of Marietta. The enemy made a strong effort to drive them away, but failed signally, leaving more than two hundred dead on the field. Our lines are now in close contact, and the fighting is incessant, with a good deal of artillery-fire. As fast as we gain one position the enemy has another all ready, but I think he will soon have to let go Kenesaw, which is the key to the whole country. The weather is now better, and the roads are drying up fast. Our losses are light, and, not-withstanding the repeated breaks of the road to our rear, supplies are ample.

During the 24th and 25th of June General Schofield extended his right as far as prudent, so as to compel the enemy to thin out his lines correspondingly, with the intention to make two strong assaults at points where success would give us the greatest advantage. I had consulted Generals Thomas, McPherson, and Schofield, and we all agreed that we could not with prudence stretch out any more, and therefore there was no alternative but to attack "fortified lines," a thing carefully avoided up to that time. I reasoned, if we could make a breach anywhere near the rebel centre, and thrust in a strong head of column, that with the one moiety of our army we could hold in check the corresponding wing of the enemy, and with the other sweep in flank and overwhelm the other half. The 27th of June was fixed as the day for the attempt, and in order to oversee the whole, and to be in close communication with all parts of the army, I had a place cleared on the top of a hill to the rear of Thomas's centre, and had the telegraph-wires laid to it. The points of attack were chosen, and the troops were all prepared with as little demonstration as possible. About 9 A.M. Of the day appointed, the troops moved to the assault, and all along our lines for ten miles a furious fire of artillery and musketry was kept up. At all points the enemy met us with determined courage and in great force. McPherson's attacking column fought up the face of the lesser Kenesaw, but could not reach the summit. About a mile to the right (just below the Dallas road) Thomas's assaulting column reached the parapet, where Brigadier-General Barker was shot down mortally wounded, and Brigadier-General Daniel McCook (my old law-partner) was desperately wounded, from the effects of which he afterward died. By 11.30 the assault was in fact over, and had failed. We had not broken the rebel line at either point, but our assaulting columns held their ground within a few yards of the rebel trenches, and there covered themselves with parapet. McPherson lost about five hundred men and several valuable officers, and Thomas lost nearly two thousand men. This was the hardest fight of the campaign up to that date, and it is well described by Johnston in his "Narrative" (pages 342, 343), where he admits his loss in killed and wounded as

Total 808

This, no doubt, is a true and fair statement; but, as usual, Johnston overestimates our loss, putting it at six thousand, whereas our entire loss was about twenty-five hundred, killed and wounded.

While the battle was in progress at the centre, Schofield crossed Olley's Creek on the right, and gained a position threatening Johnston's line of retreat; and, to increase the effect, I ordered Stoneman's cavalry to proceed rapidly still farther to the right, to Sweetwater. Satisfied of the bloody cost of attacking intrenched lines, I at once thought of moving the whole army to the railroad at a point (Fulton) about ten miles below Marietta, or to the Chattahoochee River itself, a movement similar to the one afterward so successfully practised at Atlanta. All the orders were issued to bring forward supplies enough to fill our wagons, intending to strip the railroad back to Allatoona, and leave that place as our depot, to be covered as well as possible by Garrard's cavalry. General Thomas, as usual, shook his head, deeming it risky to leave the railroad; but something had to be done, and I had resolved on this move, as reported in my dispatch to General Halleck on July 1st:

General Schofield is now south of Olley's Creek, and on the head of Nickajack. I have been hurrying down provisions and forage, and tomorrow night propose to move McPherson from the left to the extreme right, back of General Thomas. This will bring my right within three miles of the Chattahoochee River, and about five miles from the railroad. By this movement I think I can force Johnston to move his whole army down from Kenesaw to defend his railroad and the Chattahoochee, when I will (by the left flank) reach the railroad below Marietta; but in this I must cut loose from the railroad with ten days' supplies in wagons. Johnston may come out of his intrenchments to attack Thomas, which is exactly what I want, for General Thomas is well intrenched on a line parallel with the enemy south of Kenesaw. I think that Allatoona and the line of the Etowah are strong enough for me to venture on this move. The movement is substantially down the Sandtown road straight for Atlanta.

McPherson drew out of his lines during the night of July 2d, leaving Garrard's cavalry, dismounted, occupying his trenches, and moved to the rear of the Army of the Cumberland, stretching down the Nickajack; but Johnston detected the movement, and promptly abandoned Marietta and Kenesaw. I expected as much, for, by the earliest dawn of the 3d of July, I was up at a large spy-glass mounted on a tripod, which Colonel Poe, United States Engineers, had at his bivouac close by our camp. I directed the glass on Kenesaw, and saw some of our pickets crawling up the hill cautiously; soon they stood upon the very top, and I could plainly see their movements as they ran along the crest just abandoned by the enemy. In a minute I roused my staff, and started them off with orders in every direction for a pursuit by every possible road, hoping to catch Johnston in the confusion of retreat, especially at the crossing of the Chattahoochee River.

I must close this chapter here, so as to give the actual losses during June, which are compiled from the official returns by months. These losses, from June 1st to July 3d, were all substantially sustained about Kenesaw and Marietta, and it was really a continuous battle, lasting from the 10th day of June till the 3d of July, when the rebel army fell back from Marietta toward the Chattahoochee River. Our losses were:

	Killed and Missing	Wounded	Total

Loss in June	1,790	5,74
Aggregate	0	,530

Johnston makes his statement of losses from the report of his surgeon Foard, for pretty much the same period, viz., from June 4th to July 4th (page 576):

	K illed	Wo unded	otal
T otal	4 68	3,48 0	,948

In the tabular statement the "missing" embraces the prisoners; and, giving two thousand as a fair proportion of prisoners captured by us for the month of June (twelve thousand nine hundred and eighty-three in all the campaign), makes an aggregate loss in the rebel army of fifty-nine hundred and forty-eight, to ours of seventy-five hundred and thirty—a less proportion than in the relative strength of our two armies, viz., as six to ten, thus maintaining our relative superiority, which the desperate game of war justified.

CHAPTER XVIII.
ATLANTA CAMPAIGN—BATTLES ABOUT ATLANTA

JULY, 1864.

As before explained, on the 3d of July, by moving McPherson's entire army from the extreme left, at the base of Kenesaw to the right, below Olley's Creek, and stretching it down the Nickajack toward Turner's Ferry of the Chattahoochee, we forced Johnston to choose between a direct assault on Thomas's intrenched position, or to permit us to make a lodgment on his railroad below Marietta, or even to cross the Chattahoochee. Of course, he chose to let go Kenesaw and Marietta, and fall back on an intrenched camp prepared by his orders in advance on the north and west bank of the Chattahoochee, covering the railroad-crossing and his several pontoon-bridges. I confess I had not learned beforehand of the existence of this strong place, in the nature of a tete-du-pont, and had counted on striking him an effectual blow in the expected confusion of his crossing the Chattahoochee, a broad and deep river then to his rear. Ordering every part of the army to pursue vigorously on the morning of the 3d of July, I rode into Marietta, just quitted by the rebel rear-guard, and was terribly angry at the cautious pursuit by Garrard's cavalry, and even by the head of our infantry columns. But Johnston had in advance cleared and multiplied his roads, whereas ours had to cross at right angles from the direction of Powder Springs toward Marrietta, producing delay and confusion. By night Thomas's head of column ran up against a strong rear-guard intrenched at Smyrna camp-ground, six miles below Marietta, and there on the next day we celebrated our Fourth of July, by a noisy but not a desperate battle, designed chiefly to hold the enemy there till Generals McPherson and Schofield could get well into position below him, near the Chattahoochee crossings.

It was here that General Noyes, late Governor of Ohio, lost his leg. I came very near being shot myself while reconnoitring in the second story of a house on our picket-line, which was struck several times by cannon-shot, and perfectly riddled with musket-balls.

During the night Johnston drew back all his army and trains inside the tete-du-pont at the Chattahoochee, which proved one of the strongest pieces of field-fortification I ever saw. We closed up against it, and were promptly met by a heavy and severe fire. Thomas was on the main road in immediate pursuit; next on his right was Schofield; and McPherson on the extreme right, reaching the Chattahoochee River below Turner's Ferry. Stoneman's cavalry was still farther to the right, along down the Chattahoochee River as far as opposite Sandtown; and on that day I ordered Garrard's division of cavalry up the river eighteen miles, to secure possession of the factories at Roswell, as well as to hold an important bridge and ford at that place.

About three miles out from the Chattahoochee the main road forked, the right branch following substantially the railroad, and the left one leading straight for Atlanta, via Paice's Ferry and Buckhead. We found the latter unoccupied and unguarded, and the Fourth Corps (Howard's) reached the river at Paice's Ferry. The right-hand road was perfectly covered by the tete-du-pont before described, where the resistance was very severe, and for some time deceived me, for I was pushing Thomas with orders to fiercely assault his enemy, supposing that he was merely opposing us to gain time to get his trains and troops across the Chattahoochee; but, on personally reconnoitring, I saw the abatis and the strong redoubts, which satisfied me of the preparations that had been made by Johnston in anticipation of this very event. While I was with General Jeff. C. Davis, a poor negro came out of the abatis, blanched with fright, said he had been hidden under a log all day, with a perfect storm of shot, shells, and musket-balls, passing over him, till a short lull had enabled him to creep out and make himself known to our skirmishers, who in turn had sent him back to where we were. This negro explained that he with about a thousand slaves had been at work a month or more on these very lines, which, as he explained, extended from the river about a mile above the railroad-bridge to Turner's Ferry below,—being in extent from five to six miles.

Therefore, on the 5th of July we had driven our enemy to cover in the valley of the Chattahoochee, and we held possession of the river above for eighteen miles, as far as Roswell, and below ten miles to the mouth of the Sweetwater. Moreover, we held the high ground and could overlook his movements, instead of his looking down on us, as was the case at Kenesaw.

From a hill just back of Mining's Station I could see the houses in Atlanta, nine miles distant, and the whole intervening valley of the Chattahoochee; could observe the preparations for our reception on the other side, the camps of men and large trains of covered wagons, and supposed, as a matter of course, that Johnston had passed the river with the bulk of his army, and that he had only left on our side a corps to cover his bridges; but in fact he had only sent across his cavalry and trains. Between Howard's corps at Paice's Ferry and the rest of Thomas's army pressing up against this tete-du-pont, was a space concealed by dense woods, in crossing which I came near riding into a detachment of the enemy's cavalry; and later in the same day Colonel Frank Sherman, of Chicago, then on General Howard's staff, did actually ride straight into the enemy's camp, supposing that our lines were continuous. He was carried to Atlanta, and for some time the enemy supposed they were in possession of the commander-in-chief of the opposing army.

I knew that Johnston would not remain long on the west bank of the Chattahoochee, for I could easily practise on that ground to better advantage our former tactics of intrenching a moiety in his front, and with the rest of our army cross the river and threaten either his rear or the city of Atlanta itself, which city was of vital importance to the existence not only of his own army, but of the Confederacy itself. In my dispatch of July 6th to General Halleck, at Washington, I state that:

Johnston (in his retreat from Kenesaw) has left two breaks in the railroad—one above Marietta and one near Mining's Station. The former is already repaired, and Johnston's army has heard the sound of our locomotives. The telegraph is finished to Mining's Station, and the field-wire has just reached my bivouac, and will be ready to convey this message as soon as it is written and translated into cipher.

I propose to study the crossings of the Chattahoochee, and, when all is ready, to move quickly. As a beginning, I will keep the troops and wagons well back from the river, and only display to the enemy our picket-line, with a few field-batteries along at random. I have already shifted Schofield to a point in our left rear, whence he can in a single move reach the Chattahoochee at a point above the railroad-bridge, where there is a ford. At present the waters are turbid and swollen from recent rains; but if the present hot weather lasts, the water will run down very fast. We have pontoons enough for four bridges, but, as our crossing will be resisted, we must manoeuvre some. All the regular crossing-places are covered by forts, apparently of long construction; but we shall cross in due time, and, instead of attacking Atlanta direct, or any of its forts, I propose to make a circuit, destroying all its railroads. This is a delicate movement, and must be done with caution. Our army is in good condition and full of confidence; but the weather is intensely hot, and a good many men have fallen with sunstroke. The country is high and healthy, and the sanitary condition of the army is good.

At this time Stoneman was very active on our extreme right, pretending to be searching the river below Turner's Ferry for a crossing, and was watched closely by the enemy's cavalry on the other side, McPherson, on the right, was equally demonstrative at and near Turner's Ferry. Thomas faced substantially the intrenched tete-du-pont, and had his left on the Chattahoochee River, at Paice's Ferry. Garrard's cavalry was up at Roswell, and McCook's small division of cavalry was intermediate, above Soap's Creek. Meantime, also, the railroad-construction party was hard at work, repairing the railroad up to our camp at Vining's Station.

Of course, I expected every possible resistance in crossing the Chattahoochee River, and had made up my mind to feign on the right, but actually to cross over by the left. We had already secured a crossing place at Roswell, but one nearer was advisable; General Schofield had examined the river well, found a place just below the mouth of Soap's Creek which he deemed advantageous, and was instructed to effect an early crossing there, and to intrench a good position on the other side, viz., the east bank. But, preliminary thereto, I had ordered General Rousseau, at Nashville, to collect, out of the scattered detachments of cavalry in Tennessee, a force of a couple of thousand men, to rendezvous at Decatur, Alabama, thence to make a rapid march for Opelika, to break up the railroad links between Georgia and Alabama, and then to make junction with me about Atlanta; or, if forced, to go on to Pensacola, or even to swing across to some of our posts in Mississippi. General Rousseau asked leave to command this expedition himself, to which I consented, and on the 6th of July he reported that he was all ready at Decatur, and I gave him orders to start. He moved promptly on the 9th, crossed the Coosa below the "Ten Islands" and the Tallapoosa below "Horseshoe Bend," having passed through Talladega. He struck the railroad west of Opelika, tore it up for twenty miles, then turned north and came to Marietta on the 22d of July, whence he reported to me. This expedition was in the nature of a raid, and must have disturbed the enemy somewhat; but, as usual, the cavalry did not work hard, and their destruction of the railroad was soon repaired. Rousseau, when he reported to me in person before Atlanta, on the 28d of July, stated his entire loss to have been only twelve killed and thirty wounded. He brought in four hundred captured mules and three hundred horses, and also told me a good story. He said he was far down in Alabama, below Talladega, one hot, dusty day, when the blue clothing of his men was gray with dust; he had halted his column along a road, and he in person, with his staff, had gone to the house of a planter, who met him kindly on the front-porch. He asked for water, which was brought, and as the party sat on the porch in conversation he saw, in a stable-yard across the road, quite a number of good mules. He remarked to the planter, "My good sir, I fear I must take some of your mules." The planter remonstrated, saying he had already contributed liberally to the good cause; that it was only last week he had given to General Roddy ten mules. Rousseau replied, "Well, in this war you should be at least neutral—that is, you should be as liberal to us as to Roddy" (a rebel cavalry general). "Well, ain't you on our side?" "No," said Rousseau; "I am General Rousseau, and all these men you see are Yanks." "Great God! is it possible! Are these Yanks! Who ever supposed they would come away down here in Alabama?" Of course, Rousseau took his ten mules.

Schofield effected his crossing at Soap's Creek very handsomely on the 9th, capturing the small guard that was watching the crossing. By night he was on the high ground beyond, strongly intrenched, with two good pontoon-bridges finished, and was prepared, if necessary, for an assault by the whole Confederate army. The same day Garrard's cavalry also crossed over at Roswell, drove away the cavalry-pickets, and held its ground till relieved by Newton's division of Howard's corps, which was sent up temporarily, till it in turn was relieved by Dodge's corps (Sixteenth) of the Army of the Tennessee, which was the advance of the whole of that army.

That night Johnston evacuated his trenches, crossed over the Chattahoochee, burned the railroad bridge and his pontoon and trestle bridges, and left us in full possession of the north or west bank-besides which, we had already secured possession of the two good crossings at Roswell and Soap's Creek. I have always thought Johnston neglected his opportunity there, for he had lain comparatively idle while we got control of both banks of the river above him.

On the 13th I ordered McPherson, with the Fifteenth Corps, to move up to Roswell, to cross over, prepare good bridges, and to make a strong tete-du-pont on the farther side. Stoneman had been sent down to Campbellton, with orders to cross over and to threaten the railroad below Atlanta, if he could do so without too much risk; and General Blair, with the Seventeenth Corps, was to remain at Turner's Ferry, demonstrating as much as possible, thus keeping up the feint below while we were actually crossing above. Thomas was also ordered to prepare his bridges at Powers's and Paice's Ferries. By crossing the Chattahoochee above the railroad bridge, we were better placed to cover our railroad and depots than below, though a movement across the river below the railroad, to the south of Atlanta, might have been more decisive. But we were already so far from home, and would be compelled to accept battle whenever offered, with the Chattahoochee to our rear, that it became imperative for me to take all prudential measures the case admitted of, and I therefore determined to pass the river above the railroad-bridge-McPherson on the left, Schofield in the centre, and Thomas on the right. On the 13th I reported to General Halleck as follows:

All is well. I have now accumulated stores at Allatoona and Marietta, both fortified and garrisoned points. Have also three places at which to cross the Chattahoochee in our possession, and only await General Stoneman's return from a trip down the river, to cross the army in force and move on Atlanta.

Stoneman is now out two days, and had orders to be back on the fourth or fifth day at furthest.

From the 10th to the 15th we were all busy in strengthening the several points for the proposed passage of the Chattahoochee, in increasing the number and capacity of the bridges, rearranging the garrisons to our rear, and in bringing forward supplies. On the 15th General Stoneman got back to Powder Springs, and was ordered to replace General Blair at Turner's Ferry, and Blair, with the Seventeenth Corps, was ordered up to Roswell to join McPherson. On the 17th we began the general movement against Atlanta, Thomas crossing the Chattahoochee at Powers's and Paice's, by pontoon-bridges; Schofield moving out toward Cross Keys, and McPherson toward Stone Mountain. We encountered but little opposition except by cavalry. On the 18th all the armies moved on a general right wheel, Thomas to Buckhead, forming line of battle facing Peach-Tree Creek; Schofield was on his left, and McPherson well over toward the railroad between Stone Mountain and Decatur, which he reached at 2 p.m. of that day, about four miles from Stone Mountain, and seven miles east of Decatur, and there he turned toward Atlanta, breaking up the railroad as he progressed, his advance-guard reaching Ecatur about night, where he came into communication with Schofield's troops, which had also reached Decatur. About 10 A.M. of that day (July 18th), when the armies were all in motion, one of General Thomas's staff-officers brought me a citizen, one of our spies, who had just come out of Atlanta, and had brought a newspaper of the same day, or of the day before, containing Johnston's order relinquishing the command of the Confederate forces in Atlanta, and Hood's order assuming the command. I immediately inquired of General Schofield, who was his classmate at West Point, about Hood, as to his general character, etc., and learned that he was bold even to rashness, and courageous in the extreme; I inferred that the change of commanders meant "fight." Notice of this important change was at once sent to all parts of the army, and every division commander was cautioned to be always prepared for battle in any shape. This was just what we wanted, viz., to fight in open ground, on any thing like equal terms, instead of being forced to run up against prepared intrenchments; but, at the same time, the enemy having Atlanta behind him, could choose the time and place of attack, and could at pleasure mass a superior force on our weakest points. Therefore, we had to be constantly ready for sallies.

On the 19th the three armies were converging toward Atlanta, meeting such feeble resistance that I really thought the enemy intended to evacuate the place. McPherson was moving astride of the railroad, near Decatur; Schofield along a road leading toward Atlanta, by Colonel Howard's house and the distillery; and Thomas was crossing "Peach-Tree" in line of battle, building bridges for nearly every division as deployed. There was quite a gap between Thomas and Schofield, which I endeavored to close by drawing two of Howard's divisions nearer Schofield. On the 20th I was with General Schofield near the centre, and soon after noon heard heavy firing in front of Thomas's right, which lasted an hour or so, and then ceased.

I soon learned that the enemy had made a furious sally, the blow falling on Hooker's corps (the Twentieth), and partially on Johnson's division of the Fourteenth, and Newton's of the Fourth. The troops had crossed Peach-Tree Creek, were deployed, but at the time were resting for noon, when, without notice, the enemy came pouring out of their trenches down upon them, they became commingled, and fought in many places hand to hand. General Thomas happened to be near the rear of Newton's division, and got some field-batteries in a good position, on the north side of Peach-Tree Creek, from which he directed a furious fire on a mass of the enemy, which was passing around Newton's left and exposed flank. After a couple of hours of hard and close conflict, the enemy retired slowly within his trenches, leaving his dead and many wounded on the field. Johnson's and Newton's losses were light, for they had partially covered their fronts with light parapet; but Hooker's whole corps fought in open ground, and lost about fifteen hundred men. He reported four hundred rebel dead left on the ground, and that the rebel wounded would number four thousand; but this was conjectural, for most of them got back within their own lines. We had, however, met successfully a bold sally, had repelled it handsomely, and were also put on our guard; and the event illustrated the future tactics of our enemy. This sally came from the Peach-Tree line, which General Johnston had carefully prepared in advance, from which to fight us outside of Atlanta. We then advanced our lines in compact order, close up to these finished intrenchments, overlapping them on our left. From various parts of our lines the houses inside of Atlanta were plainly visible, though between us were the strong parapets, with ditch, fraise, chevaux-de-frise, and abatis, prepared long in advance by Colonel Jeremy F. Gilmer, formerly of the United States Engineers. McPherson had the Fifteenth Corps astride the Augusta Railroad, and the Seventeenth deployed on its left. Schofield was next on his right, then came Howard's, Hooker's, and Palmer's corps, on the extreme right. Each corps was deployed with strong reserves, and their trains were parked to their rear. McPherson's trains were in Decatur, guarded by a brigade commanded by Colonel Sprague of the Sixty-third Ohio. The Sixteenth Corps (Dodge's) was crowded out of position on the right of McPherson's line, by the contraction of the circle of investment; and, during the previous afternoon, the Seventeenth Corps (Blair's) had pushed its operations on the farther side of the Augusta Railroad, so as to secure possession of a hill, known as Leggett's Hill, which Leggett's and Force's divisions had carried by assault. Giles A. Smith's division was on Leggett's left, deployed with a weak left flank "in air," in military phraseology. The evening before General Gresham, a great favorite, was badly wounded; and there also Colonel Tom Reynolds, now of Madison, Wisconsin, was shot through the leg. When the surgeons were debating the propriety of amputating it in his hearing, he begged them to spare the leg, as it was very valuable, being an "imported leg." He was of Irish birth, and this well-timed piece of wit saved his leg, for the surgeons thought, if he could perpetrate a joke at such a time, they would trust to his vitality to save his limb.

During the night, I had full reports from all parts of our line, most of which was partially intrenched as against a sally, and finding that McPherson was stretching out too much on his left flank, I wrote him a note early in the morning not to extend so much by his left; for we had not troops enough to completely invest the place, and I intended to destroy utterly all parts of the Augusta Railroad to the east of Atlanta, then to withdraw from the left flank and add to the right. In that letter I ordered McPherson not to extend any farther to the left, but to employ General Dodge's corps (Sixteenth), then forced out of position, to destroy every rail and tie of the railroad, from Decatur up to his skirmish-line, and I wanted him (McPherson) to be ready, as soon as General Garrard returned from Covington (whither I had sent him), to move to the extreme right of Thomas, so as to reach if possible the railroad below Atlanta, viz., the Macon road. In the morning we found the strong line of parapet, "Peach-Tree line," to the front of Schofield and Thomas, abandoned, and our lines were advanced rapidly close up to Atlanta. For some moments I supposed the enemy intended to evacuate, and in person was on horseback at the head of Schofield's troops, which had advanced in front of the Howard House to some open ground, from which we could plainly see the whole rebel line of parapets, and I saw their men dragging up from the intervening valley, by the distillery, trees and saplings for abatis. Our skirmishers found the enemy down in this valley, and we could see the rebel main line strongly manned, with guns in position at intervals. Schofield was dressing forward his lines, and I could hear Thomas farther to the right engaged, when General McPherson and his staff rode up. We went back to the Howard House, a double frame-building with a porch, and sat on the steps, discussing the chances of battle, and of Hood's general character. McPherson had also been of the same class at West Point with Hood, Schofield, and Sheridan. We agreed that we ought to be unusually cautious and prepared at all times for sallies and for hard fighting, because Hood, though not deemed much of a scholar, or of great mental capacity, was undoubtedly a brave, determined, and rash man; and the change of commanders at that particular crisis argued the displeasure of the Confederate Government with the cautious but prudent conduct of General Jos. Johnston.

McPherson was in excellent spirits, well pleased at the progress of events so far, and had come over purposely to see me about the order I had given him to use Dodge's corps to break up the railroad, saying that the night before he had gained a position on Leggett's Hill from which he could look over the rebel parapet, and see the high smoke-stack of a large foundery in Atlanta; that before receiving my order he had diverted Dodge's two divisions (then in motion) from the main road, along a diagonal one that led to his extreme left flank, then held by Giles A. Smith's division (Seventeenth Corps), for the purpose of strengthening that flank; and that he had sent some intrenching-tools there, to erect some batteries from which he intended to knock down that foundery, and otherwise to damage the buildings inside of Atlanta. He said he could put all his pioneers to work, and do with them in the time indicated all I had proposed to do with General Dodge's two divisions. Of course I assented at once, and we walked down the road a short distance, sat down by the foot of a tree where I had my map, and on it pointed out to him Thomas's position and his own. I then explained minutely that, after we had sufficiently broken up the Augusta road, I wanted to shift his whole army around by the rear to Thomas's extreme right, and hoped thus to reach the other railroad at East Point. While we sat there we could hear lively skirmishing going on near us (down about the distillery), and occasionally round-shot from twelve or twenty-four pound guns came through the trees in reply to those of Schofield, and we could hear similar sounds all along down the lines of Thomas to our right, and his own to the left; but presently the firing appeared a little more brisk (especially over about Giles G. Smith's division), and then we heard an occasional gun back toward Decatur. I asked him what it meant. We took my pocket-compass (which I always carried), and by noting the direction of the sound, we became satisfied that the firing was too far to our left rear to be explained by known facts, and he hastily called for his horse, his staff, and his orderlies.

McPherson was then in his prime (about thirty-four years old), over six feet high, and a very handsome man in every way, was universally liked, and had many noble qualities. He had on his boots outside his pantaloons, gauntlets on his hands, had on his major-general's uniform, and wore a sword-belt, but no sword. He hastily gathered his papers (save one, which I now possess) into a pocket-book, put it in his breast-pocket, and jumped on his horse, saying he would hurry down his line and send me back word what these sounds meant. His adjutant-general, Clark, Inspector-General Strong, and his aides, Captains Steele and Gile, were with him. Although the sound of musketry on our left grew in volume, I was not so much disturbed by it as by the sound of artillery back toward Decatur. I ordered Schofield at once to send a brigade back to Decatur (some five miles) and was walking up and down the porch of the Howard House, listening, when one of McPherson's staff, with his horse covered with sweat, dashed up to the porch, and reported that General McPherson was either "killed or a prisoner." He explained that when they had left me a few minutes before, they had ridden rapidly across to the railroad, the sounds of battle increasing as they neared the position occupied by General Giles A. Smith's division, and that McPherson had sent first one, then another of his staff to bring some of the reserve brigades of the Fifteenth Corps over to the exposed left flank; that he had reached the head of Dodge's corps (marching by the flank on the diagonal road as described), and had ordered it to hurry forward to the same point; that then, almost if not entirely alone, he had followed this road leading across the wooded valley behind the Seventeenth Corps, and had disappeared in these woods, doubtless with a sense of absolute security. The sound of musketry was there heard, and McPherson's horse came back, bleeding, wounded, and riderless. I ordered the staff-officer who brought this message to return at once, to find General Logan (the senior officer present with the Army of the Tennessee), to report the same facts to him, and to instruct him to drive back this supposed small force, which had evidently got around the Seventeenth Corps through the blind woods in rear of our left flank. I soon dispatched one of my own staff (McCoy, I think) to General Logan with similar orders, telling him to refuse his left flank, and to fight the battle (holding fast to Leggett's Hill) with the Army of the Tennessee; that I would personally look to Decatur and to the safety of his rear, and would reenforce him if he needed it. I dispatched orders to General Thomas on our right, telling him of this strong sally, and my inference that the lines in his front had evidently been weakened by reason thereof, and that he ought to take advantage of the opportunity to make a lodgment in Atlanta, if possible.

Meantime the sounds of the battle rose on our extreme left more and more furious, extending to the place where I stood, at the Howard House. Within an hour an ambulance came in (attended by Colonels Clark and Strong, and Captains Steele and Gile), bearing McPherson's body. I had it carried inside of the Howard House, and laid on a door wrenched from its hinges. Dr. Hewitt, of the army, was there, and I asked him to examine the wound. He opened the coat and shirt, saw where the ball had entered and where it came out, or rather lodged under the skin, and he reported that McPherson must have died in a few seconds after being hit; that the ball had ranged upward across his body, and passed near the heart. He was dressed just as he left me, with gauntlets and boots on, but his pocket-book was gone. On further inquiry I learned that his body must have been in possession of the enemy some minutes, during which time it was rifled of the pocket-book, and I was much concerned lest the letter I had written him that morning should have fallen into the hands of some one who could read and understand its meaning. Fortunately the spot in the woods where McPherson was shot was regained by our troops in a few minutes, and the pocket-book found in the haversack of a prisoner of war captured at the time, and it and its contents were secured by one of McPherson's staff.

While we were examining the body inside the house, the battle was progressing outside, and many shots struck the building, which I feared would take fire; so I ordered Captains Steele and Gile to carry the body to Marietta. They reached that place the same night, and, on application, I ordered his personal staff to go on and escort the body to his home, in Clyde, Ohio, where it was received with great honor, and it is now buried in a small cemetery, close by his mother's house, which cemetery is composed in part of the family orchard, in which he used to play when a boy. The foundation is ready laid for the equestrian monument now in progress, under the auspices of the Society of the Army of the Tennessee.

The reports that came to me from all parts of the field revealed clearly what was the game of my antagonist, and the ground somewhat favored his. The railroad and wagon-road from Decatur to Atlanta lie along the summit, from which the waters flow, by short, steep valleys, into the "Peach-Tree" and Chattahoochee, to the west, and by other valleys, of gentler declivity, toward the east (Ocmulgee). The ridges and level ground were mostly cleared, and had been cultivated as corn or cotton fields; but where the valleys were broken, they were left in a state of nature—wooded, and full of undergrowth. McPherson's line of battle was across this railroad, along a general ridge, with a gentle but cleared valley to his front, between him and the defenses of Atlanta; and another valley, behind him, was clear of timber in part, but to his left rear the country was heavily wooded. Hood, during the night of July 21st, had withdrawn from his Peach-Tree line, had occupied the fortified line of Atlanta, facing north and east, with Stewart's—formerly Polk's—corps and part of Hardee's, and with G. W. Smith's division of militia. His own corps, and part of Hardee's, had marched out to the road leading from McDonough to Decatur, and had turned so as to strike the left and, rear of McPherson's line "in air." At the same time he had sent Wheeler's division of cavalry against the trains parked in Decatur. Unluckily for us, I had sent away the whole of Garrard's division of cavalry during the night of the 20th, with orders to proceed to Covington, thirty miles east, to burn two important bridges across the Ulcofauhatchee and Yellow Rivers, to tear up the railroad, to damage it as much as possible from Stone Mountain eastward, and to be gone four days; so that McPherson had no cavalry in hand to guard that flank.

The enemy was therefore enabled, under cover or the forest, to approach quite near before he was discovered; indeed, his skirmish-line had worked through the timber and got into the field to the rear of Giles A. Smith's division of the Seventeenth Corps unseen, had captured Murray's battery of regular artillery, moving through these woods entirely unguarded, and had got possession of several of the hospital camps. The right of this rebel line struck Dodge's troops in motion; but, fortunately, this corps (Sixteenth) had only to halt, face to the left, and was in line of battle; and this corps not only held in check the enemy, but drove him back through the woods. About the same time this same force had struck General Giles A. Smith's left flank, doubled it back, captured four guns in position and the party engaged in building the very battery which was the special object of McPherson's visit to me, and almost enveloped the entire left flank. The men, however, were skillful and brave, and fought for a time with their backs to Atlanta. They gradually fell back, compressing their own line, and gaining strength by making junction with Leggett's division of the Seventeenth Corps, well and strongly posted on the hill. One or two brigades of the Fifteenth Corps, ordered by McPherson, came rapidly across the open field to the rear, from the direction of the railroad, filled up the gap from Blair's new left to the head of Dodge's column—now facing to the general left—thus forming a strong left flank, at right angles to the original line of battle. The enemy attacked, boldly and repeatedly, the whole of this flank, but met an equally fierce resistance; and on that ground a bloody battle raged from little after noon till into the night. A part of Hood's plan of action was to sally from Atlanta at the same moment; but this sally was not, for some reason, simultaneous, for the first attack on our extreme left flank had been checked and repulsed before the sally came from the direction of Atlanta. Meantime, Colonel Sprague, in Decatur, had got his teams harnessed up, and safely conducted his train to the rear of Schofield's position, holding in check Wheeler's cavalry till he had got off all his trains, with the exception of three or four wagons. I remained near the Howard House, receiving reports and sending orders, urging Generals Thomas and Schofield to take advantage of the absence from their front of so considerable a body as was evidently engaged on our left, and, if possible, to make a lodgment in Atlanta itself; but they reported that the lines to their front, at all accessible points, were strong, by nature and by art, and were fully manned. About 4 p.m. the expected, sally came from Atlanta, directed mainly against Leggett's Hill and along the Decatur road. At Leggett's Hill they were met and bloodily repulsed. Along the railroad they were more successful. Sweeping over a small force with two guns, they reached our main line, broke through it, and got possession of De Gress's battery of four twenty-pound Parrotts, killing every horse, and turning the guns against us. General Charles R. Wood's division of the Fifteenth Corps was on the extreme right of the Army of the Tennessee, between the railroad and the Howard House, where he connected with Schofield's troops. He reported to me in person that the line on his left had been swept back, and that his connection with General Logan, on Leggett's Hill, was broken. I ordered him to wheel his brigades to the left, to advance in echelon, and to catch the enemy in flank. General Schofield brought forward all his available batteries, to the number of twenty guns, to a position to the left front of the Howard House, whence we could overlook the field of action, and directed a heavy fire over the heads of General Wood's men against the enemy; and we saw Wood's troops advance and encounter the enemy, who had secured possession of the old line of parapet which had been held by our men. His right crossed this parapet, which he swept back, taking it in flank; and, at the same time, the division which had been driven back along the railroad was rallied by General Logan in person, and fought for their former ground. These combined forces drove the enemy into Atlanta, recovering the twenty pound Parrott guns but one of them was found "bursted" while in the possession of the enemy. The two six-pounders farther in advance were, however, lost, and had been hauled back by the enemy into Atlanta. Poor Captain de Gress came to me in tears, lamenting the loss of his favorite guns; when they were regained he had only a few men left, and not a single horse. He asked an order for a reequipment, but I told him he must beg and borrow of others till he could restore his battery, now reduced to three guns. How he did so I do not know, but in a short time he did get horses, men, and finally another gun, of the same special pattern, and served them with splendid effect till the very close of the war. This battery had also been with me from Shiloh till that time.

The battle of July 22d is usually called the battle of Atlanta. It extended from the Howard House to General Giles A. Smith's position, about a mile beyond the Augusta Railroad, and then back toward Decatur, the whole extent of ground being fully seven miles. In part the ground was clear and in part densely wooded. I rode over the whole of it the next day, and it bore the marks of a bloody conflict. The enemy had retired during the night inside of Atlanta, and we remained masters of the situation outside. I purposely allowed the Army of the Tennessee to fight this battle almost unaided, save by demonstrations on the part of General Schofield and Thomas against the fortified lines to their immediate fronts, and by detaching, as described, one of Schofield's brigades to Decatur, because I knew that the attacking force could only be a part of Hood's army, and that, if any assistance were rendered by either of the other armies, the Army of the Tennessee would be jealous. Nobly did they do their work that day, and terrible was the slaughter done to our enemy, though at sad cost to ourselves, as shown by the following reports:

*HEADQUARTERS MILITARY DIVISION OF THE MISSISSIPPI
IN THE FIELD NEAR ATLANTA, July 23,1864.*

General HALLECK, Washington, D. C.

Yesterday morning the enemy fell back to the intrenchments proper of the city of Atlanta, which are in a general circle, with a radius of one and a half miles, and we closed in. While we were forming our lines, and selecting positions for our batteries, the enemy appeared suddenly out of the dense woods in heavy masses on our extreme left, and struck the Seventeenth Corps (General Blair) in flank, and was forcing it back, when the Sixteenth Corps (General Dodge) came up and checked the movement, but the enemy's cavalry got well to our rear, and into Decatur, and for some hours our left flank was completely enveloped. The fight that resulted was continuous until night, with heavy loss on both sides. The enemy took one of our batteries (Murray's, of the Regular Army) that was marching in its place in column in the road, unconscious of danger. About 4 p.m. the enemy sallied against the division of General Morgan L. Smith, of the Fifteenth Corps, which occupied an abandoned line of rifle-trench near the railroad east of the city, and forced it back some four hundred yards, leaving in his hands for the time two batteries, but the ground and batteries were immediately after recovered by the same troops reenforced. I cannot well approximate our loss, which fell heavily on the Fifteenth and Seventeenth Corps, but count it as three thousand; I know that, being on the defensive, we have inflicted equally heavy loss on the enemy.

General McPherson, when arranging his troops about 11.00 A.M., and passing from one column to another, incautiously rode upon an ambuscade without apprehension, at some distance ahead of his staff and orderlies, and was shot dead.

W. T. SHERMAN, Major-General commanding.

*HEADQUARTERS MILITARY DIVISION OF THE MISSISSIPPI IN THE FIELD NEAR ATLANTA,
July 26,1864.*

Major-General HALLECK, Washington, D. C.

GENERAL: I find it difficult to make prompt report of results, coupled with some data or information, without occasionally making mistakes. McPherson's sudden death, and Logan succeeding to the command as it were in the midst of battle, made some confusion on our extreme left; but it soon recovered and made sad havoc with the enemy, who had practised one of his favorite games of attacking our left when in motion, and before it had time to cover its weak flank. After riding over the ground and hearing the varying statements of the actors, I directed General Logan to make an official report of the actual result, and I herewith inclose it.

Though the number of dead rebels seems excessive, I am disposed to give full credit to the report that our loss, though only thirty-five hundred and twenty-one killed, wounded, and missing, the enemy's dead alone on the field nearly equaled that number, viz., thirty-two hundred and twenty. Happening at that point of the line when a flag of truce was sent in to ask permission for each party to bury its dead, I gave General Logan authority to permit a temporary truce on that flank alone, while our labors and fighting proceeded at all others.

I also send you a copy of General Garrard's report of the breaking of the railroad toward Augusta. I am now grouping my command to attack the Macon road, and with that view will intrench a strong line of circumvallation with flanks, so as to have as large an infantry column as possible, with all the cavalry to swing round to the south and east, to strike that road at or below East Point.

I have the honor to be, your obedient servant,

W. T. SHERMAN, Major-General commanding.

HEADQUARTERS DEPARTMENT AND ARMY OF THE TENNESSEE BEFORE ATLANTA GEORGIA, July 24, 1864

Major-General W. T. SHERMAN, commanding Military Division of the Mississippi.

GENERAL: I have the honor to report the following general summary of the result of the attack of the enemy on this army on the 22d inst.

Total loss, killed, wounded, and missing, thirty-five hundred and twenty-one, and ten pieces of artillery.

We have buried and delivered to the enemy, under a flag of truce sent in by them, in front of the Third Division, Seventeenth Corps, one thousand of their killed.

The number of their dead in front of the Fourth Division of the same corps, including those on the ground not now occupied by our troops, General Blair reports, will swell the number of their dead on his front to two thousand.

The number of their dead buried in front of the Fifteenth Corps, up to this hour, is three hundred and sixty, and the commanding officer reports that at least as many more are yet unburied; burying-parties being still at work.

The number of dead buried in front of the Sixteenth Corps is four hundred and twenty-two. We have over one thousand of their wounded in our hands, the larger number of the wounded being carried off during the night, after the engagement, by them.

We captured eighteen stands of colors, and have them now. We also captured five thousand stands of arms.

The attack was made on our lines seven times, and was seven times repulsed. Hood's and Hardee's corps and Wheeler's cavalry engaged us.

We have sent to the rear one thousand prisoners, including thirty-three commissioned officers of high rank.

We still occupy the field, and the troops are in fine spirits. A detailed and full report will be furnished as soon as completed.

Recapitulation.

Our total loss	,521
Enemy's dead, thus far reported, buried, and delivered to them	,220

Very respectfully, your obedient servant,
Joan A. Logan, Major-General.

On the 22d of July General Rousseau reached Marietta, having returned from his raid on the Alabama road at Opelika, and on the next day General Garrard also returned from Covington, both having been measurably successful. The former was about twenty-five hundred strong, the latter about four thousand, and both reported that their horses were jaded and tired, needing shoes and rest. But, about this time, I was advised by General Grant (then investing Richmond) that the rebel Government had become aroused to the critical condition of things about Atlanta, and that I must look out for Hood being greatly reenforced. I therefore was resolved to push matters, and at once set about the original purpose of transferring the whole of the Army of the Tennessee to our right flank, leaving Schofield to stretch out so as to rest his left on the Augusta road, then torn up for thirty miles eastward; and, as auxiliary thereto, I ordered all the cavalry to be ready to pass around Atlanta on both flanks, to break up the Macon road at some point below, so as to cut off all supplies to the rebel army inside, and thus to force it to evacuate, or come out and fight us on equal terms.

But it first became necessary to settle the important question of who should succeed General McPherson? General Logan had taken command of the Army of the Tennessee by virtue of his seniority, and had done well; but I did not consider him equal to the command of three corps. Between him and General Blair there existed a natural rivalry. Both were men of great courage and talent, but were politicians by nature and experience, and it may be that for this reason they were mistrusted by regular officers like Generals Schofield, Thomas, and myself. It was all-important that there should exist a perfect understanding among the army commanders, and at a conference with General George H. Thomas at the headquarters of General Thomas J. Woods, commanding a division in the Fourth Corps, he (Thomas) remonstrated warmly against my recommending that General Logan should be regularly assigned to the command of the Army of the Tennessee by reason of his accidental seniority. We discussed fully the merits and qualities of every officer of high rank in the army, and finally settled on Major-General O. O. Howard as the best officer who was present and available for the purpose; on the 24th of July I telegraphed to General Halleck this preference, and it was promptly ratified by the President. General Howard's place in command of the Fourth Corps was filled by General Stanley, one of his division commanders, on the recommendation of General Thomas. All these promotions happened to fall upon West-Pointers, and doubtless Logan and Blair had some reason to believe that we intended to monopolize the higher honors of the war for the regular officers. I remember well my own thoughts and feelings at the time, and feel sure that I was not intentionally partial to any class, I wanted to succeed in taking Atlanta, and needed commanders who were purely and technically soldiers, men who would obey orders and execute them promptly and on time; for I knew that we would have to execute some most delicate manoeuvres, requiring the utmost skill, nicety, and precision. I believed that General Howard would do all these faithfully and well, and I think the result has justified my choice. I regarded both Generals Logan and Blair as "volunteers," that looked to personal fame and glory as auxiliary and secondary to their political ambition, and not as professional soldiers.

As soon as it was known that General Howard had been chosen to command the Army of the Tennessee; General Hooker applied to General Thomas to be relieved of the command of the Twentieth Corps, and General Thomas forwarded his application to me approved and heartily recommended. I at once telegraphed to General Halleck, recommending General Slocum (then at Vicksburg) to be his successor, because Slocum had been displaced from the command of his corps at the time when the Eleventh and Twelfth were united and made the Twentieth.

General Hooker was offended because he was not chosen to succeed McPherson; but his chances were not even considered; indeed, I had never been satisfied with him since his affair at the Gulp House, and had been more than once disposed to relieve him of his corps, because of his repeated attempts to interfere with Generals McPherson and Schofield. I had known Hooker since 1836, and was intimately associated with him in California, where we served together on the staff of General Persifer F. Smith. He had come to us from the East with a high reputation as a "fighter," which he had fully justified at Chattanooga and Peach-Tree Creek; at which latter battle I complimented him on the field for special gallantry, and afterward in official reports. Still, I did feel a sense of relief when he left us. We were then two hundred and fifty miles in advance of our base, dependent on a single line of railroad for our daily food. We had a bold, determined foe in our immediate front, strongly intrenched, with communication open to his rear for supplies and reenforcements, and every soldier realized that we had plenty of hard fighting ahead, and that all honors had to be fairly earned.

Until General Slocum joined (in the latter part of August), the Twentieth Corps was commanded by General A. S. Williams, the senior division commander present. On the 25th of July the army, therefore, stood thus: the Army of the Tennessee (General O. O. Howard commanding) was on the left, pretty much on the same ground it had occupied during the battle of the 22d, all ready to move rapidly by the rear to the extreme right beyond Proctor's Creek; the Army of the Ohio (General Schofield) was next in order, with its left flank reaching the Augusta Railroad; next in order, conforming closely with the rebel intrenchments of Atlanta, was General Thomas's Army of the Cumberland, in the order of—the Fourth Corps (Stanley's), the Twentieth Corps (Williams's), and the Fourteenth Corps (Palmer's). Palmer's right division (Jefferson C. Davis's) was strongly refused about five miles out, and was intrenched as against a sally about as strong as was our enemy. The cavalry was assembled in two strong divisions; that of McCook (including the brigade of Harrison which had been brought in from Opelika by General Rousseau) numbered about thirty-five hundred effective cavalry, and was posted to our right rear, at Turner's Ferry, where we had a good pontoon-bridge; and to our left rear, at and about Decatur, were the two cavalry divisions of Stoneman, twenty-five hundred, and Garrard, four thousand, united for the time and occasion under the command of Major-General George Stoneman, a cavalry-officer of high repute. My plan of action was to move the Army of the Tennessee to the right rapidly and boldly against the railroad below Atlanta, and at the same time to send all the cavalry around by the right and left to make a lodgment on the Macon road about Jonesboro.

All the orders were given, and the morning of the 27th was fixed for commencing the movement. On the 26th I received from General Stoneman a note asking permission (after having accomplished his orders to break up the railroad at Jonesboro) to go on to Macon to rescue our prisoners of war known to be held there, and then to push on to Andersonville, where was the great depot of Union prisoners, in which were penned at one time as many as twenty-three thousand of our men, badly fed and harshly treated. I wrote him an answer consenting substantially to his proposition, only modifying it by requiring him to send back General Garrard's division to its position on our left flank after he had broken up the railroad at Jonesboro. Promptly, and on time, all got off, and General Dodge's corps (the Sixteenth, of the Army of the Tennessee) reached its position across Proctor's Creek the same evening, and early the next morning (the 28th) Blair's corps (the Seventeenth) deployed on his right, both corps covering their front with the usual parapet; the Fifteenth Corps (General Logan's) came up that morning on the right of Blair, strongly refused, and began to prepare the usual cover. As General Jeff. C. Davis's division was, as it were, left out of line, I ordered it on the evening before to march down toward Turner's Ferry, and then to take a road laid down on our maps which led from there toward East Point, ready to engage any enemy that might attack our general right flank, after the same manner as had been done to the left flank on the 22d.

Personally on the morning of the 28th I followed the movement, and rode to the extreme right, where we could hear some skirmishing and an occasional cannon-shot. As we approached the ground held by the Fifteenth Corps, a cannon-ball passed over my shoulder and killed the horse of an orderly behind; and seeing that this gun enfiladed the road by which we were riding, we turned out of it and rode down into a valley, where we left our horses and walked up to the hill held by Morgan L. Smith's division of the Fifteenth Corps. Near a house I met Generals Howard and Logan, who explained that there was an intrenched battery in their front, with the appearance of a strong infantry support. I then walked up to the ridge, where I found General Morgan L. Smith. His men were deployed and engaged in rolling logs and fence-rails, preparing a hasty cover. From this ridge we could overlook the open fields near a meeting-house known as "Ezra Church," close by the Poor-House. We could see the fresh earth of a parapet covering some guns (that fired an occasional shot), and there was also an appearance of activity beyond. General Smith was in the act of sending forward a regiment from, his right flank to feel the position of the enemy, when I explained to him and to Generals Logan and Howard that they must look out for General Jeff. C. Davis's division, which was coming up from the direction of Turner's Ferry.

As the skirmish-fire warmed up along the front of Blair's corps, as well as along the Fifteenth Corps (Logan's), I became convinced that Hood designed to attack this right flank, to prevent, if possible, the extension of our line in that direction. I regained my horse, and rode rapidly back to see that Davis's division had been dispatched as ordered. I found General Davis in person, who was unwell, and had sent his division that morning early, under the command of his senior brigadier, Morgan; but, as I attached great importance to the movement, he mounted his horse, and rode away to overtake and to hurry forward the movement, so as to come up on the left rear of the enemy, during the expected battle.

By this time the sound of cannon and musketry denoted a severe battle as in progress, which began seriously at 11.30 a.m., and ended substantially by 4 p.m. It was a fierce attack by the enemy on our extreme right flank, well posted and partially covered. The most authentic account of the battle is given by General

Logan, who commanded the Fifteenth Corps, in his official report to the Adjutant-General of the Army of the Tennessee, thus:

HEADQUARTERS FIFTEENTH ARMY CORPS
BEFORE ATLANTA, GEORGIA, July 29, 1864

Lieutenant-Colonel WILLIAM T. CLARK, Assistant Adjutant-General, Army of the Tennessee, present.

COLONEL: I have the honor to report that, in pursuance of orders, I moved my command into position on the right of the Seventeenth Corps, which was the extreme right of the army in the field, during the night of the 27th and morning of the 28th; and, while advancing in line of battle to a more favorable position, we were met by the rebel infantry of Hardee's and Lee's corps, who made a determined and desperate attack on us at 11 A.M. of the 28th (yesterday).

My lines were only protected by logs and rails, hastily thrown up in front of them.

The first onset was received and checked, and the battle commenced and lasted until about three o'clock in the evening. During that time six successive charges were made, which were six times gallantly repulsed, each time with fearful loss to the enemy.

Later in the evening my lines were several times assaulted vigorously, but each time with like result. The worst of the fighting occurred on General Harrow's and Morgan L. Smith's fronts, which formed the centre and right of the corps. The troops could not have displayed greater courage, nor greater determination not to give ground; had they shown less, they would have been driven from their position.

Brigadier-Generals C. R. Woods, Harrow, and Morgan L. Smith, division commanders, are entitled to equal credit for gallant conduct and skill in repelling the assault. My thanks are due to Major-Generals Blair and Dodge for sending me reenforcements at a time when they were much needed. My losses were fifty killed, four hundred and forty-nine wounded, and seventy-three missing: aggregate, five hundred and seventy-two.

The division of General Harrow captured five battle-flags. There were about fifteen hundred or two thousand muskets left on the ground. One hundred and six prisoners were captured, exclusive of seventy-three wounded, who were sent to our hospital, and are being cared for by our surgeons. Five hundred and sixty-five rebels have up to this time been buried, and about two hundred are supposed to be yet unburied. A large number of their wounded were undoubtedly carried away in the night, as the enemy did not withdraw till near daylight. The enemy's loss could not have been less than six or seven thousand men. A more detailed report will hereafter be made.

I am, very respectfully,
Your obedient servant,

JOHN A. LOGAN,
Major-General, commanding Fifteenth Army Corps.

General Howard, in transmitting this report, added:

I wish to express my high gratification with the conduct of the troops engaged. I never saw better conduct in battle. General Logan, though ill and much worn out, was indefatigable, and the success of the day is as much attributable to him as to any one man.

This was, of coarse, the first fight in which General Howard had commanded the Army of the Tennessee, and he evidently aimed to reconcile General Logan in his disappointment, and to gain the heart of his army, to which he was a stranger. He very properly left General Logan to fight his own corps, but exposed himself freely; and, after the firing had ceased, in the afternoon he walked the lines; the men, as reported to me, gathered about him in the most affectionate way, and he at once gained their respect and confidence. To this fact I at the time attached much importance, for it put me at ease as to the future conduct of that most important army.

At no instant of time did I feel the least uneasiness about the result on the 28th, but wanted to reap fuller results, hoping that Davis's division would come up at the instant of defeat, and catch the enemy in flank; but the woods were dense, the roads obscure, and as usual this division got on the wrong road, and did not come into position until about dark. In like manner, I thought that Hood had greatly weakened his main lines inside of Atlanta, and accordingly sent repeated orders to Schofield and Thomas to make an attempt to break in; but both reported that they found the parapets very strong and full manned.

Our men were unusually encouraged by this day's work, for they realized that we could compel Hood to come out from behind his fortified lines to attack us at a disadvantage. In conversation with me, the soldiers of the Fifteenth Corps, with whom I was on the most familiar terms, spoke of the affair of the 28th as the easiest thing in the world; that, in fact, it was a common slaughter of the enemy; they pointed out where the rebel lines had been, and how they themselves had fired deliberately, had shot down their antagonists, whose bodies still lay unburied, and marked plainly their lines of battle, which must have halted within easy musket-range of our men, who were partially protected by their improvised line of logs and fence-rails. All bore willing testimony to the courage and spirit of the foe, who, though repeatedly repulsed, came back with increased determination some six or more times.

The next morning the Fifteenth Corps wheeled forward to the left over the battle-field of the day before, and Davis's division still farther prolonged the line, which reached nearly to the ever-to-be-remembered "Sandtown road."

Then, by further thinning out Thomas's line, which was well entrenched, I drew another division of Palmer's corps (Baird's) around to the right, to further strengthen that flank. I was impatient to hear from the cavalry raid, then four days out, and was watching for its effect, ready to make a bold push for the possession of East Point. General Garrard's division returned to Decatur on the 31st, and reported that General Stoneman had posted him at Flat Rock, while he (Stoneman) went on. The month of July therefore closed with our infantry line strongly entrenched, but drawn out from the Augusta road on the left to the Sandtown road on the right, a distance of full ten measured miles.

The enemy, though evidently somewhat intimidated by the results of their defeats on the 22d and 28th, still presented a bold front at all points, with fortified lines that defied a direct assault. Our railroad was done to the rear of our camps, Colonel W. P. Wright having reconstructed the bridge across the Chattahoochee in six days; and our garrisons and detachments to the rear had so effectually guarded the railroad that the trains from Nashville arrived daily, and our substantial wants were well supplied.

The month, though hot in the extreme, had been one of constant conflict, without intermission, and on four several occasions —viz., July 4th, 20th, 22d, and 28th—these affairs had amounted to real battles, with casualty lists by the thousands. Assuming the correctness of the rebel surgeon Foard's report, on page 577 of Johnston's "Narrative," commencing with July 4th and terminating with July 31st, we have:

Aggregate loss of the enemy......... 10,841

Our losses, as compiled from the official returns for July, 1864, are:

	Killed and Missing.	Wounded.	Total.
Aggregate loss of July	3,804	5,915	9,719

In this table the column of "killed and missing" embraces the prisoners that fell into the hands of the enemy, mostly lost in the Seventeenth Corps, on the 22d of July, and does not embrace the losses in the cavalry divisions of Garrard and McCook, which, however, were small for July. In all other respects the statement is absolutely correct. I am satisfied, however, that Surgeon Foard could not have been in possession of data sufficiently accurate to enable him to report the losses in actual battle of men who never saw the hospital. During the whole campaign I had rendered to me tri-monthly statements of "effective strength," from which I carefully eliminated the figures not essential for my conduct, so that at all times I knew the exact fighting-strength of each corps, division, and brigade, of the whole army, and also endeavored to bear in mind our losses both on the several fields of battle and by sickness, and well remember that I always estimated that during the month of July we had inflicted heavier loss on the enemy than we had sustained ourselves, and the above figures prove it conclusively. Before closing this chapter, I must record one or two minor events that occurred about this time, that may prove of interest.

On the 24th of July I received a dispatch from Inspector-General James A. Hardie, then on duty at the War Department in Washington, to the effect that Generals Osterhaus and Alvan P. Hovey had been appointed major-generals. Both of these had begun the campaign with us in command of divisions, but had gone to the rear—the former by reason of sickness, and the latter dissatisfied with General Schofield and myself about the composition of his division of the Twenty-third Corps. Both were esteemed as first-class officers, who had gained special distinction in the Vicksburg campaign. But up to that time, when the newspapers announced daily promotions elsewhere, no prominent officers serving with me had been advanced a peg, and I felt hurt. I answered Hardie on the 25th, in a dispatch which has been made public, closing with this language: "If the rear be the post of honor, then we had better all change front on Washington." To my amazement, in a few days I received from President Lincoln himself an answer, in which he caught me fairly. I have not preserved a copy of that dispatch, and suppose it was burned up in the Chicago fire; but it was characteristic of Mr. Lincoln, and was dated the 26th or 27th day of July, contained unequivocal expressions of respect for those who were fighting hard and unselfishly, offering us a full share of the honors and rewards of the war, and saying that, in the cases of Hovey and Osterhaus, he was influenced mainly by the recommendations of Generals Grant and Sherman. On the 27th I replied direct, apologizing somewhat for my message to General Hardie, saying that I did not suppose such messages ever reached him personally, explaining that General Grant's and Sherman's recommendations for Hovey and Osterhaus had been made when the events of the Vicksburg campaign were fresh with us, and that my dispatch of the 25th to General Hardie had reflected chiefly the feelings of the officers then present with me before Atlanta. The result of all this, however, was good, for another dispatch from General Hardie, of the 28th, called on me to nominate eight colonels for promotion as brigadier-generals. I at once sent a circular note to the army-commanders to nominate two colonels from the Army of the Ohio and three from each of the others; and the result was, that on the 29th of July I telegraphed the names of —Colonel William Gross, Thirty-sixth Indiana; Colonel Charles C. Walcutt, Forty-sixth Ohio; Colonel James W. Riley, One Hundred and Fourth Ohio; Colonel L. P. Bradley, Fifty-first Illinois; Colonel J. W. Sprague, Sixty-third Ohio; Colonel Joseph A. Cooper, Sixth East Tennessee; Colonel John T. Croxton, Fourth Kentucky; Colonel William W. Belknap, Fifteenth Iowa. These were promptly appointed brigadier-generals, were already in command of brigades or divisions; and I doubt if eight promotions were ever made fairer, or were more honestly earned, during the whole war.

CHAPTER XIX.
CAPTURE OF ATLANTA.

AUGUST AND SEPTEMBER, 1864

The month of August opened hot and sultry, but our position before Atlanta was healthy, with ample supply of wood, water, and provisions. The troops had become habituated to the slow and steady progress of the siege; the skirmish-lines were held close up to the enemy, were covered by rifle-trenches or logs, and kept up a continuous clatter of musketry. The mainlines were held farther back, adapted to the shape of the ground, with muskets loaded and stacked for instant use. The field-batteries were in select positions, covered by handsome parapets, and occasional shots from them gave life and animation to the scene. The men loitered about the trenches carelessly, or busied themselves in constructing ingenious huts out of the abundant timber, and seemed as snug, comfortable, and happy, as though they were at home. General Schofield was still on the extreme left, Thomas in the centre, and Howard on the right. Two divisions of the Fourteenth Corps (Baird's and Jeff. C. Davis's) were detached to the right rear, and held in reserve.

I thus awaited the effect of the cavalry movement against the railroad about Jonesboro, and had heard from General Garrard that Stoneman had gone on to Mason; during that day (August 1st) Colonel Brownlow, of a Tennessee cavalry regiment, came in to Marietta from General McCook, and reported that McCook's whole division had been overwhelmed, defeated, and captured at Newnan. Of course, I was disturbed by this wild report, though I discredited it, but made all possible preparations to strengthen our guards along the railroad to the rear, on the theory that the force of cavalry which had defeated McCook would at once be on the railroad about Marietta. At the same time Garrard was ordered to occupy the trenches on our left, while Schofield's whole army moved to the extreme right, and extended the line toward East Point. Thomas was also ordered still further to thin out his lines, so as to set free the other division (Johnson's) of the Fourteenth Corps (Palmer's), which was moved to the extreme right rear, and held in reserve ready to make a bold push from that flank to secure a footing on the Mason Railroad at or below East Point.

These changes were effected during the 2d and 3d days of August, when General McCook came in and reported the actual results of his cavalry expedition. He had crossed the Chattahoochee River below Campbellton, by his pontoon-bridge; had then marched rapidly across to the Mason Railroad at Lovejoy's Station, where he had reason to expect General Stoneman; but, not hearing of him, he set to work, tore up two miles of track, burned two trains of cars, and cut away five miles of telegraph-wire. He also found the wagon-train belonging to the rebel army in Atlanta, burned five hundred wagons, killed eight hundred mules; and captured seventy-two officers and three hundred and fifty men. Finding his progress eastward, toward McDonough, barred by a superior force, he turned back to Newnan, where he found himself completely surrounded by infantry and cavalry. He had to drop his prisoners and fight his way out, losing about six hundred men in killed and captured, and then returned with the remainder to his position at Turner's Ferry. This was bad enough, but not so bad as had been reported by Colonel Brownlow. Meantime, rumors came that General Stoneman was down about Mason, on the east bank of the Ocmulgee. On the 4th of August Colonel Adams got to Marietta with his small brigade of nine hundred men belonging to Stoneman's cavalry, reporting, as usual, all the rest lost, and this was partially confirmed by a report which came to me all the way round by General Grant's headquarters before Richmond. A few days afterward Colonel Capron also got in, with another small brigade perfectly demoralized, and confirmed the report that General Stoneman had covered the escape of these two small brigades, himself standing with a reserve of seven hundred men, with which he surrendered to a Colonel Iverson. Thus another of my cavalry divisions was badly damaged, and out of the fragments we hastily reorganized three small divisions under Brigadier-Generals Garrard, McCook, and Kilpatrick.

Stoneman had not obeyed his orders to attack the railroad first before going to Macon and Andersonville, but had crossed the Ocmulgee River high up near Covington, and had gone down that river on the east bank. He reached Clinton, and sent out detachments which struck the railroad leading from Macon to Savannah at Griswold Station, where they found and destroyed seventeen locomotives and over a hundred cars; then went on and burned the bridge across the Oconee, and reunited the division before Macon. Stoneman shelled the town across the river, but could not cross over by the bridge, and returned to Clinton, where he found his retreat obstructed, as he supposed, by a superior force. There he became bewildered, and sacrificed himself for the safety of his command. He occupied the attention of his enemy by a small force of seven hundred men, giving Colonels Adams and Capron leave, with their brigades, to cut their way back to me at Atlanta. The former reached us entire, but the latter was struck and scattered at some place farther north, and came in by detachments. Stoneman surrendered, and remained a prisoner until he was exchanged some time after, late in September, at Rough and Ready.

I now became satisfied that cavalry could not, or would not, make a sufficient lodgment on the railroad below Atlanta, and that nothing would suffice but for us to reach it with the main army. Therefore the most urgent efforts to that end were made, and to Schofield, on the right, was committed the charge of this special object. He had his own corps (the Twenty-third), composed of eleven thousand and seventy-five infantry and eight hundred and eighty-five artillery, with McCook's broken division of cavalry, seventeen hundred and fifty-four men and horses. For this purpose I also placed the Fourteenth Corps (Palmer) under his orders. This corps numbered at the time seventeen thousand two hundred and eighty-eight infantry and eight hundred and twenty-six artillery; but General Palmer claimed to rank General Schofield in the date of his commission as major-general, and denied the latter's right to exercise command over him. General Palmer was a man of ability, but was not enterprising. His three divisions were compact and strong, well commanded, admirable on the defensive, but slow to move or to act on the offensive. His corps (the Fourteenth) had sustained, up to that time, fewer hard knocks than any other corps in the whole army, and I was anxious to give it a chance. I always expected to have a desperate fight to get possession of the Macon road, which was then the vital objective of the campaign. Its possession by us would, in my judgment, result in the capture of Atlanta, and give us the fruits of victory, although the destruction of Hood's army was the real object to be desired. Yet Atlanta was known as the "Gate-City of the South," was full of founderies, arsenals, and machine-shops, and I knew that its capture would be the death-knell of the Southern Confederacy.

On the 4th of August I ordered General Schofield to make a bold attack on the railroad, anywhere about East Point, and ordered General Palmer to report to him for duty. He at once denied General Schofield's right to command him; but, after examining the dates of their respective commissions, and hearing their arguments, I wrote to General Palmer.

August 4th.-10.45 p.m.

From the statements made by yourself and General Schofield to-day, my decision is, that he ranks you as a major-general, being of the same date of present commission, by reason of his previous superior rank as brigadier-general. The movements of to-morrow are so important that the orders of the superior on that flank must be regarded as military orders, and not in the nature of co-operation. I did hope that there would be no necessity for my making this decision; but it is better for all parties interested that no question of rank should occur in actual battle. The Sandtown road, and the railroad, if possible, must be gained to-morrow, if it costs half your command. I regard the loss of time this afternoon as equal to the loss of two thousand men.

I also communicated the substance of this to General Thomas, to whose army Palmer's corps belonged, who replied on the 5th:

I regret to hear that Palmer has taken the course he has, and I know that he intends to offer his resignation as soon as he can properly do so. I recommend that his application be granted.

And on the 5th I again wrote to General Palmer, arguing the point with him, advising him, as a friend, not to resign at that crisis lest his motives might be misconstrued, and because it might damage his future career in civil life; but, at the same time, I felt it my duty to say to him that the operations on that flank, during the 4th and 5th, had not been satisfactory—not imputing to him, however, any want of energy or skill, but insisting that "the events did not keep pace with my desires." General Schofield had reported to me that night:

I am compelled to acknowledge that I have totally failed to make any aggressive movement with the Fourteenth Corps. I have ordered General Johnson's division to replace General Hascall's this evening, and I propose to-morrow to take my own troops (Twenty-third Corps) to the right, and try to recover what has been lost by two days' delay. The force may likely be too small.

I sanctioned the movement, and ordered two of Palmers divisions—Davis's and Baird's—to follow en echelon in support of Schofield, and summoned General Palmer to meet me in person: He came on the 6th to my headquarters, and insisted on his resignation being accepted, for which formal act I referred him to General Thomas. He then rode to General Thomas's camp, where he made a written resignation of his office as commander of the Fourteenth Corps, and was granted the usual leave of absence to go to his home in Illinois, there to await further orders. General Thomas recommended that the resignation be accepted; that Johnson, the senior division commander of the corps, should be ordered back to Nashville as chief of cavalry, and that Brigadier-General Jefferson C. Davis, the next in order, should be promoted major general, and assigned to command the corps. These changes had to be referred to the President, in Washington, and were, in due time, approved and executed; and thenceforward I had no reason to complain of the slowness or inactivity of that splendid corps. It had been originally formed by General George H. Thomas, had been commanded by him in person, and had imbibed some what his personal character, viz., steadiness, good order, and deliberation nothing hasty or rash, but always safe, "slow, and sure." On August 7th I telegraphed to General Halleck:

Have received to-day the dispatches of the Secretary of War and of General Grant, which are very satisfactory. We keep hammering away all the time, and there is no peace, inside or outside of Atlanta. To-day General Schofield got round the line which was assaulted yesterday by General Reilly's brigade, turned it and gained the ground where the assault had been made, and got possession of all our dead and wounded. He continued to press on that flank, and brought on a noisy but not a bloody battle. He drove the enemy behind his main breastworks, which cover the railroad from Atlanta to East Point, and captured a good many of the skirmishers, who are of his best troops—for the militia hug the breastworks close. I do not deem it prudent to extend any more to the right, but will push forward daily by parallels, and make the inside of Atlanta too hot to be endured. I have sent back to Chattanooga for two thirty-pound Parrotts, with which we can pick out almost any house in town. I am too impatient for a siege, and don't know but this is as good a place to fight it out on, as farther inland. One thing is certain, whether we get inside of Atlanta or not, it will be a used-up community when we are done with it.

In Schofield's extension on the 5th, General Reilly's brigade had struck an outwork, which he promptly attacked, but, as usual, got entangled in the trees and bushes which had been felled, and lost about five hundred men, in killed and wounded; but, as above reported, this outwork was found abandoned the next day, and we could see from it that the rebels were extending their lines, parallel with the railroad, about as fast as we could add to our line of investment. On the 10th of August the Parrott thirty-pounders were received and placed in Position; for a couple of days we kept up a sharp fire from all our batteries converging on Atlanta, and at every available point we advanced our infantry-lines, thereby shortening and strengthening the investment; but I was not willing to order a direct assault, unless some accident or positive neglect on the part of our antagonist should reveal an opening. However, it was manifest that no such opening was intended by Hood, who felt secure behind his strong defenses. He had repelled our cavalry attacks on his railroad, and had damaged us seriously thereby, so I expected that he would attempt the same game against our rear. Therefore I made extraordinary exertions to recompose our cavalry divisions, which were so essential, both for defense and offense. Kilpatrick was given that on our right rear, in support of Schofield's exposed flank; Garrard retained that on our general left; and McCook's division was held somewhat in reserve, about Marietta and the railroad. On the 10th, having occasion to telegraph to General Grant, then in Washington, I used this language:

Since July 28th Hood has not attempted to meet us outside his parapets. In order to possess and destroy effectually his communications, I may have to leave a corps at the railroad-bridge, well intrenched, and cut loose with the balance to make a circle of desolation around Atlanta. I do not propose to assault the works, which are too strong, nor to proceed by regular approaches. I have lost a good many regiments, and will lose more, by the expiration of service; and this is the only reason why I want reenforcements. We have killed, crippled, and captured more of the enemy than we have lost by his acts.

On the 12th of August I heard of the success of Admiral Farragut in entering Mobile Bay, which was regarded as a most valuable auxiliary to our operations at Atlanta; and learned that I had been commissioned a major-general in the regular army, which was unexpected, and not desired until successful in the capture of Atlanta. These did not change the fact that we were held in check by the stubborn defense of the place, and a conviction was forced on my mind that our enemy would hold fast, even though every house in the town should be battered down by our artillery. It was evident that we most decoy him out to fight us on something like equal terms, or else, with the whole army, raise the siege and attack his communications. Accordingly, on the 13th of August, I gave general orders for the Twentieth Corps to draw back to the railroad-bridge at the Chattahoochee, to protect our trains, hospitals, spare artillery, and the railroad-depot, while the rest of the army should move bodily to some point on the Macon Railroad below East Point.

Luckily, I learned just then that the enemy's cavalry, under General Wheeler, had made a wide circuit around our left flank, and had actually reached our railroad at Tilton Station, above Resaca, captured a drove of one thousand of our beef-cattle, and was strong enough to appear before Dalton, and demand its commander, Colonel Raum, the surrender of the place. General John E. Smith, who was at Kingston, collected together a couple of thousand men, and proceeded in cars to the relief of Dalton when Wheeler retreated northward toward Cleveland. On the 16th another detachment of the enemy's cavalry appeared in force about Allatoona and the Etowah bridge, when I became fully convinced that Hood had sent all of his cavalry to raid upon our railroads. For some days our communication with Nashville was interrupted by the destruction of the telegraph-lines, as well as railroad. I at once ordered strong reconnoissances forward from our flanks on the left by Garrard, and on the right by Kilpatrick. The former moved with so much caution that I was displeased; but Kilpatrick, on the contrary, displayed so much zeal and activity that I was attracted to him at once. He reached Fairburn Station, on the West Point road, and tore it up, returning safely to his position on our right flank. I summoned him to me, and was so pleased with his spirit and confidence, that I concluded to suspend the general movement of the main army, and to send him with his small division of cavalry to break up the Macon road about Jonesboro, in the hopes that it would force Hood to evacuate Atlanta, and that I should thereby not only secure possession of the city itself, but probably could catch Hood in the confusion of retreat; and, further to increase the chances of success.

I ordered General Thomas to detach two brigades of Garrard's division of cavalry from the left to the right rear, to act as a reserve in support of General Kilpatrick. Meantime, also, the utmost activity was ordered along our whole front by the infantry and artillery. Kilpatrick got off during the night of the 18th, and returned to us on the 22d, having made the complete circuit of Atlanta. He reported that he had destroyed three miles of the railroad about Jonesboro, which he reckoned would take ten days to repair; that he had encountered a division of infantry and a brigade of cavalry (Ross's); that he had captured a battery and destroyed three of its guns, bringing one in as a trophy, and he also brought in three battle-flags and seventy prisoners. On the 23d, however, we saw trains coming into Atlanta from the south, when I became more than ever convinced that cavalry could not or would not work hard enough to disable a railroad properly, and therefore resolved at once to proceed to the execution of my original plan. Meantime, the damage done to our own railroad and telegraph by Wheeler, about Resaca and Dalton, had been repaired, and Wheeler himself was too far away to be of any service to his own army, and where he could not do us much harm, viz., up about the Hiawaesee. On the 24th I rode down to the Chattahoochee bridge, to see in person that it could be properly defended by the single corps proposed to be left there for that purpose, and found that the rebel works, which had been built by Johnston to resist us, could be easily utilized against themselves; and on returning to my camp, at that same evening, I telegraphed to General Halleck as follows:

Heavy fires in Atlanta all day, caused by our artillery. I will be all ready, and will commence the movement around Atlanta by the south, tomorrow night, and for some time you will hear little of us. I will keep open a courier line back to the Chattahoochee bridge, by way of Sandtown. The Twentieth Corps will hold the railroad-bridge, and I will move with the balance of the army, provisioned for twenty days.

Meantime General Dodge (commanding the Sixteenth Corps) had been wounded in the forehead, had gone to the rear, and his two divisions were distributed to the Fifteenth and Seventeenth Corps. The real movement commenced on the 25th, at night. The Twentieth Corps drew back and took post at the railroad-bridge, and the Fourth Corps (Stanley) moved to his right rear, closing up with the Fourteenth Corps (Jeff. C. Davis) near Utoy Creek; at the same time Garrard's cavalry, leaving their horses out of sight, occupied the vacant trenches, so that the enemy did not detect the change at all. The next night (26th) the Fifteenth and Seventeenth Corps, composing the Army of the Tennessee (Howard), drew out of their trenches, made a wide circuit, and came up on the extreme right of the Fourth and Fourteenth Corps of the Army of the Cumberland (Thomas) along Utoy Creek, facing south. The enemy seemed to suspect something that night, using his artillery pretty freely; but I think he supposed we were going to retreat altogether. An artillery-shot, fired at random, killed one man and wounded another, and the next morning some of his infantry came out of Atlanta and found our camps abandoned. It was afterward related that there was great rejoicing in Atlanta "that the Yankees were gone;" the fact was telegraphed all over the South, and several trains of cars (with ladies) came up from Macon to assist in the celebration of their grand victory.

On the 28th (making a general left-wheel, pivoting on Schofield) both Thomas and Howard reached the West Point Railroad, extending from East Point to Red-Oak Station and Fairburn, where we spent the next day (29th) in breaking it up thoroughly. The track was heaved up in sections the length of a regiment, then separated rail by rail; bonfires were made of the ties and of fence-rails on which the rails were heated, carried to trees or telegraph-poles, wrapped around and left to cool. Such rails could not be used again; and, to be still more certain, we filled up many deep cuts with trees, brush, and earth, and commingled with them loaded shells, so arranged that they would explode on an attempt to haul out the bushes. The explosion of one such shell would have demoralized a gang of negroes, and thus would have prevented even the attempt to clear the road.

Meantime Schofield, with the Twenty-third Corps, presented a bold front toward East Point, daring and inviting the enemy to sally out to attack him in position. His first movement was on the 30th, to Mount Gilead Church, then to Morrow's Mills, facing Rough and Ready. Thomas was on his right, within easy support, moving by cross-roads from Red Oak to the Fayetteville road, extending from Couch's to Renfrew's; and Howard was aiming for Jonesboro.

I was with General Thomas that day, which was hot but otherwise very pleasant. We stopped for a short noon-rest near a little church (marked on our maps as Shoal-Creek Church), which stood back about a hundred yards from the road, in a grove of native oaks. The infantry column had halted in the road, stacked their arms, and the men were scattered about—some lying in the shade of the trees, and others were bringing corn-stalks from a large corn-field across the road to feed our horses, while still others had arms full of the roasting-ears, then in their prime. Hundreds of fires were soon started with the fence-rails, and the men were busy roasting the ears. Thomas and I were walking up and down the road which led to the church, discussing the chances of the movement, which he thought were extra-hazardous, and our path carried us by a fire at which a soldier was roasting his corn. The fire was built artistically; the man was stripping the ears of their husks, standing them in front of his fire, watching them carefully, and turning each ear little by little, so as to roast it nicely. He was down on his knees intent on his business, paying little heed to the stately and serious deliberations of his leaders. Thomas's mind was running on the fact that we had cut loose from our base of supplies, and that seventy thousand men were then dependent for their food on the chance supplies of the country (already impoverished by the requisitions of the enemy), and on the contents of our wagons. Between Thomas and his men there existed a most kindly relation, and he frequently talked with them in the most familiar way. Pausing awhile, and watching the operations of this man roasting his corn, he said, "What are you doing?" The man looked up smilingly "Why, general, I am laying in a supply of provisions." "That is right, my man, but don't waste your provisions." As we resumed our walk, the man remarked, in a sort of musing way, but loud enough for me to hear: "There he goes, there goes the old man, economizing as usual." "Economizing" with corn, which cost only the labor of gathering and roasting!

As we walked, we could hear General Howard's guns at intervals, away off to our right front, but an ominous silence continued toward our left, where I was expecting at each moment to hear the sound of battle. That night we reached Renfrew's, and had reports from left to right (from General Schofield, about Morrow's Mills, to General Howard, within a couple of miles of Jonesboro). The next morning (August 31st) all moved straight for the railroad. Schofield reached it near Rough and Ready, and Thomas at two points between there and Jonesboro. Howard found an intrenched foe (Hardee's corps) covering Jonesboro, and his men began at once to dig their accustomed rifle-pits. Orders were sent to Generals Thomas and Schofield to turn straight for Jonesboro, tearing up the railroad-track as they advanced. About 3.00 p.m. the enemy sallied from Jonesboro against the Fifteenth corps, but was easily repulsed, and driven back within his lines. All hands were kept busy tearing up the railroad, and it was not until toward evening of the 1st day of September that the Fourteenth Corps (Davis) closed down on the north front of Jonesboro, connecting on his right with Howard, and his left reaching the railroad, along which General Stanley was moving, followed by Schofield. General Davis formed his divisions in line about 4 p.m., swept forward over some old cotton-fields in full view, and went over the rebel parapet handsomely, capturing the whole of Govan's brigade, with two field-batteries of ten guns. Being on the spot, I checked Davis's movement, and ordered General Howard to send the two divisions of the Seventeenth Corps (Blair) round by his right rear, to get below Jonesboro, and to reach the railroad, so as to cut off retreat in that direction. I also dispatched orders after orders to hurry forward Stanley, so as to lap around Jonesboro on the east, hoping thus to capture the whole of Hardee's corps. I sent first Captain Audenried (aide-de-camp), then Colonel Poe, of the Engineers, and lastly General Thomas himself (and that is the only time during the campaign I can recall seeing General Thomas urge his horse into a gallop). Night was approaching, and the country on the farther side of the railroad was densely wooded. General Stanley had come up on the left of Davis, and was deploying, though there could not have been on his front more than a skirmish-line. Had he moved straight on by the flank, or by a slight circuit to his left, he would have inclosed the whole ground occupied by Hardee's corps, and that corps could not have escaped us; but night came on, and Hardee did escape.

Meantime General Slocum had reached his corps (the Twentieth), stationed at the Chattahoochee bridge, had relieved General A. S. Williams in command, and orders had been sent back to him to feel forward occasionally toward Atlanta, to observe the effect when we had reached the railroad. That night I was so restless and impatient that I could not sleep, and about midnight there arose toward Atlanta sounds of shells exploding, and other sound like that of musketry. I walked to the house of a farmer close by my bivouac, called him out to listen to the reverberations which came from the direction of Atlanta (twenty miles to the north of us), and inquired of him if he had resided there long. He said he had, and that these sounds were just like those of a battle. An interval of quiet then ensued, when again, about 4 a.m., arose other similar explosions, but I still remained in doubt whether the enemy was engaged in blowing up his own magazines, or whether General Slocum had not felt forward, and become engaged in a real battle.

The next morning General Hardee was gone, and we all pushed forward along the railroad south, in close pursuit, till we ran up against his lines at a point just above Lovejoy's Station. While bringing forward troops and feeling the new position of our adversary, rumors came from the rear that the enemy had evacuated Atlanta, and that General Slocum was in the city. Later in the day I received a note in Slocum's own handwriting, stating that he had heard during the night the very sounds that I have referred to; that he had moved rapidly up from the bridge about daylight, and had entered Atlanta unopposed. His letter was dated inside the city, so there was no doubt of the fact. General Thomas's bivouac was but a short distance from mine, and, before giving notice to the army in general orders, I sent one of my staff-officers to show him the note. In a few minutes the officer returned, soon followed by Thomas himself, who again examined the note, so as to be perfectly certain that it was genuine. The news seemed to him too good to be true. He snapped his fingers, whistled, and almost danced, and, as the news spread to the army, the shouts that arose from our men, the wild hallooing and glorious laughter, were to us a full recompense for the labor and toils and hardships through which we had passed in the previous three months.

A courier-line was at once organized, messages were sent back and forth from our camp at Lovejoy's to Atlanta, and to our telegraph-station at the Chattahoochee bridge. Of course, the glad tidings flew on the wings of electricity to all parts of the North, where the people had patiently awaited news of their husbands, sons, and brothers, away down in "Dixie Land;" and congratulations came pouring back full of good-will and patriotism. This victory was most opportune; Mr. Lincoln himself told me afterward that even he had previously felt in doubt, for the summer was fast passing away; that General Grant seemed to be checkmated about Richmond and Petersburg, and my army seemed to have run up against an impassable barrier, when, suddenly and unexpectedly, came the news that "Atlanta was ours, and fairly won." On this text many a fine speech was made, but none more eloquent than that by Edward Everett, in Boston. A presidential election then agitated the North. Mr. Lincoln represented the national cause, and General McClellan had accepted the nomination of the Democratic party, whose platform was that the war was a failure, and that it was better to allow the South to go free to establish a separate government, whose corner-stone should be slavery. Success to our arms at that instant was therefore a political necessity; and it was all-important that something startling in our interest should occur before the election in November. The brilliant success at Atlanta filled that requirement, and made the election of Mr. Lincoln certain. Among the many letters of congratulation received, those of Mr. Lincoln and General Grant seem most important:

EXECUTIVE MANSION
WASHINGTON, D.C. September 3, 1864.

The national thanks are rendered by the President to Major-General W. T. Sherman and the gallant officers and soldiers of his command before Atlanta, for the distinguished ability and perseverance displayed in the campaign in Georgia, which, under Divine favor, has resulted in the capture of Atlanta. The marches, battles, sieges, and other military operations, that have signalized the campaign, must render it famous in the annals of war, and have entitled those who have participated therein to the applause and thanks of the nation.

ABRAHAM LINCOLN
President of the United States

CITY POINT VIRGINIA, September 4, 1864-9 P.M.

Major-General SHERMAN: I have just received your dispatch announcing the capture of Atlanta. In honor of your great victory, I have ordered a salute to be fired with shotted guns from every battery bearing upon the enemy. The salute will be fired within an hour, amid great rejoicing.

U. S. GRANT, Lieutenant-General.

These dispatches were communicated to the army in general orders, and we all felt duly encouraged and elated by the praise of those competent to bestow it.

The army still remained where the news of success had first found us, viz., Lovejoy's; but, after due refection, I resolved not to attempt at that time a further pursuit of Hood's army, but slowly and deliberately to move back, occupy Atlanta, enjoy a short period of rest, and to think well over the next step required in the progress of events. Orders for this movement were made on the 5th September, and three days were given for each army to reach the place assigned it, viz.: the Army of the Cumberland in and about Atlanta; the Army of the Tennessee at East Point; and the Army of the Ohio at Decatur.

Personally I rode back to Jonesboro on the 6th, and there inspected the rebel hospital, full of wounded officers and men left by Hardee in his retreat. The next night we stopped at Rough and Ready, and on the 8th of September we rode into Atlanta, then occupied by the Twentieth Corps (General Slocum). In the Court-House Square was encamped a brigade, embracing the Massachusetts Second and Thirty-third Regiments, which had two of the finest bands of the army, and their music was to us all a source of infinite pleasure during our sojourn in that city. I took up my headquarters in the house of Judge Lyons, which stood opposite one corner of the Court-House Square, and at once set about a measure already ordered, of which I had thought much and long, viz., to remove the entire civil population, and to deny to all civilians from the rear the expected profits of civil trade. Hundreds of sutlers and traders were waiting at Nashville and Chattanooga, greedy to reach Atlanta with their wares and goods, with, which to drive a profitable trade with the inhabitants. I gave positive orders that none of these traders, except three (one for each separate army), should be permitted to come nearer than Chattanooga; and, moreover, I peremptorily required that all the citizens and families resident in Atlanta should go away, giving to each the option to go south or north, as their interests or feelings dictated. I was resolved to make Atlanta a pure military garrison or depot, with no civil population to influence military measures. I had seen Memphis, Vicksburg, Natchez, and New Orleans, all captured from the enemy, and each at once was garrisoned by a full division of troops, if not more; so that success was actually crippling our armies in the field by detachments to guard and protect the interests of a hostile population.

I gave notice of this purpose, as early as the 4th of September, to General Halleck, in a letter concluding with these words:

If the people raise a howl against my barbarity and cruelty, I will answer that war is war, and not popularity-seeking. If they want peace, they and their relatives most stop the war.

I knew, of course, that such a measure would be strongly criticised, but made up my mind to do it with the absolute certainty of its justness, and that time would sanction its wisdom. I knew that the people of the South would read in this measure two important conclusions: one, that we were in earnest; and the other, if they were sincere in their common and popular clamor "to die in the last ditch," that the opportunity would soon come.

Soon after our reaching Atlanta, General Hood had sent in by a flag of truce a proposition, offering a general exchange of prisoners, saying that he was authorized to make such an exchange by the Richmond authorities, out of the vast number of our men then held captive at Andersonville, the same whom General Stoneman had hoped to rescue at the time of his raid. Some of these prisoners had already escaped and got in, had described the pitiable condition of the remainder, and, although I felt a sympathy for their hardships and sufferings as deeply as any man could, yet as nearly all the prisoners who had been captured by us during the campaign had been sent, as fast as taken, to the usual depots North, they were then beyond my control. There were still about two thousand, mostly captured at Jonesboro, who had been sent back by cars, but had not passed Chattanooga. These I ordered back, and offered General Hood to exchange them for Stoneman, Buell, and such of my own army as would make up the equivalent; but I would not exchange for his prisoners generally, because I knew these would have to be sent to their own regiments, away from my army, whereas all we could give him could at once be put to duty in his immediate army. Quite an angry correspondence grew up between us, which was published at the time in the newspapers, but it is not to be found in any book of which I have present knowledge, and therefore is given here, as illustrative of the events referred to, and of the feelings of the actors in the game of war at that particular crisis, together with certain other original letters of Generals Grant and Halleck, never hitherto published.

HEADQUARTERS ARMIES OF THE UNITED STATES CITY POINT, VIRGINIA, September 12, 1864

Major-General W. T. SHERMAN, commanding Military Division of the Mississippi

GENERAL: I send Lieutenant-Colonel Horace Porter, of my staff, with this. Colonel Porter will explain to you the exact condition of affairs here, better than I can do in the limits of a letter. Although I feel myself strong enough now for offensive operations, I am holding on quietly, to get advantage of recruits and convalescents, who are coming forward very rapidly. My lines are necessarily very long, extending from Deep Bottom, north of the James, across the peninsula formed by the Appomattox and the James, and south of the Appomattox to the Weldon road. This line is very strongly fortified, and can be held with comparatively few men; but, from its great length, necessarily takes many in the aggregate. I propose, when I do move, to extend my left so as to control what is known as the Southside, or Lynchburg & Petersburg road; then, if possible, to keep the Danville road out. At the same time this move is made, I want to send a force of from six to ten thousand men against Wilmington. The way I propose to do this is to land the men north of Fort Fisher, and hold that point. At the same time a large naval fleet will be assembled there, and the iron-clads will run the batteries as they did at Mobile. This will give us the same control of the harbor of Wilmington that we now have of the harbor of Mobile. What you are to do with the forces at your command, I do not exactly see. The difficulties of supplying your army, except when they are constantly moving beyond where you are, I plainly see. If it had not been for Price's movement, Canby could have sent twelve thousand more men to Mobile. From your command on the Mississippi, an equal number could have been taken. With these forces, my idea would have been to divide them, sending one-half to Mobile, and the other half to Savannah. You could then move as proposed in your telegram, so as to threaten Macon and Augusta equally. Whichever one should be abandoned by the enemy, you could take and open up a new base of supplies. My object now in sending a staff-officer to you is not so much to suggest operations for you as to get your views, and to have plans matured by the time every thing can be got ready. It would probably be the 5th of October before any of the plans here indicated will be executed. If you have any promotions to recommend, send the names forward, and I will approve them.

In conclusion, it is hardly necessary for me to say that I feel you have accomplished the most gigantic undertaking given to any general in this war, and with a skill and ability that will be acknowledged in history as unsurpassed, if not unequaled. It gives me as much pleasure to record this in your favor as it world in favor of any living man, myself included. Truly yours,

41

U. S. GRANT, *Lieutenant-General.*

HEADQUARTERS MILITARY DIVISION OF THE MISSISSIPPI IN THE FIELD, ATLANTA, GEORGIA, September 20, 1864.

Lieutenant-General U. S. GRANT, Commander-in-Chief, City Point, Virgina.

GENERAL: I have the honor to acknowledge, at the hands of Lieutenant Colonel Porter, of your staff, your letter of September 12th, and accept with thanks the honorable and kindly mention of the services of this army in the great cause in which we are all engaged.

I send by Colonel Porter all official reports which are completed, and will in a few days submit a list of names which are deemed worthy of promotion.

I think we owe it to the President to save him the invidious task of selection among the vast number of worthy applicants, and have ordered my army commanders to prepare their lists with great care, and to express their preferences, based upon claims of actual capacity and services rendered.

These I will consolidate, and submit in such a form that, if mistakes are made, they will at least be sanctioned by the best contemporaneous evidence of merit, for I know that vacancies do not exist equal in number to that of the officers who really deserve promotion.

As to the future, I am pleased to know that your army is being steadily reinforced by a good class of men, and I hope it will go on until you have a force that is numerically double that of your antagonist, so that with one part you can watch him, and with the other push out boldly from your left flank, occupy the Southside Railroad, compel him to attack you in position, or accept battle on your own terms.

We ought to ask our country for the largest possible armies that can be raised, as so important a thing as the self-existence of a great nation should not be left to the fickle chances of war.

Now that Mobile is shut out to the commerce of our enemy, it calls for no further effort on our part, unless the capture of the city can be followed by the occupation of the Alabama River and the railroad to Columbus, Georgia, when that place would be a magnificent auxiliary to my further progress into Georgia; but, until General Canby is much reinforced, and until he can more thoroughly subdue the scattered armies west of the Mississippi, I suppose that much cannot be attempted by him against the Alabama River and Columbus, Georgia.

The utter destruction of Wilmington, North Carolina, is of importance only in connection with the necessity of cutting off all foreign trade to our enemy, and if Admiral Farragut can get across the bar, and move quickly, I suppose he will succeed. From my knowledge of the mouth of Cape Fear River, I anticipate more difficulty in getting the heavy ships across the bar than in reaching the town of Wilmington; but, of course, the soundings of the channel are well known at Washington, as well as the draught of his iron-clads, so that it must be demonstrated to be feasible, or else it would not be attempted. If successful, I suppose that Fort Caswell will be occupied, and the fleet at once sent to the Savannah River. Then the reduction of that city is the next question. It once in our possession, and the river open to us, I would not hesitate to cross the State of Georgia with sixty thousand men, hauling some stores, and depending on the country for the balance. Where a million of people find subsistence, my army won't starve; but, as you know, in a country like Georgia, with few roads and innumerable streams, an inferior force can so delay an army and harass it, that it would not be a formidable object; but if the enemy knew that we had our boats in the Savannah River I could rapidly move to Milledgeville, where there is abundance of corn and meat, and could so threaten Macon and Augusta that the enemy world doubtless give up Macon for Augusta; then I would move so as to interpose between Augusta and Savannah, and force him to give us Augusta, with the only powder-mills and factories remaining in the South, or let us have the use of the Savannah River. Either horn of the dilemma will be worth a battle. I would prefer his holding Augusta (as the probabilities are); for then, with the Savannah River in our possession, the taking of Augusta would be a mere matter of time. This campaign can be made in the winter.

But the more I study the game, the more am I convinced that it would be wrong for us to penetrate farther into Georgia without an objective beyond. It would not be productive of much good. I can start east and make a circuit south and back, doing vast damage to the State, but resulting in no permanent good; and by mere threatening to do so, I hold a rod over the Georgians, who are not over-loyal to the South. I will therefore give it as my opinion that your army and Canby's should be reinforced to the maximum; that, after you get Wilmington, you should strike for Savannah and its river; that General Canby should hold the Mississippi River, and send a force to take Columbus, Georgia, either by way of the Alabama or Appalachicola River; that I should keep Hood employed and put my army in fine order for a march on Augusta, Columbia, and Charleston; and start as soon as Wilmington is sealed to commerce, and the city of Savannah is in our possession.

42

I think it will be found that the movements of Price and Shelby, west of the Mississippi, are mere diversions. They cannot hope to enter Missouri except as raiders; and the truth is, that General Rosecrans should be ashamed to take my troops for such a purpose. If you will secure Wilmington and the city of Savannah from your centre, and let General Canby leave command over the Mississippi River and country west of it, I will send a force to the Alabama and Appalachicola, provided you give me one hundred thousand of the drafted men to fill up my old regiments; and if you will fix a day to be in Savannah, I will insure our possession of Macon and a point on the river below Augusta. The possession of the Savannah River is more than fatal to the possibility of Southern independence. They may stand the fall of Richmond, but not of all Georgia.

I will have a long talk with Colonel Porter, and tell him every thing that may occur to me of interest to you.

In the mean time, know that I admire your dogged perseverance and pluck more than ever. If you can whip Lee and I can march to the Atlantic, I think Uncle Abe will give us a twenty days' leave of absence to see the young folks.

Yours as ever,

W. T. SHERMAN, Major-General.

HEADQUARTERS OF THE ARMY,
WASHINGTON, September 16, 1864.

General W. T. SHERMAN, Atlanta, Georgia.

My DEAR GENERAL: Your very interesting letter of the 4th is just received. Its perusal has given me the greatest pleasure. I have not written before to congratulate you on the capture of Atlanta, the objective point of your brilliant campaign, for the reason that I have been suffering from my annual attack of "coryza," or hay-cold. It affects my eyes so much that I can scarcely see to write. As you suppose, I have watched your movements most attentively and critically, and I do not hesitate to say that your campaign has been the most brilliant of the war. Its results are less striking and less complete than those of General Grant at Vicksburg, but then you have had greater difficulties to encounter, a longer line of communications to keep up, and a longer and more continuous strain upon yourself and upon your army.

You must have been very considerably annoyed by the State negro recruiting-agents. Your letter was a capital one, and did much good. The law was a ridiculous one; it was opposed by the War Department, but passed through the influence of Eastern manufacturers, who hoped to escape the draft in that way. They were making immense fortunes out of the war, and could well afford to purchase negro recruits, and thus save their employees at home.

I fully agree with you in regard to the policy of a stringent draft; but, unfortunately, political influences are against us, and I fear it will not amount to much. Mr. Seward's speech at Auburn, again prophesying, for the twentieth time, that the rebellion would be crushed in a few months, and saying that there would be no draft, as we now had enough soldiers to end the war, etc., has done much harm, in a military point of view. I have seen enough of politics here to last me for life. You are right in avoiding them. McClellan may possibly reach the White House, but he will lose the respect of all honest, high-minded patriots, by his affiliation with such traitors and Copperheads as B——, V——, W——, S——, & Co. He would not stand upon the traitorous Chicago platform, but he had not the manliness to oppose it. A major-general in the United States Army, and yet not one word to utter against rebels or the rebellion! I had much respect for McClellan before he became a politician, but very little after reading his letter accepting the nomination.

Hooker certainly made a mistake in leaving before the capture of Atlanta. I understand that, when here, he said that you would fail; your army was discouraged and dissatisfied, etc., etc. He is most unmeasured in his abuse of me. I inclose you a specimen of what he publishes in Northern papers, wherever he goes. They are dictated by himself and written by W. B. and such worthies. The funny part of the business is, that I had nothing whatever to do with his being relieved on either occasion. Moreover, I have never said any thing to the President or Secretary of War to injure him in the slightest degree, and he knows that perfectly well. His animosity arises from another source. He is aware that I know some things about his character and conduct in California, and, fearing that I may use that information against him, he seeks to ward off its effect by making it appear that I am his personal enemy, am jealous of him, etc. I know of no other reason for his hostility to me. He is welcome to abuse me as much as he pleases; I don't think it will do him much good, or me much harm. I know very little of General Howard, but believe him to be a true, honorable man. Thomas is also a noble old war-horse. It is true, as you say, that he is slow, but he is always sure.

I have not seen General Grant since the fall of Atlanta, and do not know what instructions he has sent you. I fear that Canby has not the means to do much by way of Mobile. The military effects of Banks's disaster are now showing themselves by the threatened operations of Price & Co. toward Missouri, thus keeping in check our armies west of the Mississippi.

With many thanks for your kind letter, and wishes for your future success, yours truly,

H. W. HALLECK.

HEADQUARTERS MILITARY DIVISION OF THE MISSISSIPPI ATLANTA, GEORGIA, September 20, 1864.

Major General HALLECK, Chief of Staff, Washington D.C.

GENERAL: I have the honor herewith to submit copies of a correspondence between General Hood, of the Confederate Army, the Mayor of Atlanta, and myself, touching the removal of the inhabitants of Atlanta.

In explanation of the tone which marks some of these letters, I will only call your attention to the fact that, after I had announced my determination, General Hood took upon himself to question my motives. I could not tamely submit to such impertinence; and I have also seen that, in violation of all official usage, he has published in the Macon newspapers such parts of the correspondence as suited his purpose. This could have had no other object than to create a feeling on the part of the people; but if he expects to resort to such artifices, I think I can meet him there too.

It is sufficient for my Government to know that the removal of the inhabitants has been made with liberality and fairness, that it has been attended with no force, and that no women or children have suffered, unless for want of provisions by their natural protectors and friends.

My real reasons for this step were:

We want all the houses of Atlanta for military storage and occupation.

We want to contract the lines of defense, so as to diminish the garrison to the limit necessary to defend its narrow and vital parts, instead of embracing, as the lines now do, the vast suburbs. This contraction of the lines, with the necessary citadels and redoubts, will make it necessary to destroy the very houses used by families as residences.

Atlanta is a fortified town, was stubbornly defended, and fairly captured. As captors, we have a right to it.

The residence here of a poor population would compel us, sooner or later, to feed them or to see them starve under our eyes.

The residence here of the families of our enemies would be a temptation and a means to keep up a correspondence dangerous and hurtful to our cause; a civil population calls for provost-guards, and absorbs the attention of officers in listening to everlasting complaints and special grievances that are not military.

These are my reasons; and, if satisfactory to the Government of the United States, it makes no difference whether it pleases General Hood and his people or not. I am, with respect, your obedient servant,

W. T. SHERMAN, Major-General commanding.

HEADQUARTERS MILITARY DIVISION OF THE MISSISSIPPI IN THE FIELD, ATLANTA, GEORGIA, September 7, 1864.

General HOOD, commanding Confederate Army.

GENERAL: I have deemed it to the interest of the United States that the citizens now residing in Atlanta should remove, those who prefer it to go south, and the rest north. For the latter I can provide food and transportation to points of their election in Tennessee, Kentucky, or farther north. For the former I can provide transportation by cars as far as Rough and Ready, and also wagons; but, that their removal may be made with as little discomfort as possible, it will be necessary for you to help the families from Rough and Ready to the care at Lovejoy's. If you consent, I will undertake to remove all the families in Atlanta who prefer to go south to Rough and Ready, with all their movable effects, viz., clothing, trunks, reasonable furniture, bedding, etc., with their servants, white and black, with the proviso that no force shall be used toward the blacks, one way or the other. If they want to go with their masters or mistresses, they may do so; otherwise they will be sent away, unless they be men, when they may be employed by our quartermaster. Atlanta is no place for families or non-combatants, and I have no desire to send them north if you will assist in conveying them south. If this proposition meets your views, I will consent to a truce in the neighborhood of Rough and Ready, stipulating that any wagons, horses, animals, or persons sent there for the purposes herein stated, shall in no manner be harmed or molested; you in your turn agreeing that any care, wagons, or carriages, persons or animals sent to the same point, shall not be interfered with. Each of us might send a guard of, say, one hundred men, to maintain order, and limit the truce to, say, two days after a certain time appointed.

I have authorized the mayor to choose two citizens to convey to you this letter, with such documents as the mayor may forward in explanation, and shall await your reply. I have the honor to be your obedient servant.

W. T. SHERMAN, Major-General commanding.

Major General W. T. SHERMAN, commanding United States Forces in Georgia

GENERAL: Your letter of yesterday's date, borne by James M. Ball and James R. Crew, citizens of Atlanta, is received. You say therein, "I deem it to be to the interest of the United States that the citizens now residing in Atlanta should remove," etc. I do not consider that I have any alternative in this matter. I therefore accept your proposition to declare a truce of two days, or such time as may be necessary to accomplish the purpose mentioned, and shall render all assistance in my power to expedite the transportation of citizens in this direction. I suggest that a staff-officer be appointed by you to superintend the removal from the city to Rough and Ready, while I appoint a like officer to control their removal farther south; that a guard of one hundred men be sent by either party as you propose, to maintain order at that place, and that the removal begin on Monday next.

And now, sir, permit me to say that the unprecedented measure you propose transcends, in studied and ingenious cruelty, all acts ever before brought to my attention in the dark history of war.

In the name of God and humanity, I protest, believing that you will find that you are expelling from their homes and firesides the wives and children of a brave people. I am, general, very respectfully, your obedient servant,

J. B. HOOD, General.

HEADQUARTERS MILITARY DIVISION OF THE MISSISSIPPI IN THE FIELD, ATLANTA, GEORGIA, September 10, 1864.

General J. B. HOOD, commanding Army of Tennessee, Confederate Army.

GENERAL: I have the honor to acknowledge the receipt of your letter of this date, at the hands of Messrs. Ball and Crew, consenting to the arrangements I had proposed to facilitate the removal south of the people of Atlanta, who prefer to go in that direction. I inclose you a copy of my orders, which will, I am satisfied, accomplish my purpose perfectly.

You style the measures proposed "unprecedented," and appeal to the dark history of war for a parallel, as an act of "studied and ingenious cruelty." It is not unprecedented; for General Johnston himself very wisely and properly removed the families all the way from Dalton down, and I see no reason why Atlanta should be excepted. Nor is it necessary to appeal to the dark history of war, when recent and modern examples are so handy. You yourself burned dwelling-houses along your parapet, and I have seen to-day fifty houses that you have rendered uninhabitable because they stood in the way of your forts and men. You defended Atlanta on a line so close to town that every cannon-shot and many musket-shots from our line of investment, that overshot their mark, went into the habitations of women and children. General Hardee did the same at Jonesboro, and General Johnston did the same, last summer, at Jackson, Mississippi. I have not accused you of heartless cruelty, but merely instance these cases of very recent occurrence, and could go on and enumerate hundreds of others, and challenge any fair man to judge which of us has the heart of pity for the families of a "brave people."

I say that it is kindness to these families of Atlanta to remove them now, at once, from scenes that women and children should not be exposed to, and the "brave people" should scorn to commit their wives and children to the rude barbarians who thus, as you say, violate the laws of war, as illustrated in the pages of its dark history.

In the name of common-sense, I ask you not to appeal to a just God in such a sacrilegious manner. You who, in the midst of peace and prosperity, have plunged a nation into war—dark and cruel war—who dared and badgered us to battle, insulted our flag, seized our arsenals and forts that were left in the honorable custody of peaceful ordnance-sergeants, seized and made "prisoners of war" the very garrisons sent to protect your people against negroes and Indians, long before any overt act was committed by the (to you) hated Lincoln Government; tried to force Kentucky and Missouri into rebellion, spite of themselves; falsified the vote of

45

Louisiana; turned loose your privateers to plunder unarmed ships; expelled Union families by the thousands, burned their houses, and declared, by an act of your Congress, the confiscation of all debts due Northern men for goods had and received! Talk thus to the marines, but not to me, who have seen these things, and who will this day make as much sacrifice for the peace and honor of the South as the best-born Southerner among you! If we must be enemies, let us be men, and fight it out as we propose to do, and not deal in arch hypocritical appeals to God and humanity. God will judge us in due time, and he will pronounce whether it be more humane to fight with a town full of women and the families of a brave people at our back or to remove them in time to places of safety among their own friends and people. I am, very respectfully, your obedient servant,

W. T. SHERMAN, Major-General commanding.

HEADQUARTERS ARMY OF THE TENNESSEE September 12, 1864

Major-General W. T, SHERMAN, commanding Military Division of the Mississippi.

GENERAL: I have the honor to acknowledge the receipt of your letter of the 9th inst., with its inclosure in reference to the women, children, and others, whom you have thought proper to expel from their homes in the city of Atlanta. Had you seen proper to let the matter rest there, I would gladly have allowed your letter to close this correspondence, and, without your expressing it in words, would have been willing to believe that, while "the interests of the United States," in your opinion, compelled you to an act of barbarous cruelty, you regretted the necessity, and we would have dropped the subject; but you have chosen to indulge in statements which I feel compelled to notice, at least so far as to signify my dissent, and not allow silence in regard to them to be construed as acquiescence.

I see nothing in your communication which induces me to modify the language of condemnation with which I characterized your order. It but strengthens me in the opinion that it stands "preeminent in the dark history of war for studied and ingenious cruelty." Your original order was stripped of all pretenses; you announced the edict for the sole reason that it was "to the interest of the United States." This alone you offered to us and the civilized world as an all-sufficient reason for disregarding the laws of God and man. You say that "General Johnston himself very wisely and properly removed the families all the way from Dalton down." It is due to that gallant soldier and gentleman to say that no act of his distinguished career gives the least color to your unfounded aspersions upon his conduct. He depopulated no villages, nor towns, nor cities, either friendly or hostile. He offered and extended friendly aid to his unfortunate fellow-citizens who desired to flee from your fraternal embraces. You are equally unfortunate in your attempt to find a justification for this act of cruelty, either in the defense of Jonesboro, by General Hardee, or of Atlanta, by myself. General Hardee defended his position in front of Jonesboro at the expense of injury to the houses; an ordinary, proper, and justifiable act of war. I defended Atlanta at the same risk and cost. If there was any fault in either case, it was your own, in not giving notice, especially in the case of Atlanta, of your purpose to shell the town, which is usual in war among civilized nations. No inhabitant was expelled from his home and fireside by the orders of General Hardee or myself, and therefore your recent order can find no support from the conduct of either of us. I feel no other emotion other than pain in reading that portion of your letter which attempts to justify your shelling Atlanta without notice under pretense that I defended Atlanta upon a line so close to town that every cannon-shot and many musket-balls from your line of investment, that overshot their mark, went into the habitations of women and children. I made no complaint of your firing into Atlanta in any way you thought proper. I make none now, but there are a hundred thousand witnesses that you fired into the habitations of women and children for weeks, firing far above and miles beyond my line of defense. I have too good an opinion, founded both upon observation and experience, of the skill of your artillerists, to credit the insinuation that they for several weeks unintentionally fired too high for my modest field-works, and slaughtered women and children by accident and want of skill.

The residue of your letter is rather discussion. It opens a wide field for the discussion of questions which I do not feel are committed to me. I am only a general of one of the armies of the Confederate States, charged with military operations in the field, under the direction of my superior officers, and I am not called upon to discuss with you the causes of the present war, or the political questions which led to or resulted from it. These grave and important questions have been committed to far abler hands than mine, and I shall only refer to them so far as to repel any unjust conclusion which might be drawn from my silence. You charge my country with "daring and badgering you to battle." The truth is, we sent commissioners to you, respectfully offering a peaceful separation, before the first gun was fired on either aide. You say we insulted your flag. The truth is, we fired upon it, and those who fought under it, when you came to our doors upon the mission of subjugation. You say we seized upon your forts and arsenals, and made prisoners of the garrisons sent to protect us against negroes and Indians. The truth is, we, by force of arms, drove out insolent intruders and took possession of our own forts and arsenals, to resist your claims to dominion over masters, slaves, and Indians, all of whom are to this day, with a unanimity unexampled in the history of the world, warring against your attempts to become their masters. You say that we tried to force Missouri and Kentucky into rebellion in spite of themselves. The truth is, my Government, from the beginning of this struggle to this hour, has again and again offered, before the whole world, to leave it to the unbiased will of these States, and all others, to determine for themselves whether they will cast their destiny with your Government or ours; and your Government has resisted this fundamental principle of free institutions with the bayonet, and labors daily, by force and fraud, to fasten its hateful tyranny upon the unfortunate freemen of these States. You say we falsified the vote of Louisiana. The truth is, Louisiana not only separated herself from your Government by nearly a unanimous vote of her people, but has vindicated the act upon every battle-field from Gettysburg to the Sabine, and has exhibited an heroic devotion to her decision which challenges the admiration and respect of every man capable of feeling sympathy for the oppressed or admiration for heroic valor. You say that we turned loose pirates to plunder your unarmed ships. The truth is, when you robbed us of our part of the navy, we built and bought a few vessels, hoisted the flag of our country, and swept the seas, in defiance of your navy, around the whole circumference of the globe. You say we have expelled Union families by thousands. The truth is, not a single family has been expelled from the Confederate States, that I am aware of; but, on the contrary, the moderation of our Government toward traitors has been a fruitful theme of denunciation by its enemies and well-meaning friends of our cause. You say my Government, by acts of Congress, has confiscated "all debts due Northern men for goods sold and delivered." The truth is, our Congress gave due and ample time to your merchants and traders to depart from our shores with their ships, goods, and effects, and only sequestrated the property of our enemies in retaliation for their acts—declaring us traitors, and confiscating our property wherever their power extended, either in their country or our own. Such are your accusations, and such are the facts known of all men to be true.

You order into exile the whole population of a city; drive men, women and children from their homes at the point of the bayonet, under the plea that it is to the interest of your Government, and on the claim that it is "an act of kindness to these families of Atlanta." Butler only banished from New Orleans the registered enemies of his Government, and acknowledged that he did it as a punishment. You issue a sweeping edict, covering all the inhabitants of a city, and add insult to the injury heaped upon the defenseless by assuming that you have done them a kindness. This you follow by the assertion that you will "make as much sacrifice for the peace and honor of the South as the best-born Southerner." And, because I characterize what you call as kindness as being real cruelty, you presume to sit in judgment between me and my God; and you decide that my earnest prayer to the Almighty Father to save our women and children from what you call kindness, is a "sacrilegious, hypocritical appeal."

You came into our country with your army, avowedly for the purpose of subjugating free white men, women, and children, and not only intend to rule over them, but you make negroes your allies, and desire to place over us an inferior race, which we have raised from barbarism to its present position, which is the highest ever attained by that race, in any country, in all time. I must, therefore, decline to accept your statements in reference to your kindness toward the people of Atlanta, and your willingness to sacrifice every thing for the peace and honor of the South, and refuse to be governed by your decision in regard to matters between myself, my country, and my God.

You say, "Let us fight it out like men." To this my reply is—for myself, and I believe for all the free men, ay, and women and children, in my country—we will fight you to the death! Better die a thousand deaths than submit to live under you or your Government and your negro allies!

Having answered the points forced upon me by your letter of the 9th of September, I close this correspondence with you; and, notwithstanding your comments upon my appeal to God in the cause of humanity, I again humbly and reverently invoke his almighty aid in defense of justice and right. Respectfully, your obedient servant,

J. B. HOOD, General.

ATLANTA, GEORGIA, September 11, 1864
Major-General W. T. SHERMAN.

Sir: We the undersigned, Mayor and two of the Council for the city of Atlanta, for the time being the only legal organ of the people of the said city, to express their wants and wishes, ask leave most earnestly but respectfully to petition you to reconsider the order requiring them to leave Atlanta.

At first view, it struck us that the measure would involve extraordinary hardship and loss, but since we have seen the practical execution of it so far as it has progressed, and the individual condition of the people, and heard their statements as to the inconveniences, loss, and suffering attending it, we are satisfied that the amount of it will involve in the aggregate consequences appalling and heart-rending.

Many poor women are in advanced state of pregnancy, others now having young children, and whose husbands for the greater part are either in the army, prisoners, or dead. Some say: "I have such a one sick at my house; who will wait on them when I am gone?" Others say: "What are we to do? We have no house to go to, and no means to buy, build, or rent any; no parents, relatives, or friends, to go to." Another says: "I will try and take this or that article of property, but such and such things I must leave behind, though I need them much." We reply to them: "General Sherman will carry your property to Rough and Ready, and General Hood will take it thence on." And they will reply to that: "But I want to leave the railroad at such a place, and cannot get conveyance from there on."

We only refer to a few facts, to try to illustrate in part how this measure will operate in practice. As you advanced, the people north of this fell back; and before your arrival here, a large portion of the people had retired south, so that the country south of this is already crowded, and without houses enough to accommodate the people, and we are informed that many are now staying in churches and other out-buildings.

This being so, how is it possible for the people still here (mostly women and children) to find any shelter? And how can they live through the winter in the woods—no shelter or subsistence, in the midst of strangers who know them not, and without the power to assist them much, if they were willing to do so?

This is but a feeble picture of the consequences of this measure. You know the woe, the horrors, and the suffering, cannot be described by words; imagination can only conceive of it, and we ask you to take these things into consideration.

We know your mind and time are constantly occupied with the duties of your command, which almost deters us from asking your attention to this matter, but thought it might be that you had not considered this subject in all of its awful consequences, and that on more reflection you, we hope, would not make this people an exception to all mankind, for we know of no such instance ever having occurred—surely never in the United States—and what has this helpless people done, that they should be driven from their homes, to wander strangers and outcasts, and exiles, and to subsist on charity?

We do not know as yet the number of people still here; of those who are here, we are satisfied a respectable number, if allowed to remain at home, could subsist for several months without assistance, and a respectable number for a much longer time, and who might not need assistance at any time.

In conclusion, we most earnestly and solemnly petition you to reconsider this order, or modify it, and suffer this unfortunate people to remain at home, and enjoy what little means they have.
Respectfully submitted
JAMES M. CALHOUN, Mayor.
E. E. RAWSON, Councilman.
S. C. Warns, Councilman.

HEADQUARTERS MILITARY DIVISION OF THE MISSISSIPPI IN THE FIELD, ATLANTA, GEORGIA, September 12, 1864.

JAMES M. CALHOUN, Mayor, E. E. RAWSON and S. C. Wares, representing City Council of Atlanta.

GENTLEMEN: I have your letter of the 11th, in the nature of a petition to revoke my orders removing all the inhabitants from Atlanta. I have read it carefully, and give full credit to your statements of the distress that will be occasioned, and yet shall not revoke my orders, because they were not designed to meet the humanities of the case, but to prepare for the future struggles in which millions of good people outside of Atlanta have a deep interest. We must have peace, not only at Atlanta, but in all America. To secure this, we must stop the war that now desolates our once happy and favored country. To stop war, we must defeat the rebel armies which are arrayed against the laws and Constitution that all must respect and obey. To defeat those armies, we must prepare the way to reach them in their recesses, provided with the arms and instruments which enable us to accomplish our purpose. Now, I know the vindictive nature of our enemy, that we may have many years of military operations from this quarter; and, therefore, deem it wise and prudent to prepare in time. The use of Atlanta for warlike purposes is inconsistent with its character as a home for families. There will be no manufactures, commerce, or agriculture here, for the maintenance of families, and sooner or later want will compel the inhabitants to go. Why not go now, when all the arrangements are completed for the transfer,—instead of waiting till the plunging shot of contending armies will renew the scenes of the past months. Of course, I do not apprehend any such thing at this moment, but you do not suppose this army will be here until the war is over. I cannot discuss this subject with you fairly, because I cannot impart to you what we propose to do, but I assert that our military plans make it necessary for the inhabitants to go away, and I can only renew my offer of services to make their exodus in any direction as easy and comfortable as possible.

You cannot qualify war in harsher terms than I will. War is cruelty, and you cannot refine it; and those who brought war into our country deserve all the curses and maledictions a people can pour out. I know I had no hand in making this war, and I know I will make more sacrifices to-day than any of you to secure peace. But you cannot have peace and a division of our country. If the United States submits to a division now, it will not stop, but will go on until we reap the fate of Mexico, which is eternal war. The United States does and must assert its authority, wherever it once had power; for, if it relaxes one bit to pressure, it is gone, and I believe that such is the national feeling. This feeling assumes various shapes, but always comes back to that of Union. Once admit the Union, once more acknowledge the authority of the national Government, and, instead of devoting your houses and streets and roads to the dread uses of war, I and this army become at once your protectors and supporters, shielding you from danger, let it come from what quarter it may. I know that a few individuals cannot resist a torrent of error and passion, such as swept the South into rebellion, but you can point out, so that we may know those who desire a government, and those who insist on war and its desolation.

You might as well appeal against the thunder-storm as against these terrible hardships of war. They are inevitable, and the only way the people of Atlanta can hope once more to live in peace and quiet at home, is to stop the war, which can only be done by admitting that it began in error and is perpetuated in pride.

We don't want your negroes, or your horses, or your houses, or your lands, or any thing you have, but we do want and will have a just obedience to the laws of the United States. That we will have, and, if it involves the destruction of your improvements, we cannot help it.

You have heretofore read public sentiment in your newspapers, that live by falsehood and excitement; and the quicker you seek for truth in other quarters, the better. I repeat then that, by the original compact of Government, the United States had certain rights in Georgia, which have never been relinquished and never will be; that the South began war by seizing forts, arsenals, mints, custom-houses, etc., etc., long before Mr. Lincoln was installed, and before the South had one jot or tittle of provocation. I myself have seen in Missouri, Kentucky, Tennessee, and Mississippi, hundreds and thousands of women and children fleeing from your armies and desperadoes, hungry and with bleeding feet. In Memphis, Vicksburg, and Mississippi, we fed thousands upon thousands of the families of rebel soldiers left on our hands, and whom we could not see starve. Now that war comes home to you; you feel very different. You deprecate its horrors, but did not feel them when you sent car-loads of soldiers and ammunition, and moulded shells and shot, to carry war into Kentucky and Tennessee, to desolate the homes of hundreds and thousands of good people who only asked to live in peace at their old homes, and under the Government of their inheritance. But these comparisons are idle. I want peace, and believe it can only be reached through union and war, and I will ever conduct war with a view to perfect and early success.

But, my dear sirs, when peace does come, you may call on me for any thing. Then will I share with you the last cracker, and watch with you to shield your homes and families against danger from every quarter.

Now you must go, and take with you the old and feeble, feed and nurse them, and build for them, in more quiet places, proper habitations to shield them against the weather until the mad passions of men cool down, and allow the Union and peace once more to settle over your old homes at Atlanta. Yours in haste,

W. T. SHERMAN, Major-General commanding.

HEADQUARTERS MILITARY DIVISION OF THE MISSISSIPPI
IN THE FIELD, ATLANTA, GEORGIA, September 14, 1864.

General J. B. HOOD, commanding Army of the Tennessee, Confederate Army.

GENERAL: Yours of September 12th is received, and has been carefully perused. I agree with you that this discussion by two soldiers is out of place, and profitless; but you must admit that you began the controversy by characterizing an official act of mine in unfair and improper terms. I reiterate my former answer, and to the only new matter contained in your rejoinder add: We have no "negro allies" in this army; not a single negro soldier left Chattanooga with this army, or is with it now. There are a few guarding Chattanooga, which General Steedman sent at one time to drive Wheeler out of Dalton.

I was not bound by the laws of war to give notice of the shelling of Atlanta, a "fortified town, with magazines, arsenals, founderies, and public stores;" you were bound to take notice. See the books.

This is the conclusion of our correspondence, which I did not begin, and terminate with satisfaction. I am, with respect, your obedient servant,

W. T. SHERMAN, Major-General commanding.

HEADQUARTERS OF THE ARMY
WASHINGTON, September 28, 1864,

Major-General SHERMAN, Atlanta, Georgia.

GENERAL: Your communications of the 20th in regard to the removal of families from Atlanta, and the exchange of prisoners, and also the official report of your campaign, are just received. I have not had time as yet to examine your report. The course which you have pursued in removing rebel families from Atlanta, and in the exchange of prisoners, is fully approved by the War Department. Not only are you justified by the laws and usages of war in removing these people, but I think it was your duty to your own army to do so. Moreover, I am fully of opinion that the nature of your position, the character of the war, the conduct of the enemy (and especially of non-combatants and women of the territory which we have heretofore conquered and occupied), will justify you in *gathering up all the forage and provisions which your army may require, both for a siege of Atlanta and for your supply in your march farther into the enemy's country. Let the disloyal families of the country, thus stripped, go to their husbands, fathers, and natural protectors, in the rebel ranks; we have tried three years of conciliation and kindness without any reciprocation; on the contrary, those thus treated have acted as spies and guerrillas in our rear and within our lines. The safety of our armies, and a proper regard for the lives of our soldiers, require that we apply to our inexorable foes the severe rules of war. We certainly are not required to treat the so-called non-combatant rebels better than they themselves treat each other. Even herein Virginia, within fifty miles of Washington, they strip their own families of provisions, leaving them, as our army advances, to be fed by us, or to starve within our lines. We have fed this class of people long enough. Let them go with their husbands and fathers in the rebel ranks; and if they won't go, we must send them to their friends and natural protectors. I would destroy every mill and factory within reach which I did not want for my own use. This the rebels have done, not only in Maryland and Pennsylvania, but also in Virginia and other rebel States, when compelled to fall back before our armies. In many sections of the country they have not left a mill to grind grain for their own suffering families, lest we might use them to supply our armies. We most do the same.*

I have endeavored to impress these views upon our commanders for the last two years. You are almost the only one who has properly applied them. I do not approve of General Hunter's course in burning private homes or uselessly destroying private property. That is barbarous. But I approve of taking or destroying whatever may serve as supplies to us or to the enemy's army.

Very respectfully, your obedient servant,

H. W. HALLECK, Major-General, Chief of Staff

In order to effect the exchange of prisoners, to facilitate the exodus of the people of Atlanta, and to keep open communication with the South, we established a neutral camp, at and about the railroad-station next south of Atlanta, known as "Rough and Ready," to which point I dispatched Lieutenant-Colonel Willard Warner, of my staff, with a guard of one hundred men, and General Hood sent Colonel Clare, of his staff, with a similar guard; these officers and men harmonized perfectly, and parted good friends when their work was done. In the mean time I also had reconnoitred the entire rebel lines about Atlanta, which were well built, but were entirely too extensive to be held by a single corps or division of troops, so I instructed Colonel Poe, United States Engineers, on my staff, to lay off an inner and shorter line, susceptible of defense by a smaller garrison.

By the middle of September all these matters were in progress, the reports of the past campaign were written up and dispatched to Washington, and our thoughts began to turn toward the future. Admiral Farragut had boldly and successfully run the forts at the entrance to Mobile Bay, which resulted in the capture of Fort Morgan, so that General Canby was enabled to begin his regular operations against Mobile City, with a view to open the Alabama River to navigation. My first thoughts were to concert operations with him, either by way of Montgomery, Alabama, or by the Appalachicula; but so long a line, to be used as a base for further operations eastward, was not advisable, and I concluded to await the initiative of the enemy, supposing that he would be forced to resort to some desperate campaign by the clamor raised at the South on account of the great loss to them of the city of Atlanta.

General Thomas occupied a house on Marietta Streets which had a veranda with high pillars. We were sitting there one evening, talking about things generally, when General Thomas asked leave to send his trains back to Chattanooga, for the convenience and economy of forage. I inquired of him if he supposed we would be allowed much rest at Atlanta, and he said he thought we would, or that at all events it would not be prudent for us to go much farther into Georgia because of our already long line of communication, viz., three hundred miles from Nashville. This was true; but there we were, and we could not afford to remain on the defensive, simply holding Atlanta and fighting for the safety of its railroad. I insisted on his retaining all trains, and on keeping all his divisions ready to move at a moment's warning. All the army, officers and men, seemed to relax more or less, and sink into a condition of idleness. General Schofield was permitted to go to Knoxville, to look after matters in his Department of the Ohio; and Generals Blair and Logan went home to look after politics. Many of the regiments were entitled to, and claimed, their discharge, by reason of the expiration of their term of service; so that with victory and success came also many causes of disintegration.

The rebel General Wheeler was still in Middle Tennessee, threatening our railroads, and rumors came that Forrest was on his way from Mississippi to the same theatre, for the avowed purpose of breaking up our railroads and compelling us to fall back from our conquest. To prepare for this, or any other emergency, I ordered Newton's division of the Fourth Corps back to Chattanooga, and Corse's division of the Seventeenth Corps to Rome, and instructed General Rousseau at Nashville, Granger at Decatur, and Steadman at Chattanooga, to adopt the most active measures to protect and insure the safety of our roads.

Hood still remained about Lovejoy's Station, and, up to the 15th of September, had given no signs of his future plans; so that with this date I close the campaign of Atlanta, with the following review of our relative losses during the months of August and September, with a summary of those for the whole campaign, beginning

May 6 and ending September 15, 1864. The losses for August and September are added together, so as to include those about Jonesboro:

	Killed and Missing	Wo unded	otal
Grand Aggregate	1,408	3,73 1	,139

Hood's losses, as reported for the same period, page 577, Johnston's "Narrative:"

к illed	Wo unded	otal
82	4 3,22 3	,705

To which should be added:

Prisoners captured by us:	,738

Giving his total loss	,440

On recapitulating the entire losses of each army during the entire campaign, from May to September, inclusive, we have, in the Union army, as per table appended:

Killed	,423
Wounded	2,822
Missing	,442

Aggregate Loss	1,627

In the Southern army, according to the reports of Surgeon Foard (pp 576, 577, Johnston's "Narrative ")

Total killed	,044
Total killed and wounded	1,996
Prisoners captured by us	2,983

Aggregate loss to the Southern Army	4,979

The foregoing figures are official, and are very nearly correct. I see no room for error save in the cavalry, which was very much scattered, and whose reports are much less reliable than of the infantry and artillery; but as Surgeon Foard's tables do not embrace Wheeler's, Jackson's, and Martin's divisions of cavalry, I infer that the comparison, as to cavalry losses, is a "stand-off."

I have no doubt that the Southern officers flattered themselves that they had filled and crippled of us two and even six to one, as stated by Johnston; but they were simply mistaken, and I herewith submit official tabular statements made up from the archives of the War Department, in proof thereof.

I have also had a careful tabular statement compiled from official records in the adjutant-general's office, giving the "effective strength" of the army under my command for each of the months of May, June, July, August, and September, 1864, which enumerate every man (infantry, artillery, and cavalry) for duty. The recapitulation clearly exhibits the actual truth. We opened the campaign with 98,797 (ninety-eight thousand seven hundred and ninety-seven) men. Blair's two divisions joined us early in June, giving 112,819 (one hundred and twelve thousand eight hundred and nineteen), which number gradually became reduced to 106,070 (one hundred and six thousand and seventy men), 91,675 (ninety-one thousand six hundred and seventy-five), and 81,758 (eighty-one thousand seven hundred and fifty-eight) at the end of the campaign. This gradual reduction was not altogether owing to death and wounds, but to the expiration of service, or by detachments sent to points at the rear.

51

CHAPTER XX.
ATLANTA AND AFTER—PURSUIT OF HOOD.

SEPTEMBER AND OCTOBER, 1864.

By the middle of September, matters and things had settled down in Atlanta, so that we felt perfectly at home. The telegraph and railroads were repaired, and we had uninterrupted communication to the rear. The trains arrived with regularity and dispatch, and brought us ample supplies. General Wheeler had been driven out of Middle Tennessee, escaping south across the Tennessee River at Bainbridge; and things looked as though we were to have a period of repose.

One day, two citizens, Messrs. Hill and Foster, came into our lines at Decatur, and were sent to my headquarters. They represented themselves as former members of Congress, and particular friends of my brother John Sherman; that Mr. Hill had a son killed in the rebel army as it fell back before us somewhere near Cassville, and they wanted to obtain the body, having learned from a comrade where it was buried. I gave them permission to go by rail to the rear, with a note to the commanding officer, General John E. Smith, at Cartersville, requiring him to furnish them an escort and an ambulance for the purpose. I invited them to take dinner with our mess, and we naturally ran into a general conversation about politics and the devastation and ruin caused by the war. They had seen a part of the country over which the army had passed, and could easily apply its measure of desolation to the remainder of the State, if necessity should compel us to go ahead.

Mr. Hill resided at Madison, on the main road to Augusta, and seemed to realize fully the danger; said that further resistance on the part of the South was madness, that he hoped Governor Brown, of Georgia, would so proclaim it, and withdraw his people from the rebellion, in pursuance of what was known as the policy of "separate State action." I told him, if he saw Governor Brown, to describe to him fully what he had seen, and to say that if he remained inert, I would be compelled to go ahead, devastating the State in its whole length and breadth; that there was no adequate force to stop us, etc.; but if he would issue his proclamation withdrawing his State troops from the armies of the Confederacy, I would spare the State, and in our passage across it confine the troops to the main roads, and would, moreover, pay for all the corn and food we needed. I also told Mr. Hill that he might, in my name, invite Governor Brown to visit Atlanta; that I would give him a safeguard, and that if he wanted to make a speech, I would guarantee him as full and respectable an audience as any he had ever spoken to. I believe that Mr. Hill, after reaching his home at Madison, went to Milledgeville, the capital of the State, and delivered the message to Governor Brown. I had also sent similar messages by Judge Wright of Rome, Georgia, and by Mr. King, of Marietta. On the 15th of September I telegraphed to General Halleck as follows:

My report is done, and will be forwarded as soon as I get in a few more of the subordinate reports. I am awaiting a courier from General Grant. All well; the troops are in good, healthy camps, and supplies are coming forward finely. Governor Brown has disbanded his militia, to gather the corn and sorghum of the State. I have reason to believe that he and Stephens want to visit me, and have sent them hearty invitation. I will exchange two thousand prisoners with Hood, but no more.

Governor Brown's action at that time is fully explained by the following letter, since made public, which was then only known to us in part by hearsay:

EXECUTIVE DEPARTMENT MILLEDGEVILLE, GEORGIA, September 10, 1864

General J. B. HOOD, commanding army of Tennessee.

GENERAL: As the militia of the State were called out for the defense of Atlanta during the campaign against it, which has terminated by the fall of the city into the hands of the enemy, and as many of these left their homes without preparation (expecting to be gone but a few weeks), who have remained in service over three months (most of the time in the trenches), justice requires that they be permitted, while the enemy are preparing for the winter campaign, to return to their homes, and look for a time after important interests, and prepare themselves for such service as may be required when another campaign commences against other important points in the State. I therefore hereby withdraw said organization from your command . . . .

JOSEPH C. BROWN

This militia had composed a division under command of Major-General Gustavus W. Smith, and were thus dispersed to their homes, to gather the corn and sorghum, then ripe and ready for the harvesters.

On the 17th I received by telegraph from President Lincoln this dispatch:

WASHINGTON, D.C., September 17, 1864

Major-General SHERMAN:

I feel great interest in the subjects of your dispatch, mentioning corn and sorghum, and the contemplated visit to you.

A. LINCOLN, President of the United States.

I replied at once:

*HEADQUARTERS MILITARY DIVISION OF THE MISSISSIPPI
IN THE FIELD, ATLANTA, GEORGIA, September 17, 1864.*

President LINCOLN, Washington., D. C.:

I will keep the department fully advised of all developments connected with the subject in which you feel interested.

Mr. Wright, former member of Congress from Rome, Georgia, and Mr. King, of Marietta, are now going between Governor Brown and myself. I have said to them that some of the people of Georgia are engaged in rebellion, began in error and perpetuated in pride, but that Georgia can now save herself from the devastations of war preparing for her, only by withdrawing her quota out of the Confederate Army, and aiding me to expel Hood from the borders of the State; in which event, instead of desolating the land as we progress, I will keep our men to the high-roads and commons, and pay for the corn and meat we need and take.

I am fully conscious of the delicate nature of such assertions, but it would be a magnificent stroke of policy if we could, without surrendering principle or a foot of ground, arouse the latent enmity of Georgia against Davis.

The people do not hesitate to say that Mr. Stephens was and is a Union man at heart; and they say that Davis will not trust him or let him have a share in his Government.

W. T. SHERMAN, Major-General.

I have not the least doubt that Governor Brown, at that time, seriously entertained the proposition; but he hardly felt ready to act, and simply gave a furlough to the militia, and called a special session of the Legislature, to meet at Milledgeville, to take into consideration the critical condition of affairs in the State.

On the 20th of September Colonel Horace Porter arrived from General Grant, at City Point, bringing me the letter of September 12th, asking my general views as to what should next be done. He staid several days at Atlanta, and on his return carried back to Washington my full reports of the past campaign, and my letter of September 20th to General Grant in answer to his of the 12th.

About this time we detected signs of activity on the part of the enemy. On the 21st Hood shifted his army across from the Mason road, at Lovejoy's, to the West Point road, at Palmetto Station, and his cavalry appeared on the west side of the Chattahoochee, toward Powder Springs; thus, as it were, stepping aside, and opening wide the door for us to enter Central Georgia. I inferred, however, that his real purpose was to assume the offensive against our railroads, and on the 24th a heavy force of cavalry from Mississippi, under General Forrest, made its appearance at Athena, Alabama, and captured its garrison.

General Newton's division (of the Fourth Corps), and Corse's (of the Seventeenth), were sent back by rail, the former to Chattanooga, and the latter to Rome. On the 25th I telegraphed to General Halleck:

Hood seems to be moving, as it were, to the Alabama line, leaving open the road to Mason, as also to Augusta; but his cavalry is busy on all our roads. A force, number estimated as high as eight thousand, are reported to have captured Athena, Alabama; and a regiment of three hundred and fifty men sent to its relief. I have sent Newton's division up to Chattanooga in cars, and will send another division to Rome. If I were sure that Savannah would soon be in our possession, I should be tempted to march for Milledgeville and Augusta; but I must first secure what I have. Jeff. Davis is at Macon.

On the next day I telegraphed further that Jeff. Davis was with Hood at Palmetto Station. One of our spies was there at the time, who came in the next night, and reported to me the substance of his speech to the

53

soldiers. It was a repetition of those he had made at Colombia, South Carolina, and Mason, Georgia, on his way out, which I had seen in the newspapers. Davis seemed to be perfectly upset by the fall of Atlanta, and to have lost all sense and reason. He denounced General Jos. Johnston and Governor Brown as little better than traitors; attributed to them personally the many misfortunes which had befallen their cause, and informed the soldiers that now the tables were to be turned; that General Forrest was already on our roads in Middle Tennessee; and that Hood's army would soon be there. He asserted that the Yankee army would have to retreat or starve, and that the retreat would prove more disastrous than was that of Napoleon from Moscow. He promised his Tennessee and Kentucky soldiers that their feet should soon tread their "native soil," etc., etc. He made no concealment of these vainglorious boasts, and thus gave us the full key to his future designs. To be forewarned was to be forearmed, and I think we took full advantage of the occasion.

On the 26th I received this dispatch.

CITY POINT, VIRGINIA,September 26,1864-10 a.m.

Major-General SHERMAN, Atlanta It will be better to drive Forrest out of Middle Tennessee as a first step, and do any thing else you may feel your force sufficient for. When a movement is made on any part of the sea-coast, I will advise you. If Hood goes to the Alabama line, will it not be impossible for him to subsist his army? U. S. GRANT, Lieutenant-General.

Answer:

HEADQUARTERS MILITARY DIVISION OF THE MISSISSIPPI IN THE FIELD, ATLANTA, GEORGIA, September 26, 1864.

GENERAL: I have your dispatch of to-day. I have already sent one division (Newton's) to Chattanooga, and another (Corse's) to Rome.

Our armies are much reduced, and if I send back any more, I will not be able to threaten Georgia much. There are men enough to the rear to whip Forrest, but they are necessarily scattered to defend the roads.

Can you expedite the sending to Nashville of the recruits that are in Indiana and Ohio? They could occupy the forts.

Hood is now on the West Point road, twenty-four miles south of this, and draws his supplies by that road. Jefferson Davis is there to-day, and superhuman efforts will be made to break my road.

Forrest is now lieutenant-general, and commands all the enemy's cavalry.

W. T. SHERMAN, Major-General.

General Grant first thought I was in error in supposing that Jeff. Davis was at Macon and Palmetto, but on the 27th I received a printed copy of his speech made at Macon on the 22d, which was so significant that I ordered it to be telegraphed entire as far as Louisville, to be sent thence by mail to Washington, and on the same day received this dispatch:

WASHINGTON, D. C., September 27, 1864-9 a.m.
Major-General SHERMAN, Atlanta: You say Jeff Davis is on a visit to General Hood. I judge that Brown and Stephens are the objects of his visit.
A. LINCOLN, President of the United States.

To which I replied:

HEADQUARTERS MILITARY DIVISION OF THE MISSISSIPPI
IN THE FIELD, ATLANTA, GEORGIA, September 28, 1864.

President LINCOLN, Washington, D. C.:

I have positive knowledge that Mr. Davis made a speech at Macon, on the 22d, which I mailed to General Halleck yesterday. It was bitter against General Jos. Johnston and Governor Brown. The militia are on furlough. Brown is at Milledgeville, trying to get a Legislature to meet next month, but he is afraid to act unless in concert with other Governors, Judge Wright, of Rome, has been here, and Messrs. Hill and Nelson, former members of Congress, are here now, and will go to meet Wright at Rome, and then go back to Madison and Milledgeville.

Great efforts are being made to reenforce Hood's army, and to break up my railroads, and I should have at once a good reserve force at Nashville. It would have a bad effect, if I were forced to send back any considerable part of my army to guard roads, so as to weaken me to an extent that I could not act offensively if the occasion calls for it.

W. T. SHERMAN, Major-General.

All this time Hood and I were carrying on the foregoing correspondence relating to the exchange of prisoners, the removal of the people from Atlanta, and the relief of our prisoners of war at Andersonville. Notwithstanding the severity of their imprisonment, some of these men escaped from Andersonville, and got to me at Atlanta. They described their sad condition: more than twenty-five thousand prisoners confined in a stockade designed for only ten thousand; debarred the privilege of gathering wood out of which to make huts; deprived of sufficient healthy food, and the little stream that ran through their prison pen poisoned and polluted by the offal from their cooking and butchering houses above. On the 22d of September I wrote to General Hood, describing the condition of our men at Andersonville, purposely refraining from casting odium on him or his associates for the treatment of these men, but asking his consent for me to procure from our generous friends at the North the articles of clothing and comfort which they wanted, viz., under-clothing, soap, combs, scissors, etc.—all needed to keep them in health—and to send these stores with a train, and an officer to issue them. General Hood, on the 24th, promptly consented, and I telegraphed to my friend Mr. James E. Yeatman, Vice-President of the Sanitary Commission at St. Louis, to send us all the under-clothing and soap he could spare, specifying twelve hundred fine-tooth combs, and four hundred pairs of shears to cut hair. These articles indicate the plague that most afflicted our prisoners at Andersonville.

Mr. Yeatman promptly responded to my request, expressed the articles, but they did not reach Andersonville in time, for the prisoners were soon after removed; these supplies did, however, finally overtake them at Jacksonville, Florida, just before the war closed.

On the 28th I received from General Grant two dispatches

CITY POINT, VIRGINIA; September 27, 1864-8.30 a.m. Major-General SHERMAN: It is evident, from the tone of the Richmond press and from other sources of information, that the enemy intend making a desperate effort to drive you from where you are. I have directed all new troops from the West, and from the East too, if necessary, in case none are ready in the West, to be sent to you. If General Burbridge is not too far on his way to Abingdon, I think he had better be recalled and his surplus troops sent into Tennessee. U. S. GRANT, Lieutenant-General.

CITY POINT, VIRGINIA; September 27, 1864-10.30 a.m. Major-General SHERMAN: I have directed all recruits and new troops from all the Western States to be sent to Nashville, to receive their further orders from you. I was mistaken about Jeff. Davis being in Richmond on Thursday last. He was then on his way to Macon. U. S. GRANT, Lieutenant-General.

Forrest having already made his appearance in Middle Tennessee, and Hood evidently edging off in that direction, satisfied me that the general movement against our roads had begun. I therefore determined to send General Thomas back to Chattanooga, with another division (Morgan's, of the Fourteenth Corps), to meet the danger in Tennessee. General Thomas went up on the 29th, and Morgan's division followed the same day, also by rail. And I telegraphed to General Halleck

I take it for granted that Forrest will cut our road, but think we can prevent him from making a serious lodgment. His cavalry will travel a hundred miles where ours will ten. I have sent two divisions up to Chattanooga and one to Rome, and General Thomas started to-day to drive Forrest out of Tennessee. Our roads should be watched from the rear, and I am glad that General Grant has ordered reserves to Nashville. I prefer for the future to make the movement on Milledgeville, Millen, and Savannah. Hood now rests twenty-four miles south, on the Chattahoochee, with his right on the West Point road. He is removing the iron of the Macon road. I can whip his infantry, but his cavalry is to be feared.

There was great difficulty in obtaining correct information about Hood's movements from Palmetto Station. I could not get spies to penetrate his camps, but on the 1st of October I was satisfied that the bulk of his infantry was at and across the Chattahoochee River, near Campbellton, and that his cavalry was on the west side, at Powder Springs. On that day I telegraphed to General Grant:

Hood is evidently across the Chattahoochee, below Sweetwater. If he tries to get on our road, this side of the Etowah, I shall attack him; but if he goes to the Selma & Talladega road, why will it not do to leave Tennessee to the forces which Thomas has, and the reserves soon to come to Nashville, and for me to destroy Atlanta and march across Georgia to Savannah or Charleston, breaking roads and doing irreparable damage? We cannot remain on the defensive.

The Selma & Talladega road herein referred to was an unfinished railroad from Selma, Alabama, through Talladega, to Blue Mountain, a terminus sixty-five miles southwest of Rome and about fifteen miles southeast of Gadsden, where the rebel army could be supplied from the direction of Montgomery and Mobile, and from which point Hood could easily threaten Middle Tennessee. My first impression was, that Hood would make for that point; but by the 3d of October the indications were that he would strike our railroad nearer us, viz., about Kingston or Marietta.

Orders were at once made for the Twentieth Corps (Slocum's) to hold Atlanta and the bridges of the Chattahoochee, and the other corps were put in motion for Marietta.

The army had undergone many changes since the capture of Atlanta. General Schofield had gone to the rear, leaving General J. D. Cog in command of the Army of the Ohio (Twenty-third Corps). General Thomas, also, had been dispatched to Chattanooga, with Newton's division of the Fourth Corps and Morgan's of the Fourteenth Corps, leaving General D. S. Stanley, the senior major-general of the two corps of his Army of the Cumberland, remaining and available for this movement, viz., the Fourth and Fourteenth, commanded by himself and Major-General Jeff. C. Davis; and after General Dodge was wounded, his corps (the Sixteenth) had been broken up, and its two divisions were added to the Fifteenth and Seventeenth Corps, constituting the Army of the Tennessee, commanded by Major-General O. O. Howard. Generals Logan and Blair had gone home to assist in the political canvass, leaving their corps, viz., the Fifteenth and Seventeenth, under the command of Major-Generals Osterhaus and T. E. G. Ransom.

These five corps were very much reduced in strength, by detachments and by discharges, so that for the purpose of fighting Hood I had only about sixty thousand infantry and artillery, with two small divisions of cavalry (Kilpatrick's and Garrard's). General Elliott was the chief of cavalry to the Army of the Cumberland, and was the senior officer of that arm of service present for duty with me.

We had strong railroad guards at Marietta and Kenesaw, Allatoona, Etowah Bridge, Kingston, Rome, Resaca, Dalton, Ringgold, and Chattanooga. All the important bridges were likewise protected by good block-houses, admirably constructed, and capable of a strong defense against cavalry or infantry; and at nearly all the regular railroad-stations we had smaller detachments intrenched. I had little fear of the enemy's cavalry damaging our roads seriously, for they rarely made a break which could not be repaired in a few days; but it was absolutely necessary to keep General Hood's infantry off our main route of communication and supply. Forrest had with him in Middle Tennessee about eight thousand cavalry, and Hood's army was estimated at from thirty-five to forty thousand men, infantry and artillery, including Wheeler's cavalry, then about three thousand strong.

We crossed the Chattahoochee River during the 3d and 4th of October, rendezvoused at the old battle-field of Smyrna Camp, and the next day reached Marietta and Kenesaw. The telegraph-wires had been cut above Marietta, and learning that heavy masses of infantry, artillery, and cavalry, had been seen from Kenesaw (marching north), I inferred that Allatoona was their objective point; and on the 4th of October I signaled from Mining's Station to Kenesaw, and from Kenesaw to Allatoona, over the heads of the enemy, a message for General Corse, at Rome, to hurry back to the assistance of the garrison at Allatoona. Allatoona was held by, a small brigade, commanded by Lieutenant-Colonel Tourtellotte, my present aide-de-camp. He had two small redoubts on either side of the railroad, overlooking the village of Allatoona, and the warehouses, in which were stored over a million rations of bread.

Reaching Kenesaw Mountain about 8 a.m. of October 5th (a beautiful day), I had a superb view of the vast panorama to the north and west. To the southwest, about Dallas, could be seen the smoke of camp-fires, indicating the presence of a large force of the enemy, and the whole line of railroad from Big Shanty up to Allatoona (full fifteen miles) was marked by the fires of the burning railroad. We could plainly see the smoke of battle about, Allatoona, and hear the faint reverberation of the cannon.

From Kenesaw I ordered the Twenty-third Corps (General Cox) to march due west on the Burnt Hickory road, and to burn houses or piles of brush as it progressed, to indicate the head of column, hoping to interpose this corps between Hood's main army at Dallas and the detachment then assailing Allatoona. The rest of the army was directed straight for Allatoona, northwest, distant eighteen miles. The signal-officer on Kenesaw reported that since daylight he had failed to obtain any answer to his call for Allatoona; but, while I was with him, he caught a faint glimpse of the tell-tale flag through an embrasure, and after much time he made out these letters-" C.," "R.," "S.," "E.," "H.," "E.," "R.," and translated the message—"Corse is here." It was a source of great relief, for it gave me the first assurance that General Corse had received his orders, and that the place was adequately garrisoned.

I watched with painful suspense the indications of the battle raging there, and was dreadfully impatient at the slow progress of the relieving column, whose advance was marked by the smokes which were made

56

according to orders, but about 2 p.m. I noticed with satisfaction that the smoke of battle about Allatoona grew less and less, and ceased altogether about 4 p.m. For a time I attributed this result to the effect of General Cog's march, but later in the afternoon the signal-flag announced the welcome tidings that the attack had been fairly repulsed, but that General Corse was wounded. The next day my aide, Colonel Dayton, received this characteristic dispatch:

ALLATOONA, GEORGIA, October 6, 1884-2 P.M.
Captain L. M. DAYTON, Aide-de-Camp:
I am short a cheek-bone and an ear, but am able to whip all h—l yet! My losses are very heavy. A force moving from Stilesboro' to Kingston gives me some anxiety. Tell me where Sherman is.
JOHN M. CORSE, Brigadier-General.

Inasmuch as the enemy had retreated southwest, and would probably next appear at Rome, I answered General Corse with orders to get back to Rome with his troops as quickly as possible.

General Corse's report of this fight at Allatoona is very full and graphic. It is dated Rome, October 27, 1864; recites the fact that he received his orders by signal to go to the assistance of Allatoona on the 4th, when he telegraphed to Kingston for cars, and a train of thirty empty cars was started for him, but about ten of them got off the track and caused delay. By 7 p.m. he had at Rome a train of twenty cars, which he loaded up with Colonel Rowett's brigade, and part of the Twelfth Illinois Infantry; started at 8 p.m., reached Allatoona (distant thirty-five miles) at 1 a.m. of the 5th, and sent the train back for more men; but the road was in bad order, and no more men came in time. He found Colonel Tourtellotte's garrison composed of eight hundred and ninety men; his reenforcement was one thousand and fifty-four: total for the defense, nineteen hundred and forty-four. The outposts were already engaged, and as soon as daylight came he drew back the men from the village to the ridge on which the redoubts were built.

The enemy was composed of French's division of three brigades, variously reported from four to five thousand strong. This force gradually surrounded the place by 8 a.m., when General French sent in by flag of truce this note:

AROUND ALLATOONA, October 5, 1884.

Commanding Officer, United States Forces, Allatoona:

I have placed the forces under my command in such positions that you are surrounded, and to avoid a needless effusion of blood I call on you to surrender your forces at once, and unconditionally.

Five minutes will be allowed you to decide. Should you accede to this, you will be treated in the most honorable manner as prisoners of war.

I have the honor to be, very respectfully yours,

S. G. FRENCH,
Major-General commanding forces Confederate States.

General Corse answered immediately:

HEADQUARTERS FOURTH DIVISION, FIFTEENTH CORPS
ALLATOONA, GEORGIA, October 5, 1864.

Major-General S. G. FRENCH, Confederate States, etc:

Your communication demanding surrender of my command I acknowledge receipt of, and respectfully reply that we are prepared for the "needless effusion of blood" whenever it is agreeable to you.

I am, very respectfully, your obedient servant,

Of course the attack began at once, coming from front, flank, and rear. There were two small redoubts, with slight parapets and ditches, one on each side of the deep railroad-cut. These redoubts had been located by Colonel Poe, United States Engineers, at the time of our advance on Kenesaw, the previous June. Each redoubt overlooked the storehouses close by the railroad, and each could aid the other defensively by catching in flank the attacking force of the other. Our troops at first endeavored to hold some ground outside the redoubts, but were soon driven inside, when the enemy made repeated assaults, but were always driven back. About 11 a.m., Colonel Redfield, of the Thirty-ninth Iowa, was killed, and Colonel Rowett was wounded, but never ceased to fight and encourage his men. Colonel Tourtellotte was shot through the hips, but continued to command. General Corse was, at 1 p.m., shot across the face, the ball cutting his ear, which stunned him, but he continued to encourage his men and to give orders. The enemy (about 1.30 p.m.) made a last and desperate effort to carry one of the redoubts, but was badly cut to pieces by the artillery and infantry fire from the other, when he began to draw off, leaving his dead and wounded on the ground.

Before finally withdrawing, General French converged a heavy fire of his cannon on the block-house at Allatoona Creek, about two miles from the depot, set it on fire, and captured its garrison, consisting of four officers and eighty-five men. By 4 p.m. he was in full retreat south, on the Dallas road, and got by before the head of General Cox's column had reached it; still several ambulances and stragglers were picked up by this command on that road. General Corse reported two hundred and thirty-one rebel dead, four hundred and eleven prisoners, three regimental colors, and eight hundred muskets captured.

Among the prisoners was a Brigadier-General Young, who thought that French's aggregate loss would reach two thousand. Colonel Tourtellotte says that, for days after General Corse had returned to Rome, his men found and buried at least a hundred more dead rebels, who had doubtless been wounded, and died in the woods near Allatoona. I know that when I reached Allatoona, on the 9th, I saw a good many dead men, which had been collected for burial.

Corse's entire loss, officially reported, was:

K illed.	Wou nded.	Mi ssing.	otal.
1 42	353	21 2	07

I esteemed this defense of Allatoona so handsome and important, that I made it the subject of a general order, viz., No. 86, of October 7, 1864:

The general commanding avails himself of the opportunity, in the handsome defense made of Allatoona, to illustrate the most important principle in war, that fortified posts should be defended to the last, regardless of the relative numbers of the party attacking and attacked . . . . The thanks of this army are due and are hereby accorded to General Corse, Colonel Tourtellotte, Colonel Rowett, officers, and men, for their determined and gallant defense of Allatoona, and it is made an example to illustrate the importance of preparing in time, and meeting the danger, when present, boldly, manfully, and well.

Commanders and garrisons of the posts along our railroad are hereby instructed that they must hold their posts to the last minute, sure that the time gained is valuable and necessary to their comrades at the front.

By order of Major-General W. T. Sherman,
L. M. DAYTON, Aide-A-Camp.

The rebels had struck our railroad a heavy blow, burning every tie, bending the rails for eight miles, from Big Shanty to above Acworth, so that the estimate for repairs called for thirty-five thousand new ties, and six miles of iron. Ten thousand men were distributed along the break to replace the ties, and to prepare the road-bed, while the regular repair-party, under Colonel W. W. Wright, came down from Chattanooga with iron, spikes, etc., and in about seven days the road was all right again. It was by such acts of extraordinary energy that we discouraged our adversaries, for the rebel soldiers felt that it was a waste of labor for them to march hurriedly, on wide circuits, day and night, to burn a bridge and tear up a mile or so of track, when they knew that we could lay it back so quickly. They supposed that we had men and money without limit, and that we always kept on hand, distributed along the road, duplicates of every bridge and culvert of any importance.

A good story is told of one who was on Kenesaw Mountain during our advance in the previous June or July. A group of rebels lay in the shade of a tree, one hot day, overlooking our camps about Big Shanty. One soldier remarked to his fellows:

"Well, the Yanks will have to git up and git now, for I heard General Johnston himself say that General Wheeler had blown up the tunnel near Dalton, and that the Yanks would have to retreat, because they could get no more rations."

"Oh, hell!" said a listener, "don't you know that old Sherman carries a duplicate tunnel along?"

After the war was over, General Johnston inquired of me who was our chief railroad-engineer. When I told him that it was Colonel W. W. Wright, a civilian, he was much surprised, said that our feats of bridge-building and repairs of roads had excited his admiration; and he instanced the occasion at Kenesaw in June, when an officer from Wheeler's cavalry had reported to him in person that he had come from General Wheeler, who had made a bad break in our road about Triton Station, which he said would take at least a fortnight to repair; and, while they were talking, a train was seen coming down the road which had passed that very break, and had reached me at Big Shanty as soon as the fleet horseman had reached him (General Johnston) at Marietta

I doubt whether the history of war can furnish more examples of skill and bravery than attended the defense of the railroad from Nashville to Atlanta during the year 1864.

In person I reached Allatoona on the 9th of October, still in doubt as to Hood's immediate intentions. Our cavalry could do little against his infantry in the rough and wooded country about Dallas, which masked the enemy's movements; but General Corse, at Rome, with Spencer's First Alabama Cavalry and a mounted regiment of Illinois Infantry, could feel the country south of Rome about Cedartown and Villa Rica; and reported the enemy to be in force at both places. On the 9th I telegraphed to General Thomas, at Nashville, as follows:

I came up here to relieve our road. The Twentieth Corps remains at Atlanta. Hood reached the road and broke it up between Big Shanty and Acworth. He attacked Allatoona, but was repulsed. We have plenty of bread and meat, but forage is scarce. I want to destroy all the road below Chattanooga, including Atlanta, and to make for the sea-coast. We cannot defend this long line of road.

And on the same day I telegraphed to General Grant, at City Point:

It will be a physical impossibility to protect the roads, now that Hood, Forrest, Wheeler, and the whole batch of devils, are turned loose without home or habitation. I think Hood's movements indicate a diversion to the end of the Selma & Talladega road, at Blue Mountain, about sixty miles southwest of Rome, from which he will threaten Kingston, Bridgeport, and Decatur, Alabama. I propose that we break up the railroad from Ohattanooga forward, and that we strike out with our wagons for Milledgeville, Millen, and Savannah. Until we can repopulate Georgia, it is useless for us to occupy it; but the utter destruction of its roads, houses, and people, will cripple their military resources. By attempting to hold the roads, we will lose a thousand men each month, and will gain no result. I can make this march, and make Georgia howl! We have on hand over eight thousand head of cattle and three million rations of bread, but no corn. We can find plenty of forage in the interior of the State.

Meantime the rebel General Forrest had made a bold circuit in Middle Tennessee, avoiding all fortified points, and breaking up the railroad at several places; but, as usual, he did his work so hastily and carelessly that our engineers soon repaired the damage—then, retreating before General Rousseau, he left the State of Tennessee, crossing the river near Florence, Alabama, and got off unharmed.

On the 10th of October the enemy appeared south of the Etowah River at Rome, when I ordered all the armies to march to Kingston, rode myself to Cartersville with the Twenty-third Corps (General Cox), and telegraphed from there to General Thomas at Nashville:

It looks to me as though Hood was bound for Tuscumbia. He is now crossing the Coosa River below Rome, looking west. Let me know if you can hold him with your forces now in Tennessee and the expected reenforeements, as, in that event, you know what I propose to do.

I will be at Kingston to-morrow. I think Rome is strong enough to resist any attack, and the rivers are all high. If he turns up by Summerville, I will get in behind him.

And on the same day to General Grant, at City Point:

Hood is now crossing the Coosa, twelve miles below Rome, bound west. If he passes over to the Mobile & Ohio Railroad, had I not better execute the plan of my letter sent you by Colonel Porter, and leave General Thomas, with the troops now in Tennessee, to

59

defend the State? He will have an ample force when the reenforcements ordered reach Nashville.

I found General John E. Smith at Cartersville, and on the 11th rode on to Kingston, where I had telegraphic communications in all directions.

From General Corse, at Rome, I learned that Hood's army had disappeared, but in what direction he was still in doubt; and I was so strongly convinced of the wisdom of my proposition to change the whole tactics of the campaign, to leave Hood to General Thomas, and to march across Georgia for Savannah or Charleston, that I again telegraphed to General Grant:

We cannot now remain on the defensive. With twenty-five thousand infantry and the bold cavalry he has, Hood can constantly break my road. I would infinitely prefer to make a wreck of the road and of the country from Chattanooga to Atlanta, including the latter city; send back all my wounded and unserviceable men, and with my effective army move through Georgia, smashing things to the sea. Hood may turn into Tennessee and Kentucky, but I believe he will be forced to follow me. Instead of being on the defensive, I will be on the offensive. Instead of my guessing at what he means to do, he will have to guess at my plans. The difference in war would be fully twenty-five per cent. I can make Savannah, Charleston, or the month of the Chattahoochee (Appalachicola). Answer quick, as I know we will not have the telegraph long.

I received no answer to this at the time, and the next day went on to Rome, where the news came that Hood had made his appearance at Resaca, and had demanded the surrender of the place, which was commanded by Colonel Weaver, reenforced by Brevet Brigadier-General Raum. General Hood had evidently marched with rapidity up the Chattooga Valley, by Summerville, Lafayette, Ship's Gap, and Snake-Creek Gap, and had with him his whole army, except a small force left behind to watch Rome. I ordered Resaca to be further reenforced by rail from Kingston, and ordered General Cox to make a bold reconnoissance down the Coosa Valley, which captured and brought into Rome some cavalrymen and a couple of field-guns, with their horses and men. At first I thought of interposing my whole army in the Chattooga Valley, so as to prevent Hood's escape south; but I saw at a glance that he did not mean to fight, and in that event, after damaging the road all he could, he would be likely to retreat eastward by Spring Place, which I did not want him to do; and, hearing from General Raum that he still held Resaca safe, and that General Edward McCook had also got there with some cavalry reenforcements, I turned all the heads of columns for Resaca, viz., General Cox's, from Rome; General Stanley's, from McGuire's; and General Howard's, from Kingston. We all reached Resaca during that night, and the next morning (13th) learned that Hood's whole army had passed up the valley toward Dalton, burning the railroad and doing all the damage possible.

On the 12th he had demanded the surrender of Resaca in the following letter

HEADQUARTERS ARMY OF TENNESSEE IN THE FIELD, October 12,1861.

To the officer commanding the United States Forces at Resaca, Georgia.

SIR: I demand the immediate and unconditional surrender of the post and garrison under your command, and, should this be acceded to, all white officers and soldiers will be parolled in a few days. If the place is carried by assault, no prisoners will be taken. Most respectfully, your obedient servant,

J. B. HOOD, General.

To this Colonel Weaver, then in command, replied:

HEADQUARTERS SECOND BRIGADE, THIRD DIVISION, FIFTEENTH CORPS RESACA, GEORGIA, October 12, 1884.

To General J. B. HOOD

Your communication of this date just received. In reply, I have to state that I am somewhat surprised at the concluding paragraph, to the effect that, if the place is carried by assault, no prisoners will be taken. In my opinion I can hold this post. If you want it, come and take it.

I am, general, very respectfully, your most obedient servant,

CLARK R. WEAVER, Commanding Officer.

This brigade was very small, and as Hood's investment extended only from the Oostenaula, below the town, to the Connesauga above, he left open the approach from the south, which enabled General Raum and the cavalry of Generals McCook and Watkins to reenforce from Kingston. In fact, Hood, admonished by his losses at Allatoona, did not attempt an assault at all, but limited his attack to the above threat, and to some skirmishing, giving his attention chiefly to the destruction of the railroad, which he accomplished all the way up to Tunnel Hill, nearly twenty miles, capturing en route the regiment of black troops at Dalton (Johnson's Forty-fourth United States colored). On the 14th, I turned General Howard through Snake-Creek Gap, and sent General Stanley around by Tilton, with orders to cross the mountain to the west, so as to capture, if possible, the force left by the enemy in Snake-Creek Gap. We found this gap very badly obstructed by fallen timber, but got through that night, and the next day the main army was at Villanow. On the morning of the 16th, the leading division of General Howard's column, commanded by General Charles R. Woods, carried Ship's Gap, taking prisoners part of the Twenty-fourth South Carolina Regiment, which had been left there to hold us in check.

The best information there obtained located Hood's army at Lafayette, near which place I hoped to catch him and force him to battle; but, by the time we had got enough troops across the mountain at Ship's Gap, Hood had escaped down the valley of the Chattooga, and all we could do was to follow him as closely as possible. From Ship's Gap I dispatched couriers to Chattanooga, and received word back that General Schofield was there, endeavoring to cooperate with me, but Hood had broken up the telegraph, and thus had prevented quick communication. General Schofield did not reach me till the army had got down to Gaylesville, about the 21st of October.

It was at Ship's Gap that a courier brought me the cipher message from General Halleck which intimated that the authorities in Washington were willing I should undertake the march across Georgia to the sea. The translated dispatch named "Horse-i-bar Sound" as the point where the fleet would await my arrival. After much time I construed it to mean, "Ossabaw Sound," below Savannah, which was correct.

On the 16th I telegraphed to General Thomas, at Nashville:

Send me Morgan's and Newton's old divisions. Reestablish the road, and I will follow Hood wherever he may go. I think he will move to Blue Mountain. We can maintain our men and animals on the country.

General Thomas's reply was:

NASHVILLE, October 17, 1864—10.30 a.m.

Major-General SHERMAN:

Your dispatch from Ship's Gap, 5 p.m. of the 16th, just received. Schofield, whom I placed in command of the two divisions (Wagner's and Morgan's), was to move up Lookout Valley this A.M., to intercept Hood, should he be marching for Bridgeport. I will order him to join you with the two divisions, and will reconstruct the road as soon as possible. Will also reorganize the guards for posts and block-houses .... Mower and Wilson have arrived, and are on their way to join you. I hope you will adopt Grant's idea of turning Wilson loose, rather than undertake the plan of a march with the whole force through Georgia to the sea, inasmuch as General Grant cannot cooperate with you as at first arranged.

GEORGE H. THOMAS, Major-General.

So it is clear that at that date neither General Grant nor General Thomas heartily favored my proposed plan of campaign. On the same day, I wrote to General Schofield at Chattanooga:

Hood is not at Dear Head Cove. We occupy Ship's Gap and Lafayette. Hood is moving south via Summerville, Alpine, and Gadsden. If he enters Tennessee, it will be to the west of Huntsville, but I think he has given up all such idea. I want the road repaired to Atlanta; the sick and wounded men sent north of the Tennessee; my army recomposed; and I will then make the interior of Georgia feel the weight of war. It is folly for us to be moving our armies on the reports of scouts and citizens. We must maintain the offensive. Your first move on Trenton and Valley Head was right —the move to defend Caperton's Ferry is wrong. Notify General Thomas of these my views. We must follow Hood till he is beyond the reach of mischief, and then resume the offensive.

The correspondence between me and the authorities at Washington, as well as with the several army commanders, given at length in the report of the Committee on the Conduct of the War, is full on all these points.

After striking our road at Dalton, Hood was compelled to go on to Chattanooga and Bridgeport, or to pass around by Decatur and abandon altogether his attempt to make us let go our hold of Atlanta by attacking our communications. It was clear to me that he had no intention to meet us in open battle, and the lightness and celerity of his army convinced me that I could not possibly catch him on a stern-chase. We therefore quietly followed him down the Chattooga Valley to the neighborhood of Gadsden, but halted the main armies near the Coosa River, at the mouth of the Chattooga, drawing our supplies of corn and meat from the farms of that comparatively rich valley and of the neighborhood.

General Slocum, in Atlanta, had likewise sent out, under strong escort, large trains of wagons to the east, and brought back corn, bacon, and all kinds of provisions, so that Hood's efforts to cut off our supplies only reacted on his own people. So long as the railroads were in good order, our supplies came full and regular from the North; but when the enemy broke our railroads we were perfectly justified in stripping the inhabitants of all they had. I remember well the appeal of a very respectable farmer against our men driving away his fine flock of sheep. I explained to him that General Hood had broken our railroad; that we were a strong, hungry crowd, and needed plenty of food; that Uncle Sam was deeply interested in our continued health and would soon repair these roads, but meantime we must eat; we preferred Illinois beef, but mutton would have to answer. Poor fellow! I don't believe he was convinced of the wisdom or wit of my explanation. Very soon after reaching Lafayette we organized a line of supply from Chattanooga to Ringgold by rail, and thence by wagons to our camps about Gaylesville. Meantime, also, Hood had reached the neighborhood of Gadsden, and drew his supplies from the railroad at Blue Mountain.

On the 19th of October I telegraphed to General Halleck, at Washington:

Hood has retreated rapidly by all the roads leading south. Our advance columns are now at Alpine and Melville Post-Office. I shall pursue him as far as Gaylesville. The enemy will not venture toward Tennessee except around by Decatur. I propose to send the Fourth Corps back to General Thomas, and leave him, with that corps, the garrisons, and new troops, to defend the line of the Tennessee River; and with the rest I will push into the heart of Georgia and come out at Savannah, destroying all the railroads of the State. The break in our railroad at Big Shanty is almost repaired, and that about Dalton should be done in ten days. We find abundance of forage in the country.

On the same day I telegraphed to General L. C. Easton, chief-quartermaster, who had been absent on a visit to Missouri, but had got back to Chattanooga:

Go in person to superintend the repairs of the railroad, and make all orders in my name that will expedite its completion. I want it finished, to bring back from Atlanta to Chattanooga the sick and wounded men and surplus stores. On the 1st of November I want nothing in front of Chattanooga except what we can use as food and clothing and haul in our wagons. There is plenty of corn in the country, and we only want forage for the posts. I allow ten days for all this to be done, by which time I expect to be at or near Atlanta.

I telegraphed also to General Amos Beckwith, chief-commissary in Atlanta, who was acting as chief-quartermaster during the absence of General Easton:

Hood will escape me. I want to prepare for my big raid. On the 1st of November I want nothing in Atlanta but what is necessary for war. Send all trash to the rear at once, and have on hand thirty days' food and but little forage. I propose to abandon Atlanta, and the railroad back to Chattanooga, to sally forth to ruin Georgia and bring up on the seashore. Make all dispositions accordingly. I will go down the Coosa until I am sure that Hood has gone to Blue Mountain.

On the 21st of October I reached Gaylesville, had my bivouac in an open field back of the village, and remained there till the 28th. During that time General Schofield arrived, with the two divisions of Generals Wagner (formerly Newton's) and Morgan, which were returned to their respective corps (the Fourth and Fourteenth), and General Schofield resumed his own command of the Army of the Ohio, then on the Coosa River, near Cedar Bluff. General Joseph A. Mower also arrived, and was assigned to command a division in the Seventeenth Corps; and General J. H. Wilson came, having been sent from Virginia by General Grant, for the purpose of commanding all my cavalry. I first intended to organize this cavalry into a corps of three small divisions, to be commanded by General Wilson; but the horses were well run down, and, at Wilson's instance, I concluded to retain only one division of four thousand five hundred men, with selected horses, under General Kilpatrick, and to send General Wilson back with all the rest to Nashville, to be reorganized and to act under General Thomas in the defense of Tennessee. Orders to this effect were made on the 24th of October.

General Grant, in designating General Wilson to command my cavalry, predicted that he would, by his personal activity, increase the effect of that arm "fifty per cent.," and he advised that he should be sent south, to accomplish all that I had proposed to do with the main army; but I had not so much faith in cavalry as he had, and preferred to adhere to my original intention of going myself with a competent force.

About this time I learned that General Beauregard had reached Hood's army at Gadsden; that, without assuming direct command of that army, he had authority from the Confederate Government to direct all its movements, and to call to his assistance the whole strength of the South. His orders, on assuming command, were full of alarm and desperation, dated:

HEADQUARTERS MILITARY DIVISION OF THE WEST
October 17, 1864

In assuming command, at this critical juncture, of the Military Division of the West, I appeal to my countrymen, of all classes and sections, for their generous support. In assigning me to this responsible position, the President of the Confederate States has extended to me the assurance of his earnest support. The Executives of your States meet me with similar expressions of their devotion to our cause. The noble army in the field, composed of brave men and gallant officers, are strangers to me, but I know they will do all that patriots can achieve.....

The army of Sherman still defiantly holds Atlanta. He can and must be driven from it. It is only for the good people of Georgia and surrounding states to speak the word, and the work is done, we have abundant provisions. There are men enough in the country, liable to and able for service, to accomplish the result.....

My countrymen, respond to this call as you have done in days that are past, and, with the blessing of a kind and overruling Providence, the enemy shall be driven from your soil. The security of your wives and daughters from the insults and outrages of a brutal foe shall be established soon, and be followed by a permanent and honorable peace. The claims of home and country, wife and children, uniting with the demands of honor and patriotism, summon us to the field. We cannot, dare not, will not fail to respond. Full of hope and confidence, I come to join you in your struggles, sharing your privations, and, with your brave and true men, to strike the blow that shall bring success to our arms, triumph to our cause, and peace to our country! . . .

G. T. BEAUREGARD, General.

Notwithstanding this somewhat boastful order or appeal, General Beauregard did not actually accompany General Hood on his disastrous march to Nashville, but took post at Corinth, Mississippi, to control the movement of his supplies and to watch me.

At Gaylesville the pursuit of Hood by the army under my immediate command may be said to have ceased. During this pursuit, the Fifteenth Corps was commanded by its senior major-general present, P. J. Osterhaus, in the absence of General John A. Logan; and the Seventeenth Corps was commanded by Brigadier-General T. E. G. Ransom, the senior officer present, in the absence of General Frank P. Blair.

General Ransom was a young, most gallant, and promising officer, son of the Colonel Ransom who was killed at Chapultepec, in the Mexican War. He had served with the Army of the Tennessee in 1862 and 1863, at Vicksburg, where he was severely wounded. He was not well at the time we started from Atlanta, but he insisted on going along with his command. His symptoms became more aggravated on the march, and when we were encamped near Gaylesville, I visited him in company with Surgeon John Moors, United States Army, who said that the case was one of typhoid fever, which would likely prove fatal. A few days after, viz., the 28th, he was being carried on a litter toward Rome; and as I rode from Gaylesville to Rome, I passed him by the way, stopped, and spoke with him, but did not then suppose he was so near his end. The next day, however, his escort reached Rome, bearing his dead body. The officer in charge reported that, shortly after I had passed, his symptoms became so much worse that they stopped at a farmhouse by the road-side, where he died that evening. His body was at once sent to Chicago for burial, and a monument has been ordered by the Society of the Army of the Tennessee to be erected in his memory.

On the 26th of October I learned that Hood's whole army had made its appearance about Decatur, Alabama, and at once caused a strong reconnoissance to be made down the Coosa to near Gadsden, which revealed the truth that the enemy was gone except a small force of cavalry, commanded by General Wheeler, which had been left to watch us. I then finally resolved on my future course, which was to leave Hood to be encountered by General Thomas, while I should carry into full effect the long-contemplated project of marching for the sea-coast, and thence to operate toward Richmond. But it was all-important to me and to our cause that General Thomas should have an ample force, equal to any and every emergency.

He then had at Nashville about eight or ten thousand new troops, and as many more civil employs of the Quartermaster's Department, which were not suited for the field, but would be most useful in manning the excellent forts that already covered Nashville. At Chattanooga, he had General Steedman's division, about five thousand men, besides garrisons for Chattanooga, Bridgeport, and Stevenson; at Murfreesboro' he also had General Rousseau's division, which was full five thousand strong, independent of the necessary garrisons for the railroad. At Decatur and Huntsville, Alabama, was the infantry division of General R. S. Granger, estimated at four thousand; and near Florence, Alabama, watching the crossings of the Tennessee, were General Edward Hatch's division of cavalry, four thousand; General Croxton's brigade, twenty-five hundred; and Colonel Capron's brigade, twelve hundred; besides which, General J. H. Wilson had collected in Nashville about ten thousand dismounted cavalry, for which he was rapidly collecting the necessary horses for a remount. All these aggregated about forty-five thousand men. General A. J. Smith at that time was in Missouri, with the two divisions of the Sixteenth Corps which had been diverted to that quarter to assist General Rosecrans in driving the rebel General Price out of Missouri. This object had been accomplished, and these troops, numbering from eight to ten thousand, had been ordered to Nashville. To these I proposed at first to add only the Fourth Corps (General Stanley), fifteen thousand; and that corps was ordered from Gaylesville to march to Chattanooga, and thence report for orders to General Thomas; but subsequently, on the 30th of October, at Rome, Georgia, learning from General Thomas that the new troops promised by General Grant were coming forward very slowly, I concluded to further reenforce him by General Schofield's corps (Twenty-third), twelve thousand, which corps accordingly marched for Resaca, and there took the cars for Chattanooga. I then knew that General Thomas would have an ample force with which to encounter General Hood anywhere in the open field, besides garrisons to secure the railroad to his rear and as far forward as Chattanooga. And, moreover, I was more than convinced that he would have ample time for preparation; for, on that very day, General R. S. Granger had telegraphed me from Decatur, Alabama:

I omitted to mention another reason why Hood will go to Tusomnbia before crossing the Tennessee River. He was evidently out of supplies. His men were all grumbling; the first thing the prisoners asked for was something to eat. Hood could not get any thing if he should cross this side of Rogersville.

I knew that the country about Decatur and Tuscumbia, Alabama, was bare of provisions, and inferred that General Hood would have to draw his supplies, not only of food, but of stores, clothing, and ammunition, from Mobile, Montgomery, and Selma, Alabama, by the railroad around by Meridian and Corinth, Mississippi, which we had most effectually disabled the previous winter.

General Hood did not make a serious attack on Decatur, but hung around it from October 26th to the 30th, when he drew off and marched for a point on the south side of the Tennessee River, opposite Florence, where he was compelled to remain nearly a month, to collect the necessary supplies for his contemplated invasion of Tennessee and Kentucky.

The Fourth Corps (Stanley) had already reached Chattanooga, and had been transported by rail to Pulaski, Tennessee; and General Thomas ordered General Schofield, with the Twenty-third Corps, to Columbia, Tennessee, a place intermediate between Hood (then on the Tennessee River, opposite Florence) and Forrest, opposite Johnsonville.

On the 31st of October General Croxton, of the cavalry, reported that the enemy had crossed the Tennessee River four miles above Florence, and that he had endeavored to stop him, but without success. Still, I was convinced that Hood's army was in no condition to march for Nashville, and that a good deal of further delay might reasonably be counted on. I also rested with much confidence on the fact that the Tennessee River below Muscle Shoals was strongly patrolled by gunboats, and that the reach of the river above Muscle Shoals, from Decatur as high up as our railroad at Bridgeport, was also guarded by gunboats, so that Hood, to cross over, would be compelled to select a point inaccessible to these gunboats. He actually did choose such a place, at the old railroad-piers, four miles above Florence, Alabama, which is below Muscle Shoals and above Colbert Shoals.

On the 31st of October Forrest made his appearance on the Tennessee River opposite Johnsonville (whence a new railroad led to Nashville), and with his cavalry and field pieces actually crippled and captured two gunboats with five of our transports, a feat of arms which, I confess, excited my admiration.

There is no doubt that the month of October closed to us looking decidedly squally; but, somehow, I was sustained in the belief that in a very few days the tide would turn.

On the 1st of November I telegraphed very fully to General Grant, at City Point, who must have been disturbed by the wild rumors that filled the country, and on the 2d of November received (at Rome) this dispatch:

CITY POINT, *November 1, 1864—6 P.M.*

Major-General SHERMAN:

Do you not think it advisable, now that Hood has gone so far north, to entirely ruin him before starting on your proposed campaign? With Hood's army destroyed, you can go where you please with impunity. I believed and still believe, if you had started south while Hood was in the neighborhood of you, he would have been forced to go after you. Now that he is far away he might look upon the chase as useless, and he will go in one direction while you are pushing in the other. If you can see a chance of destroying Hood's army, attend to that first, and make your other move secondary.

U. S. GRANT, Lieutenant-General.

My answer is dated:

ROME, GEORGIA, *November 2, 1864.*
Lieutenant-General U. S. GRANT, City Point, Virginia:

Your dispatch is received. If I could hope to overhaul Hood, I would turn against him with my whole force; then he would retreat to the south west, drawing me as a decoy away from Georgia, which is his chief object. If he ventures north of the Tennessee River, I may turn in that direction, and endeavor to get below him on his line of retreat; but thus far he has not gone above the Tennessee River. General Thomas will have a force strong enough to prevent his reaching any country in which we have an interest; and he has orders, if Hood turns to follow me, to push for Selma, Alabama. No single army can catch Hood, and I am convinced the best results will follow from our defeating Jeff. Davis's cherished plea of making me leave Georgia by manoeuvring. Thus far I have confined my efforts to thwart this plan, and have reduced baggage so that I can pick up and start in any direction; but I regard the pursuit of Hood as useless. Still, if he attempts to invade Middle Tennessee, I will hold Decatur, and be prepared to move in that direction; but, unless I let go of Atlanta, my force will not be equal to his.

W. T. SHERMAN, Major-General.

By this date, under the intelligent and energetic action of Colonel W. W. Wright, and with the labor of fifteen hundred men, the railroad break of fifteen miles about Dalton was repaired so far as to admit of the passage of cars, and I transferred my headquarters to Kingston as more central; and from that place, on the same day (November 2d), again telegraphed to General Grant:

KINGSTON, GEORGIA, *November 2, 1884.*
Lieutenant-General U. S. GRANT, City Point, Virginia: If I turn back, the whole effect of my campaign will be lost. By my movements I have thrown Beauregard (Hood) well to the west, and Thomas will have ample time and sufficient troops to hold him until the reenforcements from Missouri reach him. We have now ample supplies at Chattanooga and Atlanta, and can stand a month's interruption to our communications. I do not believe the Confederate army can reach our railroad-lines except by cavalry-raids, and Wilson will have cavalry enough to checkmate them. I am clearly of opinion that the best results will follow my contemplated movement through Georgia.
W. T. SHERMAN, Major-General.

That same day I received, in answer to the Rome dispatch, the following:

CITY POINT, VIRGINIA, *November 2, 1864—11.30 a.m.*

Major-General SHERMAN:

Your dispatch of 9 A.M. yesterday is just received. I dispatched you the same date, advising that Hood's army, now that it had worked so far north, ought to be looked upon now as the "object." With the force, however, that you have left with General Thomas, he must be able to take care of Hood and destroy him.

I do not see that you can withdraw from where you are to follow Hood, without giving up all we have gained in territory. I say, then, go on as you propose.

U. S. GRANT, Lieutenant-General,

This was the first time that General Grant ordered the "march to the sea," and, although many of his warm friends and admirers insist that he was the author and projector of that march, and that I simply executed his plans, General Grant has never, in my opinion, thought so or said so. The truth is fully given in an original letter of President Lincoln, which I received at Savannah, Georgia, and have at this instant before me, every word of which is in his own familiar handwriting. It is dated—

WASHINGTON, December 26, 1864.

When you were about leaving Atlanta for the Atlantic coast, I was anxious, if not fearful; but, feeling that you were the better judge, and remembering "nothing risked, nothing gained," I did not interfere. Now, the undertaking being a success, the honor is all yours; for I believe none of us went further than to acquiesce; and, taking the work of General Thomas into account, as it should be taken, it is indeed a great success. Not only does it afford the obvious and immediate military advantages, but, in showing to the world that your army could be divided, putting the stronger part to an important new service, and yet leaving enough to vanquish the old opposing force of the whole, Hood's army, it brings those who sat in darkness to see a great light. But what next? I suppose it will be safer if I leave General Grant and yourself to decide.

A. LINCOLN

Of course, this judgment; made after the event, was extremely flattering and was all I ever expected, a recognition of the truth and of its importance. I have often been asked, by well-meaning friends, when the thought of that march first entered my mind. I knew that an army which had penetrated Georgia as far as Atlanta could not turn back. It must go ahead, but when, how, and where, depended on many considerations. As soon as Hood had shifted across from Lovejoy's to Palmetto, I saw the move in my "mind's eye;" and, after Jeff. Davis's speech at Palmetto, of September 26th, I was more positive in my conviction, but was in doubt as to the time and manner. When General Hood first struck our railroad above Marietta, we were not ready, and I was forced to watch his movements further, till he had "carromed" off to the west of Decatur. Then I was perfectly convinced, and had no longer a shadow of doubt. The only possible question was as to Thomas's strength and ability to meet Hood in the open field. I did not suppose that General Hood, though rash, would venture to attack fortified places like Allatoona, Resaca, Decatur, and Nashville; but he did so, and in so doing he played into our hands perfectly.

On the 2d of November I was at Kingston, Georgia, and my four corps—the Fifteenth, Seventeenth, Fourteenth, and Twentieth—with one division of cavalry, were strung from Rome to Atlanta. Our railroads and telegraph had been repaired, and I deliberately prepared for the march to Savannah, distant three hundred miles from Atlanta. All the sick and wounded men had been sent back by rail to Chattanooga; all our wagon-trains had been carefully overhauled and loaded, so as to be ready to start on an hour's notice, and there was no serious enemy in our front.

General Hood remained still at Florence, Alabama, occupying both banks of the Tennessee River, busy in collecting shoes and clothing for his men, and the necessary ammunition and stores with which to invade Tennessee, most of which had to come from Mobile, Selma, and Montgomery, Alabama, over railroads that were still broken. Beauregard was at Corinth, hastening forward these necessary preparations.

General Thomas was at Nashville, with Wilson's dismounted cavalry and a mass of new troops and quartermaster's employs amply sufficient to defend the place. The Fourth and Twenty-third Corps, under Generals Stanley and Schofield were posted at Pulaski, Tennessee, and the cavalry of Hatch, Croxton, and Capron, were about Florence, watching Hood. Smith's (A. J.) two divisions of the Sixteenth Corps were still in Missouri, but were reported as ready to embark at Lexington for the Cumberland River and Nashville. Of course, General Thomas saw that on him would likely fall the real blow, and was naturally anxious. He still kept Granger's division at Decatur, Rousseau's at Murfreesboro', and Steedman's at Chattanooga, with strong railroad guards at all the essential points intermediate, confident that by means of this very railroad he could make his concentration sooner than Hood could possibly march up from Florence.

Meantime, General F. P. Blair had rejoined his corps (Seventeenth), and we were receiving at Kingston recruits and returned furlough-men, distributing them to their proper companies. Paymasters had come down to pay off our men before their departure to a new sphere of action, and commissioners were also on hand from the several States to take the vote of our men in the presidential election then agitating the country.

On the 6th of November, at Kingston, I wrote and telegraphed to General Grant, reviewing the whole situation, gave him my full plan of action, stated that I was ready to march as soon as the election was over, and appointed November 10th as the day for starting. On the 8th I received this dispatch:

CITY POINT, VIRGINIA, November 7, 1864-10.30 P.M.

Major-General SHERMAN:

Your dispatch of this evening received. I see no present reason for changing your plan. Should any arise, you will see it, or if I do I will inform you. I think everything here is favorable now. Great good fortune attend you! I believe you will be eminently successful, and, at worst, can only make a march less fruitful of results than hoped for.

U. S. GRANT, Lieutenant-General.

Meantime trains of cars were whirling by, carrying to the rear an immense amount of stores which had accumulated at Atlanta, and at the other stations along the railroad; and General Steedman had come down to Kingston, to take charge of the final evacuation and withdrawal of the several garrisons below Chattanooga.

On the 10th of November the movement may be said to have fairly begun. All the troops designed for the campaign were ordered to march for Atlanta, and General Corse, before evacuating his post at Rome, was ordered to burn all the mills, factories, etc., etc., that could be useful to the enemy, should he undertake to pursue us, or resume military possession of the country. This was done on the night of the 10th, and next day Corse reached Kingston. On the 11th General Thomas and I interchanged full dispatches. He had heard of the arrival of General A. J. Smith's two divisions at Paducah, which would surely reach Nashville much sooner than General Hood could possibly do from Florence, so that he was perfectly satisfied with his share of the army.

On the 12th, with a full staff, I started from Kingston for Atlanta; and about noon of that day we reached Cartersville, and sat on the edge of a porch to rest, when the telegraph operator, Mr. Van Valkenburg, or Eddy, got the wire down from the poles to his lap, in which he held a small pocket instrument. Calling "Chattanooga," he received this message from General Thomas, dated:

NASHVILLE, November 12, 1884—8.80 A.M.

Major-General SHERMAN:

Your dispatch of twelve o'clock last night is received. I have no fears that Beauregard can do us any harm now, and, if he attempts to follow you, I will follow him as far as possible. If he does not follow you, I will then thoroughly organize my troops, and believe I shall have men enough to ruin him unless he gets out of the way very rapidly.

The country of Middle Alabama, I learn, is teeming with supplies this year, which will be greatly to our advantage. I have no additional news to report from the direction of Florence. I am now convinced that the greater part of Beauregard's army is near Florence and Tuscumbia, and that you will have at least a clear road before you for several days, and that your success will fully equal your expectations.

George H. THOMAS, Major-General.

I answered simply: "Dispatch received—all right." About that instant of time, some of our men burnt a bridge, which severed the telegraph-wire, and all communication with the rear ceased thenceforth.

As we rode on toward Atlanta that night, I remember the railroad-trains going to the rear with a furious speed; the engineers and the few men about the trains waving us an affectionate adieu. It surely was a strange event—two hostile armies marching in opposite directions, each in the full belief that it was achieving a final and conclusive result in a great war; and I was strongly inspired with the feeling that the movement on our part was a direct attack upon the rebel army and the rebel capital at Richmond, though a full thousand miles of hostile country intervened, and that, for better or worse, it would end the war.

CHAPTER XXI.
THE MARCH TO THE SEA FROM ATLANTA TO SAVANNAH.

NOVEMBER AND DECEMBER, 1864.

On the 12th of November the railroad and telegraph communications with the rear were broken, and the army stood detached from all friends, dependent on its own resources and supplies. No time was to be lost; all the detachments were ordered to march rapidly for Atlanta, breaking up the railroad en route, and generally to so damage the country as to make it untenable to the enemy. By the 14th all the troops had arrived at or near Atlanta, and were, according to orders, grouped into two wings, the right and left, commanded respectively by Major-Generals O. O. Howard and H. W. Slocum, both comparatively young men, but educated and experienced officers, fully competent to their command.

The right wing was composed of the Fifteenth Corps, Major-General P. J. Osterhaus commanding, and the Seventeenth Corps, Major-General Frank P. Blair commanding.

The left wing was composed of the Fourteenth Corps, Major-General Jefferson C. Davis commanding, and the Twentieth Corps, Brigadier-General A. S. Williams commanding.

The Fifteenth Corps had four divisions, commanded by Brigadier-Generals Charles R. Woods, W. B. Hazen, John E. Smith, and John M. Gorse.

The Seventeenth Corps had three divisions, commanded by Major-General J. A. Mower, and Brigadier-Generals M. D. Leggett ad Giles A. Smith.

The Fourteenth Corps had three divisions, commanded by Brigadier-Generals W. P. Carlin, James D. Morgan, and A. Baird.

The Twentieth Corps had also three divisions, commanded by Brigadier-Generals N. J. Jackson, John W. Geary, and W. T. Ward.

The cavalry division was held separate, subject to my own orders. It was commanded by Brigadier-General Judson Kilpatrick, and was composed of two brigades, commanded by Colonels Eli H. Murray, of Kentucky, and Smith D. Atkins, of Illinois.

The strength of the army, as officially reported, is given in the following tables, and shows an aggregate of fifty-five thousand three hundred and twenty-nine infantry, five thousand and sixty-three cavalry, and eighteen hundred and twelve artillery in all, sixty-two thousand two hundred and four officers and men.

The most extraordinary efforts had been made to purge this army of non-combatants and of sick men, for we knew well that there was to be no place of safety save with the army itself; our wagons were loaded with ammunition, provisions, and forage, and we could ill afford to haul even sick men in the ambulances, so that all on this exhibit may be assumed to have been able-bodied, experienced soldiers, well armed, well equipped and provided, as far as human foresight could, with all the essentials of life, strength, and vigorous action.

The two general orders made for this march appear to me, even at this late day, so clear, emphatic, and well-digested, that no account of that historic event is perfect without them, and I give them entire, even at the seeming appearance of repetition; and, though they called for great sacrifice and labor on the part of the officers and men, I insist that these orders were obeyed as well as any similar orders ever were, by an army operating wholly in an enemy's country, and dispersed, as we necessarily were, during the subsequent period of nearly six months.

[Special Field Orders, No. 119.]

HEADQUARTERS MILITARY DIVISION OF THE MISSISSIPPI

The general commanding deems it proper at this time to inform the officers and men of the Fourteenth, Fifteenth, Seventeenth, and Twentieth Corps, that he has organized them into an army for a special purpose, well known to the War Department and to General Grant. It is sufficient for you to know that it involves a departure from our present base, and a long and difficult march to a new one. All the chances of war have been considered and provided for, as far as human sagacity can. All he asks of you is to maintain that discipline, patience, and courage, which have characterized you in the past; and he hopes, through you, to strike a blow at our enemy that will have a material effect in producing what we all so much desire, his complete overthrow. Of all things, the most important is, that the men, during marches and in camp, keep their places and do not scatter about as stragglers or foragers, to be picked up by a hostile people in detail. It is also of the utmost importance that our wagons should not be loaded with any thing but provisions and ammunition. All surplus servants, noncombatants, and refugees, should now go to the rear, and none should be encouraged to encumber us on the march. At some future time we will be able to provide for the poor whites and blacks who seek to escape the bondage under which they are now suffering. With these few simple cautions, he hopes to lead you to achievements equal in importance to those of the past.

By order of Major-General W. T. Sherman, L. M. DAYTON, Aide-de-Camp.

[Special Field Orders, No. 120.]

*HEADQUARTERS MILITARY DIVISION OF THE MISSISSIPPI
IN THE FIELD, KINGSTON, GEORGIA, November 9, 1864*

1. For the purpose of military operations, this army is divided into two wings viz.:

The right wing, Major-General O. O. Howard commanding, composed of the Fifteenth and Seventeenth Corps; the left wing, Major-General H. W. Slocum commanding, composed of the Fourteenth and Twentieth Corps.

2. The habitual order of march will be, wherever practicable, by four roads, as nearly parallel as possible, and converging at points hereafter to be indicated in orders. The cavalry, Brigadier-General Kilpatrick commanding, will receive special orders from the commander-in-chief.

3. There will be no general train of supplies, but each corps will have its ammunition-train and provision-train, distributed habitually as follows: Behind each regiment should follow one wagon and one ambulance; behind each brigade should follow a due proportion of ammunition-wagons, provision-wagons, and ambulances. In case of danger, each corps commander should change this order of march, by having his advance and rear brigades unencumbered by wheels. The separate columns will start habitually at 7 a.m., and make about fifteen miles per day, unless otherwise fixed in orders.

4. The army will forage liberally on the country during the march. To this end, each brigade commander will organize a good and sufficient foraging party, under the command of one or more discreet officers, who will gather, near the route traveled, corn or forage of any kind, meat of any kind, vegetables, corn-meal, or whatever is needed by the command, aiming at all times to keep in the wagons at least ten days' provisions for his command, and three days' forage. Soldiers must not enter the dwellings of the inhabitants, or commit any trespass; but, during a halt or camp, they may be permitted to gather turnips, potatoes, and other vegetables, and to drive in stock in sight of their camp. To regular foraging-parties must be intrusted the gathering of provisions and forage, at any distance from the road traveled.

6. To corps commanders alone is intrusted the power to destroy mills, houses, cotton-gins, etc.; and for them this general principle is laid down:

In districts and neighborhoods where the army is unmolested, no destruction of each property should be permitted; but should guerrillas or bushwhackers molest our march, or should the inhabitants burn bridges, obstruct roads, or otherwise manifest local hostility, then army commanders should order and enforce a devastation more or less relentless, according to the measure of such hostility.

6. As for horses, mules, wagons, etc., belonging to the inhabitants, the cavalry and artillery may appropriate freely and without limit; discriminating, however, between the rich, who are usually hostile, and the poor and industrious, usually neutral or friendly. Foraging-parties may also take mules or horses, to replace the jaded animals of their trains, or to serve as pack-mules for the regiments or brigades. In all foraging, of whatever kind, the parties engaged will refrain from abusive or threatening language, and may, where the officer in command thinks proper, give written certificates of the facts, but no receipts; and they will endeavor to leave with each family a reasonable portion for their maintenance,

7. Negroes who are able-bodied and can be of service to the several columns may be taken along; but each army commander will bear in mind that the question of supplies is a very important one, and that his first duty is to see to those who bear arms.

8. The organization, at once, of a good pioneer battalion for each army corps, composed if possible of negroes, should be attended to. This battalion should follow the advance-guard, repair roads and double them if possible, so that the columns will not be delayed after reaching bad places. Also, army commanders should practise the habit of giving the artillery and wagons the road, marching their troops on one side, and instruct their troops to assist wagons at steep hills or bad crossings of streams.

9. Captain O. M. Poe, chief-engineer, will assign to each wing of the army a pontoon-train, fully equipped and organized; and the commanders thereof will see to their being properly protected at all times.

By order of Major-General W. T. Sherman,

L. M. DAYTON, Aide-de-Camp.

The greatest possible attention had been given to the artillery and wagon trains. The number of guns had been reduced to sixty-five, or about one gun to each thousand men, and these were generally in batteries of four guns each.

Each gun, caisson, and forges was drawn by four teams of horses. We had in all about twenty-five hundred wagons, with teams of six mules to each, and six hundred ambulances, with two horses to each. The loads were made comparatively light, about twenty-five hundred pounds net; each wagon carrying in addition the forage needed by its own team: Each soldier carried on his person forty rounds of ammunition, and in the wagons were enough cartridges to make up about two hundred rounds per man, and in like manner two hundred rounds of assorted ammunition were carried for each gun.

The wagon-trains were divided equally between the four corps, so that each had about eight hundred wagons, and these usually on the march occupied five miles or more of road. Each corps commander managed his own train; and habitually the artillery and wagons had the road, while the men, with the exception of the advance and rear guards, pursued paths improvised by the aide of the wagons, unless they were forced to use a bridge or causeway in common.

I reached Atlanta during the afternoon of the 14th, and found that all preparations had been made-Colonel Beckwith, chief commissary, reporting one million two hundred thousand rations in possession of the troops, which was about twenty days' supply, and he had on hand a good supply of beef-cattle to be driven along on the hoof. Of forage, the supply was limited, being of oats and corn enough for five days, but I knew that within that time we would reach a country well stocked with corn, which had been gathered and stored in cribs, seemingly for our use, by Governor Brown's militia.

Colonel Poe, United States Engineers, of my staff, had been busy in his special task of destruction. He had a large force at work, had leveled the great depot, round house, and the machine-shops of the Georgia Railroad, and had applied fire to the wreck. One of these machine-shops had been used by the rebels as an arsenal, and in it were stored piles of shot and shell, some of which proved to be loaded, and that night was made hideous by the bursting of shells, whose fragments came uncomfortably, near Judge Lyon's house, in which I was quartered. The fire also reached the block of stores near the depot, and the heart of the city was in flames all night, but the fire did not reach the parts of Atlanta where the court-house was, or the great mass of dwelling houses.

The march from Atlanta began on the morning of November 15th, the right wing and cavalry following the railroad southeast toward Jonesboro', and General Slocum with the Twentieth Corps leading off to the east by Decatur and Stone Mountain, toward Madison. These were divergent lines, designed to threaten both Mason and Augusta at the same time, so as to prevent a concentration at our intended destination, or "objective," Milledgeville, the capital of Georgia, distant southeast about one hundred miles. The time allowed each column for reaching Milledgeville was seven days. I remained in Atlanta during the 15th with the Fourteenth Corps, and the rear-guard of the right wing, to complete the loading of the trains, and the destruction of the buildings of Atlanta which could be converted to hostile uses, and on the morning of the 16th started with my personal staff, a company of Alabama cavalry, commanded by Lieutenant Snelling, and an infantry company, commanded by Lieutenant McCrory, which guarded our small train of wagons.

My staff was then composed of Major L. M. Dayton, aide-de-camp and acting adjutant-general, Major J. C. McCoy, and Major J. C. Audenried, aides. Major Ward Nichols had joined some weeks before at Gaylesville, Alabama, and was attached as an acting aide-de-camp. Also Major Henry Hitchcock had joined at the same time as judge-advocate. Colonel Charles Ewing was inspector-general, and Surgeon John Moore medical director. These constituted our mess. We had no tents, only the flies, with which we nightly made bivouacs with the assistance of the abundant pine-boughs, which made excellent shelter, as well as beds.

70

Colonel L. C. Easton was chief-quartermaster; Colonel Amos Beckwith, chief-commissary; Colonel O. M. Poe, chief-engineer; and Colonel T. G. Baylor, chief of ordnance. These invariably rode with us during the day, but they had a separate camp and mess at night.

General William F. Barry had been chief of artillery in the previous campaign, but at Kingston his face was so swollen with erysipelas that he was reluctantly compelled to leave us for the rear; and he could not, on recovering, rejoin us till we had reached Savannah.

About 7 a.m. of November 16th we rode out of Atlanta by the Decatur road, filled by the marching troops and wagons of the Fourteenth Corps; and reaching the hill, just outside of the old rebel works, we naturally paused to look back upon the scenes of our past battles. We stood upon the very ground whereon was fought the bloody battle of July 22d, and could see the copse of wood where McPherson fell. Behind us lay Atlanta, smouldering and in ruins, the black smoke rising high in air, and hanging like a pall over the ruined city. Away off in the distance, on the McDonough road, was the rear of Howard's column, the gun-barrels glistening in the sun, the white-topped wagons stretching away to the south; and right before us the Fourteenth Corps, marching steadily and rapidly, with a cheery look and swinging pace, that made light of the thousand miles that lay between us and Richmond. Some band, by accident, struck up the anthem of "John Brown's soul goes marching on;" the men caught up the strain, and never before or since have I heard the chorus of "Glory, glory, hallelujah!" done with more spirit, or in better harmony of time and place.

Then we turned our horses' heads to the east; Atlanta was soon lost behind the screen of trees, and became a thing of the past. Around it clings many a thought of desperate battle, of hope and fear, that now seem like the memory of a dream; and I have never seen the place since. The day was extremely beautiful, clear sunlight, with bracing air, and an unusual feeling of exhilaration seemed to pervade all minds--a feeling of something to come, vague and undefined, still full of venture and intense interest. Even the common soldiers caught the inspiration, and many a group called out to me as I worked my way past them, "Uncle Billy, I guess Grant is waiting for us at Richmond!" Indeed, the general sentiment was that we were marching for Richmond, and that there we should end the war, but how and when they seemed to care not; nor did they measure the distance, or count the cost in life, or bother their brains about the great rivers to be crossed, and the food required for man and beast, that had to be gathered by the way. There was a "devil-may-care" feeling pervading officers and men, that made me feel the full load of responsibility, for success would be accepted as a matter of course, whereas, should we fail, this "march" would be adjudged the wild adventure of a crazy fool. I had no purpose to march direct for Richmond by way of Augusta and Charlotte, but always designed to reach the sea-coast first at Savannah or Port Royal, South Carolina, and even kept in mind the alternative of Pensacola.

The first night out we camped by the road-side near Lithonia. Stone Mountain, a mass of granite, was in plain view, cut out in clear outline against the blue sky; the whole horizon was lurid with the bonfires of rail-ties, and groups of men all night were carrying the heated rails to the nearest trees, and bending them around the trunks. Colonel Poe had provided tools for ripping up the rails and twisting them when hot; but the best and easiest way is the one I have described, of heating the middle of the iron-rails on bonfires made of the cross-ties, and then winding them around a telegraph-pole or the trunk of some convenient sapling. I attached much importance to this destruction of the railroad, gave it my own personal attention, and made reiterated orders to others on the subject.

The next day we passed through the handsome town of Covington, the soldiers closing up their ranks, the color-bearers unfurling their flags, and the bands striking up patriotic airs. The white people came out of their houses to behold the sight, spite of their deep hatred of the invaders, and the negroes were simply frantic with joy. Whenever they heard my name, they clustered about my horse, shouted and prayed in their peculiar style, which had a natural eloquence that would have moved a stone. I have witnessed hundreds, if not thousands, of such scenes; and can now see a poor girl, in the very ecstasy of the Methodist "shout," hugging the banner of one of the regiments, and jumping up to the "feet of Jesus."

I remember, when riding around by a by-street in Covington, to avoid the crowd that followed the marching column, that some one brought me an invitation to dine with a sister of Sam. Anderson, who was a cadet at West Point with me; but the messenger reached me after we had passed the main part of the town. I asked to be excused, and rode on to a place designated for camp, at the crossing of the Ulcofauhachee River, about four miles to the east of the town. Here we made our bivouac, and I walked up to a plantation-house close by, where were assembled many negroes, among them an old, gray-haired man, of as fine a head as I ever saw. I asked him if he understood about the war and its progress. He said he did; that he had been looking for the "angel of the Lord" ever since he was knee-high, and, though we professed to be fighting for the Union, he supposed that slavery was the cause, and that our success was to be his freedom. I asked him if all the negro slaves comprehended this fact, and he said they surely did. I then explained to him that we wanted the slaves to remain where they were, and not to load us down with useless mouths, which would eat up the food needed for our fighting men; that our success was their assured freedom; that we could receive a few of their young, hearty men as pioneers; but that, if they followed us in swarms of old and young, feeble and helpless, it would simply load us down and cripple us in our great task. I think Major Henry Hitchcock was with me on that occasion, and made a note of the conversation, and I believe that old man spread this message to the slaves, which was carried from mouth to mouth, to the very end of our journey, and that it in part saved us from the great danger we incurred of swelling our numbers so that famine would have attended our progress. It was at this very plantation that a soldier passed me with a ham on his musket, a jug of sorghum-molasses under his arm, and a big piece of honey in his hand, from which he was eating, and, catching my eye, he remarked sotto voce and carelessly to a comrade, "Forage liberally on the country," quoting from my general orders. On this occasion, as on many others that fell under my personal observation, I reproved the man, explained that foraging must be limited to the regular parties properly detailed, and that all provisions thus obtained must be delivered to the regular commissaries, to be fairly distributed to the men who kept their ranks.

From Covington the Fourteenth Corps (Davis's), with which I was traveling, turned to the right for Milledgeville, via Shady Dale. General Slocum was ahead at Madison, with the Twentieth Corps, having torn up the railroad as far as that place, and thence had sent Geary's division on to the Oconee, to burn the bridges across that stream, when this corps turned south by Eatonton, for Milledgeville, the common "objective" for the first stage of the "march." We found abundance of corn, molasses, meal, bacon, and sweet-potatoes. We also took a good many cows and oxen, and a large number of mules. In all these the country was quite rich, never before having been visited by a hostile army; the recent crop had been excellent, had been just gathered and laid by for the winter. As a rule, we destroyed none, but kept our wagons full, and fed our teams bountifully.

The skill and success of the men in collecting forage was one of the features of this march. Each brigade commander had authority to detail a company of foragers, usually about fifty men, with one or two commissioned officers selected for their boldness and enterprise. This party would be dispatched before daylight with a knowledge of the intended day's march and camp; would proceed on foot five or six miles from the route traveled by their brigade, and then visit every plantation and farm within range. They would usually procure a wagon or family carriage, load it with bacon, corn-meal, turkeys, chickens, ducks, and every thing that could be used as food or forage, and would then regain the main road, usually in advance of their train. When this came up, they would deliver to the brigade commissary the supplies thus gathered by the way. Often would I pass these foraging-parties at the roadside, waiting for their wagons to come up, and was amused at their strange collections--mules, horses, even cattle, packed with old saddles and loaded with hams, bags of cornmeal, and poultry of every character and description. Although this foraging was attended with great danger and hard work, there seemed to be a charm about it that attracted the soldiers, and it was a privilege to be detailed on such a party. Daily they returned mounted on all sorts of beasts, which were at once taken from them and appropriated to the general use; but the next day they would start out again on foot, only to repeat the experience of the day before. No doubt, many acts of pillage, robbery, and violence, were committed by these parties of foragers, usually called "bummers;" for I have since heard of jewelry taken from women, and the plunder of articles that never reached the commissary; but these acts were exceptional and incidental. I never heard of any cases of murder or rape; and no army could have carried along sufficient food and forage for a march of three hundred miles; so that foraging in some shape was necessary. The country was sparsely settled, with no magistrates or civil authorities who could respond to requisitions, as is done in all the wars of Europe; so that this system of foraging was simply indispensable to our success. By it our men were well supplied with all the essentials of life and health, while the wagons retained enough in case of unexpected delay, and our animals were well fed. Indeed, when we reached Savannah, the trains were pronounced by experts to be the finest in flesh and appearance ever seen with any army.

Habitually each corps followed some main road, and the foragers, being kept out on the exposed flank, served all the military uses of flankers. The main columns gathered, by the roads traveled, much forage and food, chiefly meat, corn, and sweet-potatoes, and it was the duty of each division and brigade quartermaster to fill his wagons as fast as the contents were issued to the troops. The wagon-trains had the right to the road always, but each wagon was required to keep closed up, so as to leave no gaps in the column. If for any purpose any wagon or group of wagons dropped out of place, they had to wait for the rear. And this was always dreaded, for each brigade commander wanted his train up at camp as soon after reaching it with his men as possible.

I have seen much skill and industry displayed by these quarter-masters on the march, in trying to load their wagons with corn and fodder by the way without losing their place in column. They would, while marching, shift the loads of wagons, so as to have six or ten of them empty. Then, riding well ahead, they would secure possession of certain stacks of fodder near the road, or cribs of corn, leave some men in charge, then open fences and a road back for a couple of miles, return to their trains, divert the empty wagons out of column, and conduct them rapidly to their forage, load up and regain their place in column without losing distance. On one occasion I remember to have seen ten or a dozen wagons thus loaded with corn from two or three full cribs, almost without halting. These cribs were built of logs, and roofed. The train-guard, by a lever, had raised the whole side of the crib a foot or two; the wagons drove close alongside, and the men in the cribs, lying on their backs, kicked out a wagon-load of corn in the time I have taken to describe it.

In a well-ordered and well-disciplined army, these things might be deemed irregular, but I am convinced that the ingenuity of these younger officers accomplished many things far better than I could have ordered, and the marches were thus made, and the distances were accomplished, in the most admirable way. Habitually we started from camp at the earliest break of dawn, and usually reached camp soon after noon. The marches varied from ten to fifteen miles a day, though sometimes on extreme flanks it was necessary to make as much as twenty, but the rate of travel was regulated by the wagons; and, considering the nature of the roads, fifteen miles per day was deemed the limit.

The pontoon-trains were in like manner distributed in about equal proportions to the four corps, giving each a section of about nine hundred feet. The pontoons were of the skeleton pattern, with cotton-canvas covers, each boat, with its proportion of balks and cheeses, constituting a load for one wagon. By uniting two such sections together, we could make a bridge of eighteen hundred feet, enough for any river we had to traverse; but habitually the leading brigade would, out of the abundant timber, improvise a bridge before the pontoon-train could come up, unless in the cases of rivers of considerable magnitude, such as the Ocmulgee, Oconee, Ogeechee, Savannah, etc.

On the 20th of November I was still with the Fourteenth Corps, near Eatonton Factory, waiting to hear of the Twentieth Corps; and on the 21st we camped near the house of a man named Mann; the next day, about 4 p.m., General Davis had halted his head of column on a wooded ridge, overlooking an extensive slope of cultivated country, about ten miles short of Milledgeville, and was deploying his troops for camp when I got up. There was a high, raw wind blowing, and I asked him why he had chosen so cold and bleak a position. He explained that he had accomplished his full distance for the day, and had there an abundance of wood and water. He explained further that his advance-guard was a mile or so ahead; so I rode on, asking him to let his rear division, as it came up, move some distance ahead into the depression or valley beyond. Riding on some distance to the border of a plantation, I turned out of the main road into a cluster of wild-plum bushes, that broke the force of the cold November wind, dismounted, and instructed the staff to pick out the place for our camp.

The afternoon was unusually raw and cold. My orderly was at hand with his invariable saddle-bags, which contained a change of under-clothing, my maps, a flask of whiskey, and bunch of cigars. Taking a drink and lighting a cigar, I walked to a row of negro-huts close by, entered one and found a soldier or two warming themselves by a wood-fire. I took their place by the fire, intending to wait there till our wagons had got up, and a camp made for the night. I was talking to the old negro woman, when some one came and explained to me that, if I would come farther down the road, I could find a better place. So I started on foot, and found on the main road a good double-hewed-log house, in one room of which Colonel Poe, Dr. Moore, and others, had started a fire. I sent back orders to the "plum-bushes" to bring our horses and saddles up to this house, and an orderly to conduct our headquarter wagons to the same place. In looking around the room, I saw a small box, like a candle-box, marked "Howell Cobb," and, on inquiring of a negro, found that we were at the plantation of General Howell Cobb, of Georgia, one of the leading rebels of the South, then a general in the Southern army, and who had been Secretary of the United States Treasury in Mr. Buchanan's time. Of course, we confiscated his property, and found it rich in corn, beans, pea-nuts, and sorghum-molasses. Extensive fields were all round the house; I sent word back to General David to explain whose plantation it was, and instructed him to spare nothing. That night huge bonfires consumed the fence-rails, kept our soldiers warm, and the teamsters and men, as well as the slaves, carried off an immense quantity of corn and provisions of all sorts.

In due season the headquarter wagons came up, and we got supper. After supper I sat on a chair astride, with my back to a good fire, musing, and became conscious that an old negro, with a tallow-candle in his hand, was scanning my face closely. I inquired, "What do you want, old man!" He answered, "Dey say you is Massa Sherman." I answered that such was the case, and inquired what he wanted. He only wanted to look at me, and kept muttering, "Dis nigger can't sleep dis night." I asked him why he trembled so, and he said that he wanted to be sure that we were in fact "Yankees," for on a former occasion some rebel cavalry had put on light-blue overcoats, personating Yankee troops, and many of the negroes were deceived thereby, himself among the number had shown them sympathy, and had in consequence been unmercifully beaten therefor. This time he wanted to be certain before committing himself; so I told him to go out on the porch, from which he could see the whole horizon lit up with camp-fires, and he could then judge whether he had ever seen any thing like it before. The old man became convinced that the "Yankees" had come at last, about whom he had been dreaming all his life; and some of the staff officers gave him a strong drink of whiskey, which set his tongue going. Lieutenant Spelling, who commanded my escort, was a Georgian, and recognized in this old negro a favorite slave of his uncle, who resided about six miles off; but the old slave did not at first recognize his young master in our uniform. One of my staff-officers asked him what had become of his young master, George. He did not know, only that he had gone off to the war, and he supposed him killed, as a matter of course. His attention was then drawn to Spelling's face, when he fell on his knees and thanked God that he had found his young master alive and along with the Yankees. Spelling inquired all about his uncle and the family, asked my permission to go and pay his uncle a visit, which I granted, of course, and the next morning he described to me his visit. The uncle was not cordial, by any means, to find his nephew in the ranks of the host that was desolating the land, and Spelling came back, having exchanged his tired horse for a fresher one out of his uncle's stables, explaining that surely some of the "bummers" would have got the horse had he not.

The next morning, November 23d, we rode into Milledgeville, the capital of the State, whither the Twentieth Corps had preceded us; and during that day the left wing was all united, in and around Milledgeville. From the inhabitants we learned that some of Kilpatrick's cavalry had preceded us by a couple of days, and that all of the right wing was at and near Gordon, twelve miles off, viz., the place where the branch railroad came to

73

Milledgeville from the Mason & Savannah road. The first stage of the journey was, therefore, complete, and absolutely successful.

General Howard soon reported by letter the operations of his right wing, which, on leaving Atlanta, had substantially followed the two roads toward Mason, by Jonesboro' and McDonough, and reached the Ocmulgee at Planters' Factory, which they crossed, by the aid of the pontoon-train, during the 18th and 19th of November. Thence, with the Seventeenth Corps (General Blair's) he (General Howard) had marched via Monticello toward Gordon, having dispatched Kilpatrick's cavalry, supported by the Fifteenth Corps (Osterhaus's), to feign on Mason. Kilpatrick met the enemy's cavalry about four miles out of Mason, and drove them rapidly back into the bridge-defenses held by infantry. Kilpatrick charged these, got inside the parapet, but could not hold it, and retired to his infantry supports, near Griswold Station. The Fifteenth Corps tore up the railroad-track eastward from Griswold, leaving Charles R. Wood's division behind as a rear-guard-one brigade of which was intrenched across the road, with some of Kilpatrick's cavalry on the flanks. On the 22d of November General G. W. Smith, with a division of troops, came out of Mason, attacked this brigade (Walcutt's) in position, and was handsomely repulsed and driven back into Mason. This brigade was in part armed with Spencer repeating-rifles, and its fire was so rapid that General Smith insists to this day that he encountered a whole division; but he is mistaken; he was beaten by one brigade (Walcutt's), and made no further effort to molest our operations from that direction. General Walcutt was wounded in the leg, and had to ride the rest of the distance to Savannah in a carriage.

Therefore, by the 23d, I was in Milledgeville with the left wing, and was in full communication with the right wing at Gordon. The people of Milledgeville remained at home, except the Governor (Brown), the State officers, and Legislature, who had ignominiously fled, in the utmost disorder and confusion; standing not on the order of their going, but going at once--some by rail, some by carriages, and many on foot. Some of the citizens who remained behind described this flight of the "brave and patriotic" Governor Brown. He had occupied a public building known as the "Governor's Mansion," and had hastily stripped it of carpets, curtains, and furniture of all sorts, which were removed to a train of freight-cars, which carried away these things--even the cabbages and vegetables from his kitchen and cellar--leaving behind muskets, ammunition, and the public archives. On arrival at Milledgeville I occupied the same public mansion, and was soon overwhelmed with appeals for protection. General Slocum had previously arrived with the Twentieth Corps, had taken up his quarters at the Milledgeville Hotel, established a good provost-guard, and excellent order was maintained. The most frantic appeals had been made by the Governor and Legislature for help from every quarter, and the people of the State had been called out en masse to resist and destroy the invaders of their homes and firesides. Even the prisoners and convicts of the penitentiary were released on condition of serving as soldiers, and the cadets were taken from their military college for the same purpose. These constituted a small battalion, under General Harry Wayne, a former officer of the United States Army, and son of the then Justice Wayne of the Supreme Court. But these hastily retreated east across the Oconee River, leaving us a good bridge, which we promptly secured.

At Milledgeville we found newspapers from all the South, and learned the consternation which had filled the Southern mind at our temerity; many charging that we were actually fleeing for our lives and seeking safety at the hands of our fleet on the sea-coast. All demanded that we should be assailed, "front, flank, and rear;" that provisions should be destroyed in advance, so that we would starve; that bridges should be burned, roads obstructed, and no mercy shown us. Judging from the tone of the Southern press of that day, the outside world must have supposed us ruined and lost. I give a few of these appeals as samples, which to-day must sound strange to the parties who made them:

Corinth, Mississippi, November 18, 1884.

To the People of Georgia:

Arise for the defense of your native soil! Rally around your patriotic Governor and gallant soldiers! Obstruct and destroy all the roads in Sherman's front, flank, and rear, and his army will soon starve in your midst. Be confident. Be resolute. Trust in an overruling Providence, and success will soon crown your efforts. I hasten to join you in the defense of your homes and firesides.

G. T. BEAUREGARD.

RICHMOND, November 18, 1884.

To the People of Georgia:

You have now the best opportunity ever yet presented to destroy the enemy. Put every thing at the disposal of our generals; remove all provisions from the path of the, invader, and put all obstructions in his path.

Every citizen with his gun, and every negro with his spade and axe, can do the work of a soldier. You can destroy the enemy by retarding his march.

Georgians, be firm! Act promptly, and fear not!

B. H. Hill, Senator.

I most cordially approve the above.
James A. SEDDON, Secretary of War.

Richmond, November 19,1864.

To the People of Georgia:

We have had a special conference with President Davis and the Secretary of War, and are able to assure you that they have done and are still doing all that can be done to meet the emergency that presses upon you. Let every man fly to arms! Remove your negroes, horses, cattle, and provisions from Sherman's army, and burn what you cannot carry. Burn all bridges, and block up the roads in his route. Assail the invader in front, flank, and rear, by night and by day. Let him have no rest.

JULIAN HARTRIDGE
MARK BLANDFORD,
J. H. ECHOLS
GEO. N. LESTER
JOHN T. SHUEMAKER
JAS. M. SMITH,

Members of Congress.

Of course, we were rather amused than alarmed at these threats, and made light of the feeble opposition offered to our progress. Some of the officers (in the spirit of mischief) gathered together in the vacant hall of Representatives, elected a Speaker, and constituted themselves the Legislature of the State of Georgia! A proposition was made to repeal the ordinance of secession, which was well debated, and resulted in its repeal by a fair vote! I was not present at these frolics, but heard of them at the time, and enjoyed the joke.

Meantime orders were made for the total destruction of the arsenal and its contents, and of such public buildings as could be easily converted to hostile uses. But little or no damage was done to private property, and General Slocum, with my approval, spared several mills, and many thousands of bales of cotton, taking what he knew to be worthless bonds, that the cotton should not be used for the Confederacy. Meantime the right wing continued its movement along the railroad toward Savannah, tearing up the track and destroying its iron. At the Oconee was met a feeble resistance from Harry Wayne's troops, but soon the pontoon-bridge was laid, and that wing crossed over. Gilpatrick's cavalry was brought into Milledgeville, and crossed the Oconee by the bridge near the town; and on the 23d I made the general orders for the next stage of the march as far as Millen. These were, substantially, for the right wing to follow the Savannah Railroad, by roads on its south; the left wing was to move to Sandersville, by Davisboro' and Louisville, while the cavalry was ordered by a circuit to the north, and to march rapidly for Millen, to rescue our prisoners of war confined there. The distance was about a hundred miles.

General Wheeler, with his division of rebel cavalry, had succeeded in getting ahead of us between Milledgeville and Augusta, and General P. J. Hardee had been dispatched by General Beauregard from Hood's army to oppose our progress directly in front. He had, however, brought with him no troops, but relied on his influence with the Georgians (of whose State he was a native) to arouse the people, and with them to annihilate Sherman's army!

On the 24th we renewed the march, and I accompanied the Twentieth Corps, which took the direct road to Sandersville, which we reached simultaneously with the Fourteenth Corps, on the 26th. A brigade of rebel cavalry was deployed before the town, and was driven in and through it by our skirmish-line. I myself saw the rebel cavalry apply fire to stacks of fodder standing in the fields at Sandersville, and gave orders to burn some unoccupied dwellings close by. On entering the town, I told certain citizens (who would be sure to spread the report) that, if the enemy attempted to carry out their threat to burn their food, corn, and fodder, in our route, I would most undoubtedly execute to the letter the general orders of devastation made at the outset of the campaign. With this exception, and one or two minor cases near Savannah, the people did not destroy food, for they saw clearly that it would be ruin to themselves.

At Sandersville I halted the left wing until I heard that the right wing was abreast of us on the railroad. During the evening a negro was brought to me, who had that day been to the station (Tenille), about six miles south of the town. I inquired of him if there were any Yankees there, and he answered, "Yes." He described in his own way what he had seen.

"First, there come along some cavalry-men, and they burned the depot; then come along some infantry-men, and they tore up the track, and burned it;" and just before he left they had "sot fire to the well."

The next morning, viz., the 27th, I rode down to the station, and found General Corse's division (of the Fifteenth Corps) engaged in destroying the railroad, and saw the well which my negro informant had seen "burnt." It was a square pit about twenty-five feet deep, boarded up, with wooden steps leading to the bottom, wherein was a fine copper pump, to lift the water to a tank above. The soldiers had broken up the pump, heaved in the steps and lining, and set fire to the mass of lumber in the bottom of the well, which corroborated the negro's description.

From this point Blair's corps, the Seventeenth, took up the work of destroying the railroad, the Fifteenth Corps following another road leading eastward, farther to the south of the railroad. While the left wing was marching toward Louisville, north of the railroad, General Kilpatrick had, with his cavalry division, moved rapidly toward Waynesboro', on the branch railroad leading from Millen to Augusta. He found Wheeler's division of rebel cavalry there, and had considerable skirmishing with it; but, learning that our prisoners had been removed two days before from Millen, he returned to Louisville on the 29th, where he found the left wing. Here he remained a couple of days to rest his horses, and, receiving orders from me to engage Wheeler and give him all the fighting he wanted, he procured from General Slocum the assistance of the infantry division of General Baird, and moved back for Waynesboro' on the 2d of December, the remainder of the left wing continuing its march on toward Millers. Near Waynesboro' Wheeler was again encountered, and driven through the town and beyond Brier Creek, toward Augusta, thus keeping up the delusion that the main army was moving toward Augusta. General Kilpatrick's fighting and movements about Waynesboro' and Brier Creek were spirited, and produced a good effect by relieving the infantry column and the wagon-trains of all molestation during their march on Millen. Having thus covered that flank, he turned south and followed the movement of the Fourteenth Corps to Buckhead Church, north of Millen and near it.

On the 3d of December I entered Millen with the Seventeenth Corps (General Frank P. Blair), and there paused one day, to communicate with all parts of the army. General Howard was south of the Ogeechee River, with the Fifteenth Corps, opposite Scarboro'. General Slocum was at Buckhead Church, four miles north of Millen, with the Twentieth Corps. The Fourteenth (General Davis) was at Lumpkin's Station, on the Augusta road, about ten miles north of Millen, and the cavalry division was within easy support of this wing. Thus the whole army was in good position and in good condition. We had largely subsisted on the country; our wagons were full of forage and provisions; but, as we approached the sea-coast, the country became more sandy and barren, and food became more scarce; still, with little or no loss, we had traveled two-thirds of our distance, and I concluded to push on for Savannah. At Millen I learned that General Bragg was in Augusta, and that General Wade Hampton had been ordered there from Richmond, to organize a large cavalry force with which to resist our progress.

General Hardee was ahead, between us and Savannah, with McLaw's division, and other irregular troops, that could not, I felt assured, exceed ten thousand men. I caused the fine depot at Millen to be destroyed, and other damage done, and then resumed the march directly on Savannah, by the four main roads. The Seventeenth Corps (General Blair) followed substantially the railroad, and, along with it, on the 5th of December, I reached Ogeechee Church, about fifty miles from Savannah, and found there fresh earthworks, which had been thrown up by McLaw's division; but he must have seen that both his flanks were being turned, and prudently retreated to Savannah without a fight. All the columns then pursued leisurely their march toward Savannah, corn and forage becoming more and more scarce, but rice-fields beginning to occur along the Savannah and Ogeechee Rivers, which proved a good substitute, both as food and forage. The weather was fine, the roads good, and every thing seemed to favor us. Never do I recall a more agreeable sensation than the sight of our camps by night, lit up by the fires of fragrant pine-knots. The trains were all in good order, and the men seemed to march their fifteen miles a day as though it were nothing. No enemy opposed us, and we could only occasionally hear the faint reverberation of a gun to our left rear, where we knew that General Kilpatrick was skirmishing with Wheeler's cavalry, which persistently followed him. But the infantry columns had met with no opposition whatsoever. McLaw's division was falling back before us, and we occasionally picked up a few of his men as prisoners, who insisted that we would meet with strong opposition at Savannah.

On the 8th, as I rode along, I found the column turned out of the main road, marching through the fields. Close by, in the corner of a fence, was a group of men standing around a handsome young officer, whose foot had been blown to pieces by a torpedo planted in the road. He was waiting for a surgeon to amputate his leg, and told me that he was riding along with the rest of his brigade-staff of the Seventeenth Corps, when a torpedo trodden on by his horse had exploded, killing the horse and literally blowing off all the flesh from one of his legs. I saw the terrible wound, and made full inquiry into the facts. There had been no resistance at that point, nothing to give warning of danger, and the rebels had planted eight-inch shells in the road, with friction-matches to explode them by being trodden on. This was not war, but murder, and it made me very angry. I immediately ordered a lot of rebel prisoners to be brought from the provost-guard, armed with picks and spades, and made them march in close order along the road, so as to explode their own torpedoes, or to discover and dig them up. They begged hard, but I reiterated the order, and could hardly help laughing at their stepping so gingerly along the road, where it was supposed sunken torpedoes might explode at each step, but they found no other torpedoes till near Fort McAllister. That night we reached Pooler's Station, eight miles from Savannah, and during the next two days, December 9th and 10th, the several corps reached the defenses of Savannah--the Fourteenth Corps on the left, touching the river; the Twentieth Corps next; then the Seventeenth; and the Fifteenth on the extreme right; thus completely investing the city. Wishing to reconnoitre the place in person, I rode forward by the Louisville road, into a dense wood of oak, pine, and cypress, left the horses, and walked down to the railroad-track, at a place where there was a side-track, and a cut about four feet deep. From that point the railroad was straight, leading into Savannah, and about eight hundred yards off were a rebel parapet and battery. I could see the cannoneers preparing to fire, and cautioned the officers near me to scatter, as we would likely attract a shot. Very soon I saw the white puff of smoke, and, watching close, caught sight of the ball as it rose in its flight, and, finding it coming pretty straight, I stepped a short distance to one side, but noticed a negro very near me in the act of crossing the track at right angles. Some one called to him to look out; but, before the poor fellow understood his danger, the ball (a thirty-two-pound round shot) struck the ground, and rose in its first ricochet, caught the negro under the right jaw, and literally carried away his head, scattering blood and brains about. A soldier close by spread an overcoat over the body, and we all concluded to get out of that railroad-cut. Meantime, General Mower's division of the Seventeenth Corps had crossed the canal to the right of the Louisville road, and had found the line of parapet continuous; so at Savannah we had again run up against the old familiar parapet, with its deep ditches, canals, and bayous, full of water; and it looked as though another siege was inevitable. I accordingly made a camp or bivouac near the Louisville road, about five miles from Savannah, and proceeded to invest the place closely, pushing forward reconnoissances at every available point.

As soon as it was demonstrated that Savannah was well fortified, with a good garrison, commanded by General William J. Hardee, a competent soldier, I saw that the first step was to open communication with our fleet, supposed to be waiting for us with supplies and clothing in Ossabaw Sound.

General Howard had, some nights previously, sent one of his best scouts, Captain Duncan, with two men, in a canoe, to drift past Fort McAllister, and to convey to the fleet a knowledge of our approach. General Kilpatrick's cavalry had also been transferred to the south bank of the Ogeechee, with orders to open communication with the fleet. Leaving orders with General Slocum to press the siege, I instructed General Howard to send a division with all his engineers to Grog's Bridge, fourteen and a half miles southwest from Savannah, to rebuild it. On the evening of the 12th I rode over myself, and spent the night at Mr. King's house, where I found General Howard, with General Hazen's division of the Fifteenth Corps. His engineers were hard at work on the bridge, which they finished that night, and at sunrise Hazen's division passed over. I gave General Hazen, in person, his orders to march rapidly down the right bank of the Ogeechee, and without hesitation to assault and carry Fort McAllister by storm. I knew it to be strong in heavy artillery, as against an approach from the sea, but believed it open and weak to the rear. I explained to General Hazen, fully, that on his action depended the safety of the whole army, and the success of the campaign. Kilpatrick had already felt the fort, and had gone farther down the coast to Kilkenny Bluff, or St. Catharine's Sound, where, on the same day, he had communication with a vessel belonging to the blockading fleet; but, at the time, I was not aware of this fact, and trusted entirely to General Hazen and his division of infantry, the Second of the Fifteenth Corps, the same old division which I had commanded at Shiloh and Vicksburg, in which I felt a special pride and confidence.

Having seen General Hazen fairly off, accompanied by General Howard, I rode with my staff down the left bank of the Ogeechee, ten miles to the rice-plantation of a Mr. Cheevea, where General Howard had established a signal-station to overlook the lower river, and to watch for any vessel of the blockading squadron, which the negroes reported to be expecting us, because they nightly sent up rockets, and daily dispatched a steamboat up the Ogeechee as near to Fort McAllister as it was safe.

On reaching the rice-mill at Cheevea's, I found a guard and a couple of twenty-pound Parrott gone, of De Gres's battery, which fired an occasional shot toward Fort McAllister, plainly seen over the salt-marsh, about three miles distant. Fort McAllister had the rebel flag flying, and occasionally sent a heavy shot back across the marsh to where we were, but otherwise every thing about the place looked as peaceable and quiet as on the Sabbath.

The signal-officer had built a platform on the ridge-pole of the rice-mill. Leaving our horses behind the stacks of rice-straw, we all got on the roof of a shed attached to the mill, wherefrom I could communicate with the signal-officer above, and at the same time look out toward Ossabaw Sound, and across the Ogeechee River at Fort McAllister. About 2 p.m. we observed signs of commotion in the fort, and noticed one or two guns fired inland, and some musket-skirmishing in the woods close by.

This betokened the approach of Hazen's division, which had been anxiously expected, and soon thereafter the signal-officer discovered about three miles above the fort a signal-flag, with which he conversed, and found it to belong to General Hazen, who was preparing to assault the fort, and wanted to know if I were there. On being assured of this fact, and that I expected the fort to be carried before night, I received by signal the assurance of General Hazen that he was making his preparations, and would soon attempt the assault. The sun was rapidly declining, and I was dreadfully impatient. At that very moment some one discovered a faint cloud of smoke, and an object gliding, as it were, along the horizon above the tops of the sedge toward the sea, which little by little grew till it was pronounced to be the smoke-stack of a steamer coming up the river. "It must be one of our squadron!" Soon the flag of the United States was plainly visible, and our attention was divided between this approaching steamer and the expected assault. When the sun was about an hour high, another signal-message came from General Hazen that he was all ready, and I replied to go ahead, as a friendly steamer was approaching from below. Soon we made out a group of officers on the deck of this vessel, signaling with a flag, "Who are you!" The answer went back promptly, "General Sherman." Then followed the question, "Is Fort McAllister taken?" "Not yet, but it will be in a minute!" Almost at that instant of time, we saw Hazen's troops come out of the dark fringe of woods that encompassed the fort, the lines dressed as on parade, with colors flying, and moving forward with a quick, steady pace. Fort McAllister was then all alive, its big guns belching forth dense clouds of smoke, which soon enveloped our assaulting lines. One color went down, but was up in a moment. On the lines advanced, faintly seen in the white, sulphurous smoke; there was a pause, a cessation of fire; the smoke cleared away, and the parapets were blue with our men, who fired their muskets in the air, and shouted so that we actually heard them, or felt that we did. Fort McAllister was taken, and the good news was instantly sent by the signal-officer to our navy friends on the approaching gunboat, for a point of timber had shut out Fort McAllister from their view, and they had not seen the action at all, but must have heard the cannonading.

During the progress of the assault, our little group on Cheeves's mill hardly breathed; but no sooner did we see our flags on the parapet than I exclaimed, in the language of the poor negro at Cobb's plantation, "This nigger will have no sleep this night!"

I was resolved to communicate with our fleet that night, which happened to be a beautiful moonlight one. At the wharf belonging to Cheeves's mill was a small skiff, that had been used by our men in fishing or in gathering oysters. I was there in a minute, called for a volunteer crew, when several young officers, Nichols and Merritt among the number, said they were good oarsmen, and volunteered to pull the boat down to Fort McAllister. General Howard asked to accompany me; so we took seats in the stern of the boat, and our crew of officers pulled out with a will. The tide was setting in strong, and they had a hard pull, for, though the distance was but three miles in an air-line, the river was so crooked that the actual distance was fully six miles. On the way down we passed the wreck of a steamer which had been sunk some years before, during a naval attack on Fort McAllister.

Night had fairly set in when we discovered a soldier on the beach. I hailed him, and inquired if he knew where General Hazen was. He answered that the general was at the house of the overseer of the plantation (McAllister's), and that he could guide me to it. We accordingly landed, tied our boat to a driftlog, and followed our guide through bushes to a frame-house, standing in a grove of live-oaks, near a row of negro quarters.

General Hazen was there with his staff, in the act of getting supper; he invited us to join them, which we accepted promptly, for we were really very hungry. Of course, I congratulated Hazen most heartily on his brilliant success, and praised its execution very highly, as it deserved, and he explained to me more in detail the exact results. The fort was an inclosed work, and its land-front was in the nature of a bastion and curtains, with good parapet, ditch, fraise, and chevaux-de-frise, made out of the large branches of live-oaks. Luckily, the rebels had left the larger and unwieldy trunks on the ground, which served as a good cover for the skirmish-line, which crept behind these logs, and from them kept the artillerists from loading and firing their guns accurately.

The assault had been made by three parties in line, one from below, one from above the fort, and the third directly in rear, along the capital. All were simultaneous, and had to pass a good abatis and line of torpedoes, which actually killed more of the assailants than the heavy guns of the fort, which generally overshot the mark. Hazen's entire loss was reported, killed and wounded, ninety-two. Each party reached the parapet about the same time, and the garrison inside, of about two hundred and fifty men (about fifty of them killed or wounded), were in his power. The commanding officer, Major Anderson, was at that moment a prisoner, and General Hazen invited him in to take supper with us, which he did.

Up to this time General Hazen did not know that a gunboat was in the river below the fort; for it was shut off from sight by a point of timber, and I was determined to board her that night, at whatever risk or cost, as I wanted some news of what was going on in the outer world. Accordingly, after supper, we all walked down to the fort, nearly a mile from the house where we had been, entered Fort McAllister, held by a regiment of Hazen's troops, and the sentinel cautioned us to be very careful, as the ground outside the fort was full of torpedoes. Indeed, while we were there, a torpedo exploded, tearing to pieces a poor fellow who was hunting for a dead comrade. Inside the fort lay the dead as they had fallen, and they could hardly be distinguished from their living comrades, sleeping soundly side by side in the pale moonlight. In the river, close by the fort, was a good yawl tied to a stake, but the tide was high, and it required some time to get it in to the bank; the commanding officer, whose name I cannot recall, manned the boat with a good crew of his men, and, with General Howard, I entered, and pulled down-stream, regardless of the warnings all about the torpedoes.

The night was unusually bright, and we expected to find the gunboat within a mile or so; but, after pulling down the river fully three miles, and not seeing the gunboat, I began to think she had turned and gone back to the sound; but we kept on, following the bends of the river, and about six miles below McAllister we saw her light, and soon were hailed by the vessel at anchor. Pulling alongside, we announced ourselves, and were received with great warmth and enthusiasm on deck by half a dozen naval officers, among them Captain Williamson, United States Navy. She proved to be the Dandelion, a tender of the regular gunboat Flag, posted at the mouth of the Ogeechee. All sorts of questions were made and answered, and we learned that Captain Duncan had safely reached the squadron, had communicated the good news of our approach, and they had been expecting us for some days. They explained that Admiral Dahlgren commanded the South-Atlantic Squadron, which was then engaged in blockading the coast from Charleston south, and was on his flag-ship, the Harvest Moon, lying in Wassaw Sound; that General J. G. Foster was in command of the Department of the South, with his headquarters at Hilton Head; and that several ships loaded with stores for the army were lying in Tybee Roads and in Port Royal Sound. From these officers I also learned that General Grant was still besieging Petersburg and Richmond, and that matters and things generally remained pretty much the same as when we had left Atlanta. All thoughts seemed to have been turned to us in Georgia, cut off from all communication with our friends; and the rebel papers had reported us to be harassed, defeated, starving, and fleeing for safety to the coast. I then asked for pen and paper, and wrote several hasty notes to General Foster, Admiral Dahlgren, General Grant, and the Secretary of War, giving in general terms the actual state of affairs, the fact of the capture of Fort McAllister, and of my desire that means should be taken to establish a line of supply from the vessels in port up the Ogeechee to the rear of the army. As a sample, I give one of these notes, addressed to the Secretary of War, intended for publication to relieve the anxiety of our friends at the North generally:

ON BOARD DANDELION, OSSABAW SOUND, December 13, 1864--11.50 p.m.

To Hon. E. M. STANTON, Secretary of War, Washington, D. C.:

To-day, at 6 p. m., General Hazen's division of the Fifteenth Corps carried Fort McAllister by assault, capturing its entire garrison and stores. This opened to us Ossabaw Sound, and I pushed down to this gunboat to communicate with the fleet. Before opening communication we had completely destroyed all the railroads leading into Savannah, and invested the city. The left of the army is on the Savannah River three miles above the city, and the right on the Ogeechee, at King's Bridge. The army is in splendid order, and equal to any thing. The weather has been fine, and supplies were abundant. Our march was most agreeable, and we were not at all molested by guerrillas.

We reached Savannah three days ago, but, owing to Fort McAllister, could not communicate; but, now that we have McAllister, we can go ahead.

We have already captured two boats on the Savannah river and prevented their gunboats from coming down.

I estimate the population of Savannah at twenty-five thousand, and the garrison at fifteen thousand. General Hardee commands.

We have not lost a wagon on the trip; but have gathered a large supply of negroes, mules, horses, etc., and our teams are in far better condition than when we started.

My first duty will be to clear the army of surplus negroes, mules, and horses. We have utterly destroyed over two hundred miles of rails, and consumed stores and provisions that were essential to Lee's and Hood's armies.

The quick work made with McAllister, the opening of communication with our fleet, and our consequent independence as to supplies, dissipate all their boasted threats to head us off and starve the army.

I regard Savannah as already gained.
Yours truly,

W. T. SHERMAN, Major-General.

By this time the night was well advanced, and the tide was running ebb-strong; so I asked. Captain Williamson to tow us up as near Fort McAllister as he would venture for the torpedoes, of which the navy-officers had a wholesome dread. The Dandelion steamed up some three or four miles, till the lights of Fort

McAllister could be seen, when she anchored, and we pulled to the fort in our own boat. General Howard and I then walked up to the McAllister House, where we found General Hazen and his officers asleep on the floor of one of the rooms. Lying down on the floor, I was soon fast asleep, but shortly became conscious that some one in the room was inquiring for me among the sleepers. Calling out, I was told that an officer of General Fosters staff had just arrived from a steamboat anchored below McAllister; that the general was extremely anxious to see me on important business, but that he was lame from an old Mexican-War wound, and could not possibly come to me. I was extremely weary from the incessant labor of the day and night before, but got up, and again walked down the sandy road to McAllister, where I found a boat awaiting us, which carried us some three miles down the river, to the steamer W. W. Coit (I think), on board of which we found General Foster. He had just come from Port Royal, expecting to find Admiral Dahlgren in Ossabaw Sound, and, hearing of the capture of Fort McAllister, he had come up to see me. He described fully the condition of affairs with his own command in South Carolina. He had made several serious efforts to effect a lodgment on the railroad which connects Savannah with Charleston near Pocotaligo, but had not succeeded in reaching the railroad itself, though he had a full division of troops, strongly intrenched, near Broad River, within cannon-range of the railroad. He explained, moreover, that there were at Port Royal abundant supplies of bread and provisions, as well as of clothing, designed for our use. We still had in our wagons and in camp abundance of meat, but we needed bread, sugar, and coffee, and it was all-important that a route of supply should at once be opened, for which purpose the assistance of the navy were indispensable. We accordingly steamed down the Ogeechee River to Ossabaw Sound, in hopes to meet Admiral Dahlgren, but he was not there, and we continued on by the inland channel to Warsaw Sound, where we found the Harvest Moon, and Admiral Dahlgren. I was not personally acquainted with him at the time, but he was so extremely kind and courteous that I was at once attracted to him. There was nothing in his power, he said, which he would not do to assist us, to make our campaign absolutely successful. He undertook at once to find vessels of light draught to carry our supplies from Port Royal to Cheeves's Mill, or to Grog's Bridge above, whence they could be hauled by wagons to our several camps; he offered to return with me to Fort McAllister, to superintend the removal of the torpedoes, and to relieve me of all the details of this most difficult work. General Foster then concluded to go on to Port Royal, to send back to us six hundred thousand rations, and all the rifled guns of heavy calibre, and ammunition on hand, with which I thought we could reach the city of Savannah, from the positions already secured. Admiral Dahlgren then returned with me in the Harvest Moon to Fort McAllister. This consumed all of the 14th of December; and by the 15th I had again reached Cheeves's Mill, where my horse awaited me, and rode on to General Howard's headquarters at Anderson's plantation, on the plank-road, about eight miles back of Savannah. I reached this place about noon, and immediately sent orders to my own head-quarters, on the Louisville road, to have them brought over to the plank-road, as a place more central and convenient; gave written notice to Generals Slocum and Howard of all the steps taken, and ordered them to get ready to receive the siege-guns, to put them in position to bombard Savannah, and to prepare for the general assault. The country back of Savannah is very low, and intersected with innumerable saltwater creeks, swamps, and rice-fields. Fortunately the weather was good and the roads were passable, but, should the winter rains set in, I knew that we would be much embarrassed. Therefore, heavy details of men were at once put to work to prepare a wharf and depot at Grog's Bridge, and the roads leading thereto were corduroyed in advance. The Ogeechee Canal was also cleared out for use; and boats, such as were common on the river plantations, were collected, in which to float stores from our proposed base on the Ogeechee to the points most convenient to the several camps.

Slocum's wing extended from the Savannah River to the canal, and Howard's wing from the canal to the extreme right, along down the Little Ogeechee. The enemy occupied not only the city itself, with its long line of outer works, but the many forts which had been built to guard the approaches from the sea-such as at Beaulieu, Rosedew, White Bluff, Bonaventura, Thunderbolt, Cansten's Bluff, Forts Tatnall, Boggs, etc., etc. I knew that General Hardee could not have a garrison strong enough for all these purposes, and I was therefore anxious to break his lines before he could receive reenforcements from Virginia or Augusta. General Slocum had already captured a couple of steamboats trying to pass down the Savannah River from Augusta, and had established some of his men on Argyle and Hutchinson Islands above the city, and wanted to transfer a whole corps to the South Carolina bank; but, as the enemy had iron-clad gunboats in the river, I did not deem it prudent, because the same result could be better accomplished from General Fosters position at Broad River.

Fort McAllister was captured as described, late in the evening of December 13th, and by the 16th many steamboats had passed up as high as King's Bridge; among them one which General Grant had dispatched with the mails for the army, which had accumulated since our departure from Atlanta, under charge of Colonel A. H. Markland. These mails were most welcome to all the officers and soldiers of the army, which had been cut off from friends and the world for two months, and this prompt receipt of letters from home had an excellent effect, making us feel that home was near. By this vessel also came Lieutenant Dune, aide-de-camp, with the following letter of December 3d, from General Grant, and on the next day Colonel Babcock, United States Engineers, arrived with the letter of December 6th, both of which are in General Grant's own handwriting, and are given entire:

HEADQUARTERS ARMIES OF THE UNITED STATES
CITY POINT, VIRGINIA, December 3, 1864.

Major-General W. T. SHERMAN, commanding Armies near Savannah, Georgia.

GENERAL: *The little information gleaned from the Southern press indicating no great obstacle to your progress, I have directed your mails (which had been previously collected in Baltimore by Colonel Markland, special-agent of the Post-Office Department) to be sent as far as the blockading squadron off Savannah, to be forwarded to you as soon as heard from on the coast.*

Not liking to rejoice before the victory is assured, I abstain from congratulating you and those under your command, until bottom has been struck. I have never had a fear, however, for the result.

Since you left Atlanta no very great progress has been made here. The enemy has been closely watched, though, and prevented from detaching against you. I think not one man has gone from here, except some twelve or fifteen hundred dismounted cavalry. Bragg has gone from Wilmington. I am trying to take advantage of his absence to get possession of that place. Owing to some preparations Admiral Porter and General Butler are making to blow up Fort Fisher (which, while hoping for the best, I do not believe a particle in), there is a delay in getting this expedition off. I hope they will be ready to start by the 7th, and that Bragg will not have started back by that time.

In this letter I do not intend to give you any thing like directions for future action, but will state a general idea I have, and will get your views after you have established yourself on the sea-coast. With your veteran army I hope to get control of the only two through routes from east to west possessed by the enemy before the fall of Atlanta. The condition will be filled by holding Savannah and Augusta, or by holding any other port to the east of Savannah and Branchville. If Wilmington falls, a force from there can cooperate with you.

Thomas has got back into the defenses of Nashville, with Hood close upon him. Decatur has been abandoned, and so have all the roads, except the main one leading to Chattanooga. Part of this falling back was undoubtedly necessary, and all of it may have been. It did not look so, however, to me. In my opinion, Thomas far outnumbers Hood in infantry. In cavalry Hood has the advantage in morale and numbers. I hope yet that Hood will be badly crippled, if not destroyed. The general news you will learn from the papers better than I can give it.

After all becomes quiet, and roads become so bad up here that there is likely to be a week or two when nothing can be done, I will run down the coast to see you. If you desire it, I will ask Mrs. Sherman to go with me. Yours truly,

U. S. GRANT, Lieutenant-General.

HEADQUARTERS OF THE ARMIES OF THE UNITED STATES.
CITY POINT, VIRGINIA, December 6, 1864.

Major-General W. T. SHERMAN, commanding Military Division of the Mississippi

GENERAL: *On reflection since sending my letter by the hands of Lieutenant Dunn, I have concluded that the most important operation toward closing out the rebellion will be to close out Lee and his army.*

You have now destroyed the roads of the South so that it will probably take them three months without interruption to reestablish a through line from east to west. In that time I think the job here will be effectually completed.

My idea now is that you establish a base on the sea-coast, fortify and leave in it all your artillery and cavalry, and enough infantry to protect them, and at the same time so threaten the interior that the militia of the South will have to be kept at home. With the balance of your command come here by water with all dispatch. Select yourself the officer to leave in command, but you I want in person. Unless you see objections to this plan which I cannot see, use every vessel going to you for purposes of transportation.

Hood has Thomas close in Nashville. I have said all I can to force him to attack, without giving the positive order until to-day. To-day, however, I could stand it no longer, and gave the order without any reserve. I think the battle will take place to-morrow. The result will probably be known in New York before Colonel Babcock (the bearer of this) will leave it. Colonel Babcock will give you full information of all operations now in progress. Very respectfully your obedient servant,

U. S. GRANT, Lieutenant-General.

The contents of these letters gave me great uneasiness, for I had set my heart on the capture of Savannah, which I believed to be practicable, and to be near; for me to embark for Virginia by sea was so complete a change from what I had supposed would be the course of events that I was very much concerned. I supposed, as a matter of course, that a fleet of vessels would soon pour in, ready to convey the army to Virginia, and as General Grant's orders contemplated my leaving the cavalry, trains, and artillery, behind, I judged Fort McAllister to be the best place for the purpose, and sent my chief-engineer, Colonel Poe, to that fort, to reconnoitre the ground, and to prepare it so as to make a fortified camp large enough to accommodate the vast herd of mules and horses that would thus be left behind. And as some time might be required to collect the necessary shipping, which I estimated at little less than a hundred steamers and sailing-vessels, I determined to push operations, in hopes to secure the city of Savannah before the necessary fleet could be available. All these ideas are given in my answer to General Grant's letters (dated December 16, 1864) herewith, which is a little more full than the one printed in the report of the Committee on the Conduct of the War, because in that copy I omitted the matter concerning General Thomas, which now need no longer be withheld:

HEADQUARTERS MILITARY DIVISION OF THE MISSISSIPPI,
IN THE FIELD, NEAR SAVANNAH, December 16, 1864.

Lieutenant-General U. S. GRANT, Commander-in-Chief, City Point, Virginia.

GENERAL: I received, day before yesterday, at the hands of Lieutenant Dunn, your letter of December 8d, and last night, at the hands of Colonel Babcock, that of December 6th. I had previously made you a hasty scrawl from the tugboat Dandelion, in Ogeechee River, advising you that the army had reached the sea-coast, destroying all the railroads across the State of Georgia, investing closely the city of Savannah, and had made connection with the fleet.

Since writing that note, I have in person met and conferred with General Foster and Admiral Dahlgren, and made all the arrangements which were deemed essential for reducing the city of Savannah to our possession. But, since the receipt of yours of the 6th, I have initiated measures looking principally to coming to you with fifty or Sixty thousand infantry, and incidentally to capture Savannah, if time will allow.

At the time we carried Fort McAllister by assault so handsomely, with its twenty-two guns and entire garrison, I was hardly aware of its importance; but, since passing down the river with General Foster and up with Admiral Dahlgren, I realize how admirably adapted are Ossabaw Sound and Ogeechee River to supply an army operating against Savannah. Seagoing vessels can easily come to King's Bridge, a point on Ogeechee River, fourteen and a half miles due west of Savannah, from which point we have roads leading to all our camps. The country is low and sandy, and cut up with marshes, which in wet weather will be very bad, but we have been so favored with weather that they are all now comparatively good, and heavy details are constantly employed in double-corduroying the marshes, so that I have no fears even of bad weather. Fortunately, also, by liberal and judicious foraging, we reached the sea-coast abundantly supplied with forage and provisions, needing nothing on arrival except bread. Of this we started from Atlanta, with from eight to twenty days' supply per corps and some of the troops only had one day's issue of bread during the trip of thirty days; yet they did not want, for sweet-potatoes were very abundant, as well as corn-meal, and our soldiers took to them naturally. We started with about five thousand head of cattle, and arrived with over ten thousand, of course consuming mostly turkeys, chickens, sheep, hogs, and the cattle of the country. As to our mules and horses, we left Atlanta with about twenty-five hundred wagons, many of which were drawn by mules which had not recovered from the Chattanooga starvation, all of which were replaced, the poor mules shot, and our transportation is now in superb condition. I have no doubt the State of Georgia has lost, by our operations, fifteen thousand first-rate mules. As to horses, Kilpatrick collected all his remounts, and it looks to me, in riding along our columns, as though every officer had three or four led horses, and each regiment seems to be followed by at least fifty negroes and foot-sore soldiers, riding on horses and mules. The custom was for each brigade to send out daily a foraging-party of about fifty men, on foot, who invariably returned mounted, with several wagons loaded with poultry, potatoes, etc., and as the army is composed of about forty brigades, you can estimate approximately the number of horses collected. Great numbers of these were shot by my order, because of the disorganizing effect on our infantry of having too many idlers mounted. General Euston is now engaged in collecting statistics on this subject, but I know the Government will never receive full accounts of our captures, although the result aimed at was fully attained, viz., to deprive our enemy of them. All these animals I will have sent to Port Royal, or collected behind Fort McAllister, to be used by General Saxton in his farming operations, or by the Quartermaster's Department, after they are systematically accounted for. While General Easton is collecting transportation for my troops to James River, I will throw to Port Royal Island all our means of transportation I can, and collect the rest near Fort McAllister, covered by the Ogeechee River and intrenchments to be erected, and for which Captain Poe, my chief-engineer, is now reconnoitring the ground, but in the mean time will act as I have begun, as though the city of Savannah were my objective: namely, the troops will continue to invest Savannah closely, making attacks and feints wherever we have fair ground to stand upon, and I will place some thirty-pound Parrotts, which I have got from General Foster, in position, near enough to reach the centre of the city, and then will demand its surrender. If General Hardee is alarmed, or fears starvation, he may surrender; otherwise I will bombard the city, but not risk the lives of our men by assaults across the narrow causeways, by which alone I can now reach it.

If I had time, Savannah, with all its dependent fortifications, would surely fall into our possession, for we hold all its avenues of supply.

The enemy has made two desperate efforts to get boats from above to the city, in both of which he has been foiled-General Slocum (whose left flank rests on the river) capturing and burning the first boat, and in the second instance driving back two gunboats and capturing the steamer Resolute, with seven naval officers and a crew of twenty-five seamen. General Slocum occupies Argyle Island and the upper end of Hutchinson Inland, and has a brigade on the South Carolina shore opposite, and is very urgent to pass one of his corps over to that shore. But, in view of the change of plan made necessary by your order of the 6th, I will maintain things in statu quo till I have got all my transportation to the rear and out of the way, and until I have sea-transportation for the troops you require at James River, which I will accompany and command in person. Of course, I will leave Kilpatrick, with his cavalry (say five thousand three hundred), and, it may be, a division of the Fifteenth Corps; but, before determining on this, I must see General Foster, and may arrange to shift his force (now over above the Charleston Railroad, at the head of Broad River) to the Ogeechee, where, in cooperation with Kilpatrick's cavalry, he can better threaten the State of Georgia than from the direction of Port Royal. Besides, I would much prefer not to detach from my regular corps any of its veteran divisions, and would even prefer that other less valuable troops should be sent to reenforce Foster from some other quarter. My four corps, full of experience and full of ardor, coming to you en masse, equal to sixty thousand fighting men, will be a reenforcement that Lee cannot disregard. Indeed, with my present command, I had expected, after reducing Savannah, instantly to march to Columbia, South Carolina; thence to Raleigh, and thence to report to you. But this would consume, it may be, six weeks' time after the fall of Savannah; whereas, by sea, I can probably reach you with my men and arms before the middle of January.

I myself am somewhat astonished at the attitude of things in Tennessee. I purposely delayed at Kingston until General Thomas assured me that he was all ready, and my last dispatch from him of the 12th of November was full of confidence, in which he promised me that he would ruin Hood if he dared to advance from Florence, urging me to go ahead, and give myself no concern about Hood's army in Tennessee.

Why he did not turn on him at Franklin, after checking and discomfiting him, surpasses my understanding. Indeed, I do not approve of his evacuating Decatur, but think he should have assumed the offensive against Hood from Pulaski, in the direction of Waynesburg. I know full well that General Thomas is slow in mind and in action; but he is judicious and brave and the troops feel great confidence in him. I still hope he will out-manoeuvre and destroy Hood.

As to matters in the Southeast, I think Hardee, in Savannah, has good artillerists, some five or six thousand good infantry, and, it may be, a mongrel mass of eight to ten thousand militia. In all our marching through Georgia, he has not forced us to use any thing but a skirmish-line, though at several points he had erected fortifications and tried to alarm us by bombastic threats. In Savannah he has taken refuge in a line constructed behind swamps and overflowed rice-fields, extending from a point on the Savannah River about three miles above the city, around by a branch of the Little Ogeechee, which stream is impassable from its salt-marshes and boggy swamps, crossed only by narrow causeways or common corduroy-roads.

There must be twenty-five thousand citizens, men, women, and children, in Savannah, that must also be fed, and how he is to feed them beyond a few days I cannot imagine. I know that his requisitions for corn on the interior counties were not filled, and we are in possession of the rice-fields and mills, which could alone be of service to him in this neighborhood. He can draw nothing from South Carolina, save from a small corner down in the southeast, and that by a disused wagon-road. I could easily get possession of this, but hardly deem it worth the risk of making a detachment, which would be in danger by its isolation from the main army. Our whole army is in fine condition as to health, and the weather is splendid. For that reason alone I feel a personal dislike to turning northward. I will keep Lieutenant Dunn here until I know the result of my demand for the surrender of Savannah, but, whether successful or not, shall not delay my execution of your order of the 6th, which will depend alone upon the time it will require to obtain transportation by sea.

I am, with respect, etc., your obedient servant,

W. T. SHERMAN, Major-General United States Army.

    Having concluded all needful preparations, I rode from my headquarters, on the plank-road, over to General Slocum's headquarters, on the Macon road, and thence dispatched (by flag of truce) into Savannah, by the hands of Colonel Ewing, inspector-general, a demand for the surrender of the place. The following letters give the result. General Hardee refused to surrender, and I then resolved to make the attempt to break his line of defense at several places, trusting that some one would succeed.

HEADQUARTERS MILITARY DIVISION OF THE MISSISSIPPI, IN THE FIELD, NEAR SAVANNAH, December 17, 1864.

General WILLIAM J. HARDEE, commanding Confederate Forces in Savannah.

GENERAL: You have doubtless observed, from your station at Rosedew that sea-going vessels now come through Ossabaw Sound and up the Ogeechee to the rear of my army, giving me abundant supplies of all kinds, and more especially heavy ordnance necessary for the reduction of Savannah. I have already received guns that can cast heavy and destructive shot as far as the heart of your city; also, I have for some days held and controlled every avenue by which the people and garrison of Savannah can be supplied, and I am therefore justified in demanding the surrender of the city of Savannah, and its dependent forts, and shall wait a reasonable time for your answer, before opening with heavy ordnance. Should you entertain the proposition, I am prepared to grant liberal terms to the inhabitants and garrison; but should I be forced to resort to assault, or the slower and surer process of starvation, I shall then feel justified in resorting to the harshest measures, and shall make little effort to restrain my army--burning to avenge the national wrong which they attach to Savannah and other large cities which have been so prominent in dragging our country into civil war. I inclose you a copy of General Hood's demand for the surrender of the town of Resaoa, to be used by you for what it is worth. I have the honor to be your obedient servant,

W. T. SHERMAN, Major-General.

HEADQUARTERS DEPARTMENT SOUTH CAROLINA, GEORGIA AND FLORIDA SAVANNAH, GEORGIA, December 17, 1864

Major-General W. T. SHERMAN, commanding Federal Forces near Savannah, Georgia.

GENERAL: I have to acknowledge the receipt of a communication from you of this date, in which you demand "the surrender of Savannah and its dependent forts," on the ground that you "have received guns that can cast heavy and destructive shot into the heart of the city," and for the further reason that you "have, for some days, held and controlled every avenue by which the people and garrison can be supplied." You add that, should you be "forced to resort to assault, or to the slower and surer process of starvation, you will then feel justified in resorting to the harshest measures, and will make little effort to restrain your army," etc., etc. The position of your forces (a half-mile beyond the outer line for the land-defense of Savannah) is, at the nearest point, at least four miles from the heart of the city. That and the interior line are both intact.

Your statement that you have, for some days, held and controlled every avenue by which the people and garrison can be supplied, is incorrect. I am in free and constant communication with my department.

Your demand for the surrender of Savannah and its dependent forts is refused.

With respect to the threats conveyed in the closing paragraphs of your letter (of what may be expected in case your demand is not complied with), I have to say that I have hitherto conducted the military operations intrusted to my direction in strict accordance with the rules of civilized warfare, and I should deeply regret the adoption of any course by you that may force me to deviate from them in future. I have the honor to be, very respectfully, your obedient servant,

W. J. HARDEE, Lieutenant-General.

HEADQUARTERS MILITARY DIVISION OF THE MISSISSIPPI, IN THE FIELD, NEAR SAVANNAH, December 18, 1864 8 p.m.

Lieutenant-General U. S. GRANT, City Point, Virginia.

GENERAL: I wrote you at length (by Colonel Babcock) on the 16th instant. As I therein explained my purpose, yesterday I made a demand on General Hardee for the surrender of the city of Savannah, and to-day received his answer--refusing; copies of both letters are herewith inclosed. You will notice that I claim that my lines are within easy cannon-range of the heart of Savannah; but General Hardee asserts that we are four and a half miles distant. But I myself have been to the intersection of the Charleston and Georgia Central Railroads, and the three-mile post is but a few yards beyond, within the line of our pickets. The enemy has no pickets outside of his fortified line (which is a full quarter of a mile within the three-mile post), and I have the evidence of Mr. R. R. Cuyler, President of the Georgia Central Railroad (who was a prisoner in our hands), that the mile-posts are measured from the Exchange, which is but two squares back from the river. By to-morrow morning I will have six thirty-pound Parrotts in position, and General Hardee will learn whether I am right or not. From the left of our line, which is on the Savannah River, the spires can be plainly seen; but the country is so densely wooded with pine and live-oak, and lies so flat, that we can see nothing from any other portion of our lines. General Slocum feels confident that he can make a successful assault at one or two points in front of General Davis's (Fourteenth) corps. All of General Howard's troops (the right wing) lie behind the Little Ogeechee, and I doubt if it can be passed by troops in the face of an enemy. Still, we can make strong feints, and if I can get a sufficient number of boats, I shall make a cooperative demonstration up Vernon River or Wassaw Sound. I should like very much indeed to take Savannah before coming to you; but, as I wrote to you before, I will do nothing rash or hasty, and will embark for the James River as soon as General Easton (who is gone to Port Royal for that purpose) reports to me that he has an approximate number of vessels for the transportation of the contemplated force. I fear even this will cost more delay than you anticipate, for already the movement of our transports and the gunboats has required more time than I had expected. We have had dense fogs; there are more mud-banks in the Ogeechee than were reported, and there are no pilots whatever. Admiral Dahlgren promised to have the channel buoyed and staked, but it is not done yet. We find only six feet of water up to King's Bridge at low tide, about ten feet up to the rice-mill, and sixteen to Fort McAllister. All these points may be used by us, and we have a good, strong bridge across Ogeechee at King's, by which our wagons can go to Fort McAllister, to which point I am sending all wagons not absolutely necessary for daily use, the negroes, prisoners of war, sick, etc., en route for Port Royal. In relation to Savannah, you will remark that General Hardee refers to his still being in communication with his department. This language he thought would deceive me; but I am confirmed in the belief that the route to which he refers (the Union Plank-road on the South Carolina shore) is inadequate to feed his army and the people of Savannah, and General Foster assures me that he has his force on that very road, near the head of Broad River, so that cars no longer run between Charleston and Savannah. We hold this end of the Charleston Railroad, and have destroyed it from the three-mile post back to the bridge (about twelve miles). In anticipation of leaving this country, I am continuing the destruction of their railroads, and at this moment have two divisions and the cavalry at work breaking up the Gulf Railroad from the Ogeechee to the Altamaha; so that, even if I do not take Savannah, I will leave it in a bad way. But I still hope that events will give me time to take Savannah, even if I have to assault with some loss. I am satisfied that, unless we take it, the gunboats never will, for they can make no impression upon the batteries which guard every approach from the sea. I have a faint belief that, when Colonel Babcock reaches you, you will delay operations long enough to enable me to succeed here. With Savannah in our possession, at some future time if not now, we can punish South Carolina as she deserves, and as thousands of the people in Georgia hoped we would do. I do sincerely believe that the whole United States, North and South, would rejoice to have this army turned loose on South Carolina, to devastate that State in the manner we have done in Georgia, and it would have a direst and immediate bearing on your campaign in Virginia.

I have the honor to be your obedient servant,

W. T. SHERMAN, Major-General United States Army.

As soon as the army had reached Savannah, and had opened communication with the fleet, I endeavored to ascertain what had transpired in Tennessee since our departure. We received our letters and files of newspapers, which contained full accounts of all the events there up to about the 1st of December. As before described, General Hood had three full corps of infantry--S. D. Lee's, A. P. Stewart's, and Cheatham's, at Florence, Alabama--with Forrest's corps of cavalry, numbering in the aggregate about forty-five thousand men. General Thomas was in Nashville, Tennessee, quietly engaged in reorganizing his army out of the somewhat broken forces at his disposal. He had posted his only two regular corps, the Fourth and Twenty-third, under the general command of Major-General J. M. Schofield, at Pulaski, directly in front of Florence, with the three brigades of cavalry (Hatch, Croxton, and Capron), commanded by Major-General Wilson, watching closely for Hood's initiative.

This force aggregated about thirty thousand men, was therefore inferior to the enemy; and General Schofield was instructed, in case the enemy made a general advance, to fall back slowly toward Nashville, fighting, till he should be reenforced by General Thomas in person. Hood's movement was probably hurried by reason of my advance into Georgia; for on the 17th his infantry columns marched from Florence in the direction of Waynesboro', turning, Schofield's position at Pulaski. The latter at once sent his trains to the rear, and on the 21st fell back to Columbia, Tennessee. General Hood followed up this movement, skirmished lightly with Schofield at Columbia, began the passage of Duck River, below the town, and Cheatham's corps reached the vicinity of Spring Hill, whither General Schofield had sent General Stanley, with two of his divisions, to cover the movement of his trains. During the night of November 29th General Schofield passed Spring Hill with his trains and army, and took post at Franklin, on the south side of Harpeth River. General Hood now attaches serious blame to General Cheatham for not attacking General Schofield in flank while in motion at Spring Hill, for he was bivouacked within eight hundred yards of the road at the time of the passage of our army. General Schofield reached Franklin on the morning of November 30th, and posted his army in front of the town, where some rifle-intrenchments had been constructed in advance. He had the two corps of Stanley and Cox (Fourth and Twenty-third), with Wilson's cavalry on his flanks, and sent his trains behind the Harpeth.

General Hood closed upon him the same day, and assaulted his position with vehemence, at one time breaking the line and wounding General Stanley seriously; but our men were veterans, cool and determined, and fought magnificently. The rebel officers led their men in person to the several persistent assaults, continuing the battle far into the night, when they drew off, beaten and discomfited.

Their loss was very severe, especially in general officers; among them Generals Cleburn and Adams, division commanders. Hood's loss on that day was afterward ascertained to be (Thomas's report): Buried on the field, seventeen hundred and fifty; left in hospital at Franklin, thirty-eight hundred; and seven hundred and two prisoners captured and held: aggregate, six thousand two hundred and fifty-two. General Schofields lose, reported officially, was one hundred and eighty-nine killed, one thousand and thirty-three wounded, and eleven hundred and four prisoners or missing: aggregate, twenty-three hundred and twenty-six. The next day General Schofield crossed the Harpeth without trouble, and fell back to the defenses of Nashville.

Meantime General Thomas had organized the employees of the Quartermaster's Department into a corps, commanded by the chief-quartermaster, General J. Z. Donaldson, and placed them in the fortifications of Nashville, under the general direction of Major-General Z. B. Tower, now of the United States Engineers. He had also received the two veteran divisions of the Sixteenth Corps, under General A. J. Smith, long absent and long expected; and he had drawn from Chattanooga and Decatur (Alabama) the divisions of Steedman and of R. S. Granger. These, with General Schofields army and about ten thousand good cavalry, under General J. H. Wilson, constituted a strong army, capable not only of defending Nashville, but of beating Hood in the open field. Yet Thomas remained inside of Nashville, seemingly passive, until General Hood had closed upon him and had entrenched his position.

General Thomas had furthermore held fast to the railroad leading from Nashville to Chattanooga, leaving strong guards at its principal points, as at Murfreesboro', Deckerd, Stevenson, Bridgeport, Whitesides, and Chattanooga. At Murfreesboro' the division of Rousseau was reenforced and strengthened up to about eight thousand men.

At that time the weather was cold and sleety, the ground was covered with ice and snow, and both parties for a time rested on the defensive. Those matters stood at Nashville, while we were closing down on Savannah, in the early part of December, 1864; and the country, as well as General Grant, was alarmed at the seeming passive conduct of General Thomas; and General Grant at one time considered the situation so dangerous that he thought of going to Nashville in person, but General John A. Logan, happening to be at City Point, was sent out to supersede General Thomas; luckily for the latter, he acted in time, gained a magnificent victory, and thus escaped so terrible a fate.

On the 18th of December, at my camp by the side of the plank-road, eight miles back of Savannah, I received General Hardee's letter declining to surrender, when nothing remained but to assault. The ground was difficult, and, as all former assaults had proved so bloody, I concluded to make one more effort to completely surround Savannah on all aides, so as further to excite Hardee's fears, and, in case of success, to capture the whole of his army. We had already completely invested the place on the north, west, and south, but there remained to the enemy, on the east, the use of the old dike or plank-road leading into South Carolina, and I knew that Hardee would have a pontoon-bridge across the river. On examining my maps, I thought that the division of John P. Hatch, belonging to General Fosters command, might be moved from its then position at Broad River, by water, down to Bluffton, from which it could reach this plank-road, fortify and hold it--at some risk, of course, because Hardee could avail himself of his central position to fall on this detachment with his whole army. I did not want to make a mistake like "Ball's Bluff" at that period of the war; so, taking one or two of my personal staff, I rode back to Grog's Bridge, leaving with Generals Howard and Slocum orders to make all possible preparations, but not to attack, during my two or three days' absence; and there I took a boat for Wassaw Sound, whence Admiral Dahlgren conveyed me in his own boat (the Harvest Moon) to Hilton Head, where I represented the matter to General Foster, and he promptly agreed to give his personal attention to it. During the night of the 20th we started back, the wind blowing strong, Admiral Dahlgren ordered the pilot of the Harvest Moon to run into Tybee, and to work his way through to Wassaw Sound and the Ogeechee River by the Romney Marshes. We were caught by a low tide and stuck in the mud. After laboring some time, the admiral ordered out his barge; in it we pulled through this intricate and shallow channel, and toward evening of December 21st we discovered, coming toward us, a tug, called the Red Legs, belonging to the Quarter-master's Department, with a staff-officer on board, bearing letters from Colonel Dayton to myself and the admiral, reporting that the city of Savannah had been found evacuated on the morning of December 21st, and was then in our possession. General Hardee had crossed the Savannah River by a pontoon-bridge, carrying off his men and light artillery, blowing up his iron-clads and navy-yard, but leaving for us all the heavy guns, stores, cotton, railway-cars, steamboats, and an immense amount of public and private property. Admiral Dahlgren concluded to go toward a vessel (the Sonoma) of his blockading fleet, which lay at anchor near Beaulieu, and I transferred to the Red Legs, and hastened up the Ogeechee River to Grog's Bridge, whence I rode to my camp that same night. I there learned that, early on the morning of December 21st, the skirmishers had detected the absence of the enemy, and had occupied his lines simultaneously along their whole extent; but the left flank (Slocum), especially Geary's division of the Twentieth Corps, claimed to have been the first to reach the heart of the city.

Generals Slocum and Howard moved their headquarters at once into the city, leaving the bulk of their troops in camps outside. On the morning of December 22d I followed with my own headquarters, and rode down Bull Street to the custom-house, from the roof of which we had an extensive view over the city, the river, and the vast extent of marsh and rice-fields on the South Carolina side. The navy-yard, and the wreck of the iron-clad ram Savannah, were still smouldering, but all else looked quiet enough. Turning back, we rode to the Pulaski Hotel, which I had known in years long gone, and found it kept by a Vermont man with a lame leg, who used to be a clerk in the St. Louis Hotel, New Orleans, and I inquired about the capacity of his hotel for headquarters. He was very anxious to have us for boarders, but I soon explained to him that we had a full mess equipment along, and that we were not in the habit of paying board; that one wing of the building would suffice for our use, while I would allow him to keep an hotel for the accommodation of officers and gentlemen in the remainder. I then dispatched an officer to look around for a livery-stable that could accommodate our horses, and, while waiting there, an English gentleman, Mr. Charles Green, came and said that he had a fine house completely furnished, for which he had no use, and offered it as headquarters. He explained, moreover, that General Howard had informed him, the day before, that I would want his house for headquarters. At first I felt strongly disinclined to make use of any private dwelling, lest complaints should arise of damage and lose of furniture, and so expressed myself to Mr. Green; but, after riding about the city, and finding his house so spacious, so convenient, with large yard and stabling, I accepted his offer, and occupied that house during our stay in Savannah. He only reserved for himself the use of a couple of rooms above the dining-room, and we had all else, and a most excellent house it was in all respects.

I was disappointed that Hardee had escaped with his army, but on the whole we had reason to be content with the substantial fruits of victory. The Savannah River was found to be badly obstructed by torpedoes, and by log piers stretched across the channel below the city, which piers were filled with the cobble stones that formerly paved the streets. Admiral Dahlgren was extremely active, visited me repeatedly in the city, while his fleet still watched Charleston, and all the avenues, for the blockade-runners that infested the coast, which were notoriously owned and managed by Englishmen, who used the island of New Providence (Nassau) as a sort of entrepot. One of these small blockade-runners came into Savannah after we were in full possession, and the master did not discover his mistake till he came ashore to visit the custom-house. Of coarse his vessel fell a prize to the navy. A heavy force was at once set to work to remove the torpedoes and obstructions in the main channel of the river, and, from that time forth, Savannah became the great depot of supply for the troops operating in that quarter.

Meantime, on the 15th and 16th of December, were fought, in front of Nashville, the great battles in which General Thomas so nobly fulfilled his promise to ruin Hood, the details of which are fully given in his own official reports, long-since published. Rumors of these great victories reached us at Savannah by piecemeal, but his official report came on the 24th of December, with a letter from General Grant, giving in general terms the events up to the 18th, and I wrote at once through my chief of staff, General Webster, to General Thomas, complimenting him in the highest terms. His brilliant victory at Nashville was necessary to mine at Savannah to make a complete whole, and this fact was perfectly comprehended by Mr. Lincoln, who recognized it fully in his personal letter of December 26th, hereinbefore quoted at length, and which is also claimed at the time, in my Special Field Order No. 6, of January 8, 1865, here given:

(Special Field Order No. 6.)

HEADQUARTERS MILITARY DIVISION OF THE MISSISSIPPI,
IN THE FIELD, NEAR SAVANNAH, GEORGIA, January 8, 1864.

The general commanding announces to the troops composing the Military Division of the Mississippi that he has received from the President of the United States, and from Lieutenant-General Grant, letters conveying their high sense and appreciation of the campaign just closed, resulting in the capture of Savannah and the defeat of Hood's army in Tennessee.

In order that all may understand the importance of events, it is proper to revert to the situation of affairs in September last. We held Atlanta, a city of little value to us, but so important to the enemy that Mr. Davis, the head of the rebellious faction in the South, visited his army near Palmetto, and commanded it to regain the place and also to ruin and destroy us, by a series of measures which he thought would be effectual. That army, by a rapid march, gained our railroad near Big Shanty, and afterward about Dalton. We pursued it, but it moved so rapidly that we could not overtake it, and General Hood led his army successfully far over toward Mississippi, in hope to decoy us out of Georgia. But we were not thus to be led away by him, and preferred to lead and control events ourselves. Generals Thomas and Schofield, commanding the departments to our rear, returned to their posts and prepared to decoy General Hood into their meshes, while we came on to complete the original journey. We quietly and deliberately destroyed Atlanta, and all the railroads which the enemy had used to carry on war against us, occupied his State capital, and then captured his commercial capital, which had been so strongly fortified from the sea as to defy approach from that quarter. Almost at the moment of

87

our victorious entry into Savannah came the welcome and expected news that our comrades in Tennessee had also fulfilled nobly and well their part, had decoyed General Hood to Nashville and then turned on him, defeating his army thoroughly, capturing all his artillery, great numbers of prisoners, and were still pursuing the fragments down in Alabama. So complete success in military operations, extending over half a continent, is an achievement that entitles it to a place in the military history of the world. The armies serving in Georgia and Tennessee, as well as the local garrisons of Decatur, Bridgeport, Chattanooga, and Murfreesboro', are alike entitled to the common honors, and each regiment may inscribe on its colors, at pleasure, the word "Savannah" or "Nashville." The general commanding embraces, in the same general success, the operations of the cavalry under Generals Stoneman, Burbridge, and Gillem, that penetrated into Southwest Virginia, and paralyzed the efforts of the enemy to disturb the peace and safety of East Tennessee. Instead of being put on the defensive, we have at all points assumed the bold offensive, and have completely thwarted the designs of the enemies of our country.

By order of Major-General W. T. Sherman,
L. M. DAYTON, Aide-de-Camp.

Here terminated the "March to the Sea," and I only add a few letters, selected out of many, to illustrate the general feeling of rejoicing throughout the country at the time. I only regarded the march from Atlanta to Savannah as a "shift of base," as the transfer of a strong army, which had no opponent, and had finished its then work, from the interior to a point on the sea-coast, from which it could achieve other important results. I considered this march as a means to an end, and not as an essential act of war. Still, then, as now, the march to the sea was generally regarded as something extraordinary, something anomalous, something out of the usual order of events; whereas, in fact, I simply moved from Atlanta to Savannah, as one step in the direction of Richmond, a movement that had to be met and defeated, or the war was necessarily at an end.

Were I to express my measure of the relative importance of the march to the sea, and of that from Savannah northward, I would place the former at one, and the latter at ten, or the maximum.

I now close this long chapter by giving a tabular statement of the losses during the march, and the number of prisoners captured. The property captured consisted of horses and mules by the thousand, and of quantities of subsistence stores that aggregate very large, but may be measured with sufficient accuracy by assuming that sixty-five thousand men obtained abundant food for about forty days, and thirty-five thousand animals were fed for a like period, so as to reach Savannah in splendid flesh and condition. I also add a few of the more important letters that passed between Generals Grant, Halleck, and myself, which illustrate our opinions at that stage of the war:

STATEMENT OF CASUALTIES AND PRISONERS CAPTURED,
BY THE ARMY IN THE FIELD, CAMPAIGN OF GEORGIA.

Killed		Wounded		Missing		Captured	
Officers	Men	Officers	Men	Officers	Men	Officers	Men
10	3	24	04	1	77	77	,261

HEADQUARTERS OF THE ARMY
WASHINGTON, December 16, 1864

Major-General SHERMAN (via Hilton Head).

GENERAL: Lieutenant-General Grant informs me that, in his last dispatch sent to you, he suggested the transfer of your infantry to Richmond. He now wishes me to say that you will retain your entire force, at least for the present, and, with such assistance as may be given you by General Foster and Admiral Dahlgren, operate from such base as you may establish on the coast. General Foster will obey such instructions as may be given by you.

Should you have captured Savannah, it is thought that by transferring the water-batteries to the land side that place may be made a good depot and base of operations on Augusta, Branchville, or Charleston. If Savannah should not be captured, or if captured and not deemed suitable for this purpose, perhaps Beaufort would serve as a depot. As the rebels have probably removed their most valuable property from Augusta, perhaps Branchville would be the most important point at which to strike in order to sever all connection between Virginia and the Southwestern Railroad.

General Grant's wishes, however, are, that this whole matter of your future actions should be entirely left to your discretion.

We can send you from here a number of complete batteries of field-artillery, with or without horses, as you may desire; also, as soon as General Thomas can spare them, all the fragments, convalescents, and furloughed men of your army. It is reported that Thomas defeated Hood yesterday, near Nashville, but we have no particulars nor official reports, telegraphic communication being interrupted by a heavy storm.

Our last advises from you was General Howard's note, announcing his approach to Savannah. Yours truly,

H. W. HALLECK, Major-General, Chief-of-Staff.

HEADQUARTERS OF THE ARMY
WASHINGTON, *December 18, 1864.*

Major-General W. T. SHERMAN, Savannah (via Hilton Head).

My DEAR GENERAL: Yours of the 13th, by Major Anderson, is just received. I congratulate you on your splendid success, and shall very soon expect to hear of the crowning work of your campaign--the capture of Savannah. Your march will stand out prominently as the great one of this great war. When Savannah falls, then for another wide swath through the centre of the Confederacy. But I will not anticipate. General Grant is expected here this morning, and will probably write you his own views.

I do not learn from your letter, or from Major Anderson, that you are in want of any thing which we have not provided at Hilton Head. Thinking it probable that you might want more field-artillery, I had prepared several batteries, but the great difficulty of foraging horses on the sea-coast will prevent our sending any unless you actually need them. The hay-crop this year is short, and the Quartermaster's Department has great difficulty in procuring a supply for our animals.

General Thomas has defeated Hood, near Nashville, and it is hoped that he will completely, crush his army. Breckenridge, at last accounts, was trying to form a junction near Murfreesboro', but, as Thomas is between them, Breckenridge must either retreat or be defeated.

General Rosecrans made very bad work of it in Missouri, allowing Price with a small force to overrun the State and destroy millions of property.

Orders have been issued for all officers and detachments having three months or more to serve, to rejoin your army via Savannah. Those having less than three months to serve, will be retained by General Thomas.

Should you capture Charleston, I hope that by some accident the place may be destroyed, and, if a little salt should be sown upon its site, it may prevent the growth of future crops of nullification and secession. Yours truly,

H. W. HALLECK, Major-General, Chief-of-Staff.

HEADQUARTERS OF THE ARMY
WASHINGTON, *December 18, 1864.*

To Major-General W. T. SHERMAN, commanding Military Division of the Mississippi.

My DEAR GENERAL: I have just received and read, I need not tell you with how mush gratification, your letter to General Halleck. I congratulate you and the brave officers and men under your command on the successful termination of your most brilliant campaign. I never had a doubt of the result. When apprehensions for your safety were expressed by the President, I assured him with the army you had, and you in command of it, there was no danger but you would strike bottom on salt-water some place; that I would not feel the same security--in fact, would not have intrusted the expedition to any other living commander.

It has been very hard work to get Thomas to attack Hood. I gave him the most peremptory order, and had started to go there myself, before he got off. He has done magnificently, however, since he started. Up to last night, five thousand prisoners and forty-nine pieces of captured artillery, besides many wagons and innumerable small-arms, had been received in Nashville. This is exclusive of the enemy's loss at Franklin, which amounted to thirteen general officers killed, wounded, and captured. The enemy probably lost five thousand men at Franklin, and ten thousand in the last three days' operations. Breckenridge is said to be making for Murfreesboro'.

I think he is in a most excellent place. Stoneman has nearly wiped out John Morgan's old command, and five days ago entered Bristol. I did think the best thing to do was to bring the greater part of your army here, and wipe out Lee. The turn affairs now seem to be taking has shaken me in that opinion. I doubt whether you may not accomplish more toward that result where you are than if brought here, especially as I am informed, since my arrival in the city, that it would take about two months to get you here with all the other calls there are for ocean transportation.

I want to get your views about what ought to be done, and what can be done. If you capture the garrison of Savannah, it certainly will compel Lee to detach from Richmond, or give us nearly the whole South. My own opinion is that Lee is averse to going out of Virginia, and if the cause of the South is lost he wants Richmond to be the last place surrendered. If he has such views, it may be well to indulge him until we get every thing else in our hands.

Congratulating you and the army again upon the splendid results of your campaign, the like of which is not read of in past history, I subscribe myself, more than ever, if possible, your friend,

U. S. GRANT, Lieutenant-General.

HEADQUARTERS OF THE ARMY
CITY POINT, VIRGINIA, December 26, 1864.

Major-General W. T. SHERMAN, Savannah, Georgia.

GENERAL: Your very interesting letter of the 22d inst., brought by Major Grey of General Foster's staff; is fast at hand. As the major starts back at once, I can do no more at present than simply acknowledge its receipt. The capture of Savannah, with all its immense stores, must tell upon the people of the South. All well here.
Yours truly,

U. S. GRANT, Lieutenant-General.

HEADQUARTERS MILITARY DIVISION OF THE MISSISSIPPI
SAVANNAH, GEORGIA, December 24, 1864.

Lieutenant-General U. S. GRANT, City Point, Virginia.

GENERAL: Your letter of December 18th is just received. I feel very much gratified at receiving the handsome commendation you pay my army. I will, in general orders, convey to the officers and men the substance of your note.

I am also pleased that you have modified your former orders, for I feared that the transportation by sea would very much disturb the unity and morale of my army, now so perfect.

The occupation of Savannah, which I have heretofore reported, completes the first part of our game, and fulfills a great part of your instructions; and we are now engaged in dismantling the rebel forts which bear upon the sea-channels, and transferring the heavy ordnance and ammunition to Fort Pulaski and Hilton Head, where they can be more easily guarded than if left in the city.

The rebel inner lines are well adapted to our purpose, and with slight modifications can be held by a comparatively small force; and in about ten days I expect to be ready to sally forth again. I feel no doubt whatever as to our future plans. I have thought them over so long and well that they appear as clear as daylight. I left Augusta untouched on purpose, because the enemy will be in doubt as to my objective point, after we cross the Savannah River, whether it be Augusta or Charleston, and will naturally divide his forces. I will then move either on Branchville or Colombia, by any curved line that gives us the best supplies, breaking up in our course as much railroad as possible; then, ignoring Charleston and Augusta both, I would occupy Columbia and Camden, pausing there long enough to observe the effect. I would then strike for the Charleston & Wilmington Railroad, somewhere between the Santee and Cape Fear Rivers, and, if possible, communicate with the fleet under Admiral Dahlgren (whom I find a most agreeable gentleman, accommodating himself to our wishes and plans). Then I would favor an attack on Wilmington, in the belief that Porter and Butler will fail in their present undertaking. Charleston is now a mere desolated wreck, and is hardly worth the time it would take to starve it out. Still, I am aware that, historically and politically, much importance is attached to the place, and it may be that, apart from its military importance, both you and the Administration may prefer I should give it more attention; and it would be well for you to give me some general idea on that subject, for otherwise I would treat it as I have expressed, as a point of little importance, after all its railroads leading into the interior have been destroyed or occupied by us. But, on the hypothesis of ignoring Charleston and taking Wilmington, I would then favor a movement direct on Raleigh. The game is then up with Lee, unless he comes out of Richmond, avoids you and fights me; in which case I should reckon on your being on his heels. Now that Hood is used up by Thomas, I feel disposed to bring the matter to an issue as quick as possible. I feel confident that I can break up the whole railroad system of South Carolina and North Carolina, and be on the Roanoke, either at Raleigh or Weldon, by the time spring fairly opens; and, if you feel confident that you can whip Lee outside of his intrenchments, I feel equally confident that I can handle him in the open country.

One reason why I would ignore Charleston is this: that I believe Hardee will reduce the garrison to a small force, with plenty of provisions; I know that the neck back of Charleston can be made impregnable to assault, and we will hardly have time for siege operations.

I will have to leave in Savannah a garrison, and, if Thomas can spare them, I would like to have all detachments, convalescents, etc., belonging to these four corps, sent forward at once. I do not want to cripple Thomas, because I regard his operations as all-important, and I have ordered him to pursue Hood down into Alabama, trusting to the country for supplies.

I reviewed one of my corps to-day, and shall continue to review the whole army. I do not like to boast, but believe this army has a confidence in itself that makes it almost invincible. I wish you could run down and see us; it would have a good effect, and show to both armies that they are acting on a common plan. The weather is now cool and pleasant, and the general health very good. Your true friend,

W. T. SHERMAN Major-General.

HEADQUARTERS MILITARY DIVISION OF THE MISSISSIPPI IN THE FIELD, SAVANNAH, GEORGIA, December 24, 1864.

Major-General H. W. HALLECK, Chief-of-Staff; Washington, D. C.

GENERAL: I had the pleasure of receiving your two letters of the 16th and 18th instant to-day, and feel more than usually flattered by the high encomiums you have passed on our recent campaign, which is now complete by the occupation of Savannah.

I am also very glad that General Grant has changed his mind about embarking my troops for James River, leaving me free to make the broad swath you describe through South and North Carolina; and still more gratified at the news from Thomas, in Tennessee, because it fulfills my plans, which contemplated his being able to dispose of Hood, in case he ventured north of the Tennessee River. So, I think, on the whole, I can chuckle over Jeff. Davis's disappointment in not turning my Atlanta campaign into a "Moscow disaster."

I have just finished a long letter to General Grant, and have explained to him that we are engaged in shifting our base from the Ogeechee to the Savannah River, dismantling all the forts made by the enemy to bear upon the salt-water channels, transferring the heavy ordnance, etc., to Fort Pulaski and Hilton Head, and in remodeling the enemy's interior lines to suit our future plans and purposes. I have also laid down the programme for a campaign which I can make this winter, and which will put me in the spring on the Roanoke, in direct communication with General Grant on James River. In general terms, my plan is to turn over to General Foster the city of Savannah, to sally forth with my army resupplied, cross the Savannah, feign on Charleston and Augusta, but strike between, breaking en route the Charleston & Augusta Railroad, also a large part of that from Branchville and Camden toward North Carolina, and then rapidly to move for some point of the railroad from Charleston to Wilmington, between the Santee and Cape Fear Rivers; then, communicating with the fleet in the neighborhood of Georgetown, I would turn upon Wilmington or Charleston, according to the importance of either. I rather prefer Wilmington, as a live place, over Charleston, which is dead and unimportant when its railroad communications are broken. I take it for granted that the present movement on Wilmington will fail. If I should determine to take Charleston, I would turn across the country (which I have hunted over many a time) from Santee to Mount Pleasant, throwing one wing on the peninsula between the Ashley and Cooper. After accomplishing one or other of these ends, I would make a bee-line for Raleigh or Weldon, when Lee world be forced to come out of Richmond, or acknowledge himself beaten. He would, I think, by the use of the Danville Railroad, throw himself rapidly between me and Grant, leaving Richmond in the hands of the latter. This would not alarm me, for I have an army which I think can maneuver, and I world force him to attack me at a disadvantage, always under the supposition that Grant would be on his heels; and, if the worst come to the worst, I can fight my way down to Albermarle Sound, or Newbern.

I think the time has come now when we should attempt the boldest moves, and my experience is, that they are easier of execution than more timid ones, because the enemy is disconcerted by them--as, for instance, my recent campaign.

I also doubt the wisdom of concentration beyond a certain extent, for the roads of this country limit the amount of men that can be brought to bear in any one battle, and I do not believe that any one general can handle more than sixty thousand men in battle.

I think our campaign of the last month, as well as every step I take from this point northward, is as much a direct attack upon Lee's army as though we were operating within the sound of his artillery.

I am very anxious that Thomas should follow up his success to the very utmost point. My orders to him before I left Kingston were, after beating Hood, to follow him as far as Columbus, Mississippi, or Selma, Alabama, both of which lie in districts of country which are rich in corn and meat.

I attach more importance to these deep incisions into the enemy's country, because this war differs from European wars in this particular: we are not only fighting hostile armies, but a hostile people, and must make old and young, rich and poor, feel the hard hand of war, as well as their organized armies. I know that this recent movement of mine through Georgia has had a wonderful effect in this respect. Thousands who had been deceived by their lying newspapers to believe that we were being whipped all the time now realize the truth, and have no appetite for a repetition of the same experience. To be sure, Jeff. Davis has his people under pretty good discipline, but I think faith in him is much shaken in Georgia, and before we have done with her South Carolina will not be quite so tempestuous.

I will bear in mind your hint as to Charleston, and do not think "salt" will be necessary. When I move, the Fifteenth Corps will be on the right of the right wing, and their position will naturally bring them into Charleston first; and, if you have watched the history of that corps, you will have remarked that they generally do their work pretty well. The truth is, the whole army is burning with an insatiable desire to wreak vengeance upon South Carolina. I almost tremble at her fate, but feel that she deserves all that seems in store for her.

Many and many a person in Georgia asked me why we did not go to South Carolina; and, when I answered that we were enroute for that State, the invariable reply was, "Well, if you will make those people feel the utmost severities of war, we will pardon you for your desolation of Georgia."

I look upon Colombia as quite as bad as Charleston, and I doubt if we shall spare the public buildings there as we did at Milledgeville.

I have been so busy lately that I have not yet made my official report, and I think I had better wait until I get my subordinate reports before attempting it, as I am anxious to explain clearly not only the reasons for every step, but the amount of execution done, and this I cannot do until I get the subordinate reports; for we marched the whole distance in four or more columns, and, of course, I could only be present with one, and generally that one engaged in destroying railroads. This work of destruction was performed better than usual, because I had an engineer-regiment, provided with claws to twist the bars after being heated. Such bars can never be used again, and the only way in which a railroad line can be reconstructed across Georgia is, to make a new road from Fairburn Station (twenty-four miles southwest of Atlanta) to Madison, a distance of one hundred miles; and, before that can be done, I propose to be on the road from Augusta to Charleston, which is a continuation of the same. I felt somewhat disappointed at Hardee's escape, but really am not to blame. I moved as quickly as possible to close up the "Union Causeway," but intervening obstacles were such that, before I could get troops on the road, Hardee had slipped out. Still, I know that the men that were in Savannah will be lost in a measure to Jeff. Davis, for the Georgia troops, under G. W. Smith, declared they would not fight in South Carolina, and they have gone north, en route for Augusta, and I have reason to believe the North Carolina troops have gone to Wilmington; in other words, they are scattered. I have reason to believe that Beauregard was present in Savannah at the time of its evacuation, and think that he and Hardee are now in Charleston, making preparations for what they suppose will be my next step.

Please say to the President that I have received his kind message (through Colonel Markland), and feel thankful for his high favor. If I disappoint him in the future, it shall not be from want of zeal or love to the cause.

From you I expect a full and frank criticism of my plans for the future, which may enable me to correct errors before it is too late. I do not wish to be rash, but want to give my rebel friends no chance to accuse us of want of enterprise or courage.

Assuring you of my high personal respect, I remain, as ever, your friend,

W. T. SHERMAN, Major-General.

[General Order No. 3.]

WAR DEPARTMENT, ADJUTANT GENERAL'S OFFICE
WASHINGTON, January 14, 1865.

The following resolution of the Senate and House of Representatives is published to the army:

[PUBLIC RESOLUTION--No. 4.]

Joint resolution tendering the thanks of the people and of Congress to Major-General William T. Sherman, and the officers and soldiers of his command, for their gallant conduct in their late brilliant movement through Georgia.

Be it resolved by the Senate and House of Representatives of the United States of America in Congress assembled, That the thanks of the people and of the Congress of the United States are due and are hereby tendered to Major-General William T. Sherman, and through him to the officers and men under his command, for their gallantry and good conduct in their late campaign from Chattanooga to Atlanta, and the triumphal march thence through Georgia to Savannah, terminating in the capture and occupation of that city; and that the President cause a copy of this joint resolution to be engrossed and forwarded to Major-General Sherman.

Approved, January 10, 1865.

By order of the Secretary of War,
W. A. NICHOLS, Assistant Adjutant-General.

CHAPTER XXII.
SAVANNAH AND POCOTALIGO.

DECEMBER, 1884, AND JANUARY, 1885.

      The city of Savannah was an old place, and usually accounted a handsome one. Its houses were of brick or frame, with large yards, ornamented with shrubbery and flowers; its streets perfectly regular, crossing each other at right angles; and at many of the intersections were small inclosures in the nature of parks. These streets and parks were lined with the handsomest shade-trees of which I have knowledge, viz., the Willow-leaf live-oak, evergreens of exquisite beauty; and these certainly entitled Savannah to its reputation as a handsome town more than the houses, which, though comfortable, would hardly make a display on Fifth Avenue or the Boulevard Haussmann of Paris. The city was built on a plateau of sand about forty feet above the level of the sea, abutting against the river, leaving room along its margin for a street of stores and warehouses. The customhouse, court-house, post-office, etc., were on the plateau above. In rear of Savannah was a large park, with a fountain, and between it and the court-house was a handsome monument, erected to the memory of Count Pulaski, who fell in 1779 in the assault made on the city at the time it was held by the English during the Revolutionary War. Outside of Savannah there was very little to interest a stranger, except the cemetery of Bonaventura, and the ride along the Wilmington Channel by way of Thunderbolt, where might be seen some groves of the majestic live-oak trees, covered with gray and funeral moss, which were truly sublime in grandeur, but gloomy after a few days' camping under them:
      Within an hour of taking up my quarters in Mr. Green's house, Mr. A. G. Browne, of Salem, Massachusetts, United States Treasury agent for the Department of the South, made his appearance to claim possession, in the name of the Treasury Department, of all captured cotton, rice, buildings, etc. Having use for these articles ourselves, and having fairly earned them, I did not feel inclined to surrender possession, and explained to him that the quartermaster and commissary could manage them more to my liking than he; but I agreed, after the proper inventories had been prepared, if there remained any thing for which we had no special

use, I would turn it over to him. It was then known that in the warehouses were stored at least twenty-five thousand bales of cotton, and in the forts one hundred and fifty large, heavy sea-coast guns: although afterward, on a more careful count, there proved to be more than two hundred and fifty sea-coast or siege guns, and thirty-one thousand bales of cotton. At that interview Mr. Browne, who was a shrewd, clever Yankee, told me that a vessel was on the point of starting for Old Point Comfort, and, if she had good weather off Cape Hatteras, would reach Fortress Monroe by Christmas-day, and he suggested that I might make it the occasion of sending a welcome Christmas gift to the President, Mr. Lincoln, who peculiarly enjoyed such pleasantry. I accordingly sat down and wrote on a slip of paper, to be left at the telegraph-office at Fortress Monroe for transmission, the following:

SAVANNAH GEORGIA, December 22, 1884. To His Excellency President Lincoln, Washington, D. C.:

I beg to present you as a Christmas-gift the city of Savannah, with one hundred and fifty heavy guns and plenty of ammunition, also about twenty five thousand bales of cotton.

W. T. SHERMAN, Major-General.

This message actually reached him on Christmas-eve, was extensively published in the newspapers, and made many a household unusually happy on that festive day; and it was in the answer to this dispatch that Mr. Lincoln wrote me the letter of December 28th, already given, beginning with the words, "many, many thanks," etc., which he sent at the hands of General John A. Logan, who happened to be in Washington, and was coming to Savannah, to rejoin his command.

On the 23d of December were made the following general orders for the disposition of the troops in and about Savannah:

[Special Field Order No. 139.]

HEADQUARTERS MILITARY DIVISION OF THE MISSISSIPPI,
IN THE FIELD, NEAR SAVANNAH, GEORGIA, December 23, 1864.

Savannah, being now in our possession, the river partially cleared out, and measures having been taken to remove all obstructions, will at once be made a grand depot for future operations:

1. The chief-quartermaster, General Euston, will, after giving the necessary orders touching the transports in Ogeechee River and Oasabaw Sound, come in person to Savannah, and take possession of all public buildings, vacant storerooms, warehouses, etc., that may be now or hereafter needed for any department of the army. No rents will be paid by the Government of the United States during the war, and all buildings must be distributed according to the accustomed rates of the Quartermaster's Department, as though they were public property.

2. The chief commissary of subsistence, Colonel A. Beckwith, will transfer the grand depot of the army to the city of Savannah, secure possession of the needful buildings and offices, and give the necessary orders, to the end that the army may be supplied abundantly and well.

S. The chief-engineer, Captain Poe, will at once direct which of the enemy's forts are to be retained for our use, and which dismantled and destroyed. The chief ordnance-officer, Captain Baylor, will in like manner take possession of all property pertaining to his department captured from the enemy, and cause the same to be collected and conveyed to points of security; all the heavy coast-guns will be dismounted and carried to Fort Pulaski.

4. The troops, for the present, will be grouped about the city of Savannah, looking to convenience of camps; General Slocum taking from the Savannah River around to the seven-mile post on the Canal, and General Howard thence to the sea; General Kilpatrick will hold King's Bridge until Fort McAllister is dismantled, and the troops withdrawn from the south side of the Ogeechee, when he will take post about Anderson's plantation, on the plank-road, and picket all the roads leading from the north and west.

5. General Howard will keep a small guard at Forts Rosedale, Beaulieu, Wimberley, Thunderbolt, and Bonaventura, and he will cause that shore and Skidaway Island to be examined very closely, with a view to finding many and convenient points for the embarkation of troops and wagons on seagoing vessels.

By order of Major-General W. T. Sherman,

94

L. M. DAYTON, *Aide-de-Camp.*

HEADQUARTERS MILITARY DIVISION OF THE MISSISSIPPI,
IN THE FIELD, NEAR SAVANNAH, GEORGIA, December 26, 1864.

The city of Savannah and surrounding country will be held as a military post, and adapted to future military uses, but, as it contains a population of some twenty thousand people, who must be provided for, and as other citizens may come, it is proper to lay down certain general principles, that all within its military jurisdiction may understand their relative duties and obligations.

1. During war, the military is superior to civil authority, and, where interests clash, the civil must give way; yet, where there is no conflict, every encouragement should be given to well-disposed and peaceful inhabitants to resume their usual pursuits. Families should be disturbed as little as possible in their residences, and tradesmen allowed the free use of their shops, tools, etc.; churches, schools, and all places of amusement and recreation, should be encouraged, and streets and roads made perfectly safe to persons in their pursuits. Passes should not be exacted within the line of outer pickets, but if any person shall abuse these privileges by communicating with the enemy, or doing any act of hostility to the Government of the United States, he or she will be punished with the utmost rigor of the law. Commerce with the outer world will be resumed to an extent commensurate with the wants of the citizens, governed by the restrictions and rules of the Treasury Department.

2. The chief quartermaster and commissary of the army may give suitable employment to the people, white and black, or transport them to such points as they may choose where employment can be had; and may extend temporary relief in the way of provisions and vacant houses to the worthy and needy, until such time as they can help themselves. They will select first the buildings for the necessary uses of the army; next, a sufficient number of stores, to be turned over to the Treasury agent for trade-stores. All vacant store-houses or dwellings, and all buildings belonging to absent rebels, will be construed and used as belonging to the United States, until such time as their titles can be settled by the courts of the United States.

3. The Mayor and City Council of Savannah will continue to exercise their functions, and will, in concert with the commanding officer of the post and the chief-quartermaster, see that the fire-companies are kept in organization, the streets cleaned and lighted, and keep up a good understanding between the citizens and soldiers. They will ascertain and report to the chief commissary of subsistence, as soon as possible, the names and number of worthy families that need assistance and support. The mayor will forth with give public notice that the time has come when all must choose their course, viz., remain within our lines, and conduct themselves as good citizens, or depart in peace. He will ascertain the names of all who choose to leave Savannah, and report their names and residence to the chief-quartermaster, that measures may be taken to transport them beyond our lines.

4. Not more than two newspapers will be published in Savannah; their editors and proprietors will be held to the strictest accountability, and will be punished severely, in person and property, for any libelous publication, mischievous matter, premature news, exaggerated statements, or any comments whatever upon the acts of the constituted authorities; they will be held accountable for such articles, even though copied from other papers.

By order of Major-General W. T. Sherman,

L. M. DAYTON, Aide-de-Camp.

It was estimated that there were about twenty thousand inhabitants in Savannah, all of whom had participated more or less in the war, and had no special claims to our favor, but I regarded the war as rapidly drawing to a close, and it was becoming a political question as to what was to be done with the people of the South, both white and black, when the war was actually over. I concluded to give them the option to remain or to join their friends in Charleston or Augusta, and so announced in general orders. The mayor, Dr. Arnold, was completely "subjugated," and, after consulting with him, I authorized him to assemble his City Council to take charge generally of the interests of the people; but warned all who remained that they must be strictly subordinate to the military law, and to the interests of the General Government. About two hundred persona, mostly the families of men in the Confederate army, prepared to follow the fortunes of their husbands and fathers, and these were sent in a steamboat under a flag of truce, in charge of my aide Captain Audenried, to Charleston harbor, and there delivered to an officer of the Confederate army. But the great bulk of the inhabitants chose to remain in Savannah, generally behaved with propriety, and good social relations at once arose between them and the army. Shortly after our occupation of Savannah, a lady was announced at my headquarters by the orderly or sentinel at the front-door, who was ushered into the parlor, and proved to be the wife of General G. W. Smith, whom I had known about 1850, when Smith was on duty at West Point. She was a native of New London, Connecticut, and very handsome. She began her interview by presenting me a letter from her husband, who then commanded a division of the Georgia militia in the rebel army, which had just quitted Savannah, which letter began, "DEAR SHERMAN: The fortunes of war, etc-., compel me to leave my wife in Savannah, and I beg for her your courteous protection," etc., etc. I inquired where she lived, and if anybody was troubling her. She said she was boarding with a lady whose husband had, in like manner with her own, gone off with Hardee's army; that a part of the house had been taken for the use of Major-General Ward, of Kentucky; that her landlady was approaching her confinement, and was nervous at the noise which the younger staff-officers made at night; etc. I explained to her that I could give but little personal attention to such matters, and referred her to General Slocum, whose troops occupied the city. I afterward visited her house, and saw, personally, that she had no reason to complain. Shortly afterward Mr. Hardee, a merchant of Savannah, came to me and presented a letter from his brother, the general, to the same effect, alleging that his brother was a civilian, had never taken up arms, and asked of me protection for his family, his cotton, etc. To him I gave the general assurance that no harm was designed to any of the people of Savannah who would remain quiet and peaceable, but that I could give him no guarantee as to his cotton, for over it I had no absolute control; and yet still later I received a note from the wife of General A. P. Stewart (who commanded a corps in Hood's army), asking me to come to see her. This I did, and found her to be a native of Cincinnati, Ohio, wanting protection, and who was naturally anxious about the fate of her husband, known to be with General Hood, in Tennessee, retreating before General Thomas. I remember that I was able to assure her that he had not been killed or captured, up to that date, and think that I advised her, instead of attempting to go in pursuit of her husband, to go to Cincinnati, to her uncle, Judge Storer, there await the issue of events.

Before I had reached Savannah, and during our stay there, the rebel officers and newspapers represented the conduct of the men of our army as simply infamous; that we respected neither age nor sex; that we burned every thing we came across--barns, stables, cotton-gins, and even dwelling-houses; that we ravished the women and killed the men, and perpetrated all manner of outrages on the inhabitants. Therefore it struck me as strange that Generals Hardee and Smith should commit their, families to our custody, and even bespeak our personal care and attention. These officers knew well that these reports were exaggerated in the extreme, and yet tacitly assented to these publications, to arouse the drooping energies of the people of the South.

As the division of Major-General John W. Geary, of the Twentieth Corps, was the first to enter Savannah, that officer was appointed to command the place, or to act as a sort of governor. He very soon established a good police, maintained admirable order, and I doubt if Savannah, either before or since, has had a better government than during our stay. The guard-mountings and parades, as well as the greater reviews, became the daily resorts of the ladies, to hear the music of our excellent bands; schools were opened, and the churches every Sunday were well filled with most devout and respectful congregations; stores were reopened, and markets for provisions, meat, wood, etc., were established, so that each family, regardless of race, color, or opinion, could procure all the necessaries and even luxuries of life, provided they had money. Of course, many families were actually destitute of this, and to these were issued stores from our own stock of supplies. I remember to have given to Dr. Arnold, the mayor, an order for the contents of a large warehouse of rice, which he confided to a committee of gentlemen, who went North (to Boston), and soon returned with one or more cargoes of flour, hams, sugar, coffee, etc., for gratuitous distribution, which relieved the most pressing wants until the revival of trade and business enabled the people to provide for themselves.

A lady, whom I had known in former years as Miss Josephine Goodwin, told me that, with a barrel of flour and some sugar which she had received gratuitously from the commissary, she had baked cakes and pies, in the sale of which she realized a profit of fifty-six dollars.

Meantime Colonel Poe had reconnoitred and laid off new lines of parapet, which would enable a comparatively small garrison to hold the place, and a heavy detail of soldiers was put to work thereon; Generals Easton and Beckwith had organized a complete depot of supplies; and, though vessels arrived almost daily with mails and provisions, we were hardly ready to initiate a new and hazardous campaign. I had not yet received from General Grant or General Halleck any modification of the orders of December 6,1864, to embark my command for Virginia by sea; but on the 2d of January, 1865, General J. G. Barnard, United States Engineers, arrived direct from General Grant's headquarters, bearing the following letter, in the general's own handwriting, which, with my answer, is here given:

HEADQUARTERS ARMIES OF THE UNITED STATES
CITY POINT, VIRGINIA, December 27, 1864.

Major-General W. T. SHERMAN, commanding Military Division of the Mississippi.

GENERAL: Before writing you definite instructions for the next campaign, I wanted to receive your answer to my letter written from Washington. Your confidence in being able to march up and join this army pleases me, and I believe it can be done. The effect of such a campaign will be to disorganize the South, and prevent the organization of new armies from their broken fragments. Hood is now retreating, with his army broken and demoralized. His loss in men has probably not been far from twenty thousand, besides deserters. If time is given, the fragments may be collected together and many of the deserters reassembled. If we can, we should act to prevent this. Your spare army, as it were, moving as proposed, will do it.

In addition to holding Savannah, it looks to me that an intrenched camp ought to be held on the railroad between Savannah and Charleston. Your movement toward Branchville will probably enable Foster to reach this with his own force. This will give us a position in the South from which we can threaten the interior without marching over long, narrow causeways, easily defended, as we have heretofore been compelled to do. Could not such a camp be established about Pocotaligo or Coosawhatchie?

I have thought that, Hood being so completely wiped out for present harm, I might bring A. J. Smith here, with fourteen to fifteen thousand men. With this increase I could hold my lines, and move out with a greater force than Lee has. It would compel Lee to retain all his present force in the defenses of Richmond or abandon them entirely. This latter contingency is probably the only danger to the easy success of your expedition. In the event you should meet Lee's army, you would be compelled to beat it or find the sea-coast. Of course, I shall not let Lee's army escape if I can help it, and will not let it go without following to the best of my ability.

Without waiting further directions, than, you may make your preparations to start on your northern expedition without delay. Break up the railroads in South and North Carolina, and join the armies operating against Richmond as soon as you can. I will leave out all suggestions about the route you should take, knowing that your information, gained daily in the course of events, will be better than any that can be obtained now.

It may not be possible for you to march to the rear of Petersburg; but, failing in this, you could strike either of the sea-coast ports in North Carolina held by us. From there you could take shipping. It would be decidedly preferable, however, if you could march the whole distance.

From the best information I have, you will find no difficulty in supplying your army until you cross the Roanoke. From there here is but a few days' march, and supplies could be collected south of the river to bring you through. I shall establish communication with you there, by steamboat and gunboat. By this means your wants can be partially supplied. I shall hope to hear from you soon, and to hear your plan, and about the time of starting.

Please instruct Foster to hold on to all the property in Savannah, and especially the cotton. Do not turn it over to citizens or Treasury agents, without orders of the War Department.

Very respectfully, your obedient servant,

U. S. GRANT, Lieutenant-General.

HEADQUARTERS MILITARY DIVISION OF THE MISSISSIPPI,
IN THE FIELD, NEAR SAVANNAH, GEORGIA, January 2, 1865.

Lieutenant-General U. S. GRANT, City Point.

GENERAL: I have received, by the hands of General Barnard, your note of 26th and letter of 27th December.

I herewith inclose to you a copy of a projet which I have this morning, in strict confidence, discussed with my immediate commanders.

I shall need, however, larger supplies of stores, especially grain. I will inclose to you, with this, letters from General Easton, quartermaster, and Colonel Beckwith, commissary of subsistence, setting forth what will be required, and trust you will forward them to Washington with your sanction, so that the necessary steps may be taken at once to enable me to carry out this plan on time.

I wrote you very fully on the 24th, and have nothing to add. Every thing here is quiet, and if I can get the necessary supplies in our wagons, shall be ready to start at the time indicated in my projet (January 15th). But, until those supplies are in hand, I can do nothing; after they are, I shall be ready to move with great rapidity.

I have heard of the affair at Cape Fear. It has turned out as you will remember I expected.

I have furnished General Easton a copy of the dispatch from the Secretary of War. He will retain possession of all cotton here, and ship it as fast as vessels can be had to New York.

I shall immediately send the Seventeenth Corps over to Port Royal, by boats, to be furnished by Admiral Dahlgren and General

Foster (without interfering with General Easton's vessels), to make a lodgment on the railroad at Pocotaligo.

General Barnard will remain with me a few days, and I send this by a staff-officer, who can return on one of the vessels of the supply-fleet. I suppose that, now that General Butler has got through with them, you can spare them to us.

My report of recent operations is nearly ready, and will be sent you in a day or two, as soon as some farther subordinate reports come in.

I am, with great respect, very truly, your friend,

W. T. SHERMAN, Major-General.

[Entirely confidential]

PROJET FOR JANUARY.

1. Right wing to move men and artillery by transports to head of Broad River and Beaufort; reestablish Port Royal Ferry, and mass the wing at or in the neighborhood of Pocotaligo.

Left wing and cavalry to work slowly across the causeway toward Hardeeville, to open a road by which wagons can reach their corps about Broad River; also, by a rapid movement of the left, to secure Sister's Ferry, and Augusta road out to Robertsville.

In the mean time, all guns, shot, shell, cotton, etc., to be moved to a safe place, easy to guard, and provisions and wagons got ready for another swath, aiming to have our army in hand about the head of Broad River, say Pocotaligo, Robertsville, and Coosawhatchie, by the 15th January.

2. The whole army to move with loaded wagons by the roads leading in the direction of Columbia, which afford the best chance of forage and provisions. Howard to be at Pocotaligo by the 15th January, and Slocum to be at Robertsville, and Kilpatrick at or near Coosawhatchie about the same date. General Fosters troops to occupy Savannah, and gunboats to protect the rivers as soon as Howard gets Pocotaligo.

W. T. SHERMAN, Major-General.

Therefore, on the 2d of January, I was authorized to march with my entire army north by land, and concluded at once to secure a foothold or starting-point on the South Carolina side, selecting Pocotaligo and Hardeeville as the points of rendezvous for the two wings; but I still remained in doubt as to the wishes of the Administration, whether I should take Charleston en route, or confine my whole attention to the incidental advantages of breaking up the railways of South and North Carolina, and the greater object of uniting my army with that of General Grant before Richmond.

General Barnard remained with me several days, and was regarded then, as now, one of the first engineers of the age, perfectly competent to advise me on the strategy and objects of the new campaign. He expressed himself delighted with the high spirit of the army, the steps already taken, by which we had captured Savannah, and he personally inspected some of the forts, such as Thunderbolt and Causten's Bluff, by which the enemy had so long held at bay the whole of our navy, and had defeated the previous attempts made in April, 1862, by the army of General Gillmore, which had bombarded and captured Fort Pulaski, but had failed to reach the city of Savannah. I think General Barnard expected me to invite him to accompany us northward in his official capacity; but Colonel Poe, of my staff, had done so well, and was so perfectly competent, that I thought it unjust to supersede him by a senior in his own corps. I therefore said nothing of this to General Barnard, and soon after he returned to his post with General Grant, at City Point, bearing letters and full personal messages of our situation and wants.

We were very much in want of light-draught steamers for navigating the shallow waters of the coast, so that it took the Seventeenth Corps more than a week to transfer from Thunderbolt to Beaufort, South Carolina. Admiral Dahlgren had supplied the Harvest Moon and the Pontiac, and General Foster gave us a couple of hired steamers; I was really amused at the effect this short sea-voyage had on our men, most of whom had never before looked upon the ocean. Of course, they were fit subjects for sea-sickness, and afterward they begged me never again to send them to sea, saying they would rather march a thousand miles on the worst roads of the South than to spend a single night on the ocean. By the 10th General Howard had collected the bulk of the Seventeenth Corps (General Blair) on Beaufort Island, and began his march for Pocotaligo, twenty-five miles inland. They crossed the channel between the island and main-land during Saturday, the 14th of January, by a pontoon-bridge, and marched out to Garden's Corners, where there was some light skirmishing; the next day, Sunday, they continued on to Pocotaligo, finding the strong fort there abandoned, and accordingly made a lodgment on the railroad, having lost only two officers and eight men.

About the same time General Slocum crossed two divisions of the Twentieth Corps over the Savannah River, above the city, occupied Hardeeville by one division and Purysburg by another. Thus, by the middle of January, we had effected a lodgment in South Carolina, and were ready to resume the march northward; but we had not yet accumulated enough provisions and forage to fill the wagons, and other causes of delay occurred, of which I will make mention in due order.

On the last day of December, 1864, Captain Breese, United States Navy, flag-officer to Admiral Porter, reached Savannah, bringing the first news of General Butler's failure at Fort Fisher, and that the general had returned to James River with his land-forces, leaving Admiral Porter's fleet anchored off Cape Fear, in that tempestuous season. Captain Breese brought me a letter from the admiral, dated December 29th, asking me to send him from Savannah one of my old divisions, with which he said he would make short work of Fort Fisher; that he had already bombarded and silenced its guns, and that General Butler had failed because he was afraid to attack, or even give the order to attack, after (as Porter insisted) the guns of Fort Fisher had been actually silenced by the navy.

I answered him promptly on the 31st of December, that I proposed to march north inland, and that I would prefer to leave the rebel garrisons on the coast, instead of dislodging and piling them up in my front as we progressed. From the chances, as I then understood them, I supposed that Fort Fisher was garrisoned by a comparatively small force, while the whole division of General Hoke remained about the city of Wilmington; and that, if Fort Fisher were captured, it would leave General Hoke free to join the larger force that would naturally be collected to oppose my progress northward. I accordingly answered Admiral Porter to this effect, declining to loan him the use of one of my divisions. It subsequently transpired, however, that, as soon as General Butler reached City Point, General Grant was unwilling to rest under a sense of failure, and accordingly dispatched back the same troops, reenforced and commanded by General A. H. Terry, who, on the 15th day of January, successfully assaulted and captured Fort Fisher, with its entire garrison. After the war was over, about the 20th of May, when I was giving my testimony before the Congressional Committee on the Conduct of the War, the chairman of the committee, Senator B. F. Wade, of Ohio, told me that General Butler had been summoned before that committee during the previous January, and had just finished his demonstration to their entire satisfaction that Fort Fisher could not be carried by assault, when they heard the newsboy in the hall crying out an "extra" Calling him in, they inquired the news, and he answered, "Fort Fisher done took!" Of course, they all laughed, and none more heartily than General Butler himself.

On the 11th of January there arrived at Savannah a revenue-cutter, having on board Simeon Draper, Esq., of New York City, the Hon. E. M. Stanton, Secretary of War, Quartermaster-General Meigs, Adjutant-General Townsend, and a retinue of civilians, who had come down from the North to regulate the civil affairs of Savannah....

I was instructed by Mr. Stanton to transfer to Mr. Draper the custom house, post-office, and such other public buildings as these civilians needed in the execution of their office, and to cause to be delivered into their custody the captured cotton. This was accomplished by--

[Special Field Orders, No. 10.]

HEADQUARTERS MILITARY DIVISION OF THE MISSISSIPPI,
IN THE FIELD, NEAR SAVANNAH, GEORGIA, January 12, 1865.

1. Brevet Brigadier-General Euston, chief-quartermaster, will turn over to Simeon Draper, Esq., agent of the United States Treasury Department, all cotton now in the city of Savannah, prize of war, taking his receipt for the same in gross, and returning for it to the quartermaster-general. He will also afford Mr. Draper all the facilities in his power in the way of transportation, labor, etc., to enable him to handle the cotton with expedition.

2. General Euston will also turn over to Mr. Draper the custom-house, and such other buildings in the city of Savannah as he may need in the execution of his office.

By order of General W. T. Sherman,

L. M. DAYTON, Aide-de-Camp.

Up to this time all the cotton had been carefully guarded, with orders to General Euston to ship it by the return-vessels to New York, for the adjudication of the nearest prize-court, accompanied with invoices and all evidence of title to ownership. Marks, numbers, and other figures, were carefully preserved on the bales, so that the court might know the history of each bale. But Mr. Stanton, who surely was an able lawyer, changed all this, and ordered the obliteration of all the marks; so that no man, friend or foe, could trace his identical cotton. I thought it strange at the time, and think it more so now; for I am assured that claims, real and fictitious, have been proved up against this identical cotton of three times the quantity actually captured, and that reclamations on the Treasury have been allowed for more than the actual quantity captured, viz., thirty-one thousand bales.

Mr. Stanton staid in Savannah several days, and seemed very curious about matters and things in general. I walked with him through the city, especially the bivouacs of the several regiments that occupied the vacant squares, and he seemed particularly pleased at the ingenuity of the men in constructing their temporary huts. Four of the "dog-tents," or tentes d'abri, buttoned together, served for a roof, and the sides were made of clapboards, or rough boards brought from demolished houses or fences. I remember his marked admiration for the hut of a soldier who had made his door out of a handsome parlor mirror, the glass gone and its gilt frame serving for his door.

He talked to me a great deal about the negroes, the former slaves, and I told him of many interesting incidents, illustrating their simple character and faith in our arms and progress. He inquired particularly about General Jeff. C. Davis, who, he said, was a Democrat, and hostile to the negro. I assured him that General Davis was an excellent soldier, and I did not believe he had any hostility to the negro; that in our army we had no negro soldiers, and, as a rule, we preferred white soldiers, but that we employed a large force of them as servants, teamsters, and pioneers, who had rendered admirable service. He then showed me a newspaper account of General Davis taking up his pontoon-bridge across Ebenezer Creek, leaving sleeping negro men, women, and children, on the other side, to be slaughtered by Wheeler's cavalry. I had heard such a rumor, and advised Mr. Stanton, before becoming prejudiced, to allow me to send for General Davis, which he did, and General Davis explained the matter to his entire satisfaction. The truth was, that, as we approached the seaboard, the freedmen in droves, old and young, followed the several columns to reach a place of safety. It so happened that General Davis's route into Savannah followed what was known as the "River-road," and he had to make constant use of his pontoon-train--the head of his column reaching some deep, impassable creek before the rear was fairly over another. He had occasionally to use the pontoons both day and night. On the occasion referred to, the bridge was taken up from Ebenezer Creek while some of the camp-followers remained asleep on the farther side, and these were picked up by Wheeler's cavalry. Some of them, in their fright, were drowned in trying to swim over, and others may have been cruelly killed by Wheeler's men, but this was a mere supposition. At all events, the same thing might have resulted to General Howard, or to any other of the many most humane commanders who filled the army. General Jeff. C. Davis was strictly a soldier, and doubtless hated to have his wagons and columns encumbered by these poor negroes, for whom we all felt sympathy, but a sympathy of a different sort from that of Mr. Stanton, which was not of pure humanity, but of politics. The negro question was beginning to loom up among the political eventualities of the day, and many foresaw that not only would the slaves secure their freedom, but that they would also have votes. I did not dream of such a result then, but knew that slavery, as such, was dead forever, and did not suppose that the former slaves would be suddenly, without preparation, manufactured into voters, equal to all others, politically and socially. Mr. Stanton seemed desirous of coming into contact with the negroes to confer with them, and he asked me to arrange an interview for him. I accordingly sent out and invited the most intelligent of the negroes, mostly Baptist and Methodist preachers, to come to my rooms to meet the Secretary of War. Twenty responded, and were received in my room up-stairs in Mr. Green's house, where Mr. Stanton and Adjutant-General Townsend took down the conversation in the form of questions and answers. Each of the twenty gave his name and partial history, and then selected Garrison Frazier as their spokesman:

First Question. State what your understanding is in regard to the acts of Congress and President Lincoln's proclamation touching the colored people in the rebel States?

Answer. So far as I understand President Lincoln's proclamation to the rebel States, it is, that if they will lay down their arms and submit to the laws of the United States, before the 1st of January, 1863, all should be well; but if they did not, then all the slaves in the Southern States should be free, henceforth and forever. That is what I understood.

Second Question. State what you understand by slavery, and the freedom that was to be given by the President's proclamation?

Answer. Slavery is receiving by irresistible power the work of another man, and not by his consent. The freedom, as I understand it, promised by the proclamation, is taking us from under the yoke of bondage and placing us where we can reap the fruit of our own labor, and take care of ourselves and assist the Government in maintaining our freedom.

Fourth Question. State in what manner you would rather live--whether scattered among the whites, or in colonies by yourselves?

Answer. I would prefer to live by ourselves, for there is a prejudice against us in the South that will take years to get over; but I do not know that I can answer for my brethren.

(All but Mr. Lynch, a missionary from the North, agreed with Frazier, but he thought they ought to live together, along with the whites.)

Eighth Question. If the rebel leaders were to arm the slaves, what would be its effect?

Answer. I think they would fight as long as they were before the "bayonet," and just as soon as they could get away they would desert, in my opinion.

Tenth Question. Do you understand the mode of enlistment of colored persons in the rebel States by State agents, under the act of Congress; if yea, what is your understanding?

Answer. My understanding is, that colored persons enlisted by State agents are enlisted as substitutes, and give credit to the State and do not swell the army, because every black man enlisted by a State agent leaves a white man at home; and also that larger bounties are given, or promised, by the State agents than are given by the United States. The great object should be to push through this rebellion the shortest way; and there seems to be something wanting in the enlistment by State agents, for it don't strengthen the army, but takes one away for every colored man enlisted.

Eleventh Question. State what, in your opinion, is the best way to enlist colored men as soldiers?

Answer. I think, sir, that all compulsory operations should be put a stop to. The ministers would talk to them, and the young men would enlist. It is my opinion that it world be far better for the State agents to stay at home and the enlistments be made for the United States under the direction of General Sherman.

Up to this time I was present, and, on Mr. Stanton's intimating that he wanted to ask some questions affecting me, I withdrew, and then he put the twelfth and last question.

Twelfth Question. State what is the feeling of the colored people toward General Sherman, and how far do they regard his sentiments and actions as friendly to their rights and interests, or otherwise.

Answer. We looked upon General Sherman, prior to his arrival, as a man, in the providence of God, specially set apart to accomplish this work, and we unanimously felt inexpressible gratitude to him, looking upon him as a man who should be honored for the faithful performance of his duty. Some of us called upon him immediately upon his arrival, and it is probable he did not meet the secretary with more courtesy than he did us. His conduct and deportment toward us characterized him as a friend and gentleman. We have confidence in General Sherman, and think what concerns us could not be in better hands. This is our opinion now, from the short acquaintance and intercourse we have had.

It certainly was a strange fact that the great War Secretary should have catechized negroes concerning the character of a general who had commanded a hundred thousand men in battle, had captured cities conducted sixty-five thousand men successfully across four hundred miles of hostile territory, and had just brought tens of thousands of freedmen to a place of security; but because I had not loaded down my army by other hundreds of thousands of poor negroes, I was construed by others as hostile to the black race. I had received from General Halleck, at Washington, a letter warning me that there were certain influential parties near the President who were torturing him with suspicions of my fidelity to him and his negro policy; but I shall always believe that Mr. Lincoln, though a civilian, knew better, and appreciated my motives and character. Though this letter of General Halleck has always been treated by me as confidential, I now insert it here at length:

HEADQUARTERS OF THE ARMY
WASHINGTON, D.C., December 30, 1864.

Major-General W. T. SHERMAN, Savannah.

MY DEAR GENERAL: I take the liberty of calling your attention, in this private and friendly way, to a matter which may possibly hereafter be of more importance to you than either of us may now anticipate.

While almost every one is praising your great march through Georgia, and the capture of Savannah, there is a certain class having now great influence with the President, and very probably anticipating still more on a change of cabinet, who are decidedly disposed to make a point against you. I mean in regard to "inevitable Sambo." They say that you have manifested an almost criminal dislike to the negro, and that you are not willing to carry out the wishes of the Government in regard to him, but repulse him with contempt! They say you might have brought with you to Savannah more than fifty thousand, thus stripping Georgia of that number of laborers, and opening a road by which as many more could have escaped from their masters; but that, instead of this, you drove them from your ranks, prevented their following you by cutting the bridges in your rear, and thus caused the massacre of large numbers by Wheeler's cavalry.

To those who know you as I do, such accusation will pass as the idle winds, for we presume that you discouraged the negroes from following you because you had not the means of supporting them, and feared they might seriously embarrass your march. But there are others, and among them some in high authority, who think or pretend to think otherwise, and they are decidedly disposed to make a point against you.

I do not write this to induce you to conciliate this class of men by doing any thing which you do not deem right and proper, and for the interest of the Government and the country; but simply to call your attention to certain things which are viewed here somewhat differently than from your stand-point. I will explain as briefly as possible:

Some here think that, in view of the scarcity of labor in the South, and the probability that a part, at least, of the able-bodied slaves will be called into the military service of the rebels, it is of the greatest importance to open outlets by which these slaves can escape into our lines, and they say that the route you have passed over should be made the route of escape, and Savannah the great place of refuge. These, I know, are the views of some of the leading men in the Administration, and they now express dissatisfaction that you did not carry them out in your great raid.

Now that you are in possession of Savannah, and there can be no further fears about supplies, would it not be possible for you to reopen these avenues of escape for the negroes, without interfering with your military operations? Could not such escaped slaves find at least a partial supply of food in the rice-fields about Savannah, and cotton plantations on the coast?

I merely throw out these suggestions. I know that such a course would be approved by the Government, and I believe that a manifestation on your part of a desire to bring the slaves within our lines will do much to silence your opponents. You will appreciate my motives in writing this private letter. Yours truly,

H. W. HALLECK.

There is no doubt that Mr. Stanton, when he reached Savannah, shared these thoughts, but luckily the negroes themselves convinced him that he was in error, and that they understood their own interests far better than did the men in Washington, who tried to make political capital out of this negro question. The idea that such men should have been permitted to hang around Mr. Lincoln, to torture his life by suspicions of the officers who were toiling with the single purpose to bring the war to a successful end, and thereby to liberate all slaves, is a fair illustration of the influences that poison a political capital.

My aim then was, to whip the rebels, to humble their pride, to follow them to their inmost recesses, and make them fear and dread us. "Fear of the Lord is the beginning of wisdom." I did not want them to cast in our teeth what General Hood had once done in Atlanta, that we had to call on their slaves to help us to subdue them. But, as regards kindness to the race, encouraging them to patience and forbearance, procuring them food and clothing, and providing them with land whereon to labor, I assert that no army ever did more for that race than the one I commanded in Savannah. When we reached Savannah, we were beset by ravenous State agents from Hilton Head, who enticed and carried away our servants, and the corps of pioneers which we had organized, and which had done such excellent service. On one occasion, my own aide-de-camp, Colonel Audenried, found at least a hundred poor negroes shut up in a house and pen, waiting for the night, to be conveyed stealthily to Hilton Head. They appealed to him for protection, alleging that they had been told that they must be soldiers, that "Massa Lincoln" wanted them, etc. I never denied the slaves a full opportunity for voluntary enlistment, but I did prohibit force to be used, for I knew that the State agents were more influenced by the profit they derived from the large bounties then being paid than by any love of country or of the colored race. In the language of Mr. Frazier, the enlistment of every black man "did not strengthen the army, but took away one white man from the ranks."

During Mr. Stanton's stay in Savannah we discussed this negro question very fully; he asked me to draft an order on the subject, in accordance with my own views, that would meet the pressing necessities of the case, and I did so. We went over this order, No. 15, of January 16, 1865, very carefully. The secretary made some verbal modifications, when it was approved by him in all its details, I published it, and it went into operation at once. It provided fully for the enlistment of colored troops, and gave the freedmen certain possessory rights to land, which afterward became matters of judicial inquiry and decision. Of course, the military authorities at that day, when war prevailed, had a perfect right to grant the possession of any vacant land to which they could extend military protection, but we did not undertake to give a fee-simple title; and all that was designed by these special field orders was to make temporary provisions for the freedmen and their families during the rest of the war, or until Congress should take action in the premises. All that I now propose to assert is, that Mr. Stanton, Secretary of War, saw these orders in the rough, and approved every paragraph thereof, before they were made public:

[Special Field Orders, No. 15.]

HEADQUARTERS MILITARY DIVISION OF THE MISSISSIPPI,
IN THE FIELD, NEAR SAVANNAH, GEORGIA, January 16, 1865.

1. The islands from Charleston south, the abandoned rice-fields along the rivers for thirty miles back from the sea, and the country bordering the St. John's River, Florida, are reserved and set apart for the settlement of the negroes now made free by the acts of war and the proclamation of the President of the United States.

2. At Beaufort, Hilton Head, Savannah, Fernandina, St. Augustine, and Jacksonville, the blacks may remain in their chosen or accustomed vocations; but on the islands, and in the settlements hereafter to be established, no white person whatever, unless military officers and soldiers detailed for duty, will be permitted to reside; and the sole and exclusive management of affairs will be left to the freed people themselves, subject only to the United States military authority, and the acts of Congress. By the laws of war, and orders of the President of the United States, the negro is free, and must be dealt with as such. He cannot be subjected to conscription, or forced military service, save by the written orders of the highest military authority of the department, under such regulations as the President or Congress may prescribe. Domestic servants, blacksmiths, carpenters, and other mechanics, will be free to select their own work and residence, but the young and able-bodied negroes must be encouraged to enlist as soldiers in the service of the United States, to contribute their share toward maintaining their own freedom, and securing their rights as citizens of the United States.

Negroes so enlisted will be organized into companies, battalions, and regiments, under the orders of the United States military authorities, and will be paid, fed, and clothed; according to law. The bounties paid on enlistment may, with the consent of the recruit, go to assist his family and settlement in procuring agricultural implements, seed, tools, boots, clothing, and other articles necessary for their livelihood.

8. Whenever three respectable negroes, heads of families, shall desire to settle on land, and shall have selected for that purpose an island or a locality clearly defined within the limits above designated, the Inspector of Settlements and Plantations will himself, or, by such subordinate officer as he may appoint, give them a license to settle such island or district, and afford them such assistance as he can to enable them to establish a peaceable agricultural settlement. The three parties named will subdivide the land, under the supervision of the inspector, among themselves, and such others as may choose to settle near them, so that each family shall have a plot of not more than forty acres of tillable ground, and, when it borders on some water-channel, with not more than eight hundred feet water-front, in the possession of which land the military authorities will afford them protection until such time as they can protect themselves, or until Congress shall regulate their title. The quartermaster may, on the requisition of the Inspector of Settlements and Plantations, place at the disposal of the inspector one or more of the captured steamers to ply between the settlements and one or more of the commercial points heretofore named, in order to afford the settlers the opportunity to supply their necessary wants, and to sell the products of their land and labor.

4. Whenever a negro has enlisted in the military service of the United States, he may locate his family in any one of the settlements at pleasure, and acquire a homestead, and all other rights and privileges of a settler, as though present in person. In like manner, negroes may settle their families and engage on board the gunboats, or in fishing, or in the navigation of the inland waters, without losing any claim to land or other advantages derived from this system. But no one, unless an actual settler as above defined, or unless absent on Government service, will be entitled to claim any right to land or property in any settlement by virtue of these orders.

5. In order to carry out this system of settlement, a general officer will be detailed as Inspector of Settlements and Plantations, whose duty it shall be to visit the settlements, to regulate their police and general arrangement, and who will furnish personally to each head of a family, subject to the approval of the President of the United States, a possessory title in writing, giving as near as possible the description of boundaries; and who shall adjust all claims or conflicts that may arise under the same, subject to the like approval, treating such titles altogether as possessory. The same general officer will also be charged with the enlistment and organization of the negro recruits, and protecting their interests while absent from their settlements; and will be governed by the rules and regulations prescribed by the War Department for such purposes.

6. Brigadier-General R. Saxton is hereby appointed Inspector of Settlements and Plantations, and will at once enter on the performance of his duties. No change is intended or desired in the settlement now on Beaufort Island, nor will any rights to property heretofore acquired be affected thereby.

By order of Major-General W. T. Sherman, L. M. DAYTON, Assistant Adjutant-General.

I saw a good deal of the secretary socially, during the time of his visit to Savannah. He kept his quarters on the revenue-cutter with Simeon Draper, Esq., which cutter lay at a wharf in the river, but he came very often to my quarters at Mr. Green's house. Though appearing robust and strong, he complained a good deal of internal pains, which he said threatened his life, and would compel him soon to quit public office. He professed to have come from Washington purposely for rest and recreation, and he spoke unreservedly of the bickerings and jealousies at the national capital; of the interminable quarrels of the State Governors about their quotas, and more particularly of the financial troubles that threatened the very existence of the Government itself. He said that the price of every thing had so risen in comparison with the depreciated money, that there was danger of national bankruptcy, and he appealed to me, as a soldier and patriot, to hurry up matters so as to bring the war to a close.

He left for Port Royal about the 15th of January, and promised to go North without delay, so as to hurry back to me the supplies I had called for, as indispensable for the prosecution of the next stage of the campaign. I was quite impatient to get off myself, for a city-life had become dull and tame, and we were all anxious to get into the pine-woods again, free from the importunities of rebel women asking for protection, and of the civilians from the North who were coming to Savannah for cotton and all sorts of profit.

On the 18th of January General Slocum was ordered to turn over the city of Savannah to General J. G. Foster, commanding the Department of the South, who proposed to retain his own headquarters at Hilton Head, and to occupy Savannah by General Grovers division of the Nineteenth Corps, just arrived from James River; and on the next day, viz., January 19th, I made the first general orders for the move.

These were substantially to group the right wing of the army at Pocotaligo, already held by the Seventeenth Corps, and the left wing and cavalry at or near Robertsville, in South Carolina. The army remained substantially the same as during the march from Atlanta, with the exception of a few changes in the commanders of brigades and divisions, the addition of some men who had joined from furlough, and the loss of others from the expiration of their term of service. My own personal staff remained the same, with the exception that General W. F. Barry had rejoined us at Savannah, perfectly recovered from his attack of erysipelas, and continued with us to the end of the war. Generals Easton and Beckwith remained at Savannah, in charge of their respective depots, with orders to follow and meet us by sea with supplies when we should reach the coast at Wilmington or Newbern, North Carolina.

Of course, I gave out with some ostentation, especially among the rebels, that we were going to Charleston or Augusta; but I had long before made up my mind to waste no time on either, further than to play off on their fears, thus to retain for their protection a force of the enemy which would otherwise concentrate in our front, and make the passage of some of the great rivers that crossed our route more difficult and bloody.

Having accomplished all that seemed necessary, on the 21st of January, with my entire headquarters, officers, clerks, orderlies, etc., with wagons and horses, I embarked in a steamer for Beaufort, South Carolina, touching at Hilton Head, to see General Foster. The weather was rainy and bad, but we reached Beaufort safely on the 23d, and found some of General Blair's troops there. The pink of his corps (Seventeenth) was, however, up on the railroad about Pocotaligo, near the head of Broad River, to which their supplies were carried from Hilton Head by steamboats. General Hatch's division (of General Foster's command) was still at Coosawhatchie or Tullafinny, where the Charleston & Savannah Railroad crosses the river of that name. All the country between Beaufort and Pocotaligo was low alluvial land, cut up by an infinite number of salt-water sloughs and freshwater creeks, easily susceptible of defense by a small force; and why the enemy had allowed us to make a lodgment at Pocotaligo so easily I did not understand, unless it resulted from fear or ignorance. It seemed to me then that the terrible energy they had displayed in the earlier stages of the war was beginning to yield to the slower but more certain industry and discipline of our Northern men. It was to me manifest that the soldiers and people of the South entertained an undue fear of our Western men, and, like children, they had invented such ghostlike stories of our prowess in Georgia, that they were scared by their own inventions. Still, this was a power, and I intended to utilize it. Somehow, our men had got the idea that South Carolina was the cause of all our troubles; her people were the first to fire on Fort Sumter, had been in a great hurry to precipitate the country into civil war; and therefore on them should fall the scourge of war in its worst form. Taunting messages had also come to us, when in Georgia, to the effect that, when we should reach South Carolina, we would find a people less passive, who would fight us to the bitter end, daring us to come over, etc.; so that I saw and felt that we would not be able longer to restrain our men as we had done in Georgia.

Personally I had many friends in Charleston, to whom I would gladly have extended protection and mercy, but they were beyond my personal reach, and I would not restrain the army lest its vigor and energy should be impaired; and I had every reason to expect bold and strong resistance at the many broad and deep rivers that lay across our path.

General Foster's Department of the South had been enlarged to embrace the coast of North Carolina, so that the few troops serving there, under the command of General Innis N. Palmer, at Newbern, became subject to my command. General A. H. Terry held Fort Fisher, and a rumor came that he had taken the city of Wilmington; but this was premature. He had about eight thousand men. General Schofield was also known to be en route from Nashville for North Carolina, with the entire Twenty-third Corps, so that I had every reason to be satisfied that I would receive additional strength as we progressed northward, and before I should need it.

General W. J. Hardee commanded the Confederate forces in Charleston, with the Salkiehatchie River as his line of defense. It was also known that General Beauregard had come from the direction of Tennessee, and had assumed the general command of all the troops designed to resist our progress.

The heavy winter rains had begun early in January, rendered the roads execrable, and the Savannah River became so swollen that it filled its many channels, overflowing the vast extent of rice-fields that lay on the east bank. This flood delayed our departure two weeks; for it swept away our pontoon-bridge at Savannah, and came near drowning John E. Smith's division of the Fifteenth Corps, with several heavy trains of wagons that were en route from Savannah to Pocotaligo by the old causeway.

General Slocum had already ferried two of his divisions across the river, when Sister's Ferry, about forty miles above Savannah, was selected for the passage of the rest of his wing and of Kilpatrick's cavalry. The troops were in motion for that point before I quitted Savannah, and Captain S. B. Luce, United States Navy, had reported to me with a gunboat (the Pontiac) and a couple of transports, which I requested him to use in protecting Sister's Ferry during the passage of Slocum's wing, and to facilitate the passage of the troops all he could. The utmost activity prevailed at all points, but it was manifest we could not get off much before the 1st day of February; so I determined to go in person to Pocotaligo, and there act as though we were bound for Charleston. On the 24th of January I started from Beaufort with a part of my staff, leaving the rest to follow at leisure, rode across the island to a pontoon-bridge that spanned the channel between it and the main-land, and thence rode by Garden's Corners to a plantation not far from Pocotaligo, occupied by General Blair. There we found a house, with a majestic avenue of live-oaks, whose limbs had been cut away by the troops for firewood, and desolation marked one of those splendid South Carolina estates where the proprietors formerly had dispensed a hospitality that distinguished the old regime of that proud State. I slept on the floor of the house, but the night was so bitter cold that I got up by the fire several times, and when it burned low I rekindled it with an old mantel-clock and the wreck of a bedstead which stood in a corner of the room--the only act of vandalism that I recall done by myself personally during the war.

The next morning I rode to Pocotaligo, and thence reconnoitred our entire line down to Coosawhatchie. Pocotaligo Fort was on low, alluvial ground, and near it began the sandy pine-land which connected with the firm ground extending inland, constituting the chief reason for its capture at the very first stage of the campaign. Hatch's division was ordered to that point from Coosawhatchie, and the whole of Howard's right wing was brought near by, ready to start by the 1st of February. I also reconnoitred the point of the Salkiehatchie River, where the Charleston Railroad crossed it, found the bridge protected by a rebel battery on the farther side, and could see a few men about it; but the stream itself was absolutely impassable, for the whole bottom was overflowed by its swollen waters to the breadth of a full mile. Nevertheless, Force's and Mower's divisions of the Seventeenth Corps were kept active, seemingly with the intention to cross over in the direction of Charleston, and thus to keep up the delusion that that city was our immediate "objective." Meantime, I had reports from General Slocum of the terrible difficulties he had encountered about Sister's Ferry, where the Savannah River was reported nearly three miles wide, and it seemed for a time almost impossible for him to span it at all with his frail pontoons. About this time (January 25th), the weather cleared away bright and cold, and I inferred that the river would soon run down, and enable Slocum to pass the river before February 1st. One of the divisions of the Fifteenth Corps (Corse's) had also been cut off by the loss of the pontoon-bridge at Savannah, so that General Slocum had with him, not only his own two corps, but Corse's division and Kilpatrick's cavalry, without which it was not prudent for me to inaugurate the campaign. We therefore rested quietly about Pocotaligo, collecting stores and making final preparations, until the 1st of February, when I learned that the cavalry and two divisions of the Twentieth Corps were fairly across the river, and then gave the necessary orders for the march northward.

Before closing this chapter, I will add a few original letters that bear directly on the subject, and tend to illustrate it:

HEADQUARTERS ARMIES OF THE UNITED STATES
WASHINGTON, D. C. January 21, 1866.

Major-General W. T. SHERMAN, commanding Military Division of the Mississippi.

GENERAL: Your letters brought by General Barnard were received at City Point, and read with interest. Not having them with me, however, I cannot say that in this I will be able to satisfy you on all points of recommendation. As I arrived here at 1 p.m., and must leave at 6 p.m., having in the mean time spent over three hours with the secretary and General Halleck, I must be brief. Before your last request to have Thomas make a campaign into the heart of Alabama, I had ordered Schofield to Annapolis, Maryland, with his corps. The advance (six thousand) will reach the seaboard by the 23d, the remainder following as rapidly as railroad transportation can be procured from Cincinnati. The corps numbers over twenty-one thousand men.

Thomas is still left with a sufficient force, surplus to go to Selma under an energetic leader. He has been telegraphed to, to know whether he could go, and, if so, by which of several routes he would select. No reply is yet received. Canby has been ordered to set offensively from the seacoast to the interior, toward Montgomery and Selma. Thomas's forces will move from the north at an early day, or some of his troops will be sent to Canby. Without further reenforcement Canby will have a moving column of twenty thousand men.

Fort Fisher, you are aware, has been captured. We have a force there of eight thousand effective. At Newbern about half the number. It is rumored, through deserters, that Wilmington also has fallen. I am inclined to believe the rumor, because on the 17th we knew the enemy were blowing up their works about Fort Caswell, and that on the 18th Terry moved on Wilmington.

If Wilmington is captured, Schofield will go there. If not, he will be sent to Newbern. In either event, all the surplus forces at the two points will move to the interior, toward Goldsboro', in cooperation with your movements. From either point, railroad communications can be run out, there being here abundance of rolling-stock suited to the gauge of those roads.

There have been about sixteen thousand men sent from Lee's army south. Of these, you will have fourteen thousand against you, if Wilmington is not held by the enemy, casualties at Fort Fisher having overtaken about two thousand.

All other troops are subject to your orders as you come in communication with them. They will be so instructed. From about Richmond I will watch Lee closely, and if he detaches many men, or attempts to evacuate, will pitch in. In the meantime, should you be brought to a halt anywhere, I can send two corps of thirty thousand effective men to your support, from the troops about Richmond.

To resume: Canby is ordered to operate to the interior from the Gulf. A. J. Smith may go from the north, but I think it doubtful. A force of twenty-eight or thirty thousand will cooperate with you from Newbern or Wilmington, or both. You can call for reenforcements.

This will be handed you by Captain Hudson, of my staff, who will return with any message you may have for me. If there is any thing I can do for you in the way of having supplies on shipboard, at any point on the seacoast, ready for you, let me know it.

Yours truly,

U. S. GRANT, Lieutenant-General.

HEADQUARTERS MILITARY DIVISION OF THE MISSISSIPPI,
IN THE FIELD, POCOTALIGO, SOUTH CAROLINA, January 29, 1885.

Lieutenant-General U. S. GRANT, City Point, Virginia.

DEAR GENERAL: Captain Hudson has this moment arrived with your letter of January 21st, which I have read with interest.

The capture of Fort Fisher has a most important bearing on my campaign, and I rejoice in it for many reasons, because of its intrinsic importance, and because it gives me another point of security on the seaboard. I hope General Terry will follow it up by the capture of Wilmington, although I do not look for it, from Admiral Porter's dispatch to me. I rejoice that Terry was not a West-Pointer, that he belonged to your army, and that he had the same troops with which Butler feared to make the attempt.

Admiral Dahlgren, whose fleet is reenforced by some more ironclads, wants to make an assault a la Fisher on Fort Moultrie, but I withhold my consent, for the reason that the capture of all Sullivan's Island is not conclusive as to Charleston; the capture of James Island would be, but all pronounce that impossible at this time. Therefore, I am moving (as hitherto designed) for the railroad west of Branchville, then will swing across to Orangeburg, which will interpose my army between Charleston and the interior. Contemporaneous with this, Foster will demonstrate up the Edisto, and afterward make a lodgment at Bull's Bay, and occupy the common road which leads from Mount Pleasant toward Georgetown. When I get to Columbia, I think I shall move straight for Goldsboro', via Fayetteville. By this circuit I cut all roads, and devastate the land; and the forces along the coast, commanded by Foster, will follow my movement, taking any thing the enemy lets go, or so occupy his attention that he cannot detach all his forces against me. I feel sure of getting Wilmington, and may be Charleston, and being at Goldsboro', with its railroads finished back to Morehead City and Wilmington, I can easily take Raleigh, when it seems that Lee must come out. If Schofield comes to Beaufort, he should be pushed out to Kinston, on the Neuse, and may be Goldsboro' (or, rather, a point on the Wilmington road, south of Goldsboro'). It is not necessary to storm Goldsboro', because it is in a distant region, of no importance in itself, and, if its garrison is forced to draw supplies from its north, it, will be eating up the same stores on which Lee depends for his command.

I have no doubt Hood will bring his army to Augusta. Canby and Thomas should penetrate Alabama as far as possible, to keep employed at least a part of Hood's army; or, what would accomplish the same thing, Thomas might reoccupy the railroad from Chattanooga forward to the Etowah, viz., Rome, Kingston, and Allatoona, thereby threatening Georgia. I know that the Georgia troops are disaffected. At Savannah I met delegates from several counties of the southwest, who manifested a decidedly hostile spirit to the Confederate cause. I nursed the feeling as far as possible, and instructed Grower to keep it up.

My left wing must now be at Sister's Ferry, crossing the Savannah River to the east bank. Slocum has orders to be at Robertsville to-morrow, prepared to move on Barnwell. Howard is here, all ready to start for the Augusta Railroad at Midway.

We find the enemy on the east aide of the Salkiehatchie, and cavalry in our front; but all give ground on our approach, and seem to be merely watching us. If we start on Tuesday, in one week we shall be near Orangeburg, having broken up the Augusta road from the Edisto westward twenty or twenty-five miles. I will be sure that every rail is twisted. Should we encounter too much opposition near Orangeburg, then I will for a time neglect that branch, and rapidly move on Columbia, and fill up the triangle formed by the Congaree and Wateree (tributaries of the Santee), breaking up that great centre of the Carolina roads. Up to that point I feel full confidence, but from there may have to manoeuvre some, and will be guided by the questions of weather and supplies.

106

You remember we had fine weather last February for our Meridian trip, and my memory of the weather at Charleston is, that February is usually a fine month. Before the March storms come we should be within striking distance of the coast. The months of April and May will be the best for operations from Goldsboro' to Raleigh and the Roanoke. You may rest assured that I will keep my troops well in hand, and, if I get worsted, will aim to make the enemy pay so dearly that you will have less to do. I know that this trip is necessary; it must be made sooner or later; I am on time, and in the right position for it. My army is large enough for the purpose, and I ask no reinforcement, but simply wish the utmost activity to be kept up at all other points, so that concentration against me may not be universal.

I suspect that Jeff. Davis will move heaven and earth to catch me, for success to this column is fatal to his dream of empire. Richmond is not more vital to his cause than Columbia and the heart of South Carolina.

If Thomas will not move on Selma, order him to occupy Rome, Kingston, and Allatoona, and again threaten Georgia in the direction of Athena.

I think the "poor white trash" of the South are falling out of their ranks by sickness, desertion, and every available means; but there is a large class of vindictive Southerners who will fight to the last. The squabbles in Richmond, the howls in Charleston, and the disintegration elsewhere, are all good omens for us; we must not relax one iota, but, on the contrary, pile up our efforts: I world, ere this, have been off, but we had terrific rains, which caught us in motion, and nearly drowned some of the troops in the rice-fields of the Savannah, swept away our causeway (which had been carefully corduroyed), and made the swamps hereabout mere lakes of slimy mud. The weather is now good, and I have the army on terra firma. Supplies, too, came for a long time by daily driblets instead of in bulk; this is now all remedied, and I hope to start on Tuesday.

I will issue instructions to General Foster, based on the reenforcements of North Carolina; but if Schofield comes, you had better relieve Foster, who cannot take the field, and needs an operation on his leg. Let Schofield take command, with his headquarters at Beaufort, North Carolina, and with orders to secure Goldsboro' (with its railroad communication back to Beaufort and Wilmington). If Lee lets us get that position, he is gone up.

I will start with my Atlanta army (sixty thousand), supplied as before, depending on the country for all food in excess of thirty days. I will have less cattle on the hoof, but I hear of hogs, cows, and calves, in Barnwell and the Colombia districts. Even here we have found some forage. Of course, the enemy will carry off and destroy some forage, but I will burn the houses where the people burn their forage, and they will get tired of it.

I must risk Hood, and trust to you to hold Lee or be on his heels if he comes south. I observe that the enemy has some respect for my name, for they gave up Pocotaligo without a fight when they heard that the attacking force belonged to my army. I will try and keep up that feeling, which is a real power. With respect, your friend,

W. T. SHERMAN, Major-general commanding.

P. S.--I leave my chief-quartermaster and commissary behind to follow coastwise.
W. T. S.

[Dispatch No. 6.]

FLAG-STEAMER PHILADELPHIA
SAVANNAH RIVER, January 4, 1865.

HON. GIDEON WELLS, Secretary of the Navy.

SIR: I have already apprised the Department that the army of General Sherman occupied the city of Savannah on the 21st of December.

The rebel army, hardly respectable in numbers or condition, escaped by crossing the river and taking the Union Causeway toward the railroad.

I have walked about the city several times, and can affirm that its tranquillity is undisturbed. The Union soldiers who are stationed within its limits are as orderly as if they were in New York or Boston.... One effect of the march of General Sherman through Georgia has been to satisfy the people that their credulity has been imposed upon by the lying assertions of the rebel Government, affirming the inability of the United States Government to withstand the armies of rebeldom. They have seen the old flag of the United States carried by its victorious legions through their State, almost unopposed, and placed in their principal city without a *blow.*

Since the occupation of the city General Sherman has been occupied in making arrangements for its security after he leaves it for the march that he meditates. My attention has been directed to such measures of cooperation as the number and quality of my force permit.

On the 2d I arrived here from Charleston, whither, as I stated in my dispatch of the 29th of December, I had gone in consequence of information from the senior officer there that the rebels contemplated issuing from the harbor, and his request for my presence. Having placed a force there of seven monitors, sufficient to meet each an emergency, and not perceiving any sign of the expected raid, I returned to Savannah, to keep in communication with General Sherman and be ready to render any assistance that might be desired. General Sherman has fully informed me of his plans, and, so far as my means permit, they shall not lack assistance by water.

On the 3d the transfer of the right wing to Beaufort was began, and the only suitable vessel I had at hand (the Harvest Moon) was sent to Thunderbolt to receive the first embarkation. This took place about 3 p.m., and was witnessed by General Sherman and General Bernard (United States Engineers) and myself. The Pontiac is ordered around to assist, and the army transports also followed the first move by the Harvest Moon.

I could not help remarking the unbroken silence that prevailed in the large array of troops; not a voice was to be heard, as they gathered in masses on the bluff to look at the vessels. The notes of a solitary bugle alone came from their midst.

General Barnard made a brief visit to one of the rebel works (Cansten's Bluff) that dominated this water-course--the best approach of the kind to Savannah.

I am collecting data that will fully exhibit to the Department the powerful character of the defenses of the city and its approaches. General Sherman will not retain the extended limits they embrace, but will contract the line very much.

General Foster still holds the position near the Tullifinny. With his concurrence I have detached the fleet brigade, and the men belonging to it have returned to their vessels. The excellent service performed by this detachment has fully realized my wishes, and exemplified the efficiency of the organization--infantry and light artillery handled as skirmishers. The howitzers were always landed as quickly as the men, and were brought into action before the light pieces of the land-service could be got ashore.

I regret very much that the reduced complements of the vessels prevent me from maintaining the force in constant organization. With three hundred more marines and five hundred seamen I could frequently operate to great advantage, at the present time, when the attention of the rebels is so engrossed by General Sherman.

It is said that they have a force at Hardeeville, the pickets of which were retained on the Union Causeway until a few days since, when some of our troops crossed the river and pushed them back. Concurrently with this, I caused the Sonoma to anchor so as to sweep the ground in the direction of the causeway.

The transfer of the right-wing (thirty thousand men) to Beaufort will so imperil the rebel force at Hardeeville that it will be cut off or dispersed, if not moved in season.

Meanwhile I will send the Dai-Ching to St. Helena, to meet any want that may arise in that quarter, while the Mingo and Pontiac will be ready to act from Broad River.

The general route of the army will be northward; but the exact direction must be decided more or less by circumstances which it may not be possible to foresee....

My cooperation will be confined to assistance in attacking Charleston, or in establishing communication at Georgetown, in case the army pushes on without attacking Charleston, and time alone will show which of these will eventuate.

The weather of the winter first, and the condition of the ground in spring, would permit little advantage to be derived from the presence of the army at Richmond until the middle of May. So that General Sherman has no reason to move in haste, but can choose such objects as he prefers, and take as much time as their attainment may demand. The Department will learn the objects in view of General Sherman more precisely from a letter addressed by him to General Halleck, which he read to me a few days since.

I have the honor to be, very respectfully, your obedient servant,

J. A. DAHLGREN,
Rear-Admiral, commanding South-Atlantic Blockading-Squadron.

Major-General J. G. FOSTER, commanding Department of the South.

GENERAL: I have just received dispatches from General Grant, stating that Schofield's corps (the Twenty-third), twenty-one thousand strong, is ordered east from Tennessee, and will be sent to Beaufort, North Carolina. That is well; I want that force to secure a point on the railroad about Goldsboro', and then to build the railroad out to that point. If Goldsboro' be too strong to carry by a rapid movement, then a point near the Neuse, south of Goldsboro', will answer, but the bridge and position about Kinston, should be held and fortified strong. The movement should be masked by the troops already at Newbern. Please notify General Palmer that these troops are coming, and to be prepared to receive them. Major-General Schofield will command in person, and is admirably adapted for the work. If it is possible, I want him to secure Goldsboro', with the railroad back to Morehead City and Wilmington. As soon as General Schofield reaches Fort Macon, have him to meet some one of your staff, to explain in full the details of the situation of affairs with me; and you can give him the chief command of all troops at Cape Fear and in North Carolina. If he finds the enemy has all turned south against me, he need not follow, but turn his attention against Raleigh; if he can secure Goldsboro' and Wilmington, it will be as much as I expect before I have passed the Santee. Send him all detachments of men that have come to join my army. They can be so organized and officered as to be efficient, for they are nearly all old soldiers who have been detached or on furlough. Until I pass the Santee, you can better use these detachments at Bull's Bay, Georgetown, etc.

I will instruct General McCallum, of the Railroad Department, to take his men up to Beaufort, North Carolina, and employ them on the road out. I do not know that he can use them on any road here. I did instruct him, while awaiting information from North Carolina, to have them build a good trestle-bridge across Port Royal ferry; but I now suppose the pontoon-bridge will do. If you move the pontoons, be sure to make a good road out to Garden's Corners, and mark it with sign-boards--obstructing the old road, so that, should I send back any detachments, they would not be misled.

I prefer that Hatch's force should not be materially weakened until I am near Columbia, when you may be governed by the situation of affairs about Charleston. If you can break the railroad between this and Charleston, then this force could be reduced.

I am, with respect, etc.,

W. T. SHERMAN, Major-General commanding.

Hon. EDWIN M. STANTON, Secretary of War, Washington, D. C.

SIR: When you left Savannah a few days ago, you forgot the map which General Geary had prepared for you, showing the route by which his division entered the city of Savannah, being the first troops to occupy that city. I now send it to you.

I avail myself of the opportunity also to inclose you copies of all my official orders touching trade and intercourse with the people of Georgia, as well as for the establishment of the negro settlements.

Delegations of the people of Georgia continue to come in, and I am satisfied that, by judicious handling and by a little respect shown to their prejudices, we can create a schism in Jeff. Davis's dominions. All that I have conversed with realize the truth that slavery as an institution is defunct, and the only questions that remain are what disposition shall be made of the negroes themselves. I confess myself unable to offer a complete solution for these questions, and prefer to leave it to the slower operations of time. We have given the initiative, and can afford to await the working of the experiment.

As to trade-matters, I also think it is to our interest to keep the Southern people somewhat dependent on the articles of commerce to which they have hitherto been accustomed. General Grover is now here, and will, I think, be able to handle this matter judiciously, and may gradually relax, and invite cotton to come in in large quantities. But at first we should manifest no undue anxiety on that score; for the rebels would at once make use of it as a power against us. We should assume, a tone of perfect contempt for cotton and every thing else in comparison with the great object of the war--the restoration of the Union, with all its rights and power. It the rebels burn cotton as a war measure, they simply play into our hands by taking away the only product of value they have to exchange in foreign ports for war-ships and munitions. By such a course, also, they alienate the feelings of a large class of small farmers who look to their little parcels of cotton to exchange for food and clothing for their families. I hope the Government will not manifest too much anxiety to obtain cotton in large quantities, and especially that the President will not indorse the contracts for the purchase of large quantities of cotton. Several contracts, involving from six to ten thousand bales, indorsed by Mr. Lincoln, have been shown me, but *were not in such a form as to amount to an order to compel me to facilitate their execution.*

As to Treasury agents, and agents to take charge of confiscated and abandoned property, whose salaries depend on their fees, I can only say that, as a general rule, they are mischievous and disturbing elements to a military government, and it is almost impossible for us to study the law and regulations so as to understand fully their powers and duties. I rather think the Quartermaster's Department of the army could better fulfill all their duties and accomplish all that is aimed at by the law. Yet on this subject I will leave Generals Foster and Grover to do the best they can.

I am, with great respect, your obedient servant,

W. T. SHERMAN, Major-General commanding.

*HEADQUARTERS MILITARY DIVISION OF THE MISSISSIPPI,
IN THE FIELD, POCOTALIGO, SOUTH CAROLINA, January 2, 1865.*

Hon. EDWIN M. STANTON, Secretary of War, Washington, D. C.

SIR: I have just received from Lieutenant-General Grant a copy of that part of your telegram to him of December 26th relating to cotton, a copy of which has been immediately furnished to General Easton, chief-quartermaster, who will be strictly governed by it.

I had already been approached by all the consuls and half the people of Savannah on this cotton question, and my invariable answer was that all the cotton in Savannah was prize of war, belonged to the United States, and nobody should recover a bale of it with my consent; that, as cotton had been one of the chief causes of this war, it should help to pay its expenses; that all cotton became tainted with treason from the hour the first act of hostility was committed against the United States some time in December, 1860; and that no bill of sale subsequent to that date could convey title.

My orders were that an officer of the Quartermaster's Department, United States Army, might furnish the holder, agent, or attorney, a mere certificate of the fact of seizure, with description of the bales' marks, etc., the cotton then to be turned over to the agent of the Treasury Department, to be shipped to New York for sale. But, since the receipt of your dispatch, I have ordered General Easton to make the shipment himself to the quartermaster at New York, where you can dispose of it at pleasure. I do not think the Treasury Department ought to bother itself with the prizes or captures of war.

Mr. Barclay, former consul at New York, representing Mr. Molyneux, former consul here, but absent a long time, called on me with reference to cotton claimed by English subjects. He seemed amazed when I told him I should pay no respect to consular certificates, that in no event would I treat an English subject with more favor than one of our own deluded citizens, and that for my part I was unwilling to fight for cotton for the benefit of Englishmen openly engaged in smuggling arms and instruments of war to kill us; that, on the contrary, it would afford me great satisfaction to conduct my army to Nassau, and wipe out that nest of pirates. I explained to him, however, that I was not a diplomatic agent of the General Government of the United States, but that my opinion, so frankly expressed, was that of a soldier, which it would be well for him to heed. It appeared, also, that he owned a plantation on the line of investment of Savannah, which, of course, was pillaged, and for which he expected me to give some certificate entitling him to indemnification, which I declined emphatically.

I have adopted in Savannah rules concerning property--severe but just--founded upon the laws of nations and the practice of civilized governments, and am clearly of opinion that we should claim all the belligerent rights over conquered countries, that the people may realize the truth that war is no child's play.

I embrace in this a copy of a letter, dated December 31, 1864, in answer to one from Solomon Cohen (a rich lawyer) to General Blair, his personal friend, as follows:

Major-General F. P. BLAIR, commanding Seventeenth Army Corps.

GENERAL: Your note, inclosing Mr. Cohen's of this date, is received, and I answer frankly through you his inquiries.

1. No one can practise law as an attorney in the United States without acknowledging the supremacy of our Government. If I am not in error, an attorney is as much an officer of the court as the clerk, and it would be a novel thing in a government to have a court to administer law which denied the supremacy of the government itself.

2. No one will be allowed the privileges of a merchant, or, rather, to trade is a privilege which no one should seek of the Government

110

without in like manner acknowledging its supremacy.

3. If Mr. Cohen remains in Savannah as a denizen, his property, real and personal, will not be disturbed unless its temporary use be necessary for the military authorities of the city. The title to property will not be disturbed in any event, until adjudicated by the courts of the United States.

4. If Mr. Cohen leaves Savannah under my Special Order No. 148, it is a public acknowledgment that he "adheres to the enemies of the United States," and all his property becomes forfeited to the United States. But, as a matter of favor, he will be allowed to carry with him clothing and furniture for the use of himself, his family, and servants, and will be transported within the enemy's lines, but not by way of Port Royal.

These rules will apply to all parties, and from them no exception will be made.

I have the honor to be, general, your obedient servant,

W. T. SHERMAN, Major-General.

This letter was in answer to specific inquiries; it is clear, and covers all the points, and, should I leave before my orders are executed, I will endeavor to impress upon my successor, General Foster, their wisdom and propriety.

I hope the course I have taken in these matters will meet your approbation, and that the President will not refund to parties claiming cotton or other property, without the strongest evidence of loyalty and friendship on the part of the claimant, or unless some other positive end is to be gained.

I am, with great respect, your obedient servant,

W. T. SHERMAN, Major-General commanding.

CHAPTER XXIII.
CAMPAIGN OF THE CAROLINAS.

FEBRUARY AND MARCH, 1865.

On the 1st day of February, as before explained, the army designed for the active campaign from Savannah northward was composed of two wings, commanded respectively by Major-Generals Howard and Slocum, and was substantially the same that had marched from Atlanta to Savannah. The same general orders were in force, and this campaign may properly be classed as a continuance of the former.

The right wing, less Corse's division, Fifteenth Corps, was grouped at or near Pocotaligo, South Carolina, with its wagons filled with food, ammunition, and forage, all ready to start, and only waiting for the left wing, which was detained by the flood in the Savannah River. It was composed as follows:

Fifteenth Corps, Major-General JOHN A. LOGAN.

First Division, Brigadier-General Charles R. Woods; Second Division, Major-General W. B. Hazen; Third Division, Brigadier-General John E. Smith; Fourth Division, Brigadier-General John M. Corse. Artillery brigade, eighteen guns, Lieutenant-Colonel W. H. Ross, First Michigan Artillery.

Seventeenth. Corps, Major-General FRANK P. BLAIR, JR.

First Division, Major-General Joseph A. Mower; Second Division, Brigadier-General M. F. Force; Fourth Division, Brigadier-General Giles A. Smith. Artillery brigade, fourteen guns, Major A. C. Waterhouse, First Illinois Artillery.

The left wing, with Corse's division and Kilpatrick's cavalry, was at and near Sister's Ferry, forty miles above the city of Savannah, engaged in crossing the river, then much swollen. It was composed as follows:

Fourteenth Corps, Major-General JEFF. C. DAVIS.

111

First Division, Brigadier-General W. P. Carlin; Second Division, Brigadier-General John D. Morgan; Third Division, Brigadier-General A. Baird. Artillery brigade, sixteen guns, Major Charles Houghtaling, First Illinois Artillery.

Twentieth Corps, Brigadier-General A. S. WILLIAMS.

First Division, Brigadier-General N. I. Jackson; Second Division, Brigadier-General J. W. Geary; Third Division, Brigadier-General W. T. Ward. Artillery brigade, Sixteen gnus, Major J. A. Reynolds, First New York Artillery.

Cavalry Division, Brigadier-General JUDSON KILPATRICK.

First Brigade, Colonel T. J. Jordan, Ninth Pennsylvania Cavalry; Second Brigade, Colonel S. D. Atkins, Ninety-second Illinois Vol.; Third Brigade, Colonel George E. Spencer, First Alabama Cavalry. One battery of four guns.

The actual strength of the army, as given in the following official tabular statements, was at the time sixty thousand and seventy-nine men, and sixty-eight guns. The trains were made up of about twenty-five hundred wagons, with six mules to each wagon, and about six hundred ambulances, with two horses each. The contents of the wagons embraced an ample supply of ammunition for a great battle; forage for about seven days, and provisions for twenty days, mostly of bread, sugar, coffee, and salt, depending largely for fresh meat on beeves driven on the hoof and such cattle, hogs, and poultry, as we expected to gather along our line of march.

RECAPITULATION—CAMPAIGN OF THE CAROLINAS.

Febru ary 1.	Ma rch 1.	A pril 1.	A pril 10
60,07 9	57, 676	81 ,150	8 8,948

The enemy occupied the cities of Charleston and Augusta, with garrisons capable of making a respectable if not successful defense, but utterly unable to meet our veteran columns in the open field. To resist or delay our progress north, General Wheeler had his division of cavalry (reduced to the size of a brigade by his hard and persistent fighting ever since the beginning of the Atlanta campaign), and General Wade Hampton had been dispatched from the Army of Virginia to his native State of South Carolina, with a great flourish of trumpets, and extraordinary powers to raise men, money, and horses, with which "to stay the progress of the invader," and "to punish us for our insolent attempt to invade the glorious State of South Carolina!" He was supposed at the time to have, at and near Columbia, two small divisions of cavalry commanded by himself and General Butler.

Of course, I had a species of contempt for these scattered and inconsiderable forces, knew that they could hardly delay us an hour; and the only serious question that occurred to me was, would General Lee sit down in Richmond (besieged by General Grant), and permit us, almost unopposed, to pass through the States of South and North Carolina, cutting off and consuming the very supplies on which he depended to feed his army in Virginia, or would he make an effort to escape from General Grant, and endeavor to catch us inland somewhere between Columbia and Raleigh? I knew full well at the time that the broken fragments of Hood's army (which had escaped from Tennessee) were being hurried rapidly across Georgia, by Augusta, to make junction in my front; estimating them at the maximum twenty-five thousand men, and Hardee's, Wheeler's, and Hampton's forces at fifteen thousand, made forty thousand; which, if handled with spirit and energy, would constitute a formidable force, and might make the passage of such rivers as the Santee and Cape Fear a difficult undertaking. Therefore, I took all possible precautions, and arranged with Admiral Dahlgren and General Foster to watch our progress inland by all the means possible, and to provide for us points of security along the coast; as, at Bull's Bay, Georgetown, and the mouth of Cape Fear River. Still, it was extremely desirable in one march to reach Goldsboro' in the State of North Carolina (distant four hundred and twenty-five miles), a point of great convenience for ulterior operations, by reason of the two railroads which meet there, coming from the seacoast at Wilmington and Newbern. Before leaving Savannah I had sent to Newbern Colonel W. W. Wright, of the Engineers, with orders to look to these railroads, to collect rolling-stock, and to have the roads repaired out as far as possible in six weeks--the time estimated as necessary for us to march that distance.

The question of supplies remained still the one of vital importance, and I reasoned that we might safely rely on the country for a considerable quantity of forage and provisions, and that, if the worst came to the worst, we could live several months on the mules and horses of our trains. Nevertheless, time was equally material, and the moment I heard that General Slocum had finished his pontoon-bridge at Sister's Ferry, and that Kilpatrick's cavalry was over the river, I gave the general orders to march, and instructed all the columns to aim for the South Carolina Railroad to the west of Branchville, about Blackville and Midway.

The right wing moved up the Salkiehatchie, the Seventeenth Corps on the right, with orders on reaching Rivers's Bridge to cross over, and the Fifteenth Corps by Hickory Hill to Beaufort's Bridge. Kilpatrick was instructed to march by way of Barnwell; Corse's division and the Twentieth Corps to take such roads as would bring them into communication with the Fifteenth Corps about Beaufort's Bridge. All these columns started promptly on the 1st of February. We encountered Wheeler's cavalry, which had obstructed the road by felling trees, but our men picked these up and threw them aside, so that this obstruction hardly delayed us an hour. In person I accompanied the Fifteenth Corps (General Logan) by McPhersonville and Hickory Hill, and kept couriers going to and fro to General Slocum with instructions to hurry as much as possible, so as to make a junction of the whole army on the South Carolina Railroad about Blackville.

I spent the night of February 1st at Hickory Hill Post-Office, and that of the 2d at Duck Branch Post-Office, thirty-one miles out from Pocotaligo. On the 3d the Seventeenth Corps was opposite Rivers's Bridge, and the Fifteenth approached Beaufort's Bridge. The Salkiehatchie was still over its banks, and presented a most formidable obstacle. The enemy appeared in some force on the opposite bank, had cut away all the bridges which spanned the many deep channels of the swollen river, and the only available passage seemed to be along the narrow causeways which constituted the common roads. At Rivers's Bridge Generals Mower and Giles A. Smith led, their heads of column through this swamp, the water up to their shoulders, crossed over to the pine-land, turned upon the rebel brigade which defended the passage, and routed it in utter disorder. It was in this attack that General Wager Swayne lost his leg, and he had to be conveyed back to Pocotaligo. Still, the loss of life was very small, in proportion to the advantages gained, for the enemy at once abandoned the whole line of the Salkiehatchie, and the Fifteenth Corps passed over at Beaufort's Bridge, without opposition.

On the 5th of February I was at Beaufort's Bridge, by which time General A. S. Williams had got up with five brigades' of the Twentieth Corps; I also heard of General Kilpatrick's being abreast of us, at Barnwell, and then gave orders for the march straight for the railroad at Midway. I still remained with the Fifteenth Corps, which, on the 6th of February, was five miles from Bamberg. As a matter of course, I expected severe resistance at this railroad, for its loss would sever all the communications of the enemy in Charleston with those in Augusta.

Early on the 7th, in the midst of a rain-storm, we reached the railroad; almost unopposed, striking it at several points. General Howard told me a good story concerning this, which will bear repeating: He was with the Seventeenth Corps, marching straight for Midway, and when about five miles distant he began to deploy the leading division, so as to be ready for battle. Sitting on his horse by the road-side, while the deployment was making, he saw a man coming down the road, riding as hard as he could, and as he approached he recognized him as one of his own "foragers," mounted on a white horse, with a rope bridle and a blanket for saddle. As he came near he called out, "Hurry up, general; we have got the railroad!" So, while we, the generals, were proceeding deliberately to prepare for a serious battle, a parcel of our foragers, in search of plunder, had got ahead and actually captured the South Carolina Railroad, a line of vital importance to the rebel Government.

As soon as we struck the railroad, details of men were set to work to tear up the rails, to burn the ties and twist the bars. This was a most important railroad, and I proposed to destroy it completely for fifty miles, partly to prevent a possibility of its restoration and partly to utilize the time necessary for General Slocum to get up.

The country thereabouts was very poor, but the inhabitants mostly remained at home. Indeed, they knew not where to go. The enemy's cavalry had retreated before us, but his infantry was reported in some strength at Branchville, on the farther side of the Edisto; yet on the appearance of a mere squad of our men they burned their own bridges the very thing I wanted, for we had no use for them, and they had.

We all remained strung along this railroad till the 9th of February--the Seventeenth Corps on the right, then the Fifteenth, Twentieth, and cavalry, at Blackville. General Slocum reached Blackville that day, with Geary's division of the Twentieth Corps, and reported the Fourteenth Corps (General Jeff. C. Davis's) to be following by way of Barnwell. On the 10th I rode up to Blackville, where I conferred with Generals Slocum and Kilpatrick, became satisfied that the whole army would be ready within a day, and accordingly made orders for the next movement north to Columbia, the right wing to strike Orangeburg en route. Kilpatrick was ordered to demonstrate strongly toward Aiken, to keep up the delusion that we might turn to Augusta; but he was notified that Columbia was the next objective, and that he should cover the left flank against Wheeler, who hung around it. I wanted to reach Columbia before any part of Hood's army could possibly get there. Some of them were reported as having reached Augusta, under the command of General Dick Taylor.

Having sufficiently damaged the railroad, and effected the junction of the entire army, the general march was resumed on the 11th, each corps crossing the South Edisto by separate bridges, with orders to pause on the road leading from Orangeberg to Augusta, till it was certain that the Seventeenth Corps had got possession of Orangeburg. This place was simply important as its occupation would sever the communications between Charleston and Columbia. All the heads of column reached this road, known as the Edgefield road, during the 12th, and the Seventeenth Corps turned to the right, against Orangeburg. When I reached the head of column opposite Orangeburg, I found Giles A. Smith's division halted, with a battery unlimbered, exchanging shots with a party on the opposite side of the Edisto. He reported that the bridge was gone, and that the river was deep and impassable. I then directed General Blair to send a strong division below the town, some four or five miles, to effect a crossing there. He laid his pontoon-bridge, but the bottom on the other side was overflowed, and the men had to wade through it, in places as deep as their waists. I was with this division at the time, on foot, trying to pick my way across the overflowed bottom; but, as soon as the head of column reached the sand-hills, I knew that the enemy would not long remain in Orangeburg, and accordingly returned to my horse, on the west bank, and rode rapidly up to where I had left Giles A. Smith. I found him in possession of the broken bridge, abreast of the town, which he was repairing, and I was among the first to cross over and enter the town. By and before the time either Force's or Giles A. Smith's skirmishers entered the place, several stores were on fire, and I am sure that some of the towns-people told me that a Jew merchant had set fire to his own cotton and store, and

113

from this the fire had spread. This, however, was soon put out, and the Seventeenth Corps (General Blair) occupied the place during that night. I remember to have visited a large hospital, on the hill near the railroad depot, which was occupied by the orphan children who had been removed from the asylum in Charleston. We gave them protection, and, I think, some provisions. The railroad and depot were destroyed by order, and no doubt a good deal of cotton was burned, for we all regarded cotton as hostile property, a thing to be destroyed. General Blair was ordered to break up this railroad, forward to the point where it crossed the Santee, and then to turn for Columbia. On the morning of the 13th I again joined the Fifteenth Corps, which crossed the North Edisto by Snilling's Bridge, and moved straight for Columbia, around the head of Caw-Caw Swamp. Orders were sent to all the columns to turn for Columbia, where it was supposed the enemy had concentrated all the men they could from Charleston, Augusta, and even from Virginia. That night I was with the Fifteenth Corps, twenty-one miles from Columbia, where my aide, Colonel Audenried, picked up a rebel officer on the road, who, supposing him to be of the same service with himself, answered all his questions frankly, and revealed the truth that there was nothing in Columbia except Hampton's cavalry. The fact was, that General Hardee, in Charleston, took it for granted that we were after Charleston; the rebel troops in Augusta supposed they were "our objective;" so they abandoned poor Columbia to the care of Hampton's cavalry, which was confused by the rumors that poured in on it, so that both Beauregard and Wade Hampton, who were in Columbia, seem to have lost their heads.

On the 14th the head of the Fifteenth Corps, Charles R. Woods's division, approached the Little Congaree, a broad, deep stream, tributary to the Main Congaree; six or eight miles below Columbia. On the opposite side of this stream was a newly-constructed fort, and on our side--a wide extent of old cotton-fields, which, had been overflowed, and was covered with a deep slime. General Woods had deployed his leading brigade, which was skirmishing forward, but he reported that the bridge was gone, and that a considerable force of the enemy was on the other side. I directed General Howard or Logan to send a brigade by a circuit to the left, to see if this stream could not be crossed higher up, but at the same time knew that General Slocum's route world bring him to Colombia behind this stream, and that his approach would uncover it. Therefore, there was no need of exposing much life. The brigade, however, found means to cross the Little Congaree, and thus uncovered the passage by the main road, so that General Woods's skirmishers at once passed over, and a party was set to work to repair the bridge, which occupied less than an hour, when I passed over with my whole staff. I found the new fort unfinished and unoccupied, but from its parapet could see over some old fields bounded to the north and west by hills skirted with timber. There was a plantation to our left, about half a mile, and on the edge of the timber was drawn up a force of rebel cavalry of about a regiment, which advanced, and charged upon some, of our foragers, who were plundering the plantation; my aide, Colonel Audenried, who had ridden forward, came back somewhat hurt and bruised, for, observing this charge of cavalry, he had turned for us, and his horse fell with him in attempting to leap a ditch. General Woods's skirmish-line met this charge of cavalry, and drove it back into the woods and beyond. We remained on that ground during the night of the 15th, and I camped on the nearest dry ground behind the Little Congaree, where on the next morning were made the written' orders for the government of the troops while occupying Columbia. These are dated February 16, 1865, in these words:

General Howard will cross the Saluda and Broad Rivers as near their mouths as possible, occupy Columbia, destroy the public buildings, railroad property, manufacturing and machine shops; but will spare libraries, asylums, and private dwellings. He will then move to Winnsboro', destroying en route utterly that section of the railroad. He will also cause all bridges, trestles, water-tanks, and depots on the railroad back to the Wateree to be burned, switches broken, and such other destruction as he can find time to accomplish consistent with proper celerity.

These instructions were embraced in General Order No. 26, which prescribed the routes of march for the several columns as far as Fayetteville, North Carolina, and is conclusive that I then regarded Columbia as simply one point on our general route of march, and not as an important conquest.

During the 16th of February the Fifteenth Corps reached the point opposite Columbia, and pushed on for the Saluda Factory three miles above, crossed that stream, and the head of column reached Broad River just in time to find its bridge in flames, Butler's cavalry having just passed over into Columbia. The head of Slocum's column also reached the point opposite Columbia the same morning, but the bulk of his army was back at Lexington. I reached this place early in the morning of the 16th, met General Slocum there; and explained to him the purport of General Order No. 26, which contemplated the passage of his army across Broad River at Alston, fifteen miles above Columbia. Riding down to the river-bank, I saw the wreck of the large bridge which had been burned by the enemy, with its many stone piers still standing, but the superstructure gone. Across the Congaree River lay the city of Columbia, in plain, easy view. I could see the unfinished State-House, a handsome granite structure, and the ruins of the railroad depot, which were still smouldering. Occasionally a few citizens or cavalry could be seen running across the streets, and quite a number of negroes were seemingly busy in carrying off bags of grain or meal, which were piled up near the burned depot.

Captain De Gres had a section of his twenty-pound Parrott guns unlimbered, firing into the town. I asked him what he was firing for; he said he could see some rebel cavalry occasionally at the intersections of the streets, and he had an idea that there was a large force of infantry concealed on the opposite bank, lying low, in case we should attempt to cross over directly into the town. I instructed him not to fire any more into the town, but consented to his bursting a few shells near the depot, to scare away the negroes who were appropriating the bags of corn and meal which we wanted, also to fire three shots at the unoccupied State-House. I stood by and saw these fired, and then all firing ceased. Although this matter of firing into Columbia has been the subject of much abuse and investigation, I have yet to hear of any single person having been killed in Columbia by our cannon. On the other hand, the night before, when Woods's division was in camp in the open fields at Little Congaree, it was shelled all night by a rebel battery from the other aide of the river. This provoked me much at the time, for it was wanton mischief, as Generals Beauregard and Hampton must have been convinced that they could not prevent our entrance into Columbia. I have always contended that I would have been justified in retaliating for this unnecessary act of war, but did not, though I always characterized it as it deserved.

The night of the 16th I camped near an old prison bivouac opposite Columbia, known to our prisoners of war as "Camp Sorghum," where remained the mud-hovels and holes in the ground which our prisoners had made to shelter themselves from the winter's cold and the summer's heat. The Fifteenth Corps was then ahead, reaching to Broad River, about four miles above Columbia; the Seventeenth Corps was behind, on the river-bank opposite Columbia; and the left wing and cavalry had turned north toward Alston.

The next morning, viz., February 17th, I rode to the head of General Howard's column, and found that during the night he had ferried Stone's brigade of Woods's division of the Fifteenth Corps across by rafts made of the pontoons, and that brigade was then deployed on the opposite bank to cover the construction of a pontoon-bridge nearly finished.

I sat with General Howard on a log, watching the men lay this bridge; and about 9 or 10 A.M. a messenger came from Colonel Stone on the other aide, saying that the Mayor of Columbia had come out of the city to surrender the place, and asking for orders. I simply remarked to General Howard that he had his orders, to let Colonel Stone go on into the city, and that we would follow as soon as the bridge was ready. By this same messenger I received a note in pencil from the Lady Superioress of a convent or school in Columbia, in which she claimed to have been a teacher in a convent in Brown County, Ohio, at the time my daughter Minnie was a pupil there, and therefore asking special protection. My recollection is, that I gave the note to my brother-in-law, Colonel Ewing, then inspector-general on my staff, with instructions to see this lady, and assure her that we contemplated no destruction of any private property in Columbia at all.

As soon as the bridge was done, I led my horse over it, followed by my whole staff. General Howard accompanied me with his, and General Logan was next in order, followed by General C. R. Woods, and the whole of the Fifteenth Corps. Ascending the hill, we soon emerged into a broad road leading into Columbia, between old fields of corn and cotton, and, entering the city, we found seemingly all its population, white and black, in the streets. A high and boisterous wind was prevailing from the north, and flakes of cotton were flying about in the air and lodging in the limbs of the trees, reminding us of a Northern snow-storm. Near the market-square we found Stone's brigade halted, with arms stacked, and a large detail of his men, along with some citizens, engaged with an old fire-engine, trying to put out the fire in a long pile of burning cotton-bales, which I was told had been fired by the rebel cavalry on withdrawing from the city that morning. I know that, to avoid this row of burning cotton-bales, I had to ride my horse on the sidewalk. In the market-square had collected a large crowd of whites and blacks, among whom was the mayor of the city, Dr. Goodwin, quite a respectable old gentleman, who was extremely anxious to protect the interests of the citizens. He was on foot, and I on horseback, and it is probable I told him then not to be uneasy, that we did not intend to stay long, and had no purpose to injure the private citizens or private property. About this time I noticed several men trying to get through the crowd to speak with me, and called to some black people to make room for them; when they reached me, they explained that they were officers of our army, who had been prisoners, had escaped from the rebel prison and guard, and were of course overjoyed to find themselves safe with us. I told them that, as soon as things settled down, they should report to General Howard, who would provide for their safety, and enable them to travel with us. One of them handed me a paper, asking me to read it at my leisure; I put it in my breast-pocket and rode on. General Howard was still with me, and, riding down the street which led by the right to the Charleston depot, we found it and a large storehouse burned to the ground, but there were, on the platform and ground near by, piles of cotton bags filled with corn and corn-meal, partially burned.

A detachment of Stone's brigade was guarding this, and separating the good from the bad. We rode along the railroad-track, some three or four hundred yards, to a large foundery, when some man rode up and said the rebel cavalry were close by, and he warned us that we might get shot. We accordingly turned back to the market-square, and en route noticed that, several of the men were evidently in liquor, when I called General Howard's attention to it. He left me and rode toward General Woods's head of column, which was defiling through the town. On reaching the market-square, I again met Dr. Goodwin, and inquired where he proposed to quarter me, and he said that he had selected the house of Blanton Duncan, Esq., a citizen of Louisville, Kentucky, then a resident there, who had the contract for manufacturing the Confederate money, and had fled with Hampton's cavalry. We all rode some six or eight squares back from the new State-House, and found a very good modern house, completely furnished, with stabling and a large yard, took it as our headquarters, and occupied it during our stay. I considered General Howard as in command of the place, and referred the many applicants for guards and protection to him. Before our headquarters-wagons had got up, I strolled through the streets of Columbia, found sentinels posted at the principal intersections, and generally good order prevailing, but did not again return to the main street, because it was filled with a crowd of citizens watching the soldiers marching by.

During the afternoon of that day, February 17th, the whole of the Fifteenth Corps passed through the town and out on the Camden and Winnsboro' roads. The Seventeenth Corps did not enter the city at all, but crossed directly over to the Winnsboro' road from the pontoon bridge at Broad River, which was about four miles above the city.

After we had got, as it were, settled in Blanton Duncan's house, say about 2 p.m., I overhauled my pocket according to custom, to read more carefully the various notes and memoranda received during the day, and found the paper which had been given me, as described, by one of our escaped prisoners. It proved to be the song of "Sherman's March to the Sea," which had been composed by Adjutant S. H. M. Byers, of the Fifth Iowa Infantry, when a prisoner in the asylum at Columbia, which had been beautifully written off by a fellow-prisoner, and handed to me in person. This appeared to me so good that I at once sent for Byers, attached him to my staff, provided him with horse and equipment, and took him as far as Fayetteville, North Carolina, whence he was sent to Washington as bearer of dispatches. He is now United States consul at Zurich, Switzerland, where I have since been his guest. I insert the song here for convenient reference and preservation. Byers said that there was an excellent glee-club among the prisoners in Columbia, who used to sing it well, with an audience often of rebel ladies:

SHERMAN'S MARCH TO THE SEA.
Composed by Adjutant Byers, Fifth Iowa Infantry. Arranged and sung by the Prisoners in Columbia Prison.

I

Our camp-fires shone bright on the mountain
That frowned on the river below,
As we stood by our guns in the morning,
And eagerly watched for the foe;
When a rider came out of the darkness
That hung over mountain and tree,
And shouted, "Boys, up and be ready!
For Sherman will march to the sea!"

CHORUS:

Then sang we a song of our chieftain,
That echoed over river and lea;
And the stars of our banner shone brighter
When Sherman marched down to the sea!

II

Then cheer upon cheer for bold Sherman
Went up from each valley and glen,
And the bugles reechoed the music
That came from the lips of the men;
For we knew that the stars in our banner
More bright in their splendor would be,
And that blessings from Northland world greet us,
When Sherman marched down to the sea!
Then sang we a song, etc.

III

Then forward, boys! forward to battle!
We marched on our wearisome way,
We stormed the wild hills of Resacar
God bless those who fell on that day!
Then Kenesaw frowned in its glory,

Frowned down on the flag of the free;
But the East and the West bore our standard,
And Sherman marched on to the sea!
Then sang we a song, etc.

IV

Still onward we pressed, till our banners
Swept out from Atlanta's grim walls,
And the blood of the patriot dampened
The soil where the traitor-flag falls;
But we paused not to weep for the fallen,
Who slept by each river and tree,
Yet we twined them a wreath of the laurel,
As Sherman marched down to the sea!
Then sang we a song, etc.

V

Oh, proud was our army that morning,
That stood where the pine darkly towers,
When Sherman said, "Boys, you are weary,
But to-day fair Savannah is ours!"
Then sang we the song of our chieftain,
That echoed over river and lea,
And the stars in our banner shone brighter
When Sherman camped down by the sea!

Toward evening of February 17th, the mayor, Dr. Goodwin, came to my quarters at Duncan's house, and remarked that there was a lady in Columbia who professed to be a special friend of mine. On his giving her name, I could not recall it, but inquired as to her maiden or family name. He answered Poyas. It so happened that, when I was a lieutenant at Fort Moultrie, in 1842-'46, I used very often to visit a family of that name on the east branch of Cooper River, about forty miles from Fort Moultrie, and to hunt with the son, Mr. James Poyas, an elegant young fellow and a fine sportsman. His father, mother, and several sisters, composed the family, and were extremely hospitable. One of the ladies was very fond of painting in water-colors, which was one of my weaknesses, and on one occasion I had presented her with a volume treating of water-colors. Of course, I was glad to renew the acquaintance, and proposed to Dr. Goodwin that we should walk to her house and visit this lady, which we did. The house stood beyond the Charlotte depot, in a large lot, was of frame, with a high porch, which was reached by a set of steps outside. Entering this yard, I noticed ducks and chickens, and a general air of peace and comfort that was really pleasant to behold at that time of universal desolation; the lady in question met us at the head of the steps and invited us into a parlor which was perfectly neat and well furnished. After inquiring about her father, mother, sisters, and especially her brother James, my special friend, I could not help saying that I was pleased to notice that our men had not handled her house and premises as roughly as was their wont. "I owe it to you, general," she answered. "Not at all. I did not know you were here till a few minutes ago." She reiterated that she was indebted to me for the perfect safety of her house and property, and added, "You remember, when you were at our house on Cooper River in 1845, you gave me a book;" and she handed me the book in question, on the fly leaf of which was written: "To Miss Poyas, with the compliments of W. T. Sherman, First-lieutenant Third Artillery." She then explained that, as our army approached Columbia, there was a doubt in her mind whether the terrible Sherman who was devastating the land were W. T. Sherman or T. W. Sherman, both known to be generals in the Northern army; but, on the supposition that he was her old acquaintance, when Wade Hampton's cavalry drew out of the city, calling out that the Yankees were coming, she armed herself with this book, and awaited the crisis. Soon the shouts about the markethouse announced that the Yankees had come; very soon men were seen running up and down the streets; a parcel of them poured over the fence, began to chase the chickens and ducks, and to enter her house. She observed one large man, with full beard, who exercised some authority, and to him she appealed in the name of "his general." "What do you know of Uncle Billy?" "Why," she said, "when he was a young man he used to be our friend in Charleston, and here is a book he gave me." The officer or soldier took the book, looked at the inscription, and, turning to his fellows, said: "Boys, that's so; that's Uncle Billy's writing, for I have seen it often before." He at once commanded the party to stop pillaging, and left a man in charge of the house, to protect her until the regular provost-guard should be established. I then asked her if the regular guard or sentinel had been as good to her. She assured me that he was a very nice young man; that he had been telling her all about his family in Iowa; and that at that very instant of time he was in another room minding her baby. Now, this lady had good sense and tact, and had thus turned aside a party who, in five minutes more, would have rifled her premises of all that was good to eat or wear. I made her a long social visit, and, before leaving Columbia, gave her a half-tierce of rice and about one hundred pounds of ham from our own mess-stores.

In like manner, that same evening I found in Mrs. Simons another acquaintance--the wife of the brother of Hon. James Simons, of Charleston, who had been Miss Wragg. When Columbia was on fire that night, and her house in danger, I had her family and effects carried to my own headquarters, gave them my own room and bed, and, on leaving Columbia the next day, supplied her with a half-barrel of hams and a half-tierce of rice. I mention these specific facts to show that, personally, I had no malice or desire to destroy that city or its inhabitants, as is generally believed at the South.

Having walked over much of the suburbs of Columbia in the afternoon, and being tired, I lay down on a bed in Blanton Duncan's house to rest. Soon after dark I became conscious that a bright light was shining on the walls; and, calling some one of my staff (Major Nichols, I think) to inquire the cause, he said there seemed to be a house on fire down about the market-house. The same high wind still prevailed, and, fearing the consequences, I bade him go in person to see if the provost-guard were doing its duty. He soon returned, and reported that the block of buildings directly opposite the burning cotton of that morning was on fire, and that it was spreading; but he had found General Woods on the ground, with plenty of men trying to put the fire out, or, at least, to prevent its extension. The fire continued to increase, and the whole heavens became lurid. I dispatched messenger after messenger to Generals Howard, Logan, and Woods, and received from them repeated assurances that all was being done that could be done, but that the high wind was spreading the flames beyond all control. These general officers were on the ground all night, and Hazen's division had been brought into the city to assist Woods's division, already there. About eleven o'clock at night I went down-town myself, Colonel Dayton with me; we walked to Mr. Simons's house, from which I could see the flames rising high in the air, and could hear the roaring of the fire. I advised the ladies to move to my headquarters, had our own headquarter-wagons hitched up, and their effects carried there, as a place of greater safety. The whole air was full of sparks and of flying masses of cotton, shingles, etc., some of which were carried four or five blocks, and started new fires. The men seemed generally under good control, and certainly labored hard to girdle the fire, to prevent its spreading; but, so long as the high wind prevailed, it was simply beyond human possibility. Fortunately, about 3 or 4 a.m., the wind moderated, and gradually the fire was got under control; but it had burned out the very heart of the city, embracing several churches, the old State-House, and the school or asylum of that very Sister of Charity who had appealed for my personal protection. Nickerson's Hotel, in which several of my staff were quartered, was burned down, but the houses occupied by myself, Generals Howard and Logan, were not burned at all. Many of the people thought that this fire was deliberately planned and executed. This is not true. It was accidental, and in my judgment began with the cotton which General Hampton's men had set fire to on leaving the city (whether by his orders or not is not material), which fire was partially subdued early in the day by our men; but, when night came, the high wind fanned it again into full blaze, carried it against the frame houses, which caught like tinder, and soon spread beyond our control.

This whole subject has since been thoroughly and judicially investigated, in some cotton cases, by the mixed commission on American and British claims, under the Treaty of Washington, which commission failed to award a verdict in favor of the English claimants, and thereby settled the fact that the destruction of property in Columbia, during that night, did not result from the acts of the General Government of the United States-- that is to say, from my army. In my official report of this conflagration, I distinctly charged it to General Wade Hampton, and confess I did so pointedly, to shake the faith of his people in him, for he was in my opinion boastful, and professed to be the special champion of South Carolina.

The morning sun of February 18th rose bright and clear over a ruined city. About half of it was in ashes and in smouldering heaps. Many of the people were houseless, and gathered in groups in the suburbs, or in the open parks and spaces, around their scanty piles of furniture. General Howard, in concert with the mayor, did all that was possible to provide other houses for them; and by my authority he turned over to the Sisters of Charity the Methodist College, and to the mayor five hundred beef-cattle; to help feed the people; I also gave the mayor (Dr. Goodwin) one hundred muskets, with which to arm a guard to maintain order after we should leave the neighborhood. During the 18th and 19th we remained in Columbia, General Howard's troops engaged in tearing up and destroying the railroad, back toward the Wateree, while a strong detail, under the immediate supervision of Colonel O. M. Poe, United States Engineers, destroyed the State Arsenal, which was found to be well supplied with shot, shell, and ammunition. These were hauled in wagons to the Saluda River, under the supervision of Colonel Baylor, chief of ordnance, and emptied into deep water, causing a very serious accident by the bursting of a percussion-shell, as it struck another on the margin of the water. The flame followed back a train of powder which had sifted out, reached the wagons, still partially loaded, and exploded them, killing sixteen men and destroying several wagons and teams of mules. We also destroyed several valuable founderies and the factory of Confederate money. The dies had been carried away, but about sixty handpresses remained. There was also found an immense quantity of money, in various stages of manufacture, which our men spent and gambled with in the most lavish manner.

Having utterly ruined Columbia, the right wing began its march northward, toward Winnsboro', on the 20th, which we reached on the 21st, and found General Slocum, with the left wing, who had come by the way of Alston. Thence the right wing was turned eastward, toward Cheraw, and Fayetteville, North Carolina, to cross the Catawba River at Peay's Ferry. The cavalry was ordered to follow the railroad north as far as Chester, and then to turn east to Rocky Mount, the point indicated for the passage of the left wing. In person I reached Rocky Mount on the 22d, with the Twentieth Corps, which laid its pontoon-bridge and crossed over during the 23d. Kilpatrick arrived the next day, in the midst of heavy rain, and was instructed to cross the Catawba at once, by night, and to move up to Lancaster, to make believe we were bound for Charlotte, to which point I heard that Beauregard had directed all his detachments, including a corps of Hood's old army, which had been marching parallel with us, but had failed to make junction with, the forces immediately opposing us. Of course, I had no purpose of going to Charlotte, for the right wing was already moving rapidly toward Fayetteville, North Carolina. The rain was so heavy and persistent that the Catawba, River rose fast, and soon after I had crossed the pontoon bridge at Rocky Mount it was carried away, leaving General Davis, with the Fourteenth Corps, on the west bank. The roads were infamous, so I halted the Twentieth Corps at Hanging Rock for some days, to allow time for the Fourteenth to get over.

General Davis had infinite difficulty in reconstructing his bridge, and was compelled to use the fifth chains of his wagons for anchor-chains, so that we were delayed nearly a week in that neighborhood. While in camp at Hanging Rock two prisoners were brought to me--one a chaplain, the other a boy, son of Richard Bacot, of Charleston, whom I had known as a cadet at West Point. They were just from Charleston, and had been sent away by General Hardee in advance, because he was, they said, evacuating Charleston. Rumors to the same effect had reached me through the negroes, and it was, moreover, reported that Wilmington, North Carolina, was in possession of the Yankee troops; so that I had every reason to be satisfied that our march was fully reaping all the fruits we could possibly ask for. Charleston was, in fact, evacuated by General Hardee on the 18th of February, and was taken possession of by a brigade of General Fosters troops, commanded by General Schimmelpfennig, the same day. Hardee had availed himself of his only remaining railroad, by Florence to Cheraw; had sent there much of his ammunition and stores, and reached it with the effective part of the garrison in time to escape across the Pedee River before our arrival. Wilmington was captured by General Terry on the 22d of February; but of this important event we only knew by the vague rumors which reached us through rebel sources.

General Jeff. C. Davis got across the Catawba during the 27th, and the general march was resumed on Cheraw. Kilpatrick remained near Lancaster, skirmishing with Wheeler's and Hampton's cavalry, keeping up the delusion that we proposed to move on Charlotte and Salisbury, but with orders to watch the progress of the Fourteenth Corps, and to act in concert with it, on its left rear. On the 1st of March I was at Finlay's Bridge across Lynch's Creek, the roads so bad that we had to corduroy nearly every foot of the way; but I was in communication with all parts of the army, which had met no serious opposition from the enemy. On the 2d of March we entered the village of Chesterfield, skirmishing with Butler's cavalry, which gave ground rapidly. There I received a message from General Howard, who, reported that he was already in Cheraw with the Seventeenth Corps, and that the Fifteenth was near at hand.

General Hardee had retreated eastward across the Pedee, burning the bridge. I therefore directed the left wing to march for Sneedsboro', about ten miles above Cheraw, to cross the Pedee there, while I in person proposed to cross over and join the right wing in Cheraw. Early in the morning of the 3d of March I rode out of Chesterfield along with the Twentieth Corps, which filled the road, forded Thompson's Creek, and, at the top of the hill beyond, found a road branching off to the right, which corresponded with the one, on my map leading to Cheraw. Seeing a negro standing by the roadside, looking at the troops passing, I inquired of him what road that was. "Him lead to Cheraw, master!" "Is it a good road, and how far?" "A very good road, and eight or ten miles." "Any guerrillas?"

"Oh! no, master, dey is gone two days ago; you could have played cards on der coat-tails, dey was in such a hurry!" I was on my Lexington horse, who was very handsome and restive, so I made signal to my staff to follow, as I proposed to go without escort. I turned my horse down the road, and the rest of the staff followed. General Barry took up the questions about the road, and asked the same negro what he was doing there. He answered, "Dey say Massa Sherman will be along soon!" "Why," said General Barry, "that was General Sherman you were talking to." The poor negro, almost in the attitude of prayer, exclaimed: "De great God! just look at his

119

horse!" He ran up and trotted by my side for a mile or so, and gave me all the information he possessed, but he seemed to admire the horse more than the rider.

We reached Cheraw in a couple of hours in a drizzling rain, and, while waiting for our wagons to come up, I staid with General Blair in a large house, the property of a blockade-runner, whose family remained. General Howard occupied another house farther down-town. He had already ordered his pontoon-bridge to be laid across the Pedee, there a large, deep, navigable stream, and Mower's division was already across, skirmishing with the enemy about two miles out. Cheraw was found to be full of stores which had been sent up from Charleston prior to its evacuation, and which could not be removed. I was satisfied, from inquiries, that General Hardee had with him only the Charleston garrison, that the enemy had not divined our movements, and that consequently they were still scattered from Charlotte around to Florence, then behind us. Having thus secured the passage of the Pedee, I felt no uneasiness about the future, because there remained no further great impediment between us and Cape Fear River, which I felt assured was by that time in possession of our friends. The day was so wet that we all kept in-doors; and about noon General Blair invited us to take lunch with him. We passed down into the basement dining-room, where the regular family table was spread with an excellent meal; and during its progress I was asked to take some wine, which stood upon the table in venerable bottles. It was so very good that I inquired where it came from. General Blair simply asked, "Do you like it?" but I insisted upon knowing where he had got it; he only replied by asking if I liked it, and wanted some. He afterward sent to my bivouac a case containing a dozen bottles of the finest madeira I ever tasted; and I learned that he had captured, in Cheraw, the wine of some of the old aristocratic families of Charleston, who had sent it up to Cheraw for safety, and heard afterward that Blair had found about eight wagon-loads of this wine, which he distributed to the army generally, in very fair proportions.

After finishing our lunch, as we passed out of the dining room, General Blair asked me, if I did not want some saddle-blankets, or a rug for my tent, and, leading me into the hall to a space under the stairway, he pointed out a pile of carpets which had also been sent up from Charleston for safety. After our headquarter-wagons got up, and our bivouac was established in a field near by, I sent my orderly (Walter) over to General Blair, and he came back staggering under a load of carpets, out of which the officers and escort made excellent tent-rugs, saddle-cloths, and blankets. There was an immense amount of stores in Cheraw, which were used or destroyed; among them twenty-four guns, two thousand muskets, and thirty-six hundred barrels of gunpowder. By the carelessness of a soldier, an immense pile of this powder was exploded, which shook the town badly; and killed and maimed several of our men.

We remained in or near Cheraw till the 6th of March, by which time the army was mostly across the Pedee River, and was prepared to resume the march on Fayetteville. In a house where General Hardee had been, I found a late New York Tribune, of fully a month later date than any I had seen. It contained a mass of news of great interest to us, and one short paragraph which I thought extremely mischievous. I think it was an editorial, to the effect that at last the editor had the satisfaction to inform his readers that General Sherman would next be heard from about Goldsboro', because his supply-vessels from Savannah were known to be rendezvousing at Morehead City;--Now, I knew that General Hardee had read that same paper, and that he would be perfectly able to draw his own inferences. Up to, that moment I had endeavored so to feign to our left that we had completely, misled our antagonists; but this was no longer possible, and I concluded that we must be ready, for the concentration in our front of all the force subject to General Jos. Johnston's orders, for I was there also informed that he had been restored to the full command of the Confederate forces in South and North Carolina.

On the 6th of March I crossed the Pedee, and all the army marched for Fayetteville: the Seventeenth Corps kept well to the right, to make room; the Fifteenth Corps marched by a direct road; the Fourteenth Corps also followed a direct road from Sneedsboro', where it had crossed the Pedee; and the Twentieth Corps, which had come into Cheraw for the convenience of the pontoon-bridge, diverged to the left, so as to enter Fayetteville next after the Fourteenth Corps, which was appointed to lead into Fayetteville. Kilpatrick held his cavalry still farther to the left rear on the roads from Lancaster, by way of Wadesboro' and New Gilead, so as to cover our trains from Hampton's and Wheeler's cavalry, who had first retreated toward the north. I traveled with the Fifteenth Corps, and on the 8th of March reached Laurel Hill, North Carolina. Satisfied that our troops must be at Wilmington, I determined to send a message there; I called for my man, Corporal Pike, whom I had rescued as before described, at Columbia, who was then traveling with our escort, and instructed him in disguise to work his way to the Cape Fear River, secure a boat, and float down to Wilmington to convey a letter, and to report our approach. I also called on General Howard for another volunteer, and he brought me a very clever young sergeant, who is now a commissioned officer in the regular army. Each of these got off during the night by separate routes, bearing the following message, reduced to the same cipher we used in telegraphic messages:

HEADQUARTERS MILITARY DIVISION OF THE MISSISSIPPI IN THE FIELD, LAUREL HILL, Wednesday, March 8, 1865.

Commanding Officer, Wilmington, North Carolina:

We are marching for Fayetteville, will be there Saturday, Sunday, and Monday, and will then march for Goldsboro'.

If possible, send a boat up Cape Fear River, and have word conveyed to General Schofield that I expect to meet him about Goldsboro'. We are all well and have done finely. The rains make our roads difficult, and may delay us about Fayetteville, in which case I would like to have some bread, sugar, and coffee. We have abundance of all else. I expect to reach Goldsboro' by the 20th instant.

W. T. SHERMAN, Major-General.

On the 9th I was with the Fifteenth Corps, and toward evening reached a little church called Bethel, in the woods, in which we took refuge in a terrible storm of rain, which poured all night, making the roads awful. All the men were at work corduroying the roads, using fence-rails and split saplings, and every foot of the way had thus to be corduroyed to enable the artillery and wagons to pass. On the 10th we made some little progress; on the 11th I reached Fayetteville, and found that General Hardee, followed by Wade Hampton's cavalry, had barely escaped across Cape Fear River, burning the bridge which I had hoped to save. On reaching Fayetteville I found General Slocum already in possession with the Fourteenth Corps, and all the rest of the army was near at hand. A day or two before, General Kilpatrick, to our left rear, had divided his force into two parts, occupying roads behind the Twentieth Corps, interposing between our infantry columns and Wade Hampton's cavalry. The latter, doubtless to make junction with General Hardee, in Fayetteville, broke across this line, captured the house in which General Kilpatrick and the brigade-commander, General Spencer, were, and for a time held possession of the camp and artillery of the brigade. However, General Kilpatrick and most of his men escaped into a swamp with their arms, reorganized and returned, catching Hampton's men--in turn, scattered and drove them away, recovering most of his camp and artillery; but Hampton got off with Kilpatrick's private horses and a couple hundred prisoners, of which he boasted much in passing through Fayetteville.

It was also reported that, in the morning after Hardee's army was all across the bridge at Cape Fear River, Hampton, with a small bodyguard, had remained in town, ready to retreat and burn the bridge as soon as our forces made their appearance. He was getting breakfast at the hotel when the alarm was given, when he and his escort took saddle, but soon realized that the alarm came from a set of our foragers, who, as usual, were extremely bold and rash. On these he turned, scattered them, killing some and making others prisoners; among them General Howard's favorite scout, Captain Duncan. Hampton then crossed the bridge and burned it.

I took up my quarters at the old United States Arsenal, which was in fine order, and had been much enlarged by the Confederate authorities, who never dreamed that an invading army would reach it from the west; and I also found in Fayetteville the widow and daughter of my first captain (General Childs), of the Third Artillery, learned that her son Fred had been the ordnance-officer in charge of the arsenal, and had of course fled with Hardee's army.

During the 11th. the whole army closed down upon Fayetteville, and immediate preparations were made to lay two pontoon bridges, one near the burned bridge, and another about four miles lower down.

Sunday, March 12th, was a day of Sabbath stillness in Fayetteville. The people generally attended their churches, for they were a very pious people, descended in a large measure from the old Scotch Covenanters, and our men too were resting from the toils and labors of six weeks of as hard marching as ever fell to the lot of soldiers. Shortly after noon was heard in the distance the shrill whistle of a steamboat, which came nearer and nearer, and soon a shout, long and continuous, was raised down by the river, which spread farther and farther, and we all felt that it meant a messenger from home. The effect was electric, and no one can realize the feeling unless, like us, he has been for months cut off from all communication with friends, and compelled to listen to the croakings and prognostications of open enemies. But in a very few minutes came up through the town to the arsenal on the plateau behind a group of officers, among whom was a large, florid seafaring man, named Ainsworth, bearing a small mail-bag from General Terry, at Wilmington, having left at 2 p.m. the day before. Our couriers had got through safe from Laurel Hill, and this was the prompt reply.

As in the case of our former march from Atlanta, intense anxiety had been felt for our safety, and General Terry had been prompt to open communication. After a few minutes' conference with Captain Ainsworth about the capacity of his boat, and the state of facts along the river, I instructed him to be ready to start back at 6 p.m., and ordered Captain Byers to get ready to carry dispatches to Washington. I also authorized General Howard to send back by this opportunity some of the fugitives who had traveled with his army all the way from Columbia, among whom were Mrs. Feaster and her two beautiful daughters.

I immediately prepared letters for Secretary Stanton, Generals Halleck and Grant, and Generals Schofield, Foster, Easton, and Beckwith, all of which have been published, but I include here only those to the Secretary of War, and Generals Grant and Terry, as samples of the whole:

HEADQUARTERS MILITARY DIVISION OF THE MISSISSIPPI, IN THE FIELD, FAYETTVILLE,

NORTH CAROLINA, Sunday, March. 12, 1885.

Hon. E. M. STANTON, Secretary of War.

DEAR SIR: I know you will be pleased to hear that my army has reached this point, and has opened communication with Wilmington. A tug-boat came up this morning, and will start back at 6 P. M.

I have written a letter to General Grant, the substance of which he will doubtless communicate, and it must suffice for me to tell you what I know will give you pleasure--that I have done all that I proposed, and the fruits seem to me ample for the time employed. Charleston, Georgetown, and Wilmington, are incidents, while the utter demolition of the railroad system of South Carolina, and the utter destruction of the enemy's arsenals of Columbia, Cheraw, and Fayetteville, are the principals of the movement. These points were regarded as inaccessible to us, and now no place in the Confederacy is safe against the army of the West. Let Lee hold on to Richmond, and we will destroy his country; and then of what use is Richmond. He must come out and fight us on open ground, and for that we must ever be ready. Let him stick behind his parapets, and he will perish.

I remember well what you asked me, and think I am on the right road, though a long one. My army is as united and cheerful as ever, and as full of confidence in itself and its leaders. It is utterly impossible for me to enumerate what we have done, but I inclose a slip just handed me, which is but partial. At Columbia and Cheraw we destroyed nearly all the gunpowder and cartridges which the Confederacy had in this part of the country. This arsenal is in fine order, and has been much enlarged. I cannot leave a detachment to hold it, therefore shall burn it, blow it up with gunpowder, and then with rams knock down its walls. I take it for granted the United States will never again trust North Carolina with an arsenal to appropriate at her pleasure.

Hoping that good fortune may still attend my army. I remain your servant,

W. T. SHERMAN, Major-General.

HEADQUARTERS MILITARY DIVISION OF THE MISSISSIPPI, IN THE FIELD, FAYETTVILLE, NORTH CAROLINA, Sunday, March. 12, 1885.

Lieutenant-General U. S. GRANT, commanding United States Army, City Point, Virginia.

DEAR GENERAL: We reached this place yesterday at noon; Hardee, as usual, retreating across the Cape Fear, burning his bridges; but our pontoons will be up to-day, and, with as little delay as possible, I will be after him toward Goldsboro'.

A tug has just come up from Wilmington, and before I get off from here, I hope to get from Wilmington some shoes and stockings, sugar, coffee, and flour. We are abundantly supplied with all else, having in a measure lived off the country.

The army is in splendid health, condition, and spirits, though we have had foul weather, and roads that would have stopped travel to almost any other body of men I ever heard of.

Our march, was substantially what I designed--straight on Columbia, feigning on Branchville and Augusta. We destroyed, in passing, the railroad from the Edisto nearly up to Aiken; again, from Orangeburg to the Congaree; again, from Columbia down to Kingsville on the Wateree, and up toward Charlotte as far as the Chester line; thence we turned east on Cheraw and Fayetteville. At Colombia we destroyed immense arsenals and railroad establishments, among which wore forty-three cannon. At Cheraw we found also machinery and material of war sent from Charleston, among which were twenty-five guns and thirty-six hundred barrels of powder; and here we find about twenty guns and a magnificent United States' arsenal.

We cannot afford to leave detachments, and I shall therefore destroy this valuable arsenal, so the enemy shall not have its use; and the United States should never again confide such valuable property to a people who have betrayed a trust.

I could leave here to-morrow, but want to clear my columns of the vast crowd of refugees and negroes that encumber us. Some I will send down the river in boats, and the rest to Wilmington by land, under small escort, as soon as we are across Cape Fear River.

I hope you have not been uneasy about us, and that the fruits of this march will be appreciated. It had to be made not only to destroy the valuable depots by the way, but for its incidents in the necessary fall of Charleston, Georgetown, and Wilmington. If I can now add Goldsboro' without too much cost, I will be in a position to aid you materially in the spring campaign.

Jos. Johnston may try to interpose between me here and Schofield about Newbern; but I think he will not try that, but concentrate his scattered armies at Raleigh, and I will go straight at him as soon as I get our men reclothed and our wagons reloaded.

Keep everybody busy, and let Stoneman push toward Greensboro' or Charlotte from Knoxville; even a feint in that quarter will be most important.

The railroad from Charlotte to Danville is all that is left to the enemy, and it will not do for me to go there, on account of the red-clay hills which are impassable to wheels in wet weather.

I expect to make a junction with General Schofield in ten days.

Yours truly,

W. T. SHERMAN, Major-General.

HEADQUARTERS MILITARY DIVISION OF THE MISSISSIPPI, IN THE FIELD, FAYETTVILLE, NORTH CAROLINA, Sunday, March. 12, 1885.

Major-General TERRY, commanding United States Forces, Wilmington, North Carolina.

GENERAL: I have just received your message by the tug which left Wilmington at 2 p.m. yesterday, which arrived here without trouble. The scout who brought me your cipher-message started back last night with my answers, which are superseded by the fact of your opening the river.

General Howard just reports that he has secured one of the enemy's steamboats below the city, General Slocum will try to secure two others known to be above, and we will load them with refugees (white and black) who have clung to our skirts, impeded our movements, and consumed our food.

We have swept the country well from Savannah to here, and the men and animals are in fine condition. Had it not been for the foul weather, I would have caught Hardee at Cheraw or here; but at Columbia, Cheraw, and here, we have captured immense stores, and destroyed machinery, guns, ammunition, and property, of inestimable value to our enemy. At all points he has fled from us, "standing not on the order of his going."

The people of South Carolina, instead of feeding Lee's army, will now call on Lee to feed them.

I want you to send me all the shoes, stockings, drawers, sugar, coffee, and flour, you can spare; finish the loads with oats or corn: Have the boats escorted, and let them run at night at any risk. We must not give time for Jos. Johnston to concentrate at Goldsboro'. We cannot prevent his concentrating at Raleigh, but he shall have no rest. I want General Schofield to go on with his railroad from Newbern as far as he can, and you should do the same from Wilmington. If we can get the roads to and secure Goldsboro' by April 10th, it will be soon enough; but every day now is worth a million of dollars. I can whip Jos. Johnston provided he does not catch one of my corps in flank, and I will see that the army marches hence to Goldsboro' in compact form.

I must rid our army of from twenty to thirty thousand useless mouths; as many to go down Cape Fear as possible, and the rest to go in vehicles or on captured horses via Clinton to Wilmington.

I thank you for the energetic action that has marked your course, and shall be most happy to meet you. I am, truly your friend,

W. T. SHERMAN, Major-General.

In quick succession I received other messages from General Terry, of older date, and therefore superseded by that brought by the tug Davidson, viz., by two naval officers, who had come up partly by canoes and partly by land; General Terry had also sent the Thirteenth Pennsylvania Cavalry to search for us, under Colonel Kerwin, who had dispatched Major Berks with fifty men, who reached us at Fayetteville; so that, by March 12th, I was in full communication with General Terry and the outside world. Still, I was anxious to reach Goldsboro', there to make junction with General Schofield, so as to be ready for the next and last stage of the war. I then knew that my special antagonist, General Jos. E. Johnston, was back, with part of his old army; that he would not be misled by feints and false reports, and would somehow compel me to exercise more caution than I had hitherto done. I then over-estimated his force at thirty-seven thousand infantry, supposed to be made up of S. D. Lee's corps, four thousand; Cheatham's, five thousand; Hoke's, eight thousand; Hardee's, ten thousand; and other detachments, ten thousand; with Hampton's, Wheeler's, and Butler's cavalry, about eight thousand. Of these, only Hardee and the cavalry were immediately in our front, while the bulk of Johnston's army was supposed to be collecting at or near Raleigh. I was determined, however, to give him as little time for organization as possible, and accordingly crossed Cape Fear River, with all the army, during the 13th and 14th, leaving one division as a rearguard, until the arsenal could be completely destroyed. This was deliberately and completely leveled on the 14th, when fire was applied to the wreck. Little other damage was done at Fayetteville.

On the 14th the tug Davidson again arrived from Wilmington, with General Dodge, quartermaster, on board, reporting that there was no clothing to be had at Wilmington; but he brought up some sugar and coffee, which were most welcome, and some oats. He was followed by a couple of gunboats, under command of Captain Young, United States Navy, who reached Fayetteville after I had left, and undertook to patrol the river as long as the stage of water would permit; and General Dodge also promised to use the captured steamboats for a like purpose. Meantime, also, I had sent orders to General Schofield, at Newbern, and to General Terry, at Wilmington, to move with their effective forces straight for Goldsboro', where I expected to meet them by the 20th of March.

On the 15th of March the whole army was across Cape Fear River, and at once began its march for Goldsboro'; the Seventeenth Corps still on the right, the Fifteenth next in order, then the Fourteenth and Twentieth on the extreme left; the cavalry, acting in close concert with the left flank. With almost a certainty of being attacked on this flank, I had instructed General Slocum to send his corps-trains under strong escort by an interior road, holding four divisions ready for immediate battle. General Howard was in like manner ordered to keep his trains well to his right, and to have four divisions unencumbered, about six miles ahead of General Slocum, within easy support.

In the mean time, I had dispatched by land to Wilmington a train of refugees who had followed the army all the way from Columbia, South Carolina, under an escort of two hundred men, commanded by Major John A. Winson (One Hundred and Sixteenth Illinois Infantry), so that we were disencumbered, and prepared for instant battle on our left and exposed flank.

In person I accompanied General Slocum, and during the night of March 15th was thirteen miles out on the Raleigh road. This flank followed substantially a road along Cape Fear River north, encountered pretty stubborn resistance by Hardee's infantry, artillery, and cavalry, and the ground favored our enemy; for the deep river, Cape Fear, was on his right, and North River on his left, forcing us to attack him square in front. I proposed to drive Hardee well beyond Averysboro', and then to turn to the right by Bentonville for Goldsboro'. During the day it rained very hard, and I had taken refuge in an old cooper-shop, where a prisoner of war was brought to me (sent back from the skirmish-line by General Kilpatrick), who proved to be Colonel Albert Rhett, former commander of Fort Sumter. He was a tall, slender, and handsome young man, dressed in the most approved rebel uniform, with high jackboots beautifully stitched, and was dreadfully mortified to find himself a prisoner in our hands. General Frank Blair happened to be with me at the moment, and we were much amused at Rhett's outspoken disgust at having been captured without a fight. He said he was a brigade commander, and that his brigade that day was Hardee's rear-guard; that his command was composed mostly of the recent garrisons of the batteries of Charleston Harbor, and had little experience in woodcraft; that he was giving ground to us as fast as Hardee's army to his rear moved back, and during this operation he was with a single aide in the woods, and was captured by two men of Kilpatrick's skirmish-line that was following up his retrograde movement. These men called on him to surrender, and ordered him, in language more forcible than polite, to turn and ride back. He first supposed these men to be of Hampton's cavalry, and threatened to report them to General Hampton for disrespectful language; but he was soon undeceived, and was conducted to Kilpatrick, who sent him back to General Slocum's guard.

The rain was falling heavily, and, our wagons coming up, we went into camp there, and had Rhett and General Blair to take supper with us, and our conversation was full and quite interesting. In due time, however, Rhett was passed over by General Slocum to his provost-guard, with orders to be treated with due respect,--and was furnished with a horse to ride.

The next day (the 16th) the opposition continued stubborn, and near Averysboro' Hardee had taken up a strong position, before which General Slocum deployed Jackson's division (of the Twentieth Corps), with part of Ward's. Kilpatrick was on his right front. Coming up, I advised that a brigade should make a wide circuit by the left, and, if possible, catch this line in flank. The movement was completely successful, the first line of the enemy was swept away, and we captured the larger part of Rhett's brigade, two hundred and seventeen men, including Captain Macbeth's battery of three guns, and buried one hundred and eight dead.

The deployed lines (Ward's and Jackson's) pressed on, and found Hardee again intrenched; but the next morning he was gone, in full retreat toward Smithfield. In this action, called the battle of Averysboro', we lost twelve officers and sixty-five men killed, and four hundred and seventy-seven men wounded; a serious loss, because every wounded man had to be carried in an ambulance. The rebel wounded (sixty-eight) were carried to a house near by, all surgical operations necessary were performed by our surgeons, and then these wounded men were left in care of an officer and four men of the rebel prisoners, with a scanty supply of food, which was the best we could do for them. In person I visited this house while the surgeons were at work, with arms and legs lying around loose, in the yard and on the porch; and in a room on a bed lay a pale, handsome young fellow, whose left arm had just been cut off near the shoulder. Some one used my name, when he asked, in a feeble voice, if I were General Sherman. He then announced himself as Captain Macbeth, whose battery had just been captured; and said that he remembered me when I used to visit his father's house, in Charleston. I inquired about his family, and enabled him to write a note to his mother, which was sent her afterward from Goldsboro'. I have seen that same young gentleman since in St. Louis, where he was a clerk in an insurance-office.

While the battle of Averysboro' was in progress, and I was sitting on my horse, I was approached by a man on foot, without shoes or coat, and his head bandaged by a handkerchief. He announced himself as the Captain Duncan who had been captured by Wade Hampton in Fayetteville, but had escaped; and, on my inquiring how he happened to be in that plight, he explained that when he was a prisoner Wade Hampton's men had made him "get out of his coat, hat, and shoes," which they appropriated to themselves. He said Wade Hampton had seen them do it, and he had appealed to him personally for protection, as an officer, but Hampton answered him with a curse. I sent Duncan to General Kilpatrick, and heard afterward that Kilpatrick had applied to General Slocum for his prisoner, Colonel Rhett, whom he made march on foot the rest of the way to Goldsboro', in retaliation. There was a story afloat that Kilpatrick made him get out of those fine boots, but restored them because none of his own officers had feet delicate enough to wear them. Of course, I know nothing of this personally, and have never seen Rhett since that night by the cooper-shop; and suppose that he is the editor who recently fought a duel in New Orleans.

From Averysboro' the left wing turned east, toward Goldsboro', the Fourteenth Corps leading. I remained with this wing until the night of the 18th, when we were within twenty-seven miles of Goldsboro' and five from Bentonsville; and, supposing that all danger was over, I crossed over to join Howard's column, to the right, so as to be nearer to Generals Schofield and Terry, known to be approaching Goldsboro'. I overtook General Howard at Falling-Creek Church, and found his column well drawn out, by reason of the bad roads. I had heard some cannonading over about Slocum's head of column, and supposed it to indicate about the same measure of opposition by Hardee's troops and Hampton's cavalry before experienced; but during the day a messenger overtook me, and notified me that near Bentonsville General Slocum had run up against Johnston's whole army. I sent back orders for him to fight defensively to save time, and that I would come up with reenforcements from the direction of Cog's Bridge, by the road which we had reached near Falling-Creek Church. The country was very obscure, and the maps extremely defective.

By this movement I hoped General Slocum would hold Johnston's army facing west, while I would come on his rear from the east. The Fifteenth Corps, less one division (Hazen's), still well to the rear, was turned at once toward Bentonsville; Hazen's division was ordered to Slocum's flank, and orders were also sent for General Blair, with the Seventeenth Corps, to come to the same destination. Meantime the sound of cannon came from the direction of Bentonsville.

The night of the 19th caught us near Falling-Creek Church; but early the next morning the Fifteenth Corps, General C. R. Woods's division leading, closed down on Bentonsville, near which it was brought up by encountering a line of fresh parapet, crossing the road and extending north, toward Mill Creek.

After deploying, I ordered General Howard to proceed with due caution, using skirmishers alone, till he had made junction with General Slocum, on his left. These deployments occupied all day, during which two divisions of the Seventeenth Corps also got up. At that time General Johnston's army occupied the form of a V, the angle reaching the road leading from Averysboro' to Goldsboro', and the flanks resting on Mill Creek, his lines embracing the village of Bentonsville.

General Slocum's wing faced one of these lines and General Howard's the other; and, in the uncertainty of General Johnston's strength, I did not feel disposed to invite a general battle, for we had been out from Savannah since the latter part of January, and our wagon-trains contained but little food. I had also received messages during the day from General Schofield, at Kinston, and General Terry, at Faison's Depot, approaching Goldsboro', both expecting to reach it by March 21st. During the 20th we simply held our ground and started our trains back to Kinston for provisions, which would be needed in the event of being forced to fight a general battle at Bentonsville. The next day (21st) it began to rain again, and we remained quiet till about noon, when General Mower, ever rash, broke through the rebel line on his extreme left flank, and was pushing straight for Bentonsville and the bridge across Mill Creek. I ordered him back to connect with his own corps; and, lest the enemy should concentrate on him, ordered the whole rebel line to be engaged with a strong skirmish-fire.

I think I made a mistake there, and should rapidly have followed Mower's lead with the whole of the right wing, which would have brought on a general battle, and it could not have resulted otherwise than successfully to us, by reason of our vastly superior numbers; but at the moment, for the reasons given, I preferred to make junction with Generals Terry and Schofield, before engaging Johnston's army, the strength of which was utterly unknown. The next day he was gone, and had retreated on Smithfield; and, the roads all being clear, our army moved to Goldsboro'. The heaviest fighting at Bentonsville was on the first day, viz., the 19th, when Johnston's army struck the head of Slocum's columns, knocking back Carlin's division; but, as soon as General Slocum had brought up the rest of the Fourteenth Corps into line, and afterward the Twentieth on its left, he received and repulsed all attacks, and held his ground as ordered, to await the coming back of the right wing. His loss, as reported, was nine officers and one hundred and forty-five men killed, eight hundred and sixteen wounded, and two hundred and twenty-six missing. He reported having buried of the rebel dead one hundred and sixty-seven, and captured three hundred and thirty-eight prisoners.

125

The loss of the right wing was two officers and thirty-five men killed, twelve officers and two hundred and eighty-nine men wounded, and seventy missing. General Howard reported that he had buried one hundred of the rebel dead, and had captured twelve hundred and eighty-seven prisoners.

Our total loss, therefore, at Bentonsville was: 1,604

General Johnston, in his "Narrative" (p. 392), asserts that his entire force at Bentonsville, omitting Wheeler's and Butler's cavalry, only amounted to fourteen thousand one hundred infantry and artillery; and (p. 393) states his losses as: 2,343

Wide discrepancies exist in these figures: for instance, General Slocum accounts for three hundred and thirty-eight prisoners captured, and General Howard for twelve hundred and eighty-seven, making sixteen hundred and twenty-five in all, to Johnston's six hundred and fifty three--a difference of eight hundred and seventy-two. I have always accorded to General Johnston due credit for boldness in his attack on our exposed flank at Bentonville, but I think he understates his strength, and doubt whether at the time he had accurate returns from his miscellaneous army, collected from Hoke, Bragg, Hardee, Lee, etc. After the first attack on Carlin's division, I doubt if the fighting was as desperate as described by him, p. 385, et seq. I was close up with the Fifteenth Corps, on the 20th and 21st, considered the fighting as mere skirmishing, and know that my orders were to avoid a general battle, till we could be sure of Goldsboro', and of opening up a new base of supply. With the knowledge now possessed of his small force, of course I committed an error in not overwhelming Johnston's army on the 21st of March, 1865. But I was content then to let him go, and on the 22d of March rode to Cog's Bridge, where I met General Terry, with his two divisions of the Tenth Corps; and the next day we rode into Goldsboro', where I found General Schofield with the Twenty-third Corps, thus effecting a perfect junction of all the army at that point, as originally contemplated. During the 23d and 24th the whole army was assembled at Goldsboro'; General Terry's two divisions encamped at Faison's Depot to the south, and General Kilpatrick's cavalry at Mount Olive Station, near him, and there we all rested, while I directed my special attention to replenishing the army for the next and last stage of the campaign. Colonel W. W. Wright had been so indefatigable, that the Newbern Railroad was done, and a locomotive arrived in Goldsboro' on the 25th of March.

Thus was concluded one of the longest and most important marches ever made by an organized army in a civilized country. The distance from Savannah to Goldsboro' is four hundred and twenty-five miles, and the route traversed embraced five large navigable rivers, viz., the Edisto, Broad, Catawba, Pedee, and Cape Fear, at either of which a comparatively small force, well-handled, should have made the passage most difficult, if not impossible. The country generally was in a state of nature, with innumerable swamps, with simply mud roads, nearly every mile of which had to be corduroyed. In our route we had captured Columbia, Cheraw, and Fayetteville, important cities and depots of supplies, had compelled the evacuation of Charleston City and Harbor, had utterly broken up all the railroads of South Carolina, and had consumed a vast amount of food and forage, essential to the enemy for the support of his own armies. We had in mid-winter accomplished the whole journey of four hundred and twenty-five miles in fifty days, averaging ten miles per day, allowing ten lay-days, and had reached Goldsboro' with the army in superb order, and the trains almost as fresh as when we had started from Atlanta.

It was manifest to me that we could resume our march, and come within the theatre of General Grant's field of operations in all April, and that there was no force in existence that could delay our progress, unless General Lee should succeed in eluding General Grant at Petersburg, make junction with General Johnston, and thus united meet me alone; and now that we had effected a junction with Generals Terry and Schofield, I had no fear even of that event. On reaching Goldsboro, I learned from General Schofield all the details of his operations about Wilmington and Newbern; also of the fight of the Twenty-third Corps about Kinston, with General Bragg. I also found Lieutenant Dunn, of General Grant's staff, awaiting me, with the general's letter of February 7th, covering instructions to Generals Schofield and Thomas; and his letter of March 16th, in answer to mine of the 12th, from Fayetteville.

These are all given here to explain the full reasons for the events of the war then in progress, with two or three letters from myself, to fill out the picture.

HEADQUARTERS OF THE ARMIES OF THE UNITED STATES
CITY POINT, VIRGINIA, February 7, 1865

Major-General W. T. SHERMAN, commanding Military Division of the Mississippi.

GENERAL: Without much expectation of it reaching you in time to be of any service, I have mailed to you copies of instructions to Schofield and Thomas. I had informed Schofield by telegraph of the departure of Mahone's division, south from the Petersburg front. These troops marched down the Weldon road, and, as they apparently went without baggage, it is doubtful whether they have not returned. I was absent from here when they left. Just returned yesterday morning from Cape Fear River. I went there to determine where Schofield's corps had better go to operate against Wilmington and Goldsboro'. The instructions with this will inform you of the conclusion arrived at.

Schofield was with me, and the plan of the movement against Wilmington fully determined before we started back; hence the absence of more detailed instructions to him. He will land one division at Smithville, and move rapidly up the south side of the river, and secure the Wilmington & Charlotte Railroad, and with his pontoon train cross over to the island south of the city, if he can. With the aid of the gunboats, there is no doubt but this move will drive the enemy from their position eight miles east of the city, either back to their line or away altogether. There will be a large force on the north bank of Cape Fear River, ready to follow up and invest the garrison, if they should go inside.

The railroads of North Carolina are four feet eight and one-half inches gauge. I have sent large parties of railroad-men there to build them up, and have ordered stock to run them. We have abundance of it idle from the non-use of the Virginia roads. I have taken every precaution to have supplies ready for you wherever you may turn up. I did this before when you left Atlanta, and regret that they did not reach you promptly when you reached salt-water....

Alexander Stephens, R. M. T. Hunter, and Judge Campbell, are now at my headquarters, very desirous of going to Washington to see Mr. Lincoln, informally, on the subject of peace. The peace feeling within the rebel lines is gaining ground rapidly. This, however, should not relax our energies in the least, but should stimulate us to greater activity.

I have received your very kind letters, in which you say you would decline, or are opposed to, promotion. No one world be more pleased at your advancement than I, and if you should be placed in my position, and I put subordinate, it would not change our personal relations in the least. I would make the same exertions to support you that you have ever done to support me, and would do all in my power to make our cause win.

Yours truly,

U. S. GRANT, Lieutenant-General.

HEADQUARTERS OF THE ARMIES OF THE UNITED STATES
CITY POINT, VIRGINIA, January 81, 1865.

Major-General G. H. THOMAS, commanding Army of the Cumberland.

GENERAL: With this I send you a letter from General Sherman. At the time of writing it, General Sherman was not informed of the depletion of your command by my orders. It will, be impossible at present for you to move south as he contemplated, with the force of infantry indicated. General Slocum is advised before this of the changes made, and that for the winter you will be on the defensive. I think, however, an expedition from East Tennessee, under General Stoneman might penetrate South Carolina, well down toward Columbia, destroying the railroad and military resources of the country, thus visiting a portion of the State which will not be reached by Sherman's forces. He might also be able to return to East Tennessee by way of Salisbury, North Carolina, thus releasing home our prisoners of war in rebel hands.

Of the practicability of doing this, General Stoneman will have to be the judge, making up his mind from information obtained while executing the first part of his instructions. Sherman's movements will attract the attention of all the force the enemy can collect, thus facilitating the execution of this.

Three thousand cavalry would be a sufficient force to take. This probably can be raised in the old Department of the Ohio, without taking any now under General Wilson. It would require, though, the reorganization of the two regiments of Kentucky Cavalry, which Stoneman had in his very successful raid into Southwestern Virginia.

It will be necessary, probably, for you to send, in addition to the force now in East Tennessee, a small division of infantry, to enable General Gillem to hold the upper end of Holston Valley, and the mountain-passes in rear of Stevenson.

You may order such an expedition. To save time, I will send a copy of this to General Stoneman, so that he can begin his preparations without loss of time, and can commence his correspondence with you as to these preparations.

As this expedition goes to destroy and not to fight battles, but to avoid them when practicable, particularly against any thing like equal forces, or where a great object is to be gained, it should go as light as possible. Stoneman's experience, in raiding will teach him in this matter better than he can be directed.

Let there be no delay in the preparations for this expedition, and keep me advised of its progress. Very respectfully, your obedient servant,

U. S. GRANT, Lieutenant-General.

HEADQUARTERS OF THE ARMIES OF THE UNITED STATES
CITY POINT, VIRGINIA, January 81, 1865.

Major-General J. M. SCHOFIELD, commanding army of the Ohio.

GENERAL: I have requested by telegraph that, for present purposes, North Carolina be erected into a department, and that you be placed in command of it, subject to Major-General Sherman's orders. Of course, you will receive orders from me direct until such time as General Sherman gets within communicating distance of you. This obviates the necessity of my publishing the order which I informed you would meet you at Fortress Monroe. If the order referred to should not be published from the Adjutant-General's office, you will read these instructions as your authority to assume command of all the troops in North Carolina, dating all official communications, "Headquarters Army of the Ohio." Your headquarters will be in the field, and with the portion of the army where you feel yourself most needed. In the first move you will go to Cape Fear River.

Your movements are intended as cooperative with Sherman's movement through the States of South and North Carolina. The first point to be obtained is to secure Wilmington. Goldsboro' will then be your objective point, moving either from Wilmington or Newbern, or both, as you may deem best. Should you not be able to reach Goldsboro', you will advance on the line or lines of railway connecting that place with the sea-coast, as near to it as you can, building the road behind you. The enterprise under you has two objects: the first is, to give General Sherman material aid, if needed, in his march north; the second, to open a base of supplies for him on the line of his march. As soon, therefore, as you can determine which of the two points, Wilmington or Newbern, you can best use for throwing supplies from to the interior, you will commence the accumulation of twenty days rations and forage for sixty thousand men and twenty thousand animals. You will get of these as many as you can house and protect, to such point in the interior as you may be able to occupy.

I believe General Innis N. Palmer has received some instructions directly from General Sherman, on the subject of securing supplies for his army. You can learn what steps he has taken, and be governed in your requisitions accordingly. A supply of ordnance-stores will also be necessary.

Make all your requisitions upon the chiefs of their respective departments, in the field, with me at City Point. Communicate with me by every opportunity, and, should you deem it necessary at any time, send a special boat to Fortress Monroe, from which point you can communicate by telegraph.

The supplies referred to in these instructions are exclusive of those required by your own command.

The movements of the enemy may justify you, or even make it your imperative duty, to cut loose from your base and strike for the interior, to aid Sherman. In such case you will act on your own judgment, without waiting for instructions. You will report, however, what you propose doing. The details for carrying out these instructions are necessarily left to you. I would urge, however, if I did not know that you are already fully alive to the importance of it, prompt action. Sherman may be looked for in the neighborhood of Goldsboro' any time from the 22d to the 28th of February. This limits your time very materially.

If rolling-stock is not secured in the capture of Wilmington, it can be supplied from Washington: A large force of railroad-men has already been sent to Beaufort, and other mechanics will go to Fort Fisher in a day or two. On this point I have informed you by telegraph.

Very respectfully, your obedient servant,

U. S. GRANT, Lieutenant-General.

HEADQUARTERS OF THE ARMIES OF THE UNITED STATES
CITY POINT, VIRGINIA, March 16, 1865.

Major-General W. T. SHERMAN, commanding military Division of the Mississippi.

GENERAL: Your interesting letter of the 12th inst. is just received. I have never felt any uneasiness for your safety, but I have felt great anxiety to know just how you were progressing. I knew, or thought I did, that, with the magnificent army with you, you would come out safely somewhere.

To secure certain success, I deemed the capture of Wilmington of the greatest importance. Butler came near losing that prize to us. But Terry and Schofield have since retrieved his blunders, and I do not know but the first failure has been as valuable a success for the country as the capture of Fort Fisher. Butler may not see it in that light.

Ever since you started on the last campaign, and before, I have been attempting to get something done in the West, both to cooperate with you and to take advantage of the enemy's weakness there--to accomplish results favorable to us. Knowing Thomas to be slow beyond excuse, I depleted his army to reinforce Canby, so that he might act from Mobile Bay on the interior. With all I have said, he has not moved at last advices. Canby was sending a cavalry force, of about seven thousand, from Vicksburg toward Selma. I ordered Thomas to send Wilson from Eastport toward the same point, and to get him off as soon after the 20th of February as possible. He telegraphed me that he would be off by that date. He has not yet started, or had not at last advices. I ordered him to send Stoneman from East Tennessee into Northwest South Carolina, to be there about the time you would reach Columbia. He would either have drawn off the enemy's cavalry from you, or would have succeeded in destroying railroads, supplies, and other material, which you could not reach. At that time the Richmond papers were full of the accounts of your movements, and gave daily accounts of movements in West North Carolina. I supposed all the time it was Stoneman. You may judge my surprise when I afterward learned that Stoneman was still in Louisville, Kentucky, and that the troops in North Carolina were Kirk's forces! In order that Stoneman might get off without delay, I told Thomas that three thousand men would be sufficient for him to take. In the mean time I had directed Sheridan to get his cavalry ready, and, as soon as the snow in the mountains melted sufficiently, to start for Staunton, and go on and destroy the Virginia Central Railroad and canal. Time advanced, until he set the 28th of February for starting. I informed Thomas, and directed him to change the course of Stoneman toward Lynchburg, to destroy the road in Virginia up as near to that place as possible. Not hearing from Thomas, I telegraphed to him about the 12th, to know if Stoneman was yet off. He replied not, but that he (Thomas) would start that day for Knoxville, to get him off as soon as possible.

Sheridan has made his raid, and with splendid success, so far as heard. I am looking for him at "White House" to-day. Since about the 20th of last month the Richmond papers have been prohibited from publishing accounts of army movements. We are left to our own resources, therefore, for information. You will see from the papers what Sheridan has done; if you do not, the officer who bears this will tell you all.

Lee has depleted his army but very little recently, and I learn of none going south. Some regiments may have been detached, but I think no division or brigade. The determination seems to be to hold Richmond as long as possible. I have a force sufficient to leave enough to hold our lines (all that is necessary of them), and move out with plenty to whip his whole army. But the roads are entirely impassable. Until they improve, I shall content myself with watching Lee, and be prepared to pitch into him if he attempts to evacuate the place. I may bring Sheridan over--think I will--and break up the Danville and Southside Railroads. These are the last avenues left to the enemy.

Recruits have come in so rapidly at the West that Thomas has now about as much force as he had when he attacked Hood. I have stopped all who, under previous orders, would go to him, except those from Illinois.

Fearing the possibility of the enemy falling back to Lynchburg, and afterward attempting to go into East Tennessee or Kentucky, I have ordered Thomas to move the Fourth Corps to Bull's Gap, and to fortify there, and to hold out to the Virginia line, if he can. He has accumulated a large amount of supplies in Knoxville, and has been ordered not to destroy any of the railroad west of the Virginia Hue. I told him to get ready for a campaign toward Lynchburg, if it became necessary. He never can make one there or elsewhere; but the steps taken will prepare for any one else to take his troops and come east or go toward Rome, whichever may be necessary. I do not believe either will.

When I hear that you and Schofield are together, with your back upon the coast, I shall feel that you are entirely safe against any thing the enemy can do. Lee may evacuate Richmond, but he cannot get there with force enough to touch you. His army is now demoralized and deserting very fast, both to us and to their homes. A retrograde movement would cost him thousands of men, even if we did not follow.

Five thousand men, belonging to the corps with you, are now on their way to join you. If more reenforcements are necessary, I will send them. My notion is, that you should get Raleigh as soon as possible, and hold the railroad from there back. This may take more force than you now have.

From that point all North Carolina roads can be made useless to the enemy, without keeping up communications with the rear.

Hoping to hear soon of your junction with the forces from Wilmington and Newborn, I remain, very respectfully, your obedient servant,

U. S. GRANT, Lieutenant-General.

HEADQUARTERS MILITARY DIVISION OF THE MISSISSIPPI IN THE FIELD,
COX'S BRIGADE, NEUSE RIVER, NORTH CAROLINA, March 22, 1865

Lieutenant-General U. S. GRANT, Commander-in-Chief, City Point, Virginia.

GENERAL: I wrote you from Fayetteville, North Carolina, on Tuesday, the 14th instant, that I was all ready to start for Goldsboro', to which point I had also ordered General Schofield, from Newbern, and General Terry, from Wilmington. I knew that General Jos. Johnston was supreme in command against me, and that he would have time to concentrate a respectable army to oppose the last stage of this march. Accordingly, General Slocum was ordered to send his main supply-train, under escort of two divisions, straight for Bentonsville, while he, with his other four divisions, disencumbered of all unnecessary wagons, should march toward Raleigh, by way of threat, as far as Averysboro'. General Howard, in like manner, sent his trains with the Seventeenth Corps, well to the right, and, with the four divisions of the Fifteenth Corps, took roads which would enable him to come promptly to the exposed left flank. We started on the 16th, but again the rains set in, and the roads, already bad enough, became horrible.

On Tuesday, the 16th, General Slocum found Hardee's army, from Charleston, which had retreated before us from Cheraw, in position across the narrow, swampy neck between Cape Fear and North Rivers, where the road branches off to Goldsboro'. There a pretty severe fight occurred, in which General Slocum's troops carried handsomely the advanced line, held by a South Carolina brigade, commanded by a Colonel Butler. Its Commander, Colonel Rhett, of Fort Sumter notoriety, with one of his staff, had the night before been captured, by Kilpatrick's scouts, from his very skirmish-line. The next morning Hardee was found gone, and was pursued through and beyond Averysboro'. General Slocum buried one hundred and eight dead rebels, and captured and destroyed three guns. Some eighty wounded rebels were left in our hands, and, after dressing their wounds, we left them in a house, attended by a Confederate officer and four privates, detailed out of our prisoners and paroled for the purpose.

We resumed the march toward Goldsboro'. I was with the left wing until I supposed all danger had passed; but, when General Slocum's head of column was within four miles of Bentonsville, after skirmishing as usual with cavalry, he became aware that there was infantry in his front. He deployed a couple of brigades, which, on advancing, sustained a partial repulse, but soon rallied, when he formed a line of the two leading divisions (Morgan's and Carlin's) of Jeff. C. Davis's corps. The enemy attacked these with violence, but was repulsed. This was in the forenoon of Sunday, the 19th. General Slocum brought forward the two divisions of the Twentieth Corps, hastily disposed of them for defense, and General Kilpatrick massed his cavalry on the left.

General Jos. Johnston had, the night before, marched his whole army (Bragg, Cheatham, S. D. Lee, Hardee, and all the troops he had drawn from every quarter), determined, as he told his men, to crash one of our corps, and then defeat us in detail. He attacked General Slocum in position from 3 P. M. on the 19th till dark; but was everywhere repulsed, and lost heavily. At the time, I was with the Fifteenth Corps, marching on a road more to the right; but, on hearing of General Slocum's danger, directed that corps toward Cox's Bridge, in the night brought Blair's corps over, and on the 20th marched rapidly on Johnston's flank and rear. We struck him about noon, forced him to assume the defensive, and to fortify. Yesterday we pushed him hard, and came very near crushing him, the right division of the Seventeenth Corps (Mower's) having broken in to within a hundred yards of where Johnston himself was, at the bridge across Mill Creek. Last night he retreated, leaving us in possession of the field, dead, and wounded. We have over two thousand prisoners from this affair and the one at Averysboro', and I am satisfied that Johnston's army was so roughly handled yesterday that we could march right on to Raleigh; but we have now been out six weeks, living precariously upon the collections of our foragers, our men dirty, ragged, and saucy, and we must rest and fix up a little. Our entire losses thus far (killed, wounded, and prisoners) will be covered by twenty-five hundred, a great part of which are, as usual, slight wounds. The enemy has lost more than double as many, and we have in prisoners alone full two thousand.

I limited the pursuit, this morning, to Mill Creek, and will forthwith march the army to Goldsboro', there to rest, reclothe, and get some rations.

Our combinations were such that General Schofield entered Goldsboro' from Newborn; General Terry got Cox's Bridge, with pontoons laid, and a brigade across Neuse River intrenched; and we whipped Jos. Johnston--all on the same day.

After riding over the field of battle to-day, near Bentonsville, and making the necessary orders, I have ridden down to this place (Cox's Bridge) to see General Terry, and to-morrow shall ride into Goldsboro.

I propose to collect there my army proper; shall post General Terry about Faison's Depot, and General Schofield about Kinston, partly to protect the road, but more to collect such food and forage as the country affords, until the railroads are repaired leading into Goldsboro'.

I fear these have not been pushed with the vigor I had expected; but I will soon have them both going. I shall proceed at once to organize three armies of twenty-five thousand men each, and will try and be all ready to march to Raleigh or Weldon, as we may determine, by or before April 10th.

130

I inclose you a copy of my orders of to-day. I would like to be more specific, but have not the data. We have lost no general officers nor any organization. General Slocum took three guns at Averysboro', and lost three others at the first dash on him at Bentonsville. We have all our wagons and trains in good order.

Yours truly,

W. T. SHERMAN, Major-General.

HEADQUARTERS MILITARY DIVISION OF THE MISSISSIPPI IN THE FIELD, COX'S BRIGADE, GOLDSBORO', NORTH CAROLINA, March 23, 1865.

Lieutenant-General U. S. GRANT, commanding the Armies of the United States, City Point, Virginia.

GENERAL: On reaching Goldsboro' this morning, I found Lieutenant Dunn awaiting me with your letter of March 18th and dispatch of the 17th. I wrote you fully from Cox's Bridge yesterday, and since reaching Goldsboro' have learned that my letter was sent punctually to Newborn, whence it will be dispatched to you.

I am very glad to hear that General Sheridan did such good service between Richmond and Lynchburg, and hope he will keep the ball moving, I know that these raids and dashes disconcert our enemy and discourage him much.

General Slocum's two corps (Fourteenth and Twentieth) are now coming in. I will dispose of them north of Goldsboro', between the Weldon road and Little River. General Howard to-day is marching south of the Nenae, and to-morrow will come in and occupy ground north of Goldsboro', extending from the Weldon Railroad to that leading to Kinston.

I have ordered all the provisional divisions, made up of troops belonging to the regular corps, to be broken up, and the men to join their proper regiments and organizations; and have ordered General Schofield to guard the railroads back to Newborn and Wilmington, and to make up a movable column equal to twenty-five thousand men, with which to take the field. His army will be the centre, as on the Atlanta campaign. I do not think I want any more troops (other than absentees and recruits) to fill up the present regiments, and I can make up an army of eighty thousand men by April 10th. I will post General Kilpatrick at Mount Olive Station on the Wilmington road, and then allow the army some rest.

We have sent all our empty wagons, under escort, with the proper staff-officers, to bring up from Kinston clothing and provisions. As long as we move we can gather food and forage; but, the moment we stop, trouble begins.

I feel sadly disappointed that our railroads are not done. I do not like to say there has been any neglect until I make inquiries; but it does seem to me the repairs should have been made ere this, and the road properly stocked. I can only hear of one locomotive (besides the four old ones) on the Newbern road, and two damaged locomotives (found by General Terry) on the Wilmington road. I left Generals Easton and Beckwith purposely to make arrangements in anticipation of my arrival, and have heard from neither, though I suppose them both to be at Morehead City.

At all events, we have now made a junction of all the armies, and if we can maintain them, will, in a short time, be in a position to march against Raleigh, Gaston, Weldon, or even Richmond, as you may determine.

If I get the troops all well planed, and the supplies working well, I may run up to see you for a day or two before diving again into the bowels of the country.

I will make, in a very short time, accurate reports of our operations for the past two months. Yours truly,

W. T. SHERMAN, Major-General commanding.

HEADQUARTERS MILITARY DIVISION OF THE MISSISSIPPI IN THE FIELD, COX'S BRIGADE, GOLDSBORO', NORTH CAROLINA, March 24, 1865.

Lieutenant-General U. S. GRANT, City Point, Virginia.

GENERAL: I have kept Lieutenant Dunn over to-day that I might report farther. All the army is now in, save the cavalry (which I have posted at Mount Olive Station, south of the Nenae) and General Terry's command (which--to-morrow will move from

Cog's Ferry to Faison's Depot, also on the Wilmington road). I send you a copy of my orders of this morning, the operation of which will, I think, soon complete our roads. The telegraph is now done to Morehead City, and by it I learn that stores have been sent to Kinston in boats, and that our wagons are loading with rations and clothing. By using the Neuse as high up as Kinston, hauling from there twenty-six miles, and by equipping the two roads to Morehead City and Wilmington, I feel certain we can not only feed and equip the army, but in a short time fill our wagons for another start. I feel certain, from the character of the fighting, that we have got Johnston's army afraid of us. He himself acts with timidity and caution. His cavalry alone manifests spirit, but limits its operations to our stragglers and foraging-parties. My marching columns of infantry do not pay the cavalry any attention, but walk right through it.

I think I see pretty clearly how, in one more move, we can checkmate Lee, forcing him to unite Johnston with him in the defense of Richmond, or to abandon the cause. I feel certain, if he leaves Richmond, Virginia leaves the Confederacy. I will study my maps a little more before giving my positive views. I want all possible information of the Roanoke as to navigability, how far up, and with what draught.

We find the country sandy, dry, with good roads, and more corn and forage than I had expected. The families remain, but I will gradually push them all out to Raleigh or Wilmington. We will need every house in the town. Lieutenant Dunn can tell you of many things of which I need not write. Yours truly,

W. T. SHERMAN, Major-General.

HEADQUARTERS MILITARY DIVISION OF THE MISSISSIPPI IN THE FIELD, COX'S BRIGADE, GOLDSBORO', NORTH CAROLINA, April 5,1865

Major-General George H. Thomas, commanding Department of the Cumberland.

DEAR GENERAL: I can hardly help smiling when I contemplate my command--it is decidedly mixed. I believe, but am not certain, that you are in my jurisdiction, but I certainly cannot help you in the way of orders or men; nor do I think you need either. General Cruft has just arrived with his provisional division, which will at once be broken up and the men sent to their proper regiments, as that of Meagher was on my arrival here.

You may have some feeling about my asking that General Slocum should have command of the two corps that properly belong to you, viz., the Fourteenth and Twentieth, but you can recall that he was but a corps commander, and could not legally make orders of discharge, transfer, etc., which was imperatively necessary. I therefore asked that General Slocum should be assigned to command "an army in the field," called the Army of Georgia, composed of the Fourteenth and Twentieth Corps. The order is not yet made by the President, though I have recognized it because both, General Grant and the President have sanctioned it, and promised to have the order made.

My army is now here, pretty well clad and provided, divided into three parts, of two corps each--much as our old Atlanta army was.

I expect to move on in a few days, and propose (if Lee remains in Richmond) to pass the Roanoke, and open communication with the Chowan and Norfolk. This will bring me in direct communication with General Grant.

This is an admirable point--country open, and the two railroads in good order back to Wilmington and Beaufort. We have already brought up stores enough to fill our wagons, and only await some few articles, and the arrival of some men who are marching up from the coast, to be off.

General Grant explained to me his orders to you, which, of course, are all right. You can make reports direct to Washington or to General Grant, but keep me advised occasionally of the general state of affairs, that I may know what is happening. I must give my undivided attention to matters here. You will hear from a thousand sources pretty fair accounts of our next march. Yours truly,

W. T. SHERMAN, Major-General.

[LETTER FROM ADMIRAL DAHLGREN]

SOUTH ATLANTIC SQUADRON
FLAG-SHIP PHILADELPHIA, CHARLESTON, April 20, 1865

Major-General W. T. SHERMAN, commanding Armies of the Tennessee, Georgia, and Mississippi.

132

Mr DEAR GENERAL: I was much gratified by a sight of your handwriting, which has just reached me from Goldsboro'; it was very suggestive of a past to me, when these regions were the scene of your operations.

As you progressed through South Carolina, there was no manifestation of weakness or of an intention to abandon Charleston, until within a few hours of the fact. On the 11th of February I was at Stono, and a spirited demonstration was made by General Schimmel-pfennig and the vessels. He drove the rebels from their rifle-pits in front of the lines, extending from Fort Pringle, and pushed them vigorously. The next day I was at Bull's Bay, with a dozen steamers, among them the finest of the squadron. General Potter had twelve to fifteen hundred men, the object being to carry out your views. We made as much fuss as possible, and with better success than I anticipated, for it seems that the rebs conceived Stono to be a feint, and the real object at Bull's Bay, supposing, from the number of steamers and boats, that we had several thousand men. Now came an aide from General Gillmore, at Port Royal, with your cipher-dispatch from Midway, so I steamed down to Port Royal to see him. Next day was spent in vain efforts to decipher- finally it was accomplished. You thought that the state of the roads might force you to turn upon Charleston; so I went there on the 15th, but there was no sign yet of flinching. Then I went to Bull's Bay next day (16th), and found that the troops were not yet ashore, owing to the difficulties of shoal water. One of the gunboats had contrived to get up to within shelling range, and both soldiers and sailors were working hard. On the evening of the 18th I steamed down to Stono to see how matters were going there. Passing Charleston, I noticed two large fires, well inside--probably preparing to leave. On the 17th, in Stono, rumors were flying about loose of evacuation. In course of the morning, General Schimmelpfennig telegraphed me, from Morris Island, that there were symptoms of leaving; that he would again make a push at Stono, and asked for monitors. General Schimmelpfennig came down in the afternoon, and we met in the Folly Branch, near Secessionville. He was sore that the rebs would be off that night, so he was to assault them in front, while a monitor and gunboats stung their flanks both sides. I also sent an aide to order my battery of five eleven-inch guns, at Cumming's Point, to fire steadily all night on Sullivan's Island, and two monitors to close up to the island for the same object. Next morning (18th) the rascals were found to be off, and we broke in from all directions, by land and water. The main bodies had left at eight or nine in the evening, leaving detachments to keep up a fire from the batteries. I steamed round quickly, and soon got into the city, threading the streets with a large group of naval captains who had joined me. All was silent as the grave. No one to be seen but a few firemen.

No one can question the excellence of your judgment in taking the track you did, and I never had any misgivings, but it was natural to desire to go into the place with a strong hand, for, if any one spot in the land was foremost in the trouble, it was Charleston.

Your campaign was the final blow, grand in conception, complete in execution; and now it is yours to secure the last army which rebeldom possesses. I hear of your being in motion by the 9th, and hope that the result may be all that you wish.

Tidings of the murder of the President have just come, and shocked every mind. Can it be that such a resort finds root in any stratum of American opinion? Evidently it has not been the act of one man, nor of a madman. Who have prompted him?

I am grateful for your remembrance of my boy; the thought of him is ever nearest to my heart. Generous, brave, and noble, as I ever knew him to be, that he should close his young life so early, even under the accepted conditions of a soldier's life, as a son of the Union, would have been grief sufficient for me to bear; but that his precious remains should have been so treated by the brutes into whose hands they fell, adds even to the bitterness of death. I am now awaiting the hour when I can pay my last duties to his memory.

With my best and sincere wishes, my dear general, for your success and happiness, I am, most truly, your friend,

J. A. DAHLGREN.

[General Order No. 50.]

WAR DEPARTMENT, ADJUTANT-GENERAL'S OFFICE
WASHINGTON, March 27, 1865

Ordered--1. That at the hour of noon, on the 14th day of April, 1885, Brevet Major-General Anderson will raise and plant upon the ruins of Fort Sumter, in Charleston Harbor, the same United States flag which floated over the battlements of that fort during the rebel assault, and which was lowered and saluted by him and the small force of his command when the works were evacuated on the 14th day of April, 1861.

2. That the flag, when raised, be saluted by one hundred guns from Fort Sumter, and by a national salute from every fort and rebel battery that fired upon Fort Sumter.

3. That suitable ceremonies be had upon the occasion, under the direction of Major-General William T. Sherman, whose military operations compelled the rebels to evacuate Charleston, or, in his absence, under the charge of Major-General Q. A. Gilmore, commanding the department. Among the ceremonies will be the delivery of a public address by the Rev. Henry Ward Beecher.

4. That the naval forces at Charleston, and their commander on that station, be invited to participate in the ceremonies of the occasion.

By order of the President of the United States,

EDWIN M. STANTON, Secretary of War.

[General Order No. 41.]

HEADQUARTERS DEPARTMENT OF THE SOUTH
HILTON HEAD, SOUTH CAROLINA, April 10, 1865

Friday next, the 14th inst., will be the fourth anniversary of the capture of Fort Sumter by the rebels. A befitting celebration on that day, in honor of its reoccupation by the national forces, has been ordered by the President, in pursuance of which Brevet Major-General Robert Anderson, United States Army, will restore to its original place on the fort the identical flag which, after an honorable and gallant defense, he was compelled to lower to the insurgents in South Carolina, in April, 1861.

The ceremonies for the occasion will commence with prayer, at thirty minutes past eleven o'clock a.m.

At noon precisely, the flag will be raised and saluted with one hundred guns from Fort Sumter, and with a national salute from Fort Moultrie and Battery Bee on Sullivan's Island, Fort Putnam on Morris Island, and Fort Johnson on James's Island; it being eminently appropriate that the places which were so conspicuous in the inauguration of the rebellion should take a part not less prominent in this national rejoicing over the restoration of the national authority.

After the salutes, the Rev. Henry Ward Beecher will deliver an address.

The ceremonies will close with prayer and a benediction.

Colonel Stewart L. Woodford, chief of staff, under such verbal instructions as he may receive, is hereby charged with the details of the celebration, comprising all the arrangements that it may be necessary to make for the accommodation of the orator of the day, and the comfort and safety of the invited guests from the army and navy, and from civil life.

By command of Major-General Q. A. Gillmore,
W. L. M. BURGER, Assistant Adjutant-General.

Copy of Major ANDERSON's Dispatch, announcing the Surrender of Fort Sumter, April 14, 1861.

STEAMSHIP BALTIC, OFF SANDY HOOK
April 10, 1861, 10.30 a.m. via New York

Honorable S. Cameron, Secretary of War, Washington

Having defended Fort Sumter for thirty-four hours, until the quarters were entirely burned, the main gates destroyed by fire, the gorge-walls seriously injured, the magazine surrounded by flames, and its door closed from the effect of heat, four barrels and three cartridges of powder only being available, and no provisions remaining but pork, I accepted terms of evacuation offered by General Beauregard, being the same offered by him on the 11th inst., prior to the commencement of hostilities, and marched out of the fort, Sunday afternoon, the 14th inst., with colors flying and drums beating, bringing away company and private property, and saluting my flag with fifty guns.

ROBERT ANDERSON, Major First Artillery, commanding.

CHAPTER XXIV.
END OF THE WAR--FROM GOLDSBORO' TO RALEIGH AND WASHINGTON.

APRIL AND MAY, 1865.

As before described, the armies commanded respectively by Generals J. M. Schofield, A. H. Terry, and myself, effected a junction in and about Goldsboro', North Carolina, during the 22d and 23d of March, 1865, but it required a few days for all the troops and trains of wagons to reach their respective camps. In person I reached Goldsboro' on the 23d, and met General Schofield, who described fully his operations in North Carolina up to that date; and I also found Lieutenant Dunn, aide-de-camp to General Grant, with a letter from him of March 16th, giving a general description of the state of facts about City Point. The next day I received another letter, more full, dated the 22d, which I give herewith.

Nevertheless, I deemed it of great importance that I should have a personal interview with the general, and determined to go in person to City Point as soon as the repairs of the railroad, then in progress under the personal direction of Colonel W. W. Wright, would permit:

HEADQUARTERS OF THE ARMIES OF THE UNITED STATES VCITY POINT, VIRGINIA, March 22, 1865

Major-General SHERMAN, Commanding Military Division of the Mississippi.

GENERAL: Although the Richmond papers do not communicate the fact, yet I saw enough in them to satisfy me that you occupied Goldsboro' on the 19th inst. I congratulate you and the army on what may be regarded as the successful termination of the third campaign since leaving the Tennessee River, less than one year ago.

Since Sheridan's very successful raid north of the James, the enemy are left dependent on the Southside and Danville roads for all their supplies. These I hope to cut next week. Sheridan is at White House, "shoeing up" and resting his cavalry. I expect him to finish by Friday night and to start the following morning, raid Long Bridge, Newmarket, Bermuda Hundred, and the extreme left of the army around Petersburg. He will make no halt with the armies operating here, but will be joined by a division of cavalry, five thousand five hundred strong, from the Army of the Potomac, and will proceed directly to the Southside and Danville roads. His instructions will be to strike the Southside road as near Petersburg as he can, and destroy it so that it cannot be repaired for three or four days, and push on to the Danville road, as near to the Appomattox as he can get. Then I want him to destroy the road toward Burkesville as far as he can; then push on to the Southside road, west of Burkesville, and destroy it effectually. From that point I shall probably leave it to his discretion either to return to this army, crossing the Danville road south of Burkesville, or go and join you, passing between Danville and Greensboro'. When this movement commences I shall move out by my left, with all the force I can, holding present intrenched lines. I shall start with no distinct view, further than holding Lee's forces from following Sheridan. But I shall be along myself, and will take advantage of any thing that turns up. If Lee detaches, I will attack; or if he comes out of his lines I will endeavor to repulse him, and follow it up to the best advantage.

It is most difficult to understand what the rebels intend to do; so far but few troops have been detached from Lee's army. Much machinery has been removed, and material has been sent to Lynchburg, showing a disposition to go there. Points, too, have been fortified on the Danville road.

Lee's army is much demoralized, and great numbers are deserting. Probably, from returned prisoners, and such conscripts as can be picked up, his numbers may be kept up. I estimate his force now at about sixty-five thousand men.

Wilson started on Monday, with twelve thousand cavalry, from Eastport. Stoneman started on the same day, from East Tennessee, toward Lynchburg. Thomas is moving the Fourth Corps to Bull's Gap. Canby is moving with a formidable force on Mobile and the interior of Alabama.

I ordered Gilmore, as soon as the fall of Charleston was known, to hold all important posts on the sea-coast, and to send to Wilmington all surplus forces. Thomas was also directed to forward to Newbern all troops belonging to the corps with you. I understand this will give you about five thousand men, besides those brought east by Meagher.

I have been telegraphing General Meigs to hasten up locomotives and cars for you. General McCallum, he informs me, is attending to it. I fear they are not going forward as fast as I world like.

Let me know if you want more troops, or any thing else.

Very respectfully, your obedient servant,

U. S. GRANT, Lieutenant-General.

The railroad was repaired to Goldsboro' by the evening of March 25th, when, leaving General Schofield in chief command, with a couple of staff-officers I started for City Point, Virginia, in a locomotive, in company with Colonel Wright, the constructing engineer. We reached Newbern that evening, which was passed in the company of General Palmer and his accomplished lady, and early the next morning we continued on to Morehead City, where General Easton had provided for us the small captured steamer Russia, Captain Smith. We put to sea at once and steamed up the coast, reaching Fortress Monroe on the morning of the 27th, where I landed and telegraphed to my brother, Senator Sherman, at Washington, inviting him to come down and return with me to Goldsboro. We proceeded on up James River to City Point, which we reached the same afternoon. I found General Grant, with his family and staff, occupying a pretty group of huts on the bank of James River, overlooking the harbor, which was full of vessels of all classes, both war and merchant, with wharves and warehouses on an extensive scale. The general received me most heartily, and we talked over matters very fully. After I had been with him an hour or so, he remarked that the President, Mr. Lincoln, was then on board the steamer River Queen, lying at the wharf, and he proposed that we should call and see him. We walked down to the wharf, went on board, and found Mr. Lincoln alone, in the after-cabin. He remembered me perfectly, and at once engaged in a most interesting conversation. He was full of curiosity about the many incidents of our great march, which had reached him officially and through the newspapers, and seemed to enjoy very much the more ludicrous parts-about the "bummers," and their devices to collect food and forage when the outside world supposed us to be starving; but at the same time he expressed a good deal of anxiety lest some accident might happen to the army in North Carolina during my absence. I explained to him that that army was snug and comfortable, in good camps, at Goldsboro'; that it would require some days to collect forage and food for another march; and that General Schofield was fully competent to command it in my absence. Having made a good, long, social visit, we took our leave and returned to General Grant's quarters, where Mrs. Grant had provided tea. While at the table, Mrs. Grant inquired if we had seen Mrs. Lincoln. "No," said the general, "I did not ask for her;" and I added that I did not even know that she was on board. Mrs. Grant then exclaimed, "Well, you are a pretty pair!" and added that our neglect was unpardonable; when the general said we would call again the next day, and make amends for the unintended slight.

Early the next day, March 28th, all the principal officers of the army and navy called to see me, Generals Meade, Ord, Ingalls, etc., and Admiral Porter. At this time the River Queen was at anchor out in the river, abreast of the wharf, and we again started to visit Mr. and Mrs. Lincoln. Admiral Porter accompanied us. We took a small, tug at the wharf, which conveyed us on board, where we were again received most courteously by the President, who conducted us to the after-cabin. After the general compliments, General Grant inquired after Mrs. Lincoln, when the President went to her stateroom, returned, and begged us to excuse her, as she was not well. We then again entered upon a general conversation, during which General Grant explained to the President that at that very instant of time General Sheridan was crossing James River from the north, by a pontoon-bridge below City Point; that he had a large, well-appointed force of cavalry, with which he proposed to strike the Southside and Danville Railroads, by which alone General Lee, in Richmond, supplied his army; and that, in his judgment, matters were drawing to a crisis, his only apprehension being that General Lee would not wait long enough. I also explained that my army at Goldsboro' was strong enough to fight Lee's army and Johnston's combined, provided that General Grant could come up within a day or so; that if Lee would only remain in Richmond another fortnight, I could march up to Burkesville, when Lee would have to starve inside of his lines, or come out from his intrenchments and fight us on equal terms.

Both General Grant and myself supposed that one or the other of us would have to fight one more bloody battle, and that it would be the last. Mr. Lincoln exclaimed, more than once, that there had been blood enough shed, and asked us if another battle could not be avoided. I remember well to have said that we could not control that event; that this necessarily rested with our enemy; and I inferred that both Jeff. Davis and General Lee would be forced to fight one more desperate and bloody battle. I rather supposed it would fall on me, somewhere near Raleigh; and General Grant added that, if Lee would only wait a few more days, he would have his army so disposed that if the enemy should abandon Richmond, and attempt to make junction with General Jos. Johnston in North Carolina, he (General Grant) would be on his heels. Mr. Lincoln more than once expressed uneasiness that I was not with my army at Goldsboro', when I again assured him that General Schofield was fully competent to command in my absence; that I was going to start back that very day, and that Admiral Porter had kindly provided for me the steamer Bat, which he said was much swifter than my own vessel, the Russia. During this interview I inquired of the President if he was all ready for the end of the war. What was to be done with the rebel armies when defeated? And what should be done with the political leaders, such as Jeff. Davis, etc.? Should we allow them to escape, etc.? He said he was all ready; all he wanted of us was to defeat the opposing armies, and to get the men composing the Confederate armies back to their homes, at work on their farms and in their shops. As to Jeff. Davis, he was hardly at liberty to speak his mind fully, but intimated that he ought to clear out, "escape the country," only it would not do for him to say so openly. As usual, he illustrated his meaning by a story:

A man once had taken the total-abstinence pledge. When visiting a friend, he was invited to take a drink, but declined, on the score of his pledge; when his friend suggested lemonade, which was accepted. In preparing the lemonade, the friend pointed to the brandy-bottle, and said the lemonade would be more palatable if he were to pour in a little brandy; when his guest said, if he could do so "unbeknown" to him, he would "not object." From which illustration I inferred that Mr. Lincoln wanted Davis to escape, "unbeknown" to him.

I made no notes of this conversation at the time, but Admiral Porter, who was present, did, and in 1866 he furnished me an account thereof, which I insert below, but the admiral describes the first visit, of the 27th, whereas my memory puts Admiral Porter's presence on the following day. Still he may be right, and he may have been with us the day before, as I write this chiefly from memory. There were two distinct interviews; the first was late in the afternoon of March 27th, and the other about noon of the 28th, both in the after-cabin of the steamer River Queen; on both occasions Mr. Lincoln was full and frank in his conversation, assuring me that in his mind he was all ready for the civil reorganization of affairs at the South as soon as the war was over; and he distinctly authorized me to assure Governor Vance and the people of North Carolina that, as soon as the rebel armies laid down their arms, and resumed their civil pursuits, they would at once be guaranteed all their rights as citizens of a common country; and that to avoid anarchy the State governments then in existence, with their civil functionaries, would be recognized by him as the government de facto till Congress could provide others.

I know, when I left him, that I was more than ever impressed by his kindly nature, his deep and earnest sympathy with the afflictions of the whole people, resulting from the war, and by the march of hostile armies through the South; and that his earnest desire seemed to be to end the war speedily, without more bloodshed or devastation, and to restore all the men of both sections to their homes. In the language of his second inaugural address, he seemed to have "charity for all, malice toward none," and, above all, an absolute faith in the courage, manliness, and integrity of the armies in the field. When at rest or listening, his legs and arms seemed to hang almost lifeless, and his face was care-worn and haggard; but, the moment he began to talk, his face lightened up, his tall form, as it were, unfolded, and he was the very impersonation of good-humor and fellowship. The last words I recall as addressed to me were that he would feel better when I was back at Goldsboro'. We parted at the gangway of the River Queen, about noon of March 28th, and I never saw him again. Of all the men I ever met, he seemed to possess more of the elements of greatness, combined with goodness, than any other.

ADMIRAL PORTER'S ACCOUNT OF THE INTERVIEW WITH Mr. LINCOLN.

The day of General Sherman's arrival at City Point (I think the 27th of March, 1866), I accompanied him and General Grant on board the President's flagship, the Queen, where the President received us in the upper saloon, no one but ourselves being present.

The President was in an exceedingly pleasant mood, and delighted to meet General Sherman, whom he cordially greeted.

It seems that this was the first time he had met Sherman, to remember him, since the beginning of the war, and did not remember when he had seen him before, until the general reminded him of the circumstances of their first meeting.

This was rather singular on the part of Mr. Lincoln, who was, I think, remarkable for remembering people, having that kingly quality in an eminent degree. Indeed, such was the power of his memory, that he seemed never to forget the most minute circumstance.

The conversation soon turned on the events of Sherman's campaign through the South, with every movement of which the President seemed familiar.

He laughed over some of the stories Sherman told of his "bummers," and told others in return, which illustrated in a striking manner the ideas he wanted to convey. For example, he would often express his wishes by telling an apt story, which was quite a habit with him, and one that I think he adopted to prevent his committing himself seriously.

The interview between the two generals and the President lasted about an hour and a half, and, as it was a remarkable one, I jotted down what I remembered of the conversation, as I have made a practice of doing during the rebellion, when any thing interesting occurred.

I don't regret having done so, as circumstances afterward occurred (Stanton's ill conduct toward Sherman) which tended to cast odium on General Sherman for allowing such liberal terms to Jos. Johnston.

Could the conversation that occurred on board the Queen, between the President and General Sherman, have been known, Sherman would not, and could not, have been censored. Mr. Lincoln, had he lived, would have acquitted the general of any blame, for he was only carrying out the President's wishes.

My opinion is, that Mr. Lincoln came down to City Point with the most liberal views toward the rebels. He felt confident that we would be successful, and was willing that the enemy should capitulate on the most favorable terms.

I don't know what the President would have done had he been left to himself, and had our army been unsuccessful, but he was than wrought up to a high state of excitement. He wanted peace on almost any terms, and there is no knowing what proposals he might have been willing to listen to. His heart was tenderness throughout, and, as long as the rebels laid down their arms, he did not care how it was done. I do not know how far he was influenced by General Grant, but I presume, from their long conferences, that they must have understood each other perfectly, and that the terms given to Lee after his surrender were authorized by Mr. Lincoln. I know that the latter was delighted when he heard that they had been given, and exclaimed, a dozen times, "Good!" "All right!" "Exactly the thing!" and other similar expressions. Indeed, the President more than once told me what he supposed the terms would be: if Lee and Johnston surrendered, he considered the war ended, and that all the other rebel forces world lay down their arms at once.

In this he proved to be right. Grant and Sherman were both of the same opinion, and so was everyone else who knew anything about the matter.

What signified the terms to them, so long as we obtained the actual surrender of people who only wanted a good opportunity to give up gracefully? The rebels had fought "to the last ditch," and all that they had left them was the hope of being handed down in history as having received honorable terms.

After hearing General Sherman's account of his own position, and that of Johnston, at that time, the President expressed fears that the rebel general would escape south again by the railroads, and that General Sherman would have to chase him anew, over the same ground; but the general pronounced this to be impracticable. He remarked: "I have him where he cannot move without breaking up his army, which, once disbanded, can never again be got together; and I have destroyed the Southern railroads, so that they cannot be used again for a long time." General Grant remarked, "What is to prevent their laying the rails again?" "Why," said General Sherman, "my bummers don't do things by halves. Every rail, after having been placed over a hot fire, has been twisted as crooked as a ram's-horn, and they never can be used again."

This was the only remark made by General Grant during the interview, as he sat smoking a short distance from the President, intent, no doubt, on his own plans, which were being brought to a successful termination.

The conversation between the President and General Sherman, about the terms of surrender to be allowed Jos. Johnston, continued. Sherman energetically insisted that he could command his own terms, and that Johnston would have to yield to his demands; but the President was very decided about the matter, and insisted that the surrender of Johnston's army most be obtained on any terms.

General Grant was evidently of the same way of thinking, for, although he did not join in the conversation to any extent, yet he made no objections, and I presume had made up his mind to allow the best terms himself.

He was also anxious that Johnston should not be driven into Richmond, to reenforce the rebels there, who, from behind their strong intrenchments, would have given us incalculable trouble.

Sherman, as a subordinate officer, yielded his views to those of the President, and the terms of capitulation between himself and Johnston were exactly in accordance with Mr. Lincoln's wishes. He could not have done any thing which would have pleased the President better.

Mr. Lincoln did, in fact, arrange the (so considered) liberal terms offered General Jos. Johnston, and, whatever may have been

General Sherman's private views, I feel sure that he yielded to the wishes of the President in every respect. It was Mr. Lincoln's policy that was carried out, and, had he lived long enough, he would have been but too glad to have acknowledged it. Had Mr. Lincoln lived, Secretary Stanton would have issued no false telegraphic dispatches, in the hope of killing off another general in the regular army, one who by his success had placed himself in the way of his own succession.

The disbanding of Jos. Johnston's army was so complete, that the pens and ink used in the discussion of the matter were all wasted.

It was asserted, by the rabid ones, that General Sherman had given up all that we had been fighting for, had conceded every thing to Jos. Johnston, and had, as the boys say, "knocked the fat into the fire;" but sober reflection soon overruled these harsh expressions, and, with those who knew General Sherman, and appreciated him, he was still the great soldier, patriot, and gentleman. In future times this matter will be looked at more calmly and dispassionately. The bitter animosities that have been engendered during the rebellion will have died out for want of food on which to live, and the very course Grant, Sherman, and others pursued, in granting liberal terms to the defeated rebels, will be applauded. The fact is, they met an old beggar in the road, whose crutches had broken from under him: they let him have only the broken crutches to get home with!

I sent General Sherman back to Newbern, North Carolina, in the steamer Bat.

While he was absent from his command he was losing no time, for he was getting his army fully equipped with stores and clothing; and, when he returned, he had a rested and regenerated army, ready to swallow up Jos. Johnston and all his ragamuffins.

Johnston was cornered, could not move without leaving every thing behind him, and could not go to Richmond without bringing on a famine in that destitute city.

I was with Mr. Lincoln all the time he was at City Point, and until he left for Washington. He was more than delighted with the surrender of Lee, and with the terms Grant gave the rebel general; and would have given Jos. Johnston twice as much, had the latter asked for it, and could he have been certain that the rebel world have surrendered without a fight. I again repeat that, had Mr. Lincoln lived, he would have shouldered all the responsibility.

One thing is certain: had Jos. Johnston escaped and got into Richmond, and caused a larger list of killed and wounded than we had, General Sherman would have been blamed. Then why not give him the full credit of capturing on the best terms the enemy's last important army and its best general, and putting an end to the rebellion.

It was a finale worthy of Sherman's great march through the swamps and deserts of the South, a march not excelled by any thing we read of in modern military history.

D. D. PORTER, *Vice-Admiral.*

(Written by the admiral in 1866, at the United States Naval Academy at Annapolis, Md., and mailed to General Sherman at St. Louis, Mo.)

As soon as possible, I arranged with General Grant for certain changes in the organization of my army; and the general also undertook to send to North Carolina some tug-boat and barges to carry stores from Newbern up as far as Kinston, whence they could be hauled in wagons to our camps, thus relieving our railroads to that extent. I undertook to be ready to march north by April 10th, and then embarked on the steamer Bat, Captain Barnes, for North Carolina. We steamed down James River, and at Old Point Comfort took on board my brother, Senator Sherman, and Mr. Edwin Stanton, son of the Secretary of War, and proceeded at once to our destination. On our way down the river, Captain Barnes expressed himself extremely obliged to me for taking his vessel, as it had relieved him of a most painful dilemma. He explained that he had been detailed by Admiral Porter to escort the President's unarmed boat, the River Queen, in which capacity it became his special duty to look after Mrs. Lincoln. The day before my arrival at City Point, there had been a grand review of a part of the Army of the James, then commanded by General Ord. The President rode out from City Point with General Grant on horseback, accompanied by a numerous staff, including Captain Barnes and Mrs. Ord; but Mrs. Lincoln and Mrs. Grant had followed in a carriage.

The cavalcade reached the review-ground some five or six miles out from City Point, found the troops all ready, drawn up in line, and after the usual presentation of arms, the President and party, followed by Mrs. Ord and Captain Barnes on horseback, rode the lines, and returned to the reviewing stand, which meantime had been reached by Mrs. Lincoln and Mrs. Grant in their carriage, which had been delayed by the driver taking a wrong road. Mrs. Lincoln, seeing Mrs. Ord and Captain Barnes riding with the retinue, and supposing that Mrs. Ord had personated her, turned on Captain Barnes and gave him a fearful scolding; and even indulged in some pretty sharp upbraidings to Mrs. Ord.

This made Barne's position very unpleasant, so that he felt much relieved when he was sent with me to North Carolina. The Bat was very fast, and on the morning of the 29th we were near Cape Hatteras; Captain Barnes, noticing a propeller coming out of Hatteras Inlet, made her turn back and pilot us in. We entered safely, steamed up Pamlico Sound into Neuse River, and the next morning,--by reason of some derangement of machinery, we anchored about seven miles below Newbern, whence we went up in Captain Barnes's barge. As soon as we arrived at Newbern, I telegraphed up to General Schofield at Goldsboro' the fact of my return, and that I had arranged with General Grant for the changes made necessary in the reorganization of the army, and for the boats necessary to carry up the provisions and stores we needed, prior to the renewal of our march northward.

These changes amounted to constituting the left wing a distinct army, under the title of "the Army of Georgia," under command of General Slocum, with his two corps commanded by General Jeff. C. Davis and General Joseph A. Mower; the Tenth and Twenty-third Corps already constituted another army, "of the Ohio," under the command of Major-General Schofield, and his two corps were commanded by Generals J. D. Cox and A. H. Terry. These changes were necessary, because army commanders only could order courts-martial, grant discharges, and perform many other matters of discipline and administration which were indispensable; but my chief purpose was to prepare the whole army for what seemed among the probabilities of the time--to fight both Lee's and Johnston's armies combined, in case their junction could be formed before General Grant could possibly follow Lee to North Carolina.

General George H. Thomas, who still remained at Nashville, was not pleased with these changes, for the two corps with General Slocum, viz., the Fourteenth and Twentieth, up to that time, had remained technically a part of his "Army of the Cumberland;" but he was so far away, that I had to act to the best advantage with the troops and general officers actually present. I had specially asked for General Mower to command the Twentieth Corps, because I regarded him as one of the boldest and best fighting generals in the whole army. His predecessor, General A. S. Williams, the senior division commander present, had commanded the corps well from Atlanta to Goldsboro', and it may have seemed unjust to replace him at that precise moment; but I was resolved to be prepared for a most desperate and, as then expected, a final battle, should it fall on me.

I returned to Goldsboro' from Newbern by rail the evening of March 30th, and at once addressed myself to the task of reorganization and replenishment of stores, so as to be ready to march by April 10th, the day agreed on with General Grant.

The army was divided into the usual three parts, right and left wings, and centre. The tabular statements herewith will give the exact composition of these separate armies, which by the 10th of April gave the following effective strength:

Infantry	0,968
Artillery	,448
Cavalry	,587
Aggregate	8,948
Total number of guns	1

The railroads to our rear had also been repaired, so that stores were arriving very fast, both from Morehead City and Wilmington. The country was so level that a single locomotive could haul twenty-five and thirty cars to a train, instead of only ten, as was the case in Tennessee and Upper Georgia.

By the 5th of April such progress had been made, that I issued the following Special Field Orders, No. 48, prescribing the time and manner of the next march

[Special Field Orders, No. 48.]

HEADQUARTERS MILITARY DIVISION OF THE MISSISSIPPI IN THE FIELD, GOLDSBORO', NORTH CAROLINA, April 5, 1865.

Confidential to Army Commanders, Corps Commanders, and Chiefs of Staff Departments:

The next grand objective is to place this army (with its full equipment) north of Roanoke River, facing west, with a base for supplies at Norfolk, and at Winton or Murfreesboro' on the Chowan, and in full communication with the Army of the Potomac, about Petersburg; and also to do the enemy as much harm as possible en route:

1. To accomplish this result the following general plan will be followed, or modified only by written orders from these headquarters, should events require a change:

(1.) On Monday, the 10th of April, all preparations are presumed to be complete, and the outlying detachments will be called in, or given directions to meet on the next march. All preparations will also be complete to place the railroad-stock back of Kinston on the one road, and below the Northeast Branch on the other.

(2.) On Tuesday, the 11th, the columns will draw out on their lines of march, say, about seven miles, and close up.

(3.) On Wednesday the march will begin in earnest, and will be kept up at the rate, say, of about twelve miles a day, or according to the amount of resistance. All the columns will dress to the left (which is the exposed flank), and commanders will study always to find roads by which they can, if necessary, perform a general left wheel, the wagons to be escorted to some place of security on the direct route of march. Foraging and other details may continue as heretofore, only more caution and prudence should be observed; and foragers should not go in advance of the advance-guard, but look more to our right rear for corn, bacon, and meal.

2. The left wing (Major-General Slocum commanding) will aim straight for the railroad-bridge near Smithfield; thence along up the Neuse River to the railroad-bridge over Neuse River, northeast of Raleigh (Powell's); thence to Warrenton, the general point of concentration.

The centre (Major-General Schofield commanding) will move to Whitley's Mill, ready to support the left until it is past Smithfield, when it will follow up (substantially) Little River to about Rolesville, ready at all times to move to the support of the left; after passing Tar River, to move to Warrenton.

The right wing (Major-General Howard commanding), preceded by the cavalry, will move rapidly on Pikeville and Nahunta, then swing across to Bulah to Folk's Bridge, ready to make junction with the other armies in case the enemy offers battle this side of Neuse River, about Smithfield; thence, in case of no serious opposition on the left, will work up toward Earpsboro', Andrews, B----, and Warrenton.

The cavalry (General Kilpatrick commanding), leaving its encumbrances with the right wing, will push as though straight for Weldon, until the enemy is across Tar River, and that bridge burned; then it will deflect toward Nashville and Warrenton, keeping up communication with general headquarters.

3. As soon as the army starts, the chief-quartermaster and commissary will prepare a resupply of stores at some point on Pamlico or Albemarle Sounds, ready to be conveyed to Kinston or Winton and Murfreesboro', according to developments. As soon as they have satisfactory information that the army is north of the Roanoke, they will forthwith establish a depot at Winton, with a sub-depot at Murfreesboro'. Major-General Schofield will hold, as heretofore, Wilmington (with the bridge across Northern Branch as an outpost), Newborn (and Kinston as its outpost), and will be prepared to hold Winton and Murfreesboro' as soon as the time arrives for that move. The navy has instructions from Admiral Porter to cooperate, and any commanding officer is authorized to call on the navy for assistance and cooperation, always in writing, setting forth the reasons, of which necessarily the naval commander must be the judge.

4. The general-in-chief will be with the centre habitually, but may in person shift to either flank where his presence may be needed, leaving a staff-officer to receive reports. He requires, absolutely, a report of each army or grand detachment each night, whether any thing material has occurred or not, for often the absence of an enemy is a very important fact in military prognostication.

By order of Major-General W. T. Sherman,

L. M. DAYTON, Assistant Adjutant-General.

But the whole problem became suddenly changed by the news of the fall of Richmond and Petersburg, which reached as at Goldsboro', on the 6th of April. The Confederate Government, with Lee's army, had hastily abandoned Richmond, fled in great disorder toward Danville, and General Grant's whole army was in close pursuit. Of course, I inferred that General Lee would succeed in making junction with General Johnston, with at least a fraction of his army, somewhere to my front. I at once altered the foregoing orders, and prepared on the day appointed, viz., April 10th, to move straight on Raleigh, against the army of General Johnston, known to be at Smithfield, and supposed to have about thirty-five thousand men. Wade Hampton's cavalry was on his left front and Wheeler's on his right front, simply watching us and awaiting our initiative. Meantime the details of the great victories in Virginia came thick and fast, and on the 8th I received from General Grant this communication, in the form of a cipher-dispatch:

HEADQUARTERS ARMIES OF THE UNITED STATES
WILSON'S STATION, *April 5, 1865*

Major-General SHERMAN, Goldsboro', North Carolina:

All indications now are that Lee will attempt to reach Danville with the remnant of his force. Sheridan, who was up with him last night, reports all that is left with him--horse, foot, and dragoons--at twenty thousand, much demoralized. We hope to reduce this number one-half. I will push on to Burkesville, and, if a stand is made at Danville, will, in a very few days, go there. If you can possibly do so, push on from where you are, and let us see if we cannot finish the job with Lee's and Johnston's armies. Whether it will be better for you to strike for Greensboro' or nearer to Danville, you will be better able to judge when you receive this. Rebel armies now are the only strategic points to strike at.

U. S. GRANT, *Lieutenant-General.*

I answered immediately that we would move on the 10th, prepared to follow Johnston wherever he might go. Promptly on Monday morning, April 10th, the army moved straight on Smithfield; the right wing making a circuit by the right, and the left wing, supported by the centre, moving on the two direct roads toward Raleigh, distant fifty miles. General Terry's and General Kilpatrick's troops moved from their positions on the south or west bank of the Neuse River in the same general direction, by Cox's Bridge. On the 11th we reached Smithfield, and found it abandoned by Johnston's army, which had retreated hastily on Raleigh, burning the bridges. To restore these consumed the remainder of the day, and during that night I received a message from General Grant, at Appomattox, that General Lee had surrendered to him his whole army, which I at once announced to the troops in orders:

[Special Field Orders, No. 54]

HEADQUARTERS MILITARY DIVISION OF THE MISSISSIPPI
IN THE FIELD, SMITHFIELD, NORTH CAROLINA, *April 12, 1865.*

The general commanding announces to the army that he has official notice from General Grant that General Lee surrendered to him his entire army, on the 9th inst., at Appomattox Court-House, Virginia.

Glory to God and our country, and all honor to our comrades in arms, toward whom we are marching!

A little more labor, a little more toil on our part, the great race is won, and our Government stands regenerated, after four long years of war.

W. T. SHERMAN, *Major-General commanding.*

Of course, this created a perfect furore, of rejoicing, and we all regarded the war as over, for I knew well that General Johnston had no army with which to oppose mine. So that the only questions that remained were, would he surrender at Raleigh? or would he allow his army to disperse into guerrilla bands, to "die in the last ditch," and entail on his country an indefinite and prolonged military occupation, and of consequent desolation? I knew well that Johnston's army could not be caught; the country was too open; and, without wagons, the men could escape us, disperse, and assemble again at some place agreed on, and thus the war might be prolonged indefinitely.

I then remembered Mr. Lincoln's repeated expression that he wanted the rebel soldiers not only defeated, but "back at their homes, engaged in their civil pursuits." On the evening of the 12th I was with the head of Slocum's column, at Gulley's, and General Kilpatrick's cavalry was still ahead, fighting Wade Hampton's rear-guard, with orders to push it through Raleigh, while I would give a more southerly course to the infantry columns, so as, if possible, to prevent a retreat southward. On the 13th, early, I entered Raleigh, and ordered the several heads of column toward Ashville in the direction of Salisbury or Charlotte. Before reaching Raleigh, a locomotive came down the road to meet me, passing through both Wade Hampton's and Kilpatrick's cavalry, bringing four gentlemen, with a letter from Governor Vance to me, asking protection for the citizens of Raleigh. These gentlemen were, of course, dreadfully excited at the dangers through which they had passed. Among them were ex-Senator Graham, Mr. Swain, president of Chapel Hill University, and a Surgeon Warren, of the Confederate army. They had come with a flag of truce, to which they were not entitled; still, in the interest of peace, I respected it, and permitted them to return to Raleigh with their locomotive, to assure the Governor and the people that the war was substantially over, and that I wanted the civil authorities to remain in the execution of their office till the pleasure of the President could be ascertained. On reaching Raleigh I found these same gentlemen, with Messrs. Badger, Bragg, Holden, and others, but Governor Vance had fled, and could not be prevailed on to return, because he feared an arrest and imprisonment. From the Raleigh newspapers of the 10th I learned that General Stoneman, with his division of cavalry, had come across the mountains from East Tennessee, had destroyed the railroad at Salisbury, and was then supposed to be approaching Greensboro'. I also learned that General Wilson's cavalry corps was "smashing things" down about Selma and Montgomery, Alabama, and was pushing for Columbus and Macon, Georgia; and I also had reason to expect that General Sheridan would come down from Appomattox to join us at Raleigh with his superb cavalry corps. I needed more cavalry to check Johnston's retreat, so that I could come up to him with my infantry, and therefore had good reason to delay. I ordered the railroad to be finished up to Raleigh, so that I could operate from it as a base, and then made:

[Special Field Orders, No. 55]

HEADQUARTERS MILITARY DIVISION OF THE MISSISSIPPI IN THE FIELD,
RALEIGH, NORTH CAROLINA, April 14, 1865.

The next movement will be on Ashboro', to turn the position of the enemy at the "Company's Shops" in rear of Haw River Bridge, and at Greensboro', and to cut off his only available line of retreat by Salisbury and Charlotte:

1. General Kilpatrick will keep up a show of pursuit in the direction of Hillsboro' and Graham, but be ready to cross Haw River on General Howard's bridge, near Pittsboro', and thence will operate toward Greensboro', on the right front of the right wing.

2. The right wing, Major-General Howard commanding, will move out on the Chapel Hill road, and send a light division up in the direction of Chapel Hill University to act in connection with the cavalry; but the main columns and trains will move via Hackney's Cross-Roads, and Trader's Hill, Pittsboro', St. Lawrence, etc., to be followed by the cavalry and light division, as soon as the bridge is laid over Haw River.

8. The centre, Major-General Schofield commanding, will move via Holly Springs, New Hill, Haywood, and Moffitt's Mills.

4. The left wing, Major-General Slocum commanding, will move rapidly by the Aven's Ferry road, Carthage, Caledonia, and Cox's Mills.

5. All the troops will draw well out on the roads designated during today and to-morrow, and on the following day will move with all possible rapidity for Ashboro'. No further destruction of railroads, mills, cotton, and produce, will be made without the specific orders of an army commander, and the inhabitants will be dealt with kindly, looking to an early reconciliation. The troops will be permitted, however, to gather forage and provisions as heretofore; only more care should be taken not to strip the poorer classes too closely.

By order of General W. T. Sherman,

L. M. DAYTON, Assistant Adjutant-General.

Thus matters stood, when on the morning of the 14th General Kilpatrick reported from Durham's Station, twenty-six miles up the railroad toward Hillsboro', that a flag of truce had come in from the enemy with a package from General Johnston addressed to me. Taking it for granted that this was preliminary to a surrender, I ordered the message to be sent me at Raleigh, and on the 14th received from General Johnston a letter dated April 13, 1865, in these words:

The results of the recent campaign in Virginia have changed the relative military condition of the belligerents. I am, therefore, induced to address you in this form the inquiry whether, to stop the further effusion of blood and devastation of property, you are willing to make a temporary suspension of active operations, and to communicate to Lieutenant-General Grant, commanding the armies of the United States, the request that he will take like action in regard to other armies, the object being to permit the civil authorities to enter into the needful arrangements to terminate the existing war.

To which I replied as follows:

HEADQUARTERS MILITARY DIVISION OF THE MISSISSIPPI
IN THE FIELD, RALEIGH, NORTH CAROLINA, April 14, 1865.

General J. E. JOHNSTON, commanding Confederate Army.

GENERAL: I have this moment received your communication of this date. I am fully empowered to arrange with you any terms for the suspension of farther hostilities between the armies commanded by you and those commanded by myself, and will be willing to confer with you to that end. I will limit the advance of my main column, to-morrow, to Morrisville, and the cavalry to the university, and expect that you will also maintain the present position of your forces until each has notice of a failure to agree.

That a basis of action may be had, I undertake to abide by the same terms and conditions as were made by Generals Grant and Lee at Appomattox Court-House, on the 9th instant, relative to our two armies; and, furthermore, to obtain from General Grant an order to suspend the movements of any troops from the direction of Virginia. General Stoneman is under my command, and my order will suspend any devastation or destruction contemplated by him. I will add that I really desire to save the people of North Carolina the damage they would sustain by the march of this army through the central or western parts of the State.

I am, with respect, your obedient servant,

W. T. SHERMAN, Major-General.

I sent my aide-de-camp, Colonel McCoy, up to Durham's Station with this letter, with instructions to receive the answer, to telegraph its contents back to me at Raleigh, and to arrange for an interview. On the 16th I received a reply from General Johnston, agreeing to meet me the next day at a point midway between our advance at Durham and his rear at Hillsboro'. I ordered a car and locomotive to be prepared to convey me up to Durham's at eight o'clock of the morning of April 17th. Just as we were entering the car, the telegraph-operator, whose office was up-stairs in the depot-building, ran down to me and said that he was at that instant of time receiving a most important dispatch in cipher from Morehead City, which I ought to see. I held the train for nearly half an hour, when he returned with the message translated and written out. It was from Mr. Stanton, announcing the assassination of Mr. Lincoln, the attempt on the life of Mr. Seward and son, and a suspicion that a like fate was designed for General Grant and all the principal officers of the Government. Dreading the effect of such a message at that critical instant of time, I asked the operator if any one besides himself had seen it; he answered No! I then bade him not to reveal the contents by word or look till I came back, which I proposed to do the same afternoon. The train then started, and, as we passed Morris's Station, General Logan, commanding the Fifteenth Corps, came into my car, and I told him I wanted to see him on my return, as I had something very important to communicate. He knew I was going to meet General Johnston, and volunteered to say that he hoped I would succeed in obtaining his surrender, as the whole army dreaded the long march to Charlotte (one hundred and seventy-five miles), already begun, but which had been interrupted by the receipt of General Johnston's letter of the 13th. We reached Durham's, twenty-six miles, about 10 a.m., where General Kilpatrick had a squadron of cavalry drawn up to receive me. We passed into the house in which he had his headquarters, and soon after mounted some led horses, which he had prepared for myself and staff. General Kilpatrick sent a man ahead with a white flag, followed by a small platoon, behind which we rode, and were followed by the rest of the escort. We rode up the Hillsboro' road for about five miles, when our flag bearer discovered another coming to meet him: They met, and word was passed back to us that General Johnston was near at hand, when we rode forward and met General Johnston on horseback, riding side by side with General Wade Hampton. We shook hands, and introduced our respective attendants. I asked if there was a place convenient where we could be private, and General Johnston said he had passed a small farmhouse a short distance back, when we rode back to it together side by side, our staff-officers and escorts following. We had never met before, though we had been in the regular army together for thirteen years; but it so happened that we had never before come together. He was some twelve or more years my senior; but we knew enough of each other to be well acquainted at once. We soon reached the house of a Mr. Bennett, dismounted, and left our horses with orderlies in the road. Our officers, on foot, passed into the yard, and General Johnston and I entered the small frame-house. We asked the farmer if we could have the use of his house for a few minutes, and he and his wife withdrew into a smaller log-house, which stood close by.

As soon as we were alone together I showed him the dispatch announcing Mr. Lincoln's assassination, and watched him closely. The perspiration came out in large drops on his forehead, and he did not attempt to conceal his distress. He denounced the act as a disgrace to the age, and hoped I did not charge it to the Confederate Government. I told him I could not believe that he or General Lee, or the officers of the

Confederate army, could possibly be privy to acts of assassination; but I would not say as much for Jeff. Davis, George Sanders, and men of that stripe. We talked about the effect of this act on the country at large and on the armies, and he realized that it made my situation extremely delicate. I explained to him that I had not yet revealed the news to my own personal staff or to the army, and that I dreaded the effect when made known in Raleigh. Mr. Lincoln was peculiarly endeared to the soldiers, and I feared that some foolish woman or man in Raleigh might say something or do something that would madden our men, and that a fate worse than that of Columbia would befall the place.

I then told Johnston that he must be convinced that he could not oppose my army, and that, since Lee had surrendered, he could do the same with honor and propriety. He plainly and repeatedly admitted this, and added that any further fighting would be "murder;" but he thought that, instead of surrendering piecemeal, we might arrange terms that would embrace all the Confederate armies. I asked him if he could control other armies than his own; he said, not then, but intimated that he could procure authority from Mr. Davis. I then told him that I had recently had an interview with General Grant and President Lincoln, and that I was possessed of their views; that with them and the people North there seemed to be no vindictive feeling against the Confederate armies, but there was against Davis and his political adherents; and that the terms that General Grant had given to General Lee's army were certainly most generous and liberal. All this he admitted, but always recurred to the idea of a universal surrender, embracing his own army, that of Dick Taylor in Louisiana and Texas, and of Maury, Forrest, and others, in Alabama and Georgia. General Johnston's account of our interview in his "Narrative" (page 402, et seq.) is quite accurate and correct, only I do not recall his naming the capitulation of Loeben, to which he refers. Our conversation was very general and extremely cordial, satisfying me that it could have but one result, and that which we all desired, viz., to end the war as quickly as possible; and, being anxious to return to Raleigh before the news of Mr. Lincoln's assassination could be divulged, on General Johnston's saying that he thought that, during the night, he could procure authority to act in the name of all the Confederate armies in existence we agreed to meet again the next day at noon at the same place, and parted, he for Hillsboro' and I for Raleigh.

We rode back to Durham's Station in the order we had come, and then I showed the dispatch announcing Mr. Lincoln's death. I cautioned the officers to watch the soldiers closely, to prevent any violent retaliation by them, leaving that to the Government at Washington; and on our way back to Raleigh in the cars I showed the same dispatch to General Logan and to several of the officers of the Fifteenth Corps that were posted at Morrisville and Jones's Station, all of whom were deeply impressed by it; but all gave their opinion that this sad news should not change our general course of action.

As soon as I reached Raleigh I published the following orders to the army, announcing the assassination of the President, and I doubt if, in the whole land, there were more sincere mourners over his sad fate than were then in and about Raleigh. I watched the effect closely, and was gratified that there was no single act of retaliation; though I saw and felt that one single word by me would have laid the city in ashes, and turned its whole population houseless upon the country, if not worse:

[Special Field Orders, No. 56.]

HEADQUARTERS MILITARY DIVISION OF THE MISSISSIPPI IN THE FIELD, RALEIGH, NORTH CAROLINA, April 17, 1865.

The general commanding announces, with pain and sorrow, that on the evening of the 14th instant, at the theatre in Washington city, his Excellency the President of the United States, Mr. Lincoln, was assassinated by one who uttered the State motto of Virginia. At the same time, the Secretary of State, Mr. Seward, while suffering from a broken arm, was also stabbed by another murderer in his own house, but still survives, and his son was wounded, supposed fatally. It is believed, by persons capable of judging, that other high officers were designed to share the same fate. Thus it seems that our enemy, despairing of meeting us in open, manly warfare, begins to resort to the assassin's tools.

Your general does not wish you to infer that this is universal, for he knows that the great mass of the Confederate army would scorn to sanction such acts, but he believes it the legitimate consequence of rebellion against rightful authority.

We have met every phase which this war has assumed, and must now be prepared for it in its last and worst shape, that of assassins and guerrillas; but woe onto the people who seek to expend their wild passions in such a manner, for there is but one dread result!

By order of Major-General W. T. Sherman,

L. M. DAYTON, Assistant Adjutant-General.

During the evening of the 17th and morning of the 18th I saw nearly all the general officers of the army (Schofield, Slocum, Howard, Logan, Blair), and we talked over the matter of the conference at Bennett's house of the day before, and, without exception, all advised me to agree to some terms, for they all dreaded the long and harassing march in pursuit of a dissolving and fleeing army--a march that might carry us back again over the thousand miles that we had just accomplished. We all knew that if we could bring Johnston's army to bay, we could destroy it in an hour, but that was simply impossible in the country in which we found ourselves. We discussed all the probabilities, among which was, whether, if Johnston made a point of it, I should assent to the escape from the country of Jeff. Davis and his fugitive cabinet; and some one of my general officers, either Logan or Blair, insisted that, if asked for, we should even provide a vessel to carry them to Nassau from Charleston.

The next morning I again started in the cars to Durham's Station, accompanied by most of my personal staff, and by Generals Blair, Barry, Howard, etc., and, reaching General Kilpatrick's headquarters at Durham's, we again mounted, and rode, with the same escort of the day, before, to Bennett's house, reaching there punctually at noon. General Johnston had not yet arrived, but a courier shortly came, and reported him as on the way. It must have been nearly 2 p.m. when he arrived, as before, with General Wade Hampton. He had halted his escort out of sight, and we again entered Bennett's house, and I closed the door. General Johnston then assured me that he had authority over all the Confederate armies, so that they would obey his orders to surrender on the same terms with his own, but he argued that, to obtain so cheaply this desirable result, I ought to give his men and officers some assurance of their political rights after their surrender. I explained to him that Mr. Lincoln's proclamation of amnesty, of December 8, 1863, still in force; enabled every Confederate soldier and officer, below the rank of colonel, to obtain an absolute pardon, by simply laying down his arms, and taking the common oath of allegiance, and that General Grant, in accepting the surrender of General Lee's army, had extended the same principle to all the officers, General Lee included; such a pardon, I understood, would restore to them all their rights of citizenship. But he insisted that the officers and men of the Confederate army were unnecessarily alarmed about this matter, as a sort of bugbear. He then said that Mr. Breckenridge was near at hand, and he thought that it would be well for him to be present. I objected, on the score that he was then in Davis's cabinet, and our negotiations should be confined strictly to belligerents. He then said Breckenridge was a major-general in the Confederate army, and might sink his character of Secretary of War. I consented, and he sent one of his staff-officers back, who soon returned with Breckenridge, and he entered the room. General Johnston and I then again went over the whole ground, and Breckenridge confirmed what he had said as to the uneasiness of the Southern officers and soldiers about their political rights in case of surrender. While we were in consultation, a messenger came with a parcel of papers, which General Johnston said were from Mr. Reagan, Postmaster-General. He and Breckenridge looked over them, and, after some side conversation, he handed one of the papers to me. It was in Reagan's handwriting, and began with a long preamble and terms, so general and verbose, that I said they were inadmissible. Then recalling the conversation of Mr. Lincoln, at City Point, I sat down at the table, and wrote off the terms, which I thought concisely expressed his views and wishes, and explained that I was willing to submit these terms to the new President, Mr. Johnson, provided that both armies should remain in statu quo until the truce therein declared should expire. I had full faith that General Johnston would religiously respect the truce, which he did; and that I would be the gainer, for in the few days it would take to send the papers to Washington, and receive an answer, I could finish the railroad up to Raleigh, and be the better prepared for a long chase.

Neither Mr. Breckenridge nor General Johnston wrote one word of that paper. I wrote it myself, and announced it as the best I could do, and they readily assented.

While copies of this paper were being made for signature, the officers of our staffs commingled in the yard at Bennett's house, and were all presented to Generals Johnston and Breckenridge. All without exception were rejoiced that the war was over, and that in a very few days we could turn our faces toward home. I remember telling Breckenridge that he had better get away, as the feeling of our people was utterly hostile to the political element of the South, and to him especially, because he was the Vice-President of the United States, who had as such announced Mr. Lincoln, of Illinois, duly and properly elected the President of the United States, and yet that he had afterward openly rebelled and taken up arms against the Government. He answered me that he surely would give us no more trouble, and intimated that he would speedily leave the country forever. I may have also advised him that Mr. Davis too should get abroad as soon as possible.

The papers were duly signed; we parted about dark, and my party returned to Raleigh. Early the next morning, April 19th, I dispatched by telegraph to Morehead City to prepare a fleet-steamer to carry a messenger to Washington, and sent Major Henry Hitchcock down by rail, bearing the following letters, and agreement with General Johnston, with instructions to be very careful to let nothing escape him to the greedy newspaper correspondents, but to submit his papers to General Halleck, General Grant, or the Secretary of War, and to bring me back with all expedition their orders and instructions.

On their face they recited that I had no authority to make final terms involving civil or political questions, but that I submitted them to the proper quarter in Washington for their action; and the letters fully explained that the military situation was such that the delay was an advantage to us. I cared little whether they were approved, modified, or disapproved in toto; only I wanted instructions. Many of my general officers, among whom, I am almost positive, were Generals Logan and Blair, urged me to accept the "terms," without reference at all to Washington, but I preferred the latter course:

HEADQUARTERS MILITARY DIVISION OF THE MISSISSIPPI, IN THE FIELD,
RALEIGH, NORTH CAROLINA, April 18, 1886.

General H. W. HALLECK, Chief of Staff, Washington, D. C.

GENERAL: I received your dispatch describing the man Clark, detailed to assassinate me. He had better be in a hurry, or he will be too late.

The news of Mr. Lincoln's death produced a most intense effect on our troops. At first I feared it would lead to excesses; but now it has softened down, and can easily be guided. None evinced more feeling than General Johnston, who admitted that the act was calculated to stain his cause with a dark hue; and he contended that the loss was most serious to the South, who had begun to realize that Mr. Lincoln was the best friend they had.

I cannot believe that even Mr. Davis was privy to the diabolical plot, but think it the emanation of a set of young men of the South, who are very devils. I want to throw upon the South the care of this class of men, who will soon be as obnoxious to their industrial classes as to us.

Had I pushed Johnston's army to an extremity, it would have dispersed, and done infinite mischief. Johnston informed me that General Stoneman had been at Salisbury, and was now at Statesville. I have sent him orders to come to me.

General Johnston also informed me that General Wilson was at Columbia, Georgia, and he wanted me to arrest his progress. I leave that to you.

Indeed, if the President sanctions my agreement with Johnston, our interest is to cease all destruction.

Please give all orders necessary according to the views the Executive may take, and influence him, if possible, not to vary the terms at all, for I have considered every thing, and believe that, the Confederate armies once dispersed, we can adjust all else fairly and well. I am, yours, etc.,

W. T. SHERMAN, Major-General commanding.

HEADQUARTERS MILITARY DIVISION OF THE MISSISSIPPI
IN THE FIELD, RALEIGH, NORTH CAROLINA, April 18, 1865.

Lieutenant-General U. S. GRANT, or Major-General HALLECK, Washington, D. C.

GENERAL: I inclose herewith a copy of an agreement made this day between General Joseph E. Johnston and myself, which, if approved by the President of the United States, will produce peace from the Potomac to the Rio Grande. Mr. Breckenridge was present at our conference, in the capacity of major-general, and satisfied me of the ability of General Johnston to carry out to their full extent the terms of this agreement; and if you will get the President to simply indorse the copy, and commission me to carry out the terms, I will follow them to the conclusion.

You will observe that it is an absolute submission of the enemy to the lawful authority of the United States, and disperses his armies absolutely; and the point to which I attach most importance is, that the dispersion and disbandment of these armies is done in such a manner as to prevent their breaking up into guerrilla bands. On the other hand, we can retain just as much of an army as we please. I agreed to the mode and manner of the surrender of arms set forth, as it gives the States the means of repressing guerrillas, which we could not expect them to do if we stripped them of all arms.

Both Generals Johnston and Breckenridge admitted that slavery was dead, and I could not insist on embracing it in such a paper, because it can be made with the States in detail. I know that all the men of substance South sincerely want peace, and I do not believe they will resort to war again during this century. I have no doubt that they will in the future be perfectly subordinate to the laws of the United States. The moment my action in this matter is approved, I can spare five corps, and will ask for orders to leave General Schofield here with the Tenth Corps, and to march myself with the Fourteenth, Fifteenth, Seventeenth, Twentieth, and Twenty-third Corps via Burkesville and Gordonsville to Frederick or Hagerstown, Maryland, there to be paid and mustered out.

The question of finance is now the chief one, and every soldier and officer not needed should be got home at work. I would like to be able to begin the march north by May 1st.

I urge, on the part of the President, speedy action, as it is important to get the Confederate armies to their homes as well as our own.

I am, with great respect, your obedient servant,

W. T. SHERMAN, Major-General commanding.

Memorandum, or Basis of agreement, made this 18th day of April, A. D. 1865, near Durham's Station, in the State of North Carolina, by and between General Joseph E. JOHNSTON, commanding the Confederate Army, and Major-General William T. SHERMAN, commanding the army of the United States in North Carolina, both present:

1. The contending armies now in the field to maintain the statu quo until notice is given by the commanding general of any one to its opponent, and reasonable time--say, forty-eight hours--allowed.

2. The Confederate armies now in existence to be disbanded and conducted to their several State capitals, there to deposit their arms and public property in the State Arsenal; and each officer and man to execute and file an agreement to cease from acts of war, and to abide the action of the State and Federal authority. The number of arms and munitions of war to be reported to the Chief of Ordnance at Washington City, subject to the future action of the Congress of the United States, and, in the mean time, to be needed solely to maintain peace and order within the borders of the States respectively.

3. The recognition, by the Executive of the United States, of the several State governments, on their officers and Legislatures taking the oaths prescribed by the Constitution of the United States, and, where conflicting State governments have resulted from the war, the legitimacy of all shall be submitted to the Supreme Court of the United States.

4. The reestablishment of all the Federal Courts in the several States, with powers as defined by the Constitution of the United States and of the States respectively.

5. The people and inhabitants of all the States to be guaranteed, so far as the Executive can, their political rights and franchises, as well as their rights of person sad property, as defined by the Constitution of the United States and of the States respectively.

6. The Executive authority of the Government of the United States not to disturb any of the people by reason of the late war, so long as they live in peace and quiet, abstain from acts of armed hostility, and obey the laws in existence at the place of their residence.

7. In general terms--the war to cease; a general amnesty, so far as the Executive of the United States can command, on condition of the disbandment of the Confederate armies, the distribution of the arms, and the resumption of peaceful pursuits by the officers and men hitherto composing said armies.

Not being fully empowered by our respective principals to fulfill these terms, we individually and officially pledge ourselves to promptly obtain the necessary authority, and to carry out the above programme.

W. T. SHERMAN, Major-General, Commanding Army of the United States in North Carolina.

J. E. JOHNSTON, General,
Commanding Confederate States Army in North Carolina.

Major Hitchcock got off on the morning of the 20th, and I reckoned that it would take him four or five days to go to Washington and back. During that time the repairs on all the railroads and telegraph-lines were pushed with energy, and we also got possession of the railroad and telegraph from Raleigh to Weldon, in the direction of Norfolk. Meantime the troops remained statu quo, our cavalry occupying Durham's Station and Chapel Hill. General Slocum's head of column was at Aven's Ferry on Cape Fear River, and General Howard's was strung along the railroad toward Hillsboro'; the rest of the army was in and about Raleigh.

On the 20th I reviewed the Tenth Corps, and was much pleased at the appearance of General Paines's division of black troops, the first I had ever seen as a part of an organized army; and on the 21st I reviewed the Twenty-third Corps, which had been with me to Atlanta, but had returned to Nashville had formed an essential part of the army which fought at Franklin, and with which General Thomas had defeated General Hood in Tennessee. It had then been transferred rapidly by rail to Baltimore and Washington by General Grant's orders, and thence by sea to North Carolina. Nothing of interest happened at Raleigh till the evening of April 23d, when

Major Hitchcock reported by telegraph his return to Morehead City, and that he would come up by rail during the night. He arrived at 6 a.m., April 24th, accompanied by General Grant and one or two officers of his staff, who had not telegraphed the fact of their being on the train, for prudential reasons. Of course, I was both surprised and pleased to see the general, soon learned that my terms with Johnston had been disapproved, was instructed by him to give the forty-eight hours' notice required by the terms of the truce, and afterward to proceed to attack or follow him. I immediately telegraphed to General Kilpatrick, at Durham's, to have a mounted courier ready to carry the following message, then on its way up by rail, to the rebel lines:

HEADQUARTERS MILITARY DIVISION OF THE MISSISSIPPI IN THE FIELD, RALEIGH, NORTH CAROLINA, April 24, 1865 6 A.M.

General JOHNSTON, commanding Confederate Army, Greensboro':

You will take notice that the truce or suspension of hostilities agreed to between us will cease in forty-eight hours after this is received at your lines, under the first of the articles of agreement.

W. T. SHERMAN, Major-General.

At the same time I wrote another short note to General Johnston, of the same date:

I have replies from Washington to my communications of April 18th. I am instructed to limit my operations to your immediate command, and not to attempt civil negotiations. I therefore demand the surrender of your army on the same terms as were given to General Lee at Appomattox, April 9th instant, purely and simply.

Of course, both these papers were shown to General Grant at the time, before they were sent, and he approved of them.

At the same time orders were sent to all parts of the army to be ready to resume the pursuit of the enemy on the expiration of the forty-eight hours' truce, and messages were sent to General Gillmore (at Hilton Head) to the same effect, with instructions to get a similar message through to General Wilson, at Macon, by some means.

General Grant had brought with him, from Washington, written answers from the Secretary of War, and of himself, to my communications of the 18th, which I still possess, and here give the originals. They embrace the copy of a dispatch made by Mr. Stanton to General Grant, when he was pressing Lee at Appomattox, which dispatch, if sent me at the same time (as should have been done), would have saved a world of trouble. I did not understand that General Grant had come down to supersede me in command, nor did he intimate it, nor did I receive these communications as a serious reproof, but promptly acted on them, as is already shown; and in this connection I give my answer made to General Grant, at Raleigh, before I had received any answer from General Johnston to the demand for the surrender of his own army, as well as my answer to Mr. Stanton's letter, of the same date, both written on the supposition that I might have to start suddenly in pursuit of Johnston, and have no other chance to explain.

WAR DEPARTMENT, WASHINGTON CITY, April 21, 1865.

Lieutenant-General GRANT.

GENERAL: The memorandum or basis agreed upon between General Sherman and General Johnston having been submitted to the President, they are disapproved. You will give notice of the disapproval to General Sherman, and direct him to resume hostilities at the earliest moment.

The instructions given to you by the late President, Abraham Lincoln, on the 3d of March, by my telegraph of that date, addressed to you, express substantially the views of President Andrew Johnson, and will be observed by General Sherman. A copy is herewith appended.

The President desires that you proceed immediately to the headquarters of Major-General Sherman, and direct operations against the enemy.

149

Yours truly,

EDWIN M. STANTON, Secretary of War.

The following telegram was received 2 p.m., City Point, March 4, 1865 (from Washington, 12 M., March 3, 1865)

[CIPHER]

OFFICE UNITED STATES MILITARY TELEGRAPH,
HEADQUARTERS ARMIES OF THE UNITED STATES

Lieutenant-General GRANT:

The President directs me to say to you that he wishes you to have no conference with General Lee, unless it be for the capitulation of Lee's army or on solely minor and purely military matters.

He instructs me to say that you are not to decide, discuss, or confer upon any political question; such questions the President holds in his own hands, and will submit them to no military conferences or conventions.

Meantime you are to press to the utmost your military advantages.

EDWIN M. STANTON, Secretary of War.

HEADQUARTERS ARMIES OF THE UNITED STATES
WASHINGTON, D.C. April 21, 1865.

Major-General W. T. SHERMAN, commanding Military Division of the Mississippi.

GENERAL: The basis of agreement entered into between yourself and General J. E. Johnston, for the disbandment of the Southern army, and the extension of the authority of the General Government over all the territory belonging to it, sent for the approval of the President, is received.

I read it carefully myself before submitting it to the President and Secretary of War, and felt satisfied that it could not possibly be approved. My reason for these views I will give you at another time, in a more extended letter.

Your agreement touches upon questions of such vital importance that, as soon as read, I addressed a note to the Secretary of War, notifying him of their receipt, and the importance of immediate action by the President; and suggested, in view of their importance, that the entire Cabinet be called together, that all might give an expression of their opinions upon the matter. The result was a disapproval by the President of the basis laid down; a disapproval of the negotiations altogether except for the surrender of the army commanded by General Johnston, and directions to me to notify you of this decision. I cannot do no better than by sending you the inclosed copy of a dispatch (penned by the late President, though signed by the Secretary of War) in answer to me, on sending a letter received from General Lee, proposing to meet me for the purpose of submitting the question of peace to a convention of officers.

Please notify General Johnston, immediately on receipt of this, of the termination of the truce, and resume hostilities against his army at the earliest moment you can, acting in good faith.

Very respectfully your obedient servant,

U. S. GRANT, Lieutenant-General.

HEADQUARTERS MILITARY DIVISION OF THE MISSISSIPPI
IN THE FIELD, RALEIGH, NORTH CAROLINA, April 25, 1865.

150

Lieutenant-General U. S. GRANT, present.

GENERAL: I had the honor to receive your letter of April 21st, with inclosures, yesterday, and was well pleased that you came along, as you must have observed that I held the military control so as to adapt it to any phase the case might assume.

It is but just I should record the fact that I made my terms with General Johnston under the influence of the liberal terms you extended to the army of General Lee at Appomattox Court-House on the 9th, and the seeming policy of our Government, as evinced by the call of the Virginia Legislature and Governor back to Richmond, under yours and President Lincoln's very eyes.

It now appears this last act was done without any consultation with you or any knowledge of Mr. Lincoln, but rather in opposition to a previous policy well considered.

I have not the least desire to interfere in the civil policy of our Government, but would shun it as something not to my liking; but occasions do arise when a prompt seizure of results is forced on military commanders not in immediate communication with the proper authority. It is probable that the terms signed by General Johnston and myself were not clear enough on the point, well understood between us, that our negotiations did not apply to any parties outside the officers and men of the Confederate armies, which could easily have been remedied.

No surrender of any army not actually at the mercy of an antagonist was ever made without "terms," and these always define the military status of the surrendered. Thus you stipulated that the officers and men of Lee's army should not be molested at their homes so long as they obeyed the laws at the place of their residence.

I do not wish to discuss these points involved in our recognition of the State governments in actual existence, but will merely state my conclusions, to await the solution of the future.

Such action on our part in no manner recognizes for a moment the so-called Confederate Government, or makes us liable for its debts or acts.

The laws and acts done by the several States during the period of rebellion are void, because done without the oath prescribed by our Constitution of the United States, which is a "condition precedent."

We have a right to, use any sort of machinery to produce military results; and it is the commonest thing for military commanders to use the civil governments in actual existence as a means to an end. I do believe we could and can use the present State governments lawfully, constitutionally, and as the very best possible means to produce the object desired, viz., entire and complete submission to the lawful authority of the United States.

As to punishment for past crimes, that is for the judiciary, and can in no manner of way be disturbed by our acts; and, so far as I can, I will use my influence that rebels shall suffer all the personal punishment prescribed by law, as also the civil liabilities arising from their past acts.

What we now want is the new form of law by which common men may regain the positions of industry, so long disturbed by the war.

I now apprehend that the rebel armies will disperse; and, instead of dealing with six or seven States, we will have to deal with numberless bands of desperadoes, headed by such men as Mosby, Forrest, Red Jackson, and others, who know not and care not for danger and its consequences.

I am, with great respect, your obedient servant,

W. T. SHERMAN, Major-General commanding.

HEADQUARTERS MILITARY DIVISION OF THE MISSISSIPPI
IN THE FIELD, RALEIGH, NORTH CAROLINA, April 25, 1865.

Hon. E. M. STANTON, Secretary of War, Washington.

DEAR SIR: I have been furnished a copy of your letter of April 21st to General Grant, signifying your disapproval of the terms on which General Johnston proposed to disarm and disperse the insurgents, on condition of amnesty, etc. I admit my folly in embracing in a military convention any civil matters; but, unfortunately, such is the nature of our situation that they seem inextricably united, and I understood from you at Savannah that the financial state of the country demanded military success, and would warrant a little bending to policy.

When I had my conference with General Johnston I had the public examples before me of General Grant's terms to Lee's army, and General Weitzel's invitation to the Virginia Legislature to assemble at Richmond.

I still believe the General Government of the United States has made a mistake; but that is none of my business--mine is a different task; and I had flattered myself that, by four years of patient, unremitting, and successful labor, I deserved no reminder such as is contained in the last paragraph of your letter to General Grant. You may assure the President that I heed his suggestion. I am truly, etc.,

W. T. SHERMAN, Major-General commanding.

On the same day, but later, I received an answer from General Johnston, agreeing to meet me again at Bennett's house the next day, April 26th, at noon. He did not even know that General Grant was in Raleigh.

General Grant advised me to meet him, and to accept his surrender on the same terms as his with General Lee; and on the 26th I again went up to Durham's Station by rail, and rode out to Bennett's house, where we again met, and General Johnston, without hesitation, agreed to, and we executed, the following final terms:

Terms of a Military Convention, entered into this 26th day of April, 1865, at Bennett's House, near Durham's Station., North Carolina, between General JOSEPH E. JOHNSTON, commanding the Confederate Army, and Major-General W. T. SHERMAN, commanding the United States Army in North Carolina:

1. All acts of war on the part of the troops under General Johnston's command to cease from this date.

2. All arms and public property to be deposited at Greensboro', and delivered to an ordnance-officer of the United States Army.

3. Rolls of all the officers and men to be made in duplicate; one copy to be retained by the commander of the troops, and the other to be given to an officer to be designated by General Sherman. Each officer and man to give his individual obligation in writing not to take up arms against the Government of the United States, until properly released from this obligation.

4. The side-arms of officers, and their private horses and baggage, to be retained by them.

5. This being done, all the officers and men will be permitted to return to their homes, not to be disturbed by the United States authorities, so long as they observe their obligation and the laws in force where they may reside.

W. T. SHERMAN, Major-General, Commanding United States Forces in North Carolina.

J. E. JOHNSTON, General, Commanding Confederate States Forces in North Carolina.

Approved:

U. S. GRANT, Lieutenant-General.

I returned to Raleigh the same evening, and, at my request, General Grant wrote on these terms his approval, and then I thought the matter was surely at an end. He took the original copy, on the 27th returned to Newbern, and thence went back to Washington.

I immediately made all the orders necessary to carry into effect the terms of this convention, devolving on General Schofield the details of granting the parole and making the muster-rolls of prisoners, inventories of property, etc., of General Johnston's army at and about Greensboro', North Carolina, and on General Wilson the same duties in Georgia; but, thus far, I had been compelled to communicate with the latter through rebel sources, and General Wilson was necessarily confused by the conflict of orders and information. I deemed it of the utmost importance to establish for him a more reliable base of information and supply, and accordingly resolved to go in person to Savannah for that purpose. But, before starting, I received a New York Times, of April 24th, containing the following extraordinary communications:

[First Bulletin]

152

WAR DEPARTMENT WASHINGTON, April 22, 1885.

Yesterday evening a bearer of dispatches arrived from General Sherman. An agreement for a suspension of hostilities, and a memorandum of what is called a basis for peace, had been entered into on the 18th inst. by General Sherman, with the rebel General Johnston. Brigadier-General Breckenridge was present at the conference.

A cabinet meeting was held at eight o'clock in the evening, at which the action of General Sherman was disapproved by the President, by the Secretary of War, by General Grant, and by every member of the cabinet. General Sherman was ordered to resume hostilities immediately, and was directed that the instructions given by the late President, in the following telegram, which was penned by Mr. Lincoln himself, at the Capitol, on the night of the 3d of March, were approved by President Andrew Johnson, and were reiterated to govern the action of military commanders.

On the night of the 3d of March, while President Lincoln and his cabinet were at the Capitol, a telegram from General Grant was brought to the Secretary of War, informing him that General Lee had requested an interview or conference, to make an arrangement for terms of peace. The letter of General Lee was published in a letter to Davis and to the rebel Congress. General Grant's telegram was submitted to Mr. Lincoln, who, after pondering a few minutes, took up his pen and wrote with his own hand the following reply, which he submitted to the Secretary of State and Secretary of War. It was then dated, addressed, and signed, by the Secretary of War, and telegraphed to General Grant:

WASHINGTON, March 3, 1865-12 P.M.

Lieutenant-General GRANT:

The President directs me to say to you that he wishes you to have no conference with General Lee, unless it be for the capitulation of General Lee's army, or on some minor or purely military matter. He instructs me to say that you are not to decide, discuss, or confer upon any political questions. Such questions the President holds in his own hands, and will submit them to no military conferences or conventions.

Meantime you are to press to the utmost your military advantages.

EDWIN M. STANTON, Secretary of War.

The orders of General Sherman to General Stoneman to withdraw from Salisbury and join him will probably open the way for Davis to escape to Mexico or Europe with his plunder, which is reported to be very large, including not only the plunder of the Richmond banks, but previous accumulations.

A dispatch received by this department from Richmond says: "It is stated here, by respectable parties, that the amount of specie taken south by Jeff. Davis and his partisans is very large, including not only the plunder of the Richmond banks, but previous accumulations. They hope, it is said, to make terms with General Sherman, or some other commander, by which they will be permitted, with their effects, including this gold plunder, to go to Mexico or Europe. Johnston's negotiations look to this end."

After the cabinet meeting last night, General Grant started for North Carolina, to direct operations against Johnston's army.

EDWIN M. STANTON, Secretary of War.

Here followed the terms, and Mr. Stanton's ten reasons for rejecting them.

The publication of this bulletin by authority was an outrage on me, for Mr. Stanton had failed to communicate to me in advance, as was his duty, the purpose of the Administration to limit our negotiations to purely military matters; but, on the contrary, at Savannah he had authorized me to control all matters, civil and military.

By this bulletin, he implied that I had previously been furnished with a copy of his dispatch of March 3d to General Grant, which was not so; and he gave warrant to the impression, which was sown broadcast, that I might be bribed by banker's gold to permit Davis to escape. Under the influence of this, I wrote General Grant the following letter of April 28th, which has been published in the Proceedings of the Committee on the Conduct of the War.

I regarded this bulletin of Mr. Stanton as a personal and official insult, which I afterward publicly resented.

HEADQUARTERS MILITARY DIVISION OF THE MISSISSIPPI
IN THE FIELD, RALEIGH, NORTH CAROLINA, April 28,1865.

Lieutenant-General U. S. GRANT, General-in-Chief, Washington, D. C.

GENERAL: Since you left me yesterday, I have seen the New York Times of the 24th, containing a budget of military news, authenticated by the signature of the Secretary of War, Hon. E. M. Stanton, which is grouped in such a way as to give the public very erroneous impressions. It embraces a copy of the basis of agreement between myself and General Johnston, of April 18th, with comments, which it will be time enough to discuss two or three years hence, after the Government has experimented a little more in the machinery by which power reaches the scattered people of the vast country known as the "South."

In the mean time, however, I did think that my rank (if not past services) entitled me at least to trust that the Secretary of War would keep secret what was communicated for the use of none but the cabinet, until further inquiry could be made, instead of giving publicity to it along with documents which I never saw, and drawing therefrom inferences wide of the truth. I never saw or had furnished me a copy of President Lincoln's dispatch to you of the 3d of March, nor did Mr. Stanton or any human being ever convey to me its substance, or any thing like it. On the contrary, I had seen General Weitzel's invitation to the Virginia Legislature, made in Mr. Lincoln's very presence, and failed to discover any other official hint of a plan of reconstruction, or any ideas calculated to allay the fears of the people of the South, after the destruction of their armies and civil authorities would leave them without any government whatever.

We should not drive a people into anarchy, and it is simply impossible for our military power to reach all the masses of their unhappy country.

I confess I did not desire to drive General Johnston's army into bands of armed men, going about without purpose, and capable only of infinite mischief. But you saw, on your arrival here, that I had my army so disposed that his escape was only possible in a disorganized shape; and as you did not choose to "direct military operations in this quarter," I inferred that you were satisfied with the military situation; at all events, the instant I learned what was proper enough, the disapproval of the President, I acted in such a manner as to compel the surrender of General Johnston's whole army on the same terms which you had prescribed to General Lee's army, when you had it surrounded and in your absolute power.

Mr. Stanton, in stating that my orders to General Stoneman were likely to result in the escape of "Mr. Davis to Mexico or Europe," is in deep error. General Stoneman was not at "Salisbury," but had gone back to "Statesville." Davis was between us, and therefore Stoneman was beyond him. By turning toward me he was approaching Davis, and, had he joined me as ordered, I would have had a mounted force greatly needed for Davis's capture, and for other purposes. Even now I don't know that Mr. Stanton wants Davis caught, and as my official papers, deemed sacred, are hastily published to the world, it will be imprudent for me to state what has been done in that regard.

As the editor of the Times has (it may be) logically and fairly drawn from this singular document the conclusion that I am insubordinate, I can only deny the intention.

I have never in my life questioned or disobeyed an order, though many and many a time have I risked my life, health, and reputation, in obeying orders, or even hints to execute plans and purposes, not to my liking. It is not fair to withhold from me the plans and policy of Government (if any there be), and expect me to guess at them; for facts and events appear quite different from different stand-points. For four years I have been in camp dealing with soldiers, and I can assure you that the conclusion at which the cabinet arrived with such singular unanimity differs from mine. I conferred freely with the best officers in this army as to the points involved in this controversy, and, strange to say, they were singularly unanimous in the other conclusion. They will learn with pain and amazement that I am deemed insubordinate, and wanting in commonsense; that I, who for four years have labored day and night, winter and summer, who have brought an army of seventy thousand men in magnificent condition across a country hitherto deemed impassable, and placed it just where it was wanted, on the day appointed, have brought discredit on our Government! I do not wish to boast of this, but I do say that it entitled me to the courtesy of being consulted, before publishing to the world a proposition rightfully submitted to higher authority for adjudication, and then accompanied by statements which invited the dogs of the press to be let loose upon me. It is true that non-combatants, men who sleep in comfort and security while we watch on the distant lines, are better able to judge than we poor soldiers, who rarely see a newspaper, hardly hear from our families, or stop long enough to draw our pay. I envy not the task of "reconstruction," and am delighted that the Secretary of War has relieved me of it.

As you did not undertake to assume the management of the affairs of this army, I infer that, on personal inspection, your mind arrived at a different conclusion from that of the Secretary of War. I will therefore go on to execute your orders to the conclusion, and, when done, will with intense satisfaction leave to the civil authorities the execution of the task of which they seem so jealous. But, as an honest man and soldier, I invite them to go back to Nashville and follow my path, for they will see some things and hear some things that may disturb their philosophy.

With sincere respect,

W. T. SHERMAN, Major-General commanding.

P. S.--As Mr. Stanton's most singular paper has been published, I demand that this also be made public, though I am in no manner responsible to the press, but to the law, and my proper superiors.
W. T. S., Major-General.

On the 28th I summoned all the army and corps commanders together at my quarters in the Governor's mansion at Raleigh, where every thing was explained to them, and all orders for the future were completed. Generals Schofield, Terry, and Kilpatrick, were to remain on duty in the Department of North Carolina, already commanded by General Schofield, and the right and left wings were ordered to march under their respective commanding generals North by easy stages to Richmond, Virginia, there to await my return from the South.

On the 29th of April, with a part of my personal staff, I proceeded by rail to Wilmington, North Carolina, where I found Generals Hawley and Potter, and the little steamer Russia, Captain Smith, awaiting me. After a short pause in Wilmington, we embarked, and proceeded down the coast to Port Royal and the Savannah River, which we reached on the 1st of May. There Captain Hoses, who had just come from General Wilson at Macon, met us, bearing letters for me and General Grant, in which General Wilson gave a brief summary of his operations up to date. He had marched from Eastport, Mississippi, five hundred miles in thirty days, took six thousand three hundred prisoners, twenty-three colors, and one hundred and fifty-six guns, defeating Forrest, scattering the militia, and destroying every railroad, iron establishment, and factory, in North Alabama and Georgia.

He spoke in the highest terms of his cavalry, as "cavalry," claiming that it could not be excelled, and he regarded his corps as a model for modern cavalry in organization, armament, and discipline. Its strength was given at thirteen thousand five hundred men and horses on reaching Macon. Of course I was extremely gratified at his just confidence, and saw that all he wanted for efficient action was a sure base of supply, so that he need no longer depend for clothing, ammunition, food, and forage, on the country, which, now that war had ceased, it was our solemn duty to protect, instead of plunder. I accordingly ordered the captured steamer Jeff. Davis to be loaded with stores, to proceed at once up the Savannah River to Augusta, with a small detachment of troops to occupy the arsenal, and to open communication with General Wilson at Macon; and on the next day, May 2d, this steamer was followed by another with a fall cargo of clothing, sugar, coffee, and bread, sent from Hilton Head by the department commander, General Gillmore, with a stronger guard commanded by General Molineux. Leaving to General Gillmore, who was present, and in whose department General Wilson was, to keep up the supplies at Augusta, and to facilitate as far as possible General Wilson's operations inland, I began my return on the 2d of May. We went into Charleston Harbor, passing the ruins of old Forts Moultrie and Sumter without landing. We reached the city of Charleston, which was held by part of the division of General John P. Hatch, the same that we had left at Pocotaligo. We walked the old familiar streets--Broad, King, Meeting, etc.--but desolation and ruin were everywhere. The heart of the city had been burned during the bombardment, and the rebel garrison at the time of its final evacuation had fired the railroad-depots, which fire had spread, and was only subdued by our troops after they had reached the city.

I inquired for many of my old friends, but they were dead or gone, and of them all I only saw a part of the family of Mrs. Pettigru. I doubt whether any city was ever more terribly punished than Charleston, but, as her people had for years been agitating for war and discord, and had finally inaugurated the civil war by an attack on the small and devoted garrison of Major Anderson, sent there by the General Government to defend them, the judgment of the world will be, that Charleston deserved the fate that befell her. Resuming our voyage, we passed into Cape Fear River by its mouth at Fort Caswell and Smithville, and out by the new channel at Fort Fisher, and reached Morehead City on the 4th of May. We found there the revenue-cutter Wayanda, on board of which were the Chief-Justice, Mr. Chase, and his daughter Nettie, now Mrs. Hoyt. The Chief-Justice at that moment was absent on a visit to Newbern, but came back the next day. Meantime, by means of the telegraph, I was again in correspondence with General Schofield at Raleigh. He had made great progress in paroling the officers and men of Johnston's army at Greensboro', but was embarrassed by the utter confusion and anarchy that had resulted from a want of understanding on many minor points, and on the political questions that had to be met at the instant. In order to facilitate the return to their homes of the Confederate officers and men, he had been forced to make with General Johnston the following supplemental terms, which were of course ratified and approved:

155

MILITARY CONVENTION OF APRIL 26, 1865.
SUPPLEMENTAL TERMS.

1. The field transportation to be loaned to the troops for their march to their homes, and for subsequent use in their industrial pursuits. Artillery-horses may be used in field-transportation, if necessary.

2. Each brigade or separate body to retain a number of arms equal to one-seventh of its effective strength, which, when the troops reach the capitals of their states, will be disposed of as the general commanding the department may direct.

3. Private horses, and other private property of both officers and men, to be retained by them.

4. The commanding general of the Military Division of West Mississippi, Major-General Canby, will be requested to give transportation by water, from Mobile or New Orleans, to the troops from Arkansas and Texas.

5. The obligations of officers and soldiers to be signed by their immediate commanders.

6. Naval forces within the limits of General Johnston's command to be included in the terms of this convention.

J. M. SCHOFIELD, Major-General,
Commanding United States Forces in North Carolina.

J. E. JOHNSTON, General,
Commanding Confederate States Forces in North Carolina.

The total number of prisoners of war parolled by General Schofield, at Greensboro', North Carolina, as afterward officially reported, amounted to	8,817
And the total number who surrendered in Georgia and Florida, as reported by General J. H. Wilson, was	2,458
Aggregate surrendered under the capitulation of General J. E. Johnston	9,270

On the morning of the 5th I also received from General Schofield this dispatch:

RALEIGH, NORTH CAROLINA, May 5, 1866.

To Major-General W: T. SHERMAN, Morehead City:

When General Grant was here, as you doubtless recollect, he said the lines (for trade and intercourse) had been extended to embrace this and other States south. The order, it seems, has been modified so as to include only Virginia and Tennessee. I think it would be an act of wisdom to open this State to trade at once.

I hope the Government will make known its policy as to the organs of State government without delay. Affairs must necessarily be in a very unsettled state until that is done. The people are now in a mood to accept almost anything which promises a definite settlement. "What is to be done with the freedmen?" is the question of all, and it is the all important question. It requires prompt and wise notion to prevent the negroes from becoming a huge elephant on our hands. If I am to govern this State, it is important for me to know it at once. If another is to be sent here, it cannot be done too soon, for he probably will undo the most that I shall have done. I shall be glad to hear from you fully, when you have time to write. I will send your message to General Wilson at once.

J. M. SCHOFIELD, Major-General.

I was utterly without instructions from any source on the points of General Schofield's inquiry, and under the existing state of facts could not even advise him, for by this time I was in possession of the second bulletin of Mr. Stanton, published in all the Northern papers, with comments that assumed that I was a common traitor and a public enemy; and high officials had even instructed my own subordinates to disobey my lawful orders. General Halleck, who had so long been in Washington as the chief of staff, had been sent on the 21st of April to Richmond, to command the armies of the Potomac and James, in place of General Grant, who had transferred his headquarters to the national capital, and he (General Halleck) was therefore in supreme command in Virginia, while my command over North Carolina had never been revoked or modified.

[Second Bulletin.]

WAR DEPARTMENT, WASHINGTON, April 27 9.30 a.m.

To Major-General DIX:

The department has received the following dispatch from Major-General Halleck, commanding the Military Division of the James. Generals Canby and Thomas were instructed some days ago that Sherman's arrangements with Johnston were disapproved by the President, and they were ordered to disregard it and push the enemy in every direction.

E. M. STANTON, Secretary of War.

RICHMOND, VIRGINIA, April 26-9.30 p.m.

HON. E. M. STANTON, Secretary of War:

Generals Meade, Sheridan, and Wright, are acting under orders to pay no regard to any truce or orders of General Sherman respecting hostilities, on the ground that Sherman's agreement could bind his command only, and no other.

They are directed to push forward, regardless of orders from any one except from General Grant, and cut off Johnston's retreat.

Beauregard has telegraphed to Danville that a new arrangement has been made with Sherman, and that the advance of the Sixth Corps was to be suspended until further orders.

I have telegraphed back to obey no orders of Sherman, but to push forward as rapidly as possible.

The bankers here have information to-day that Jeff. Davis's specie is moving south from Goldsboro', in wagons, as fast as possible.

I suggest that orders be telegraphed, through General Thomas, that Wilson obey no orders from Sherman, and notifying him and Canby, and all commanders on the Mississippi, to take measures to intercept the rebel chiefs and their plunder.

The specie taken with them is estimated here at from six to thirteen million dollars.

H. W. HALLECK, Major-General commanding.

Subsequently, before the Committee on the Conduct of the War, in Washington, on the 22d of May, I testified fully on this whole matter, and will abide the judgment of the country on the patriotism and wisdom of my public conduct in this connection. General Halleck's measures to capture General Johnston's army, actually surrendered to me at the time, at Greensboro', on the 26th of April, simply excited my contempt for a judgment such as he was supposed to possess. The assertion that Jeff. Davis's specie-train, of six to thirteen million dollars, was reported to be moving south from Goldsboro' in wagons as fast as possible, found plenty of willing ears, though my army of eighty thousand men had been at Goldsboro' from March 22d to the date of his dispatch, April 26th; and such a train would have been composed of from fifteen to thirty-two six-mule teams to have hauled this specie, even if it all were in gold. I suppose the exact amount of treasure which Davis had with him is now known to a cent; some of it was paid to his escort, when it disbanded at and near Washington, Georgia, and at the time of his capture he had a small parcel of gold and silver coin, not to exceed ten thousand dollars, which is now retained in the United States Treasury-vault at Washington, and shown to the curious.

The thirteen millions of treasure, with which Jeff. Davis was to corrupt our armies and buy his escape, dwindled down to the contents of a hand-valise!

To say that I was merely angry at the tone and substance of these published bulletins of the War Department, would hardly express the state of my feelings. I was outraged beyond measure, and was resolved to resent the insult, cost what it might. I went to the Wayanda and showed them to Mr. Chase, with whom I had a long and frank conversation, during which he explained to me the confusion caused in Washington by the assassination of Mr. Lincoln, the sudden accession to power of Mr. Johnson, who was then supposed to be bitter and vindictive in his feelings toward the South, and the wild pressure of every class of politicians to enforce on the new President their pet schemes. He showed me a letter of his own, which was in print, dated Baltimore, April 11th, and another of April 12th, addressed to the President, urging him to recognize the freedmen as equal in all respects to the whites. He was the first man, of any authority or station, who ever informed me that the Government of the United States would insist on extending to the former slaves of the South the elective franchise, and he gave as a reason the fact that the slaves, grateful for their freedom, for which they were indebted to the armies and Government of the North, would, by their votes, offset the disaffected and rebel element of the white population of the South. At that time quite a storm was prevailing at sea, outside, and our two vessels lay snug at the wharf at Morehead City. I saw a good deal of Mr. Chase, and several notes passed between us, of which I have the originals yet. Always claiming that the South had herself freed all her slaves by rebellion, and that Mr. Lincoln's proclamation of freedom (of September 22, 1862) was binding on all officers of the General Government, I doubted the wisdom of at once clothing them with the elective franchise, without some previous preparation and qualification; and then realized the national loss in the death at that critical moment of Mr. Lincoln, who had long pondered over the difficult questions involved, who, at all events, would have been honest and frank, and would not have withheld from his army commanders at least a hint that would have been to them a guide. It was plain to me, therefore, that the manner of his assassination had stampeded the civil authorities in Washington, had unnerved them, and that they were then undecided as to the measures indispensably necessary to prevent anarchy at the South.

On the 7th of May the storm subsided, and we put to sea, Mr. Chase to the south, on his proposed tour as far as New Orleans, and I for James River. I reached Fortress Monroe on the 8th, and thence telegraphed my arrival to General Grant, asking for orders. I found at Fortress Monroe a dispatch from General Halleck, professing great friendship, and inviting me to accept his hospitality at Richmond. I answered by a cipher-dispatch that I had seen his dispatch to Mr. Stanton, of April 26th, embraced in the second bulletin, which I regarded as insulting, declined his hospitality, and added that I preferred we should not meet as I passed through Richmond. I thence proceeded to City Point in the Russia, and on to Manchester, opposite Richmond, via Petersburg, by rail. I found that both wings of the army had arrived from Raleigh, and were in camp in and around Manchester, whence I again telegraphed General Grant, an the 9th of May, for orders, and also reported my arrival to General Halleck by letter. I found that General Halleck had ordered General Davis's corps (the Fourteenth) for review by himself. This I forbade. All the army knew of the insult that had been made me by the Secretary of War and General Halleck, and watched me closely to see if I would tamely submit. During the 9th I made a full and complete report of all these events, from the last report made at Goldsboro' up to date, and the next day received orders to continue the march to Alexandria, near Washington.

On the morning of the 11th we crossed the pontoon-bridge at Richmond, marched through that city, and out on the Hanover Court House road, General Slocum's left wing leading. The right wing (General Logan) followed the next day, viz., the 12th. Meantime, General O. O. Howard had been summoned to Washington to take charge of the new Bureau of Refugees, Freedmen, and Abandoned Lands, and, from that time till the army was finally disbanded, General John A. Logan was in command of the right wing, and of the Army of the Tennessee. The left wing marched through Hanover Court House, and thence took roads well to the left by Chilesburg; the Fourteenth Corps by New Market and Culpepper, Manassas, etc.; the Twentieth Corps by Spotsylvania Court-House and Chancellorsville. The right wing followed the more direct road by Fredericksburg. On my way north I endeavored to see as much of the battle-fields of the Army of the Potomac as I could, and therefore shifted from one column to the other, visiting en route Hanover Court-House, Spotsylvania, Fredericksburg, Dumfries, etc., reaching Alexandria during the afternoon of May 19th, and pitched my camp by the road side, about half-way between Alexandria and the Long Bridge. During the same and next day the whole army reached Alexandria, and camped round about it; General Meade's Army of the Potomac had possession of the camps above, opposite Washington and Georgetown. The next day (by invitation) I went over to Washington and met many friends--among them General Grant and President Johnson. The latter occupied rooms in the house on the corner of Fifteenth and H Streets, belonging to Mr. Hooper. He was extremely cordial to me, and knowing that I was chafing under the censures of the War Department, especially of the two war bulletins of Mr. Stanton, he volunteered to say that he knew of neither of them till seen in the newspapers, and that Mr. Stanton had shown neither to him nor to any of his associates in the cabinet till they were published. Nearly all the members of the cabinet made similar assurances to me afterward, and, as Mr. Stanton made no friendly advances, and offered no word of explanation or apology, I declined General Grant's friendly offices for a reconciliation, but, on the contrary, resolved to resent what I considered an insult, as publicly as it was made. My brother, Senator Sherman, who was Mr. Stanton's neighbor, always insisted that Mr. Stanton had been frightened by the intended assassination of himself, and had become embittered thereby. At all events, I found strong military guards around his house, as well as all the houses occupied by the cabinet and by the principal officers of Government; and a sense of insecurity pervaded Washington, for which no reason existed.

On the 19th I received a copy of War Department Special Order No. 239, Adjutant-General's office, of May 18th, ordering a grand review, by the President and cabinet, of all the armies then near Washington; General Meade's to occur on Tuesday, May 23d, mine on Wednesday, the 24th; and on the 20th I made the necessary orders for my part. Meantime I had also arranged (with General Grant's approval) to remove after the review, my armies from the south side of the Potomac to the north; both for convenience and because our men had found that the grounds assigned them had been used so long for camps that they were foul and unfit.

By invitation I was on the reviewing-stand, and witnessed the review of the Army of the Potomac (on the 23d), commanded by General Meade in person. The day was beautiful, and the pageant was superb. Washington was full of strangers, who filled the streets in holiday-dress, and every house was decorated with flags. The army marched by divisions in close column around the Capitol, down Pennsylvania Avenue, past the President and cabinet, who occupied a large stand prepared for the occasion, directly in front of the White House.

I had telegraphed to Lancaster for Mrs. Sherman, who arrived that day, accompanied by her father, the Hon. Thomas Ewing, and my son Tom, then eight years old.

During the afternoon and night of the 23d, the Fifteenth, Seventeenth, and Twentieth Corps, crossed Long Bridge, bivouacked in the streets about the Capitol, and the Fourteenth Corps closed up to the bridge. The morning of the 24th was extremely beautiful, and the ground was in splendid order for our review. The streets were filled with people to see the pageant, armed with bouquets of flowers for their favorite regiments or heroes, and every thing was propitious. Punctually at 9 A.M. the signal-gun was fired, when in person, attended by General Howard and all my staff, I rode slowly down Pennsylvania Avenue, the crowds of men, women, and children, densely lining the sidewalks, and almost obstructing the way. We were followed close by General Logan and the head of the Fifteenth Corps. When I reached the Treasury-building, and looked back, the sight was simply magnificent. The column was compact, and the glittering muskets looked like a solid mass of steel, moving with the regularity of a pendulum. We passed the Treasury building, in front of which and of the White House was an immense throng of people, for whom extensive stands had been prepared on both sides of the avenue. As I neared the brick-house opposite the lower corner of Lafayette Square, some one asked me to notice Mr. Seward, who, still feeble and bandaged for his wounds, had been removed there that he might behold the troops. I moved in that direction and took off my hat to Mr. Seward, who sat at an upper window. He recognized the salute, returned it, and then we rode on steadily past the President, saluting with our swords. All on his stand arose and acknowledged the salute. Then, turning into the gate of the presidential grounds, we left our horses with orderlies, and went upon the stand, where I found Mrs. Sherman, with her father and son. Passing them, I shook hands with the President, General Grant, and each member of the cabinet. As I approached Mr. Stanton, he offered me his hand, but I declined it publicly, and the fact was universally noticed. I then took my post on the left of the President, and for six hours and a half stood, while the army passed in the order of the Fifteenth, Seventeenth, Twentieth, and Fourteenth Corps. It was, in my judgment, the most magnificent army in existence--sixty-five thousand men, in splendid physique, who had just completed a march of nearly two thousand miles in a hostile country, in good drill, and who realized that they were being closely scrutinized by thousands of their fellow-countrymen and by foreigners. Division after division passed, each commander of an army corps or division coming on the stand during the passage of his command, to be presented to the President, cabinet, and spectators. The steadiness and firmness of the tread, the careful dress on the guides, the uniform intervals between the companies, all eyes directly to the front, and the tattered and bullet-ridden flags, festooned with flowers, all attracted universal notice. Many good people, up to that time, had looked upon our Western army as a sort of mob; but the world then saw, and recognized the fact, that it was an army in the proper sense, well organized, well commanded and disciplined; and there was no wonder that it had swept through the South like a tornado. For six hours and a half that strong tread of the Army of the West resounded along Pennsylvania Avenue; not a soul of that vast crowd of spectators left his place; and, when the rear of the column had passed by, thousands of the spectators still lingered to express their sense of confidence in the strength of a Government which could claim such an army.

Some little scenes enlivened the day, and called for the laughter and cheers of the crowd. Each division was followed by six ambulances, as a representative of its baggage-train. Some of the division commanders had added, by way of variety, goats, milch-cows, and pack-mules, whose loads consisted of game-cocks, poultry, hams, etc., and some of them had the families of freed slaves along, with the women leading their children. Each division was preceded by its corps of black pioneers, armed with picks and spades. These marched abreast in double ranks, keeping perfect dress and step, and added much to the interest of the occasion. On the whole, the grand review was a splendid success, and was a fitting conclusion to the campaign and the war.

I will now conclude by a copy of my general orders taking leave of the army, which ended my connection with the war, though I afterward visited and took a more formal leave of the officers and men on July 4, 1865, at Louisville, Kentucky:

[SPECIAL FIELD ORDERS NO. 76]

HEADQUARTERS MILITARY DIVISION OF THE MISSISSIPPI, IN THE FIELD, WASHINGTON, D.C. May 30, 1865

The general commanding announces to the Armies of the Tennessee and Georgia that the time has come for us to part. Our work is done, and armed enemies no longer defy us. Some of you will go to your homes, and others will be retained in military service till further orders.

And now that we are all about to separate, to mingle with the civil world, it becomes a pleasing duty to recall to mind the situation of national affairs when, but little more than a year ago, we were gathered about the cliffs of Lookout Mountain, and all the future was wrapped in doubt and uncertainty.

Three armies had come together from distant fields, with separate histories, yet bound by one common cause--the union of our country, and the perpetuation of the Government of our inheritance. There is no need to recall to your memories Tunnel Hill, with Rocky-Face Mountain and Buzzard-Roost Gap, and the ugly forts of Dalton behind.

We were in earnest, and paused not for danger and difficulty, but dashed through Snake-Creek Gap and fell on Resaca; then on to the Etowah, to Dallas, Kenesaw; and the heats of summer found us on the banks of the Chattahoochee, far from home, and dependent on a single road for supplies. Again we were not to be held back by any obstacle, and crossed over and fought four hard battles for the possession of the citadel of Atlanta. That was the crisis of our history. A doubt still clouded our future, but we solved the problem, destroyed Atlanta, struck boldly across the State of Georgia, severed all the main arteries of life to our enemy, and Christmas found us at Savannah.

Waiting there only long enough to fill our wagons, we again began a march which, for peril, labor, and results, will compare with any ever made by an organized army. The floods of the Savannah, the swamps of the Combahee and Edisto, the "high hills" and rocks of the Santee, the flat quagmires of the Pedee and Cape Fear Rivers, were all passed in midwinter, with its floods and rains, in the face of an accumulating enemy; and, after the battles of Averysboro' and Bentonville, we once more came out of the wilderness, to meet our friends at Goldsboro'. Even then we paused only long enough to get new clothing, to reload our wagons, again pushed on to Raleigh and beyond, until we met our enemy suing for peace, instead of war, and offering to submit to the injured laws of his and our country. As long as that enemy was defiant, nor mountains nor rivers, nor swamps, nor hunger, nor cold, had checked us; but when he, who had fought us hard and persistently, offered submission, your general thought it wrong to pursue him farther, and negotiations followed, which resulted, as you all know, in his surrender.

How far the operations of this army contributed to the final overthrow of the Confederacy and the peace which now dawns upon us, must be judged by others, not by us; but that you have done all that men could do has been admitted by those in authority, and we have a right to join in the universal joy that fills our land because the war is over, and our Government stands vindicated before the world by the joint action of the volunteer armies and navy of the United States.

To such as remain in the service, your general need only remind you that success in the past was due to hard work and discipline, and that the same work and discipline are equally important in the future. To such as go home, he will only say that our favored country is so grand, so extensive, so diversified in climate, soil, and productions, that every man may find a home and occupation suited to his taste; none should yield to the natural impatience sure to result from our past life of excitement and adventure. You will be invited to seek new adventures abroad; do not yield to the temptation, for it will lead only to death and disappointment.

Your general now bids you farewell, with the full belief that, as in war you have been good soldiers, so in peace you will make good citizens; and if, unfortunately, new war should arise in our country, "Sherman's army" will be the first to buckle on its old armor, and come forth to defend and maintain the Government of our inheritance.

By order of Major-General W. T. Sherman,

L. M. DAYTON, Assistant Adjutant-General.

List of the Average Number of Miles marched by the Different Army Corps of the United States Forces under Command of Major-General W. T. SHERMAN, United States Army, during his Campaigns: 1863-'64-'65.

4th Corps.	14th Corps.	15th Corps.	16th Corps	17th Corps.	20th Corps.
10	1,586	1,289	208	5,076	2,525

CHAPTER XXV.
CONCLUSION--MILITARY LESSONS OF THE WAR.

Having thus recorded a summary of events, mostly under my own personal supervision, during the years from 1846 to 1865, it seems proper that I should add an opinion of some of the useful military lessons to be derived therefrom.

That civil war, by reason of the existence of slavery, was apprehended by most of the leading statesmen of the half-century preceding its outbreak, is a matter of notoriety. General Scott told me on my arrival at New York, as early as 1850, that the country was on the eve of civil war; and the Southern politicians openly asserted that it was their purpose to accept as a casus belli the election of General Fremont in 1856; but, fortunately or unfortunately, he was beaten by Mr. Buchanan, which simply postponed its occurrence for four years. Mr. Seward had also publicly declared that no government could possibly exist half slave and half free; yet the Government made no military preparation, and the Northern people generally paid no attention, took no warning of its coming, and would not realize its existence till Fort Sumter was fired on by batteries of artillery, handled by declared enemies, from the surrounding islands and from the city of Charleston.

General Bragg, who certainly was a man of intelligence, and who, in early life, ridiculed a thousand times, in my hearing, the threats of the people of South Carolina to secede from the Federal Union, said to me in New Orleans, in February, 1861, that he was convinced that the feeling between the slave and free States had become so embittered that it was better to part in peace; better to part anyhow; and, as a separation was inevitable, that the South should begin at once, because the possibility of a successful effort was yearly lessened by the rapid and increasing inequality between the two sections, from the fact that all the European immigrants were coming to the Northern States and Territories, and none to the Southern.

The slave population m 1860 was near four millions, and the money value thereof not far from twenty-five hundred million dollars. Now, ignoring the moral side of the question, a cause that endangered so vast a moneyed interest was an adequate cause of anxiety and preparation, and the Northern leaders surely ought to have foreseen the danger and prepared for it. After the election of Mr. Lincoln in 1860, there was no concealment of the declaration and preparation for war in the South. In Louisiana, as I have related, men were openly enlisted, officers were appointed, and war was actually begun, in January, 1861. The forts at the mouth of the Mississippi were seized, and occupied by garrisons that hauled down the United States flag and hoisted that of the State. The United States Arsenal at Baton Rouge was captured by New Orleans militia, its garrison ignominiously sent off, and the contents of the arsenal distributed. These were as much acts of war as was the subsequent firing on Fort Sumter, yet no public notice was taken thereof; and when, months afterward, I came North, I found not one single sign of preparation. It was for this reason, somewhat, that the people of the South became convinced that those of the North were pusillanimous and cowardly, and the Southern leaders were thereby enabled to commit their people to the war, nominally in defense of their slave property. Up to the hour of the firing on Fort Sumter, in April, 1861, it does seem to me that our public men, our politicians, were blamable for not sounding the note of alarm.

Then, when war was actually begun, it was by a call for seventy-five thousand "ninety-day" men, I suppose to fulfill Mr. Seward's prophecy that the war would last but ninety days.

The earlier steps by our political Government were extremely wavering and weak, for which an excuse can be found in the fact that many of the Southern representatives remained in Congress, sharing in the public councils, and influencing legislation. But as soon as Mr. Lincoln was installed, there was no longer any reason why Congress and the cabinet should have hesitated. They should have measured the cause, provided the means, and left the Executive to apply the remedy.

At the time of Mr. Lincoln's inauguration, viz., March 4, 1861, the Regular Army, by law, consisted of two regiments of dragoons, two regiments of cavalry, one regiment of mounted rifles, four regiments of artillery, and ten regiments of infantry, admitting of an aggregate strength of thirteen thousand and twenty-four officers and men. On the subsequent 4th of May the President, by his own orders (afterward sanctioned by Congress), added a regiment of cavalry, a regiment of artillery, and eight regiments of infantry, which, with the former army, admitted of a strength of thirty-nine thousand nine hundred and seventy-three; but at no time during the war did the Regular Army attain a strength of twenty-five thousand men.

To the new regiments of infantry was given an organization differing from any that had heretofore prevailed in this country--of three battalions of eight companies each; but at no time did more than one of these regiments attain its full standard; nor in the vast army of volunteers that was raised during the war were any of the regiments of infantry formed on the three-battalion system, but these were universally single battalions of ten companies; so that, on the reorganization of the Regular Army at the close of the war, Congress adopted the form of twelve companies for the regiments of cavalry and artillery, and that of ten companies for the infantry, which is the present standard.

Inasmuch as the Regular Army will naturally form the standard of organization for any increase or for new regiments of volunteers, it becomes important to study this subject in the light of past experience, and to select that form which is best for peace as well as war.

A cavalry regiment is now composed of twelve companies, usually divided into six squadrons, of two companies each, or better subdivided into three battalions of four companies each. This is an excellent form, easily admitting of subdivision as well as union into larger masses.

A single battalion of four companies, with a field-officer, will compose a good body for a garrison, for a separate expedition, or for a detachment; and, in war, three regiments would compose a good brigade, three brigades a division, and three divisions a strong cavalry corps, such as was formed and fought by Generals Sheridan and Wilson during the war.

In the artillery arm, the officers differ widely in their opinion of the true organization. A single company forms a battery, and habitually each battery acts separately, though sometimes several are united or "massed;" but these always act in concert with cavalry or infantry.

Nevertheless, the regimental organization for artillery has always been maintained in this country for classification and promotion. Twelve companies compose a regiment, and, though probably no colonel ever commanded his full regiment in the form of twelve batteries, yet in peace they occupy our heavy sea-coast forts or act as infantry; then the regimental organization is both necessary and convenient.

But the infantry composes the great mass of all armies, and the true form of the regiment or unit has been the subject of infinite discussion; and, as I have stated, during the civil war the regiment was a single battalion of ten companies. In olden times the regiment was composed of eight battalion companies and two flank companies. The first and tenth companies were armed with rifles, and were styled and used as "skirmishers;" but during 'the war they were never used exclusively for that special purpose, and in fact no distinction existed between them and the other eight companies.

The ten-company organization is awkward in practice, and I am satisfied that the infantry regiment should have the same identical organization as exists for the cavalry and artillery, viz., twelve companies, so as to be susceptible of division into three battalions of four companies each.

These companies should habitually be about a hundred one men strong, giving twelve hundred to a regiment, which in practice would settle down to about one thousand men.

Three such regiments would compose a brigade, three brigades a division, and three divisions a corps. Then, by allowing to an infantry corps a brigade of cavalry and six batteries of field-artillery, we would have an efficient corps d'armee of thirty thousand men, whose organization would be simple and most efficient, and whose strength should never be allowed to fall below twenty-five thousand men.

The corps is the true unit for grand campaigns and battle, should have a full and perfect staff, and every thing requisite for separate action, ready at all times to be detached and sent off for any nature of service. The general in command should have the rank of lieutenant-general, and should be, by experience and education, equal to any thing in war. Habitually with us he was a major-general, specially selected and assigned to the command by an order of the President, constituting, in fact, a separate grade.

The division is the unit of administration, and is the legitimate command of a major general.

The brigade is the next subdivision, and is commanded by a brigadier-general.

The regiment is the family. The colonel, as the father, should have a personal acquaintance with every officer and man, and should instill a feeling of pride and affection for himself, so that his officers and men would naturally look to him for personal advice and instruction. In war the regiment should never be subdivided, but should always be maintained entire. In peace this is impossible.

The company is the true unit of discipline, and the captain is the company. A good captain makes a good company, and he should have the power to reward as well as punish. The fact that soldiers world naturally like to have a good fellow for their captain is the best reason why he should be appointed by the colonel, or by some superior authority, instead of being elected by the men.

In the United States the people are the "sovereign," all power originally proceeds from them, and therefore the election of officers by the men is the common rule. This is wrong, because an army is not a popular organization, but an animated machine, an instrument in the hands of the Executive for enforcing the law, and maintaining the honor and dignity of the nation; and the President, as the constitutional commander-in-chief of the army and navy, should exercise the power of appointment (subject to the confirmation of the Senate) of the officers of "volunteers," as well as of "regulars."

No army can be efficient unless it be a unit for action; and the power must come from above, not from below: the President usually delegates his power to the commander-in-chief, and he to the next, and so on down to the lowest actual commander of troops, however small the detachment. No matter how troops come together, when once united, the highest officer in rank is held responsible, and should be consequently armed with the fullest power of the Executive, subject only to law and existing orders. The more simple the principle, the greater the likelihood of determined action; and the less a commanding officer is circumscribed by bounds or by precedent, the greater is the probability that he will make the best use of his command and achieve the best results.

The Regular Army and the Military Academy at West Point have in the past provided, and doubtless will in the future provide an ample supply of good officers for future wars; but, should their numbers be insufficient, we can always safely rely on the great number of young men of education and force of character throughout the country, to supplement them. At the close of our civil war, lasting four years, some of our best corps and division generals, as well as staff-officers, were from civil life; but I cannot recall any of the most successful who did not express a regret that he had not received in early life instruction in the elementary principles of the art of war, instead of being forced to acquire this knowledge in the dangerous and expensive school of actual war.

But the vital difficulty was, and will be again, to obtain an adequate number of good soldiers. We tried almost every system known to modern nations, all with more or less success--voluntary enlistments, the draft, and bought substitutes--and I think that all officers of experience will confirm my assertion that the men who voluntarily enlisted at the outbreak of the war were the best, better than the conscript, and far better than the bought substitute. When a regiment is once organized in a State, and mustered into the service of the United States, the officers and men become subject to the same laws of discipline and government as the regular troops. They are in no sense "militia," but compose a part of the Army of the United States, only retain their State title for convenience, and yet may be principally recruited from the neighborhood of their original organization: Once organized, the regiment should be kept full by recruits, and when it becomes difficult to obtain more recruits the pay should be raised by Congress, instead of tempting new men by exaggerated bounties. I believe it would have been more economical to have raised the pay of the soldier to thirty or even fifty dollars a month than to have held out the promise of three hundred and even six hundred dollars in the form of bounty. Toward the close of the war, I have often heard the soldiers complain that the "stay at-home" men got better pay, bounties, and food, than they who were exposed to all the dangers and vicissitudes of the battles and marches at the front. The feeling of the soldier should be that, in every event, the sympathy and preference of his government is for him who fights, rather than for him who is on provost or guard duty to the rear, and, like most men, he measures this by the amount of pay. Of course, the soldier must be trained to obedience, and should be "content with his wages;" but whoever has commanded an army in the field knows the difference between a willing, contented mass of men, and one that feels a cause of grievance. There is a soul to an army as well as to the individual man, and no general can accomplish the full work of his army unless he commands the soul of his men, as well as their bodies and legs.

The greatest mistake made in our civil war was in the mode of recruitment and promotion. When a regiment became reduced by the necessary wear and tear of service, instead of being filled up at the bottom, and the vacancies among the officers filled from the best noncommissioned officers and men, the habit was to raise new regiments, with new colonels, captains, and men, leaving the old and experienced battalions to dwindle away into mere skeleton organizations. I believe with the volunteers this matter was left to the States exclusively, and I remember that Wisconsin kept her regiments filled with recruits, whereas other States generally filled their quotas by new regiments, and the result was that we estimated a Wisconsin regiment equal to an ordinary brigade. I believe that five hundred new men added to an old and experienced regiment were more valuable than a thousand men in the form of a new regiment, for the former by association with good, experienced captains, lieutenants, and non-commissioned officers, soon became veterans, whereas the latter were generally unavailable for a year. The German method of recruitment is simply perfect, and there is no good reason why we should not follow it substantially.

On a road, marching by the flank, it would be considered "good order" to have five thousand men to a mile, so that a full corps of thirty thousand men would extend six miles, but with the average trains and batteries of artillery the probabilities are that it would draw out to ten miles. On a long and regular march the divisions and brigades should alternate in the lead, the leading division should be on the road by the earliest dawn, and march at the rate of about two miles, or, at most, two and a half miles an hour, so as to reach camp by noon. Even then the rear divisions and trains will hardly reach camp much before night. Theoretically, a marching column should preserve such order that by simply halting and facing to the right or left, it would be in line of battle; but this is rarely the case, and generally deployments are made "forward," by conducting each brigade by the flank obliquely to the right or left to its approximate position in line of battle, and there deployed. In such a line of battle, a brigade of three thousand infantry would occupy a mile of "front;" but for a strong line of battle five-thousand men with two batteries should be allowed to each mile, or a division would habitually constitute a double line with skirmishers and a reserve on a mile of "front."

The "feeding" of an army is a matter of the most vital importance, and demands the earliest attention of the general intrusted with a campaign. To be strong, healthy, and capable of the largest measure of physical effort, the soldier needs about three pounds gross of food per day, and the horse or mule about twenty pounds. When a general first estimates the quantity of food and forage needed for an army of fifty or one hundred thousand men, he is apt to be dismayed, and here a good staff is indispensable, though the general cannot throw off on them the responsibility. He must give the subject his personal attention, for the army reposes in him alone, and should never doubt the fact that their existence overrides in importance all other considerations. Once satisfied of this, and that all has been done that can be, the soldiers are always willing to bear the largest measure of privation. Probably no army ever had a more varied experience in this regard than the one I commanded in 1864'65.

Our base of supply was at Nashville, supplied by railways and the Cumberland River, thence by rail to Chattanooga, a "secondary base," and thence forward a single-track railroad. The stores came forward daily, but I endeavored to have on hand a full supply for twenty days in advance. These stores were habitually in the wagon-trains, distributed to corps, divisions, and regiments, in charge of experienced quartermasters and commissaries, and became subject to the orders of the generals commanding these bodies. They were generally issued on provision returns, but these had to be closely scrutinized, for too often the colonels would make requisitions for provisions for more men than they reported for battle. Of course, there are always a good many non-combatants with an army, but, after careful study, I limited their amount to twenty-five per cent. of the "effective strength," and that was found to be liberal. An ordinary army-wagon drawn by six mules may be counted on to carry three thousand pounds net, equal to the food of a full regiment for one day, but, by driving along beef-cattle, a commissary may safely count the contents of one wagon as sufficient for two days' food for a regiment of a thousand men; and as a corps should have food on hand for twenty days ready for detachment, it should have three hundred such wagons, as a provision-train; and for forage, ammunition, clothing, and other necessary stores, it was found necessary to have three hundred more wagons, or six hundred wagons in all, for a corps d'armee.

These should be absolutely under the immediate control of the corps commander, who will, however, find it economical to distribute them in due proportion to his divisions, brigades, and even regiments. Each regiment ought usually to have at least one wagon for convenience to distribute stores, and each company two pack-mules, so that the regiment may always be certain of a meal on reaching camp without waiting for the larger trains.

On long marches the artillery and wagon-trains should always have the right of way, and the troops should improvise roads to one side, unless forced to use a bridge in common, and all trains should have escorts to protect them, and to assist them in bad places. To this end there is nothing like actual experience, only, unless the officers in command give the subject their personal attention, they will find their wagon-trains loaded down with tents, personal baggage, and even the arms and knapsacks of the escort. Each soldier should, if not actually "sick or wounded," carry his musket and equipments containing from forty to sixty rounds of ammunition, his shelter-tent, a blanket or overcoat, and an extra pair of pants, socks, and drawers, in the form of a scarf, worn from the left shoulder to the right side in lieu of knapsack, and in his haversack he should carry some bread, cooked meat, salt, and coffee. I do not believe a soldier should be loaded down too much, but, including his clothing, arms, and equipment, he can carry about fifty pounds without impairing his health or activity. A simple calculation will show that by such a distribution a corps will-thus carry the equivalent of five hundred wagon-loads--an immense relief to the trains.

Where an army is near one of our many large navigable rivers, or has the safe use of a railway, it can usually be supplied with the full army ration, which is by far the best furnished to any army in America or Europe; but when it is compelled to operate away from such a base, and is dependent on its own train of wagons, the commanding officer must exercise a wise discretion in the selection of his stores. In my opinion, there is no better food for man than beef-cattle driven on the hoof, issued liberally, with salt, bacon, and bread. Coffee has also become almost indispensable, though many substitutes were found for it, such as Indian-corn, roasted, ground, and boiled as coffee; the sweet-potato, and the seed of the okra plant prepared in the same way. All these were used by the people of the South, who for years could procure no coffee, but I noticed that the women always begged of us some real coffee, which seems to satisfy a natural yearning or craving more powerful than can be accounted for on the theory of habit. Therefore I would always advise that the coffee and sugar ration be carried along, even at the expense of bread, for which there are many substitutes. Of these, Indian-corn is the best and most abundant. Parched in a frying-pan, it is excellent food, or if ground, or pounded and boiled with meat of any sort, it makes a most nutritious meal. The potato, both Irish and sweet, forms an excellent substitute for bread, and at Savannah we found that rice (was) also suitable, both for men and animals. For the former it should be cleaned of its husk in a hominy block, easily prepared out of a log, and sifted with a coarse corn bag; but for horses it should be fed in the straw. During the Atlanta campaign we were supplied by our regular commissaries with all sorts of patent compounds, such as desiccated vegetables, and concentrated milk, meat-biscuit, and sausages, but somehow the men preferred the simpler and more familiar forms of food, and usually styled these "desecrated vegetables and consecrated milk." We were also supplied liberally with lime-juice, sauerkraut, and pickles, as an antidote to scurvy, and I now recall the extreme anxiety of my medical director, Dr. Kittoe, about the scurvy, which he reported at one time as spreading and imperiling the army. This occurred at a crisis about Kenesaw, when the railroad was taxed to its utmost capacity to provide the necessary ammunition, food, and forage, and could not possibly bring us an adequate supply of potatoes and cabbage, the usual anti-scorbutics, when providentially the black berries ripened and proved an admirable antidote, and I have known the skirmish-line, without orders, to fight a respectable battle for the possession of some old fields that were full of blackberries. Soon, thereafter, the green corn or roasting-ear came into season, and I heard no more of the scurvy. Our country abounds with plants which can be utilized for a prevention to the scurvy; besides the above are the persimmon, the sassafras root and bud, the wild-mustard, the "agave," turnip tops, the dandelion cooked as greens, and a decoction of the ordinary pine-leaf.

For the more delicate and costly articles of food for the sick we relied mostly on the agents of the Sanitary Commission. I do not wish to doubt the value of these organizations, which gained so much applause during our civil war, for no one can question the motives of these charitable and generous people; but to be honest I must record an opinion that the Sanitary Commission should limit its operations to the hospitals at the rear, and should never appear at the front. They were generally local in feeling, aimed to furnish their personal friends and neighbors with a better class of food than the Government supplied, and the consequence was, that one regiment of a brigade would receive potatoes and fruit which would be denied another regiment close by: Jealousy would be the inevitable result, and in an army all parts should be equal; there should be no "partiality, favor, or affection." The Government should supply all essential wants, and in the hospitals to the rear will be found abundant opportunities for the exercise of all possible charity and generosity. During the war I several times gained the ill-will of the agents of the Sanitary Commission because I forbade their coming to the front unless they would consent to distribute their stores equally among all, regardless of the parties who had contributed them.

The sick, wounded, and dead of an army are the subjects of the greatest possible anxiety, and add an immense amount of labor to the well men. Each regiment in an active campaign should have a surgeon and two assistants always close at hand, and each brigade and division should have an experienced surgeon as a medical director. The great majority of wounds and of sickness should be treated by the regimental surgeon, on the ground, under the eye of the colonel. As few should be sent to the brigade or division hospital as possible, for the men always receive better care with their own regiment than with strangers, and as a rule the cure is more certain; but when men receive disabling wounds, or have sickness likely to become permanent, the sooner they go far to the rear the better for all. The tent or the shelter of a tree is a better hospital than a house, whose walls absorb fetid and poisonous emanations, and then give them back to the atmosphere. To men accustomed to the open air, who live on the plainest food, wounds seem to give less pain, and are attended with less danger to life than to ordinary soldiers in barracks.

Wounds which, in 1861, would have sent a man to the hospital for months, in 1865 were regarded as mere scratches, rather the subject of a joke than of sorrow. To new soldiers the sight of blood and death always has a sickening effect, but soon men become accustomed to it, and I have heard them exclaim on seeing a dead comrade borne to the rear, "Well, Bill has turned up his toes to the daisies." Of course, during a skirmish or battle, armed men should never leave their ranks to attend a dead or wounded comrade--this should be seen to in advance by the colonel, who should designate his musicians or company cooks as hospital attendants, with a white rag on their arm to indicate their office. A wounded man should go himself (if able) to the surgeon near at hand, or, if he need help, he should receive it from one of the attendants and not a comrade. It is wonderful how soon the men accustom themselves to these simple rules. In great battles these matters call for a more enlarged attention, and then it becomes the duty of the division general to see that proper stretchers and field hospitals are ready for the wounded, and trenches are dug for the dead. There should be no real neglect of the dead, because it has a bad effect on the living; for each soldier values himself and comrade as highly as though he were living in a good house at home.

The regimental chaplain, if any, usually attends the burials from the hospital, should make notes and communicate details to the captain of the company, and to the family at home. Of course it is usually impossible to mark the grave with names, dates, etc., and consequently the names of the "unknown" in our national cemeteries equal about one-half of all the dead.

Very few of the battles in which I have participated were fought as described in European text-books, viz., in great masses, in perfect order, manoeuvring by corps, divisions, and brigades. We were generally in a wooded country, and, though our lines were deployed according to tactics, the men generally fought in strong skirmish-lines, taking advantage of the shape of ground, and of every cover. We were generally the assailants, and in wooded and broken countries the "defensive" had a positive advantage over us, for they were always ready, had cover, and always knew the ground to their immediate front; whereas we, their assailants, had to grope our way over unknown ground, and generally found a cleared field or prepared entanglements that held us for a time under a close and withering fire. Rarely did the opposing lines in compact order come into actual contact, but when, as at Peach-Tree Creek and Atlanta, the lines did become commingled, the men fought individually in every possible style, more frequently with the musket clubbed than with the bayonet, and in some instances the men clinched like wrestlers, and went to the ground together. Europeans frequently criticised our war, because we did not always take full advantage of a victory; the true reason was, that habitually the woods served as a screen, and we often did not realize the fact that our enemy had retreated till he was already miles away and was again intrenched, having left a mere skirmish-line to cover the movement, in turn to fall back to the new position.

Our war was fought with the muzzle-loading rifle. Toward the close I had one brigade (Walcutt's) armed with breech-loading "Spencer's;" the cavalry generally had breach-loading carbines, "Spencer's" and "Sharp's," both of which were good arms.

The only change that breech-loading arms will probably make in the art and practice of war will be to increase the amount of ammunition to be expended, and necessarily to be carried along; to still further "thin out" the lines of attack, and to reduce battles to short, quick, decisive conflicts. It does not in the least affect the grand strategy, or the necessity for perfect organization, drill, and discipline. The companies and battalions will be more dispersed, and the men will be less under the immediate eye of their officers, and therefore a higher order of intelligence and courage on the part of the individual soldier will be an element of strength.

When a regiment is deployed as skirmishers, and crosses an open field or woods, under heavy fire, if each man runs forward from tree to tree, or stump to stump, and yet preserves a good general alignment, it gives great confidence to the men themselves, for they always keep their eyes well to the right and left, and watch their comrades; but when some few hold back, stick too close or too long to a comfortable log, it often stops the line and defeats the whole object. Therefore, the more we improve the fire-arm the more will be the necessity for good organization, good discipline and intelligence on the part of the individual soldier and officer. There is, of course, such a thing as individual courage, which has a value in war, but familiarity with danger, experience in war and its common attendants, and personal habit, are equally valuable traits, and these are the qualities with which we usually have to deal in war. All men naturally shrink from pain and danger, and only incur their risk from some higher motive, or from habit; so that I would define true courage to be a perfect sensibility of the measure of danger, and a mental willingness to incur it, rather than that insensibility to danger of which I have heard far more than I have seen. The most courageous men are generally unconscious of possessing the quality; therefore, when one professes it too openly, by words or bearing, there is reason to mistrust it. I would further illustrate my meaning by describing a man of true courage to be one who possesses all his faculties and senses perfectly when serious danger is actually present.

Modern wars have not materially changed the relative values or proportions of the several arms of service: infantry, artillery, cavalry, and engineers. If any thing, the infantry has been increased in value. The danger of cavalry attempting to charge infantry armed with breech-loading rifles was fully illustrated at Sedan, and with us very frequently. So improbable has such a thing become that we have omitted the infantry-square from our recent tactics. Still, cavalry against cavalry, and as auxiliary to infantry, will always be valuable, while all great wars will, as heretofore, depend chiefly on the infantry. Artillery is more valuable with new and inexperienced troops than with veterans. In the early stages of the war the field-guns often bore the proportion of six to a thousand men; but toward the close of the war one gun; or at most two, to a thousand men, was deemed enough. Sieges; such as characterized the wars of the last century, are too slow for this period of the world, and the Prussians recently almost ignored them altogether, penetrated France between the forts, and left a superior force "in observation," to watch the garrison and accept its surrender when the greater events of the war ahead made further resistance useless; but earth-forts, and especially field-works, will hereafter play an important part in war, because they enable a minor force to hold a superior one in check for a time, and time is a most valuable element in all wars. It was one of Prof. Mahan's maxims that the spade was as useful in war as the musket, and to this I will add the axe. The habit of intrenching certainly does have the effect of making new troops timid. When a line of battle is once covered by a good parapet, made by the engineers or by the labor of the men themselves, it does require an effort to make them leave it in the face of danger; but when the enemy is intrenched, it becomes absolutely necessary to permit each brigade and division of the troops immediately opposed to throw up a corresponding trench for their own protection in case of a sudden sally. We invariably did this in all our recent campaigns, and it had no ill effect, though sometimes our troops were a little too slow in leaving their well-covered lines to assail the enemy in position or on retreat. Even our skirmishers were in the habit of rolling logs together, or of making a lunette of rails, with dirt in front, to cover their bodies; and, though it revealed their position, I cannot say that it worked a bad effect; so that, as a rule, it may safely be left to the men themselves: On the "defensive," there is no doubt of the propriety of fortifying; but in the assailing army the general must watch closely to see that his men do not neglect an opportunity to drop his precautionary defenses, and act promptly on the "offensive" at every chance.

I have many a time crept forward to the skirmish-line to avail myself of the cover of the pickets "little fort," to observe more closely some expected result; and always talked familiarly with the men, and was astonished to see how well they comprehended the general object, and how accurately they were informed of the sate of facts existing miles away from their particular corps. Soldiers are very quick to catch the general drift and purpose of a campaign, and are always sensible when they are well commanded or well cared for. Once impressed with this fact, and that they are making progress, they bear cheerfully any amount of labor and privation.

In camp, and especially in the presence of an active enemy, it is much easier to maintain discipline than in barracks in time of peace. Crime and breaches of discipline are much less frequent, and the necessity for courts-martial far less. The captain can usually inflict all the punishment necessary, and the colonel should always. The field-officers' court is the best form for war, viz., one of the field-officers-the lieutenant-colonel or major --can examine the case and report his verdict, and the colonel should execute it. Of course, there are statutory offenses which demand a general court-martial, and these must be ordered by the division or corps commander; but, the presence of one of our regular civilian judge-advocates in an army in the field would be a first-class nuisance, for technical courts always work mischief. Too many courts-martial in any command are evidence of poor discipline and inefficient officers.

For the rapid transmission of orders in an army covering a large space of ground, the magnetic telegraph is by far the best, though habitually the paper and pencil, with good mounted orderlies, answer every purpose. I have little faith in the signal-service by flags and torches, though we always used them; because, almost invariably when they were most needed, the view was cut off by intervening trees, or by mists and fogs. There was one notable instance in my experience, when the signal-flags carried a message. of vital importance over the heads of Hood's army, which had interposed between me and Allatoona, and had broken the telegraph-wires--as recorded in Chapter XIX.; but the value of the magnetic telegraph in war cannot be exaggerated, as was illustrated by the perfect concert of action between the armies in Virginia and Georgia during 1864. Hardly a day intervened when General Grant did not know the exact state of facts with me, more than fifteen hundred miles away as the wires ran. So on the field a thin insulated wire may be run on improvised stakes or from tree to tree for six or more miles in a couple of hours, and I have seen operators so skillful, that by cutting the wire they would receive a message with their tongues from a distant station. As a matter of course, the ordinary commercial wires along the railways form the usual telegraph-lines for an army, and these are easily repaired and extended as the army advances, but each army and wing should have a small party of skilled men to put up the field-wire, and take it down when done. This is far better than the signal-flags and torches. Our commercial telegraph-lines will always supply for war enough skillful operators.

The value of railways is also fully recognized in war quite as much as, if not more so than, in peace. The Atlanta campaign would simply have been impossible without the use of the railroads from Louisville to Nashville--one hundred and eighty-five miles--from Nashville to Chattanooga--one hundred and fifty-one miles--and from Chattanooga to Atlanta--one hundred and thirty-seven miles. Every mile of this "single track" was so delicate, that one man could in a minute have broken or moved a rail, but our trains usually carried along the tools and means to repair such a break. We had, however, to maintain strong guards and garrisons at each important bridge or trestle--the destruction of which would have necessitated time for rebuilding. For the protection of a bridge, one or two log block houses, two stories high, with a piece of ordnance and a small infantry guard, usually sufficed. The block-house had a small parapet and ditch about it, and the roof was made shot proof by earth piled on. These points could usually be reached only by a dash of the enemy's cavalry, and many of these block houses successfully resisted serious attacks by both cavalry and artillery. The only block-house that was actually captured on the main was the one described near Allatoona. Our trains from Nashville forward were operated under military rules, and ran about ten miles an hour in gangs of four trains of ten cars each. Four such groups of trains daily made one hundred and sixty cars, of ten tons each, carrying sixteen hundred tons, which exceeded the absolute necessity of the army, and allowed for the accidents that were common and inevitable. But, as I have recorded, that single stem of railroad, four hundred and seventy-three miles long, supplied an army of one hundred thousand men and thirty-five thousand animals for the period of one hundred and ninety-six days, viz., from May 1 to November 12, 1864. To have delivered regularly that amount of food and forage by ordinary wagons would have required thirty-six thousand eight hundred wagons of six mules each, allowing each wagon to have hauled two tons twenty miles each day, a simple impossibility in roads such as then existed in that region of country. Therefore, I reiterate that the Atlanta campaign was an impossibility without these railroads; and only then, because we had the men and means to maintain and defend them, in addition to what were necessary to overcome the enemy. Habitually, a passenger-car will carry fifty men with their necessary baggage. Box-cars, and even platform-cars, answer the purpose well enough, but they, should always have rough board-seats. For sick and wounded men, box-cars filled with straw or bushes were usually employed. Personally, I saw but little of the practical working of the railroads, for I only turned back once as far as Resaca; but I had daily reports from the engineer in charge, and officers who came from the rear often explained to me the whole thing, with a description of the wrecked trains all the way from Nashville to Atlanta. I am convinced that the risk to life to the engineers and men on that railroad fully equaled that on the skirmish-line, called for as high an order of courage, and fully equaled it in importance. Still, I doubt if there be any necessity in time of peace to organize a corps specially to work the military railroads in time of war, because in peace these same men gain all the necessary experience, possess all the daring and courage of soldiers, and only need the occasional protection and assistance of the necessary train-guard, which may be composed of the furloughed men coming and going, or of details made from the local garrisons to the rear.

For the transfer of large armies by rail, from one theatre of action to another by the rear--the cases of the transfer of the Eleventh and Twelfth Corps--General Hooker, twenty-three thousand men--from the East to Chattanooga, eleven hundred and ninety-two miles in seven days, in the fall of 1863; and that of the Army of the Ohio--General Schofield, fifteen thousand men--from the valley of the Tennessee to Washington, fourteen hundred miles in eleven days, en route to North Carolina in January, 1865, are the best examples of which I have any knowledge, and reference to these is made in the report of the Secretary of War, Mr. Stanton, dated November 22, 1865.

Engineer troops attached to an army are habitually employed in supervising the construction of forts or field works of a nature more permanent than the lines need by the troops in motion, and in repairing roads and making bridges. I had several regiments of this kind that were most useful, but as a rule we used the infantry, or employed parties of freedmen, who worked on the trenches at night while the soldiers slept, and these in turn rested by day. Habitually the repair of the railroad and its bridges was committed to hired laborers, like the English navies, under the supervision of Colonel W. W. Wright, a railroad-engineer, who was in the military service at the time, and his successful labors were frequently referred to in the official reports of the campaign.

For the passage of rivers, each army corps had a pontoon-train with a detachment of engineers, and, on reaching a river, the leading infantry division was charged with the labor of putting it down. Generally the single pontoon-train could provide for nine hundred feet of bridge, which sufficed; but when the rivers were very wide two such trains would be brought together, or the single train was supplemented by a trestle-bridge, or bridges made on crib-work, out of timber found near the place. The pontoons in general use were skeleton frames, made with a hinge, so as to fold back and constitute a wagon-body. In this same wagon were carried the cotton canvas cover, the anchor and chains, and a due proportion of the balks, cheeses, and lashings. All the troops became very familiar with their mechanism and use, and we were rarely delayed by reason of a river, however broad. I saw, recently, in Aldershot, England, a very complete pontoon-train; the boats were sheathed with wood and felt, made very light; but I think these were more liable to chafing and damage in rough handling than were our less expensive and rougher boats. On the whole, I would prefer the skeleton frame and canvas cover to any style of pontoon that I have ever seen.

In relation to guards, pickets, and vedettes, I doubt if any discoveries or improvements were made during our war, or in any of the modern wars in Europe. These precautions vary with the nature of the country and the situation of each army. When advancing or retreating in line of battle, the usual skirmish-line constitutes the picket-line, and may have "reserves," but usually the main line of battle constitutes the reserve; and in this connection I will state that the recent innovation introduced into the new infantry tactics by General Upton is admirable, for by it each regiment, brigade, and division deployed, sends forward as "skirmishers" the one man of each set of fours, to cover its own front, and these can be recalled or reenforced at pleasure by the bugle-signal.

For flank-guards and rear-guards, one or more companies should be detached under their own officers, instead of making up the guard by detailing men from the several companies.

For regimental or camp guards, the details should be made according to existing army regulations; and all the guards should be posted early in the evening, so as to afford each sentinel or vedette a chance to study his ground before it becomes too dark.

In like manner as to the staff. The more intimately it comes into contact with the troops, the more useful and valuable it becomes. The almost entire separation of the staff from the line, as now practised by us, and hitherto by the French, has proved mischievous, and the great retinues of staff-officers with which some of our earlier generals began the war were simply ridiculous. I don't believe in a chief of staff at all, and any general commanding an army, corps, or division, that has a staff-officer who professes to know more than his chief, is to be pitied. Each regiment should have a competent adjutant, quartermaster, and commissary, with two or three medical officers. Each brigade commander should have the same staff, with the addition of a couple of young aides-de-camp, habitually selected from the subalterns of the brigade, who should be good riders, and intelligent enough to give and explain the orders of their general.

The same staff will answer for a division. The general in command of a separate army, and of a corps d'armee, should have the same professional assistance, with two or more good engineers, and his adjutant-general should exercise all the functions usually ascribed to a chief of staff, viz., he should possess the ability to comprehend the scope of operations, and to make verbally and in writing all the orders and details necessary to carry into effect the views of his general, as well as to keep the returns and records of events for the information of the next higher authority, and for history. A bulky staff implies a division of responsibility, slowness of action, and indecision, whereas a small staff implies activity and concentration of purpose. The smallness of General Grant's staff throughout the civil war forms the best model for future imitation. So of tents, officers furniture, etc., etc. In real war these should all be discarded, and an army is efficient for action and motion exactly in the inverse ratio of its impedimenta. Tents should be omitted altogether, save one to a regiment for an office, and a few for the division hospital. Officers should be content with a tent fly, improvising poles and shelter out of bushes. The tents d'abri, or shelter-tent, carried by the soldier himself, is all-sufficient. Officers should never seek for houses, but share the condition of their men.

A recent message (July 18, 1874) made to the French Assembly by Marshal MacMahon, President of the French Republic, submits a projet de loi, with a report prepared by a board of French generals on "army administration," which is full of information, and is as applicable to us as to the French. I quote from its very beginning: "The misfortunes of the campaign of 1870 have demonstrated the inferiority of our system.... Two separate organizations existed with parallel functions--the 'general' more occupied in giving direction to his troops than in providing for their material wants, which he regarded as the special province of the staff, and the 'intendant' (staff) often working at random, taking on his shoulders a crushing burden of functions and duties, exhausting himself with useless efforts, and aiming to accomplish an insufficient service, to the disappointment of everybody. This separation of the administration and command, this coexistence of two wills, each independent of the other, which paralyzed both and annulled the dualism, was condemned. It was decided by the board that this error should be "proscribed" in the new military system. The report then goes on at great length discussing the provisions. of the "new law," which is described to be a radical change from the old one on the same subject. While conceding to the Minister of War in Paris the general control and supervision of the entire military establishment primarily, especially of the annual estimates or budget, and the great depots of supply, it distributes to the commanders of the corps d'armee in time of peace, and to all army commanders generally in time of war, the absolute command of the money, provisions, and stores, with the necessary staff-officers to receive, issue, and account for them. I quote further: "The object of this law is to confer on the commander of troops whatever liberty of action the case demands. He has the power even to go beyond the regulations, in circumstances of urgency and pressing necessity. The extraordinary measures he may take on these occasions may require their execution without delay. The staff-officer has but one duty before obeying, and that is to submit his observations to the general, and to ask his orders in writing.

With this formality his responsibility ceases, and the responsibility for the extraordinary act falls solely on the general who gives the order. The officers and agents charged with supplies are placed under the orders of the general in command of the troops, that is, they are obliged both in war and peace to obey, with the single qualification above named, of first making their observations and securing the written order of the general.

With us, to-day, the law and regulations are that, no matter what may be the emergency, the commanding general in Texas, New Mexico, and the remote frontiers, cannot draw from the arsenals a pistol-cartridge, or any sort of ordnance-stores, without first procuring an order of the Secretary of War in Washington. The commanding general--though intrusted with the lives of his soldiers and with the safety of a frontier in a condition of chronic war--cannot touch or be trusted with ordnance-stores or property, and that is declared to be the law! Every officer of the old army remembers how, in 1861, we were hampered with the old blue army regulations, which tied our hands, and that to do any thing positive and necessary we had to tear it all to pieces--cut the red-tape, as it was called, a dangerous thing for an army to do, for it was calculated to bring the law and authority into contempt; but war was upon us, and overwhelming necessity overrides all law.

This French report is well worth the study of our army-officers, of all grades and classes, and I will only refer again, casually, to another part, wherein it discusses the subject of military correspondence: whether the staff-officer should correspond directly with his chief in Paris, submitting to his general copies, or whether he should be required to carry on his correspondence through his general, so that the latter could promptly forward the communication, indorsed with his own remarks and opinions. The latter is declared by the board to be the only safe role, because "the general should never be ignorant of any thing that is transpiring that concerns his command."

In this country, as in France, Congress controls the great questions of war and peace, makes all laws for the creation and government of armies, and votes the necessary supplies, leaving to the President to execute and apply these laws, especially the harder task of limiting the expenditure of public money to the amount of the annual appropriations. The executive power is further subdivided into the seven great departments, and to the Secretary of War is confided the general care of the military establishment, and his powers are further subdivided into ten distinct and separate bureaus.

The chiefs of these bureaus are under the immediate orders of the Secretary of War, who, through them, in fact commands the army from "his office," but cannot do so "in the field"--an absurdity in military if not civil law.

The subordinates of these staff-corps and departments are selected and chosen from the army itself, or fresh from West Point, and too commonly construe themselves into the elite, as made of better clay than the common soldier. Thus they separate themselves more and more from their comrades of the line, and in process of time realize the condition of that old officer of artillery who thought the army would be a delightful place for a gentleman if it were not for the d-d soldier; or, better still, the conclusion of the young lord in "Henry IV.," who told Harry Percy (Hotspur) that "but for these vile guns he would himself have been a soldier." This is all wrong; utterly at variance with our democratic form of government and of universal experience; and now that the French, from whom we had copied the system, have utterly "proscribed" it, I hope that our Congress will follow suit. I admit, in its fullest force, the strength of the maxim that the civil law should be superior to the military in time of peace; that the army should be at all times subject to the direct control of Congress; and I assert that, from the formation of our Government to the present day, the Regular Army has set the highest example of obedience to law and authority; but, for the very reason that our army is comparatively so very small, I hold that it should be the best possible, organized and governed on true military principles, and that in time of peace we should preserve the "habits and usages of war," so that, when war does come, we may not again be compelled to suffer the disgrace, confusion, and disorder of 1861.

The commanding officers of divisions, departments, and posts, should have the amplest powers, not only to command their troops, but all the stores designed for their use, and the officers of the staff necessary to administer them, within the area of their command; and then with fairness they could be held to the most perfect responsibility. The President and Secretary of War can command the army quite as well through these generals as through the subordinate staff-officers. Of course, the Secretary would, as now, distribute the funds according to the appropriation bills, and reserve to himself the absolute control and supervision of the larger arsenals and depots of supply. The error lies in the law, or in the judicial interpretation thereof, and no code of army regulations can be made that meets the case, until Congress, like the French Corps Legislatif, utterly annihilates and "proscribes" the old law and the system which has grown up under it.

It is related of Napoleon that his last words were, "Tete d'armee!" Doubtless, as the shadow of death obscured his memory, the last thought that remained for speech was of some event when he was directing an important "head of column." I believe that every general who has handled armies in battle most recall from his own experience the intensity of thought on some similar occasion, when by a single command he had given the finishing stroke to some complicated action; but to me recurs another thought that is worthy of record, and may encourage others who are to follow us in our profession. I never saw the rear of an army engaged in battle but I feared that some calamity had happened at the front the apparent confusion, broken wagons, crippled horses, men lying about dead and maimed, parties hastening to and fro in seeming disorder, and a general apprehension of something dreadful about to ensue; all these signs, however, lessened as I neared the front, and there the contrast was complete--perfect order, men and horses--full of confidence, and it was not unusual for general hilarity, laughing, and cheering. Although cannon might be firing, the musketry clattering, and the enemy's shot hitting close, there reigned a general feeling of strength and security that bore a marked contrast to the bloody signs that had drifted rapidly to the rear; therefore, for comfort and safety, I surely would rather be at the front than the rear line of battle. So also on the march, the head of a column moves on steadily, while the rear is alternately halting and then rushing forward to close up the gap; and all sorts of rumors, especially the worst, float back to the rear. Old troops invariably deem it a special privilege to be in the front --to be at the "head of column"--because experience has taught them that it is the easiest and most comfortable place, and danger only adds zest and stimulus to this fact.

The hardest task in war is to lie in support of some position or battery, under fire without the privilege of returning it; or to guard some train left in the rear, within hearing but out of danger; or to provide for the wounded and dead of some corps which is too busy ahead to care for its own.

To be at the head of a strong column of troops, in the execution of some task that requires brain, is the highest pleasure of war--a grim one and terrible, but which leaves on the mind and memory the strongest mark; to detect the weak point of an enemy's line; to break through with vehemence and thus lead to victory; or to discover some key-point and hold it with tenacity; or to do some other distinct act which is afterward recognized as the real cause of success. These all become matters that are never forgotten. Other great difficulties, experienced by every general, are to measure truly the thousand-and-one reports that come to him in the midst of conflict; to preserve a clear and well-defined purpose at every instant of time, and to cause all efforts to converge to that end.

To do these things he must know perfectly the strength and quality of each part of his own army, as well as that of his opponent, and must be where he can personally see and observe with his own eyes, and judge with his own mind. No man can properly command an army from the rear, he must be "at its front;" and when a detachment is made, the commander thereof should be informed of the object to be accomplished, and left as free as possible to execute it in his own way; and when an army is divided up into several parts, the superior should always attend that one which he regards as most important. Some men think that modern armies may be so regulated that a general can sit in an office and play on his several columns as on the keys of a piano; this is a fearful mistake. The directing mind must be at the very head of the army--must be seen there, and the effect of his mind and personal energy must be felt by every officer and man present with it, to secure the best results. Every attempt to make war easy and safe will result in humiliation and disaster.

Lastly, mail facilities should be kept up with an army if possible, that officers and men may receive and send letters to their friends, thus maintaining the home influence of infinite assistance to discipline. Newspaper correspondents with an army, as a rule, are mischievous. They are the world's gossips, pick up and retail the camp scandal, and gradually drift to the headquarters of some general, who finds it easier to make reputation at home than with his own corps or division. They are also tempted to prophesy events and state facts which, to an enemy, reveal a purpose in time to guard against it. Moreover, they are always bound to see facts colored by the partisan or political character of their own patrons, and thus bring army officers into the political controversies of the day, which are always mischievous and wrong. Yet, so greedy are the people at large for war news, that it is doubtful whether any army commander can exclude all reporters, without bringing down on himself a clamor that may imperil his own safety. Time and moderation must bring a just solution to this modern difficulty.

CHAPTER XXVI.
AFTER THE WAR

In the foregoing pages I have endeavored to describe the public events in which I was an actor or spectator before and during the civil war of 1861-'65, and it now only remains for me to treat of similar matters of general interest subsequent to the civil war. Within a few days of the grand review of May 24, 1865, I took leave of the army at Washington, and with my family went to Chicago to attend a fair held in the interest of the families of soldiers impoverished by the war. I remained there about two weeks; on the 22d of June was at South Bend, Indiana, where two of my children were at school, and reached my native place, Lancaster, Ohio, on the 24th. On the 4th of July I visited at Louisville, Kentucky, the Fourteenth, Fifteenth, Sixteenth, and Seventeenth Army Corps, which had come from Washington, under the command of General John A. Logan, for "muster out," or "further orders." I then made a short visit to General George H. Thomas at Nashville, and returned to Lancaster, where I remained with the family till the receipt of General Orders No. 118 of June 27, 1865, which divided the whole territory of the United States into nineteen departments and five military divisions, the second of which was the military division of the "Mississippi," afterward changed to "Missouri," Major-General W. T. Sherman to command, with, headquarters at St. Louis, to embrace the Departments of the Ohio, Missouri, and Arkansas.

This territorial command included the States north of the Ohio River, and the States and Territories north of Texas, as far west as the Rocky Mountains, including Montana, Utah, and New Mexico, but the part east of the Mississippi was soon transferred to another division. The department commanders were General E. O. C. Ord, at Detroit; General John Pope, at Fort Leavenworth; and General J. J. Reynolds, at Little Rock, but these also were soon changed. I at once assumed command, and ordered my staff and headquarters from Washington to St. Louis, Missouri, going there in person on the 16th of July.

My thoughts and feelings at once reverted to the construction of the great Pacific Railway, which had been chartered by Congress in the midst of war, and was then in progress. I put myself in communication with the parties engaged in the work, visiting them in person, and assured them that I would afford them all possible assistance and encouragement. Dr. Durant, the leading man of the Union Pacific, seemed to me a person of ardent nature, of great ability and energy, enthusiastic in his undertaking, and determined to build the road from Omaha to San Francisco. He had an able corps of assistants, collecting materials, letting out contracts for ties, grading, etc., and I attended the celebration of the first completed division of sixteen and a half miles, from Omaha to Papillon. When the orators spoke so confidently of the determination to build two thousand miles of railway across the plains, mountains, and desert, devoid of timber, with no population, but on the contrary raided by the bold and bloody Sioux and Cheyennes, who had almost successfully defied our power for half a century, I was disposed to treat it jocularly, because I could not help recall our California experience of 1855-'56, when we celebrated the completion of twenty-two and a half miles of the same road eastward of Sacramento; on which occasion Edward Baker had electrified us by his unequalled oratory, painting the glorious things which would result from uniting the Western coast with the East by bands of iron. Baker then, with a poet's imagination, saw the vision of the mighty future, but not the gulf which meantime was destined to swallow up half a million of the brightest and best youth of our land, and that he himself would be one of the first victims far away on the banks of the Potomac (he was killed in battle at Balls Bluff, October 21, 1861).

The Kansas Pacific was designed to unite with the main branch about the 100 deg. meridian, near Fort Kearney. Mr. Shoemaker was its general superintendent and building contractor, and this branch in 1865 was finished about forty miles to a point near Lawrence, Kansas. I may not be able to refer to these roads again except incidentally, and will, therefore, record here that the location of this branch afterward was changed from the Republican to the Smoky Hill Fork of the Kansas River, and is now the main line to Denver. The Union and Central Railroads from the beginning were pushed with a skill, vigor, and courage which always commanded my admiration, the two meeting at Promontory Point, Utah, July 15, 1869, and in my judgment constitute one of the greatest and most beneficent achievements of man on earth.

The construction of the Union Pacific Railroad was deemed so important that the President, at my suggestion, constituted on the 5th of March, 1866, the new Department of the Platte, General P. St. George

Cooke commanding, succeeded by General C. C. Augur, headquarters at Omaha, with orders to give ample protection to the working-parties, and to afford every possible assistance in the construction of the road; and subsequently in like manner the Department of Dakota was constituted, General A. H. Terry commanding, with headquarters at St. Paul, to give similar protection and encouragement to the Northern Pacific Railroad. These departments, with changed commanders, have continued up to the present day, and have fulfilled perfectly the uses for which they were designed.

During the years 1865 and 1866 the great plains remained almost in a state of nature, being the pasture-fields of about ten million buffalo, deer, elk, and antelope, and were in full possession of the Sioux, Cheyennes, Arapahoes, and Kiowas, a race of bold Indians, who saw plainly that the construction of two parallel railroads right through their country would prove destructive to the game on which they subsisted, and consequently fatal to themselves.

The troops were posted to the best advantage to protect the parties engaged in building these roads, and in person I reconnoitred well to the front, traversing the buffalo regions from south to north, and from east to west, often with a very small escort, mingling with the Indians whenever safe, and thereby gained personal knowledge of matters which enabled me to use the troops to the best advantage. I am sure that without the courage and activity of the department commanders with the small bodies of regular troops on the plains during the years 1866-'69, the Pacific Railroads could not have been built; but once built and in full operation the fate of the buffalo and Indian was settled for all time to come.

At the close of the civil war there were one million five hundred and sixteen names on the muster-rolls, of which seven hundred and ninety-seven thousand eight hundred and seven were present, and two hundred and two thousand seven hundred and nine absent, of which twenty-two thousand nine hundred and twenty-nine were regulars, the others were volunteers, colored troops, and veteran reserves. The regulars consisted of six regiments of cavalry, five of artillery, and nineteen of infantry. By the act of July 28, 1866, the peace establishment was fixed at one general (Grant), one lieutenant-general (Sherman), five major-generals (Halleck, Meade, Sheridan, Thomas, and Hancock), ten brigadiers (McDowell, Cooke, Pope, Hooker, Schofield, Howard, Terry, Ord, Canby, and Rousseau), ten regiments of cavalry, five of artillery, and forty-five of infantry, admitting of an aggregate force of fifty-four thousand six hundred and forty-one men.

All others were mustered out, and thus were remanded to their homes nearly a million of strong, vigorous men who had imbibed the somewhat erratic habits of the soldier; these were of every profession and trade in life, who, on regaining their homes, found their places occupied by others, that their friends and neighbors were different, and that they themselves had changed. They naturally looked for new homes to the great West, to the new Territories and States as far as the Pacific coast, and we realize to-day that the vigorous men who control Kansas, Nebraska, Dakota, Montana, Colorado, etc., etc., were soldiers of the civil war. These men flocked to the plains, and were rather stimulated than retarded by the danger of an Indian war. This was another potent agency in producing the result we enjoy to-day, in having in so short a time replaced the wild buffaloes by more numerous herds of tame cattle, and by substituting for the useless Indians the intelligent owners of productive farms and cattle-ranches.

While these great changes were being wrought at the West, in the East politics had resumed full sway, and all the methods of anti-war times had been renewed. President Johnson had differed with his party as to the best method of reconstructing the State governments of the South, which had been destroyed and impoverished by the war, and the press began to agitate the question of the next President. Of course, all Union men naturally turned to General Grant, and the result was jealousy of him by the personal friends of President Johnson and some of his cabinet. Mr. Johnson always seemed very patriotic and friendly, and I believed him honest and sincere in his declared purpose to follow strictly the Constitution of the United States in restoring the Southern States to their normal place in the Union; but the same cordial friendship subsisted between General Grant and myself, which was the outgrowth of personal relations dating back to 1839. So I resolved to keep out of this conflict. In September, 1866, I was in the mountains of New Mexico, when a message reached me that I was wanted at Washington. I had with me a couple of officers and half a dozen soldiers as escort, and traveled down the Arkansas, through the Kiowas, Comanches, Cheyennes, and Arapahoes, all more or less disaffected, but reached St. Louis in safety, and proceeded to Washington, where I reported to General Grant.

He explained to me that President Johnson wanted to see me. He did not know the why or wherefore, but supposed it had some connection with an order he (General Grant) had received to escort the newly appointed Minister, Hon. Lew Campbell, of Ohio, to the court of Juarez, the President-elect of Mexico, which country was still in possession of the Emperor Maximilian, supported by a corps of French troops commanded by General Bazaine. General Grant denied the right of the President to order him on a diplomatic mission unattended by troops; said that he had thought the matter over, world disobey the order, and stand the consequences. He manifested much feeling; and said it was a plot to get rid of him. I then went to President Johnson, who treated me with great cordiality, and said that he was very glad I had come; that General Grant was about to go to Mexico on business of importance, and he wanted me at Washington to command the army in General Grant's absence. I then informed him that General Grant would not go, and he seemed amazed; said that it was generally understood that General Grant construed the occupation of the territories of our neighbor, Mexico, by French troops, and the establishment of an empire therein, with an Austrian prince at its head, as hostile to republican America, and that the Administration had arranged with the French Government for the withdrawal of Bazaine's troops, which would leave the country free for the President-elect Juarez to reoccupy the city of Mexico, etc., etc.; that Mr. Campbell had been accredited to Juarez, and the fact that he was accompanied by so distinguished a soldier as General Grant would emphasize the act of the United States. I simply reiterated that General Grant would not go, and that he, Mr. Johnson, could not afford to quarrel with him at that time. I further argued that General Grant was at the moment engaged on the most delicate and difficult task of reorganizing the army under the act of July 28, 1866; that if the real object was to put Mr. Campbell in official communication with President Juarez, supposed to be at El Paso or Monterey, either General Hancock, whose command embraced New Mexico, or General Sheridan, whose command included Texas, could fulfill the object perfectly; or, in the event of neither of these alternates proving satisfactory to the Secretary of State, that I could be easier spared than General Grant. "Certainly," answered the President, "if you will go, that will answer perfectly."

The instructions of the Secretary of State, W. H. Seward, to Hon. Lewis D. Campbell, Minister to Mexico, dated October 25, 1866; a letter from President Johnson to Secretary of War Stanton, dated October 26, 1866; and the letter of Edwin M. Stanton, Secretary of War, to General Grant, dated October 27th, had been already prepared and printed, and the originals or copies were furnished me; but on the 30th of October, 1866, the following letter passed

EXECUTIVE MANSION

WASHINGTON, D. C., October 30,1866.

SIR: General Ulysses S. Grant having found it inconvenient to assume the duties specified in my letter to you of the 26th inst., you will please relieve him, and assign them in all respects to William T. Sherman, Lieutenant-General of the Army of the United States. By way of guiding General Sherman in the performance of his duties, you will furnish him with a copy of your special orders to General Grant made in compliance with my letter of the 26th inst., together with a copy of the instructions of the Secretary of State to Lewis D. Campbell, Esq., therein mentioned.

The lieutenant-general will proceed to the execution of his duties without delay.

Very respectfully yours,

ANDREW JOHNSON
To the Hon. EDWIN M. STANTON, Secretary of War.

At the Navy Department I learned that the United States ship Susquehanna, Captain Alden, was fitting out in New York for the use of this mission, and that there would be time for me to return to St. Louis to make arrangements for a prolonged absence, as also to communicate with Mr. Campbell, who was still at his home in Hamilton, Ohio. By correspondence we agreed to meet in New York, November 8th, he accompanied by Mr. Plumb, secretary of legation, and I by my aide, Colonel Audenried.

We embarked November 10th, and went to sea next day, making for Havana and Vera Cruz, and, as soon as we were outside of Sandy Hook, I explained to Captain Alden that my mission was ended, because I believed by substituting myself for General Grant I had prevented a serious quarrel between him and the Administration, which was unnecessary. We reached Havana on the 18th, with nothing to vary the monotony of an ordinary sea-voyage, except off Hatteras we picked up one woman and twenty men from open boats, who had just abandoned a propeller bound from Baltimore to Charleston which foundered. The sea was very rough, but by the personal skill and supervision of Captain Alden every soul reached our deck safely, and was carried to our consul at Havana. At Havana we were very handsomely entertained, especially by Senor Aldama, who took us by rail to his sugar-estates at Santa Ross, and back by Matanzas.

We took our departure thence on the 25th, and anchored under Isla Verde, off Vera Cruz, on the 29th.

Everything about Vera Cruz indicated the purpose of the French to withdraw, and also that the Emperor Maximilian would precede them, for the Austrian frigate Dandolo was in port, and an Austrian bark, on which were received, according to the report of our consul, Mr. Lane, as many as eleven hundred packages of private furniture to be transferred to Miramar, Maximilian's home; and Lieutenant Clarin, of the French navy, who visited the Susquehanna from the French commodore, Clouet, told me, without reserve, that, if we had delayed eight days more, we would have found Maximilian gone. General Bazaine was reported to be in the city of Mexico with about twenty-eight thousand French troops; but instead of leaving Mexico in three detachments, viz., November, 1866, March, 1867, and November, 1867, as described in Mr. Seward's letter to Mr. Campbell, of October 25, 1866, it looked to me that, as a soldier, he would evacuate at some time before November, 1867, all at once, and not by detachments. Lieutenant Clarin telegraphed Bazaine at the city of Mexico the fact of our arrival, and he sent me a most courteous and pressing invitation to come up to the city; but, as we were accredited to the government of Juarez, it was considered undiplomatic to establish friendly relations with the existing authorities. Meantime we could not hear a word of Juarez, and concluded to search for him along the coast northward. When I was in Versailles, France, July, 1872, learning that General Bazaine was in arrest for the surrender of his army and post at Metz, in 1870, I wanted to call on him to thank him for his courteous invitation to me at Vera Cruz in 1866. I inquired of President Thiers if I could with propriety call on the marshal. He answered that it would be very acceptable, no doubt, but suggested for form's sake that I should consult the Minister of War, General de Cissey, which I did, and he promptly assented. Accordingly, I called with my aide, Colonel Audenried, on Marshal Bazaine, who occupied a small, two-story stone house at Versailles, in an inclosure with a high garden wall, at the front gate or door of which was a lodge, in which was a military guard. We were shown to a good room on the second floor, where was seated the marshal in military half-dress, with large head, full face, short neck, and evidently a man of strong physique. He did not speak English, but spoke Spanish perfectly. We managed to carry on a conversation in which I endeavored to convey my sense of his politeness in inviting me so cordially up to the city of Mexico, and my regret that the peculiar duty on which I was engaged did not admit of a compliance, or even of an intelligent explanation, at the time. He spoke of the whole Mexican business as a "sad affair," that the empire necessarily fell with the result of our civil war, and that poor Maximilian was sacrificed to his own high sense of honor.

While on board the Susquehanna, on the 1st day of December, 1866, we received the proclamation made by the Emperor Maximilian at Orizaba, in which, notwithstanding the near withdrawal of the French troops, he declared his purpose to remain and "shed the last drop of his blood in defense of his dear country." Undoubtedly many of the most substantial people of Mexico, having lost all faith in the stability of the native government, had committed themselves to what they considered the more stable government of Maximilian, and Maximilian, a man of honor, concluded at the last moment he could not abandon them; the consequence was his death.

Failing to hear of Juarez, we steamed up the coast to the Island of Lobos, and on to Tampico, off which we found the United States steamer Paul Jones, which, drawing less water than the Susquehanna, carried us over the bar to the city, then in possession of the Liberal party, which recognized Juarez as their constitutional President, but of Juarez and his whereabout we could hear not a word; so we continued up the coast and anchored off Brazos Santiago, December 7th. Going ashore in small boats, we found a railroad, under the management of General J. R. West, now one of the commissioners of the city of Washington, who sent us up to Brownsville, Texas. We met on the way General Sheridan, returning from a tour of inspection of the Rio Grande frontier. On Sunday, December 9th, we were all at Matamoras, Mexico, where we met General Escobedo, one of Juarez's trusty lieutenants, who developed to us the general plan agreed on for the overthrow of the empire, and the reestablishment of the republican government of Mexico. He asked of us no assistance, except the loan of some arms, ammunition, clothing, and camp-equipage. It was agreed that Mr. Campbell should, as soon as he could get his baggage off the Susquehanna, return to Matamoras, and thence proceed to Monterey, to be received by Juarez in person as, the accredited Minister of the United States to the Republic of Mexico. Meantime the weather off the coast was stormy, and the Susquehanna parted a cable, so that we were delayed some days at Brazos; but in due time Mr. Campbell got his baggage, and we regained the deck of the Susquehanna, which got up steam and started for New Orleans. We reached New Orleans December 20th, whence I reported fully everything to General Grant, and on the 21st received the following dispatch:

WASHINGTON, December 21,1866.
Lieutenant-General SHERMAN, New Orleans.

Your telegram of yesterday has been submitted to the President. You are authorized to proceed to St. Louis at your convenience. Your proceedings in the special and delicate duties assigned you are cordially approved by the President and Cabinet and this department. EDWIN M. STANTON.

And on the same day I received this dispatch

GALVESTON, December 21, 1866.
To General SHERMAN, or General SHERIDAN.

Will be in New Orleans to-morrow. Wish to see you both on arrival, on matters of importance. LEWIS D. CAMPBELL, Minister to Mexico.

Mr. Campbell arrived on the 22d, but had nothing to tell of the least importance, save that he was generally disgusted with the whole thing, and had not found Juarez at all. I am sure this whole movement was got up for the purpose of getting General Grant away from Washington, on the pretext of his known antagonism to the French occupation of Mexico, because he was looming up as a candidate for President, and nobody understood the animus and purpose better than did Mr. Stanton. He himself was not then on good terms with President Johnson, and with several of his associates in the Cabinet. By Christmas I was back in St. Louis.

By this time the conflict between President Johnson and Congress had become open and unconcealed. Congress passed the bill known as the "Tenure of Civil Office" on the 2d of March, 1867 (over the President's veto), the first clause of which, now section 1767 of the Revised Statutes, reads thus: "Every person who holds any civil office to which he has been or hereafter may be appointed, by and with the advice and consent of the Senate, and who shall have become duly qualified to act therein, shall be entitled to hold such office during the term for which he was appointed, unless sooner removed by and with the advice and consent of the Senate, or by the appointment with the like advice and consent of a successor in his place, except as herein otherwise provided."

General E. D. Townsend, in his "Anecdotes of the Civil War," states tersely and correctly the preliminary circumstances of which I must treat. He says: "On Monday morning, August 5, 1867, President Johnson invited Mr. Stanton to resign as Secretary of War. Under the tenure-of-civil-office law, Mr. Stanton declined. The President a week after suspended him, and appointed General Grant, General-in-Chief of the Army, to exercise the functions. This continued until January 13, 1868, when according to the law the Senate passed a resolution not sustaining the President's action. The next morning General Grant came to my office and handed me the key of the Secretary's room, saying: 'I am to be found over at my office at army headquarters. I was served with a copy of the Senate resolution last evening.' I then went up-stairs and delivered the key of his room to Mr. Stanton."

The mode and manner of Mr. Stanton's regaining his office, and of General Grant's surrendering it, were at the time subjects of bitter controversy. Unhappily I was involved, and must bear testimony. In all January, 1868, I was a member of a board ordered to compile a code of articles of war and army regulations, of which Major-General Sheridan and Brigadier-General C. C. Augur were associate members. Our place of meeting was in the room of the old War Department, second floor, next to the corner room occupied by the Secretary of War, with a door of communication. While we were at work it was common for General Grant and, afterward, for Mr. Stanton to drop in and chat with us on the social gossip of the time.

On Saturday, January 11th, General Grant said that he had more carefully read the law (tenure of civil office), and it was different from what he had supposed; that in case the Senate did not consent to the removal of Secretary of War Stanton, and he (Grant) should hold on, he should incur a liability of ten thousand dollars and five years' imprisonment. We all expected the resolution of Senator Howard, of Michigan, virtually restoring Mr. Stanton to his office, would pass the Senate, and knowing that the President expected General Grant to hold on, I inquired if he had given notice of his change of purpose; he answered that there was no hurry, because he supposed Mr. Stanton would pursue toward him (Grant) the same course which he (Stanton) had required of him the preceding August, viz., would address him a letter claiming the office, and allow him a couple of days for the change. Still, he said he would go to the White House the same day and notify the President of his intended action.

That afternoon I went over to the White House to present General Pope, who was on a visit to Washington, and we found the President and General Grant together. We made our visit and withdrew, leaving them still together, and I always supposed the subject of this conference was the expected decision of the Senate, which would in effect restore Mr. Stanton to his civil office of Secretary of War. That evening I dined with the Hon. Reverdy Johnson, Senator from Maryland, and suggested to him that the best way to escape a conflict was for the President to nominate some good man as Secretary of War whose confirmation by the Senate would fall within the provisions of the law, and named General J. D. Cox, then Governor of Ohio, whose term of office was drawing to a close, who would, I knew, be acceptable to General Grant and the army generally. Mr. Johnson was most favorably impressed with this suggestion, and promised to call on the President the next day (Sunday), which he did, but President Johnson had made up his mind to meet the conflict boldly. I saw General Grant that afternoon at his house on I Street, and told him what I had done, and so anxious was he about it that he came to our room at the War Department the next morning (Monday), the 13th, and asked me to go in person to the White House to urge the President to send in the name of General Cox. I did so, saw the President, and inquired if he had seen Mr. Reverdy Johnson the day before about General Cox. He answered that he had, and thought well of General Cox, but would say no further.

Tuesday, January 14, 1868, came, and with it Mr. Stanton. He resumed possession of his former office; came into that where General Sheridan, General Augur, and I were at work, and greeted us very cordially. He said he wanted to see me when at leisure, and at half-past 10 A.M. I went into his office and found him and

General Grant together. Supposing they had some special matters of business, I withdrew, with the remark that I was close at hand, and could come in at any moment. In the afternoon I went again into Mr. Stanton's office, and we had a long and most friendly conversation; but not one word was spoken about the "tenure-of-office" matter. I then crossed over Seventeenth Street to the headquarters of the army, where I found General Grant, who expressed himself as by no means pleased with the manner in which Mr. Stanton had regained his office, saying that he had sent a messenger for him that morning as of old, with word that "he wanted to see him." We then arranged to meet at his office the next morning at half-past nine, and go together to see the President.

That morning the National Intelligencer published an article accusing General Grant of acting in bad faith to the President, and of having prevaricated in making his personal explanation to the Cabinet, so that General Grant at first felt unwilling to go, but we went. The President received us promptly and kindly. Being seated, General Grant said, "Mr. President, whoever gave the facts for the article of the Intelligencer of this morning has made some serious mistakes." The President: "General Grant, let me interrupt you just there. I have not seen the Intelligencer of this morning, and have no knowledge of the contents of any article therein" General Grant then went on: "Well, the idea is given there that I have not kept faith with you. Now, Mr. President, I remember, when you spoke to me on this subject last summer, I did say that, like the case of the Baltimore police commissioners, I did suppose Mr. Stanton could not regain his office except by a process through the courts." To this the President assented, saying he "remembered the reference to the case of the Baltimore commissioners," when General Grant resumed: "I said if I changed my opinion I would give you notice, and put things as they were before my appointment as Secretary of War ad interim."

We then entered into a general friendly conversation, both parties professing to be satisfied, the President claiming that he had always been most friendly to General Grant, and the latter insisting that he had taken the office, not for honor or profit, but in the general interests of the army.

As we withdrew, at the very door, General Grant said, "Mr. President, you should make some order that we of the army are not bound to obey the orders of Mr. Stanton as Secretary of War," which the President intimated he would do.

No such "orders" were ever made; many conferences were held, and the following letters are selected out of a great mass to show the general feeling at the time:

1321 K STREET, WASHINGTON,
January 28,1868, Saturday.

To the President:

I neglected this morning to say that I had agreed to go down to Annapolis to spend Sunday with Admiral Porter. General Grant also has to leave for Richmond on Monday morning at 6 A.M.

At a conversation with the General after our interview, wherein I offered to go with him on Monday morning to Mr. Stanton, and to say that it was our joint opinion he should resign, it was found impossible by reason of his (General Grant) going to Richmond and my going to Annapolis. The General proposed this course: He will call on you to-morrow, and offer to go to Mr. Stanton to say, for the good of the Army and of the country, he ought to resign. This on Sunday. On Monday I will again call on you, and, if you think it necessary, I will do the same, viz., go to Mr. Stanton and tell him he should resign.

If he will not, then it will be time to contrive ulterior measures. In the mean time it so happens that no necessity exists for precipitating matters.

Yours truly,

W. T. SHERMAN, Lieutenant-General.

DEAR GENERAL: On the point of starting, I have written the above, and will send a fair copy of it to the President. Please retain this, that in case of necessity I may have a copy. The President clearly stated to me that he relied on us in this category.

Think of the propriety of your putting in writing what you have to say tomorrow, even if you have to put it in the form of a letter to hand him in person, retaining a copy. I'm afraid that acting as a go-between for three persons, I may share the usual fate of meddlers, at last get kinks from all. We ought not to be involved in politics, but for the sake of the Army we are justified in trying at least to cut this Gordian knot, which they do not appear to have any practicable plan to do. In haste as usual,

W. T. SHERMAN.

HEADQUARTERS ARMIES OF THE UNITED STATES,
January 29, 1888.

DEAR SHERMAN: I called on the President and Mr. Stanton to-day, but without any effect.

I soon found that to recommend resignation to Mr. Stanton would have no effect, unless it was to incur further his displeasure; and, therefore, did not directly suggest it to him. I explained to him, however, the course I supposed he would pursue, and what I expected to do in that case, namely, to notify the President of his intentions, and thus leave him to violate the "Tenure-of-Office Bill" if he chose, instead of having me do it.

I would advise that you say nothing to Mr. Stanton on the subject unless he asks your advice. It will do no good, and may embarrass you. I did not mention your name to him, at least not in connection with his position, or what you thought upon it.

All that Mr. Johnson said was pacific and compromising. While I think he wanted the constitutionality of the "Tenure Bill" tested, I think now he would be glad either to get the vacancy of Secretary of War, or have the office just where it was during suspension. Yours truly,

U. S. GRANT.

WASHINGTON D. C., January 27, 1868.

To the President.

DEAR SIR: As I promised, I saw Mr. Ewing yesterday, and after a long conversation asked him to put down his opinion in writing, which he has done and which I now inclose.

I am now at work on these Army Regulations, and in the course of preparation have laid down the Constitution and laws now in force, clearer than I find them elsewhere; and beg leave herewith to inclose you three pages of printed matter for your perusal. My opinion is, if you will adopt these rules and make them an executive order to General Grant, they will so clearly define the duties of all concerned that no conflict can arise. I hope to get through this task in the course of this week, and want very much to go to St. Louis. For eleven years I have been tossed about so much that I really do want to rest, study, and make the acquaintance of my family. I do not think, since 1857, I have averaged thirty days out of three hundred and sixty-five at home.

Next summer also, in fulfillment of our promise to the Sioux, I must go to Fort Phil Kearney early in the spring, so that, unless I can spend the next two months at home, I might as well break up my house at St. Louis, and give up all prospect of taking care of my family.

For these reasons especially I shall soon ask leave to go to St. Louis, to resume my proper and legitimate command. With great respect,

W. T. SHERMAN, Lieutenant-General.

[Inclosure]

WASHINGTON, D. C., January 25, 1868.

MY DEAR GENERAL: I am quite clear in the opinion that it is not expedient for the President to take any action now in the case of Stanton. So far as he and his interests are concerned, things are in the best possible condition. Stanton is in the Department, got his secretary, but the secretary of the Senate, who have taken upon themselves his sins, and who place him there under a large salary to annoy and obstruct the operations of the Executive. This the people well enough understand, and he is a stench in the nostrils of their own party.

I thought the nomination of Cox at the proper juncture would have been wise as a peace-offering, but perhaps it would have let off the Senate too easily from the effect of their arbitrary act. Now the dislodging of Stanton and filling the office even temporarily without the consent of the Senate would raise a question as to the legality of the President's acts, and he would belong to the attacked instead of the attacking party. If the war between Congress and the President is to go on, as I suppose it is, Stanton should be ignored by the

President, left to perform his clerical duties which the law requires him to perform, and let the party bear the odium which is already upon them for placing him where he is. So much for the President.

As to yourself, I wish you as far as possible to keep clear of political complications. I do not think the President will require you to do an act of doubtful legality. Certainly he will not without sanction of the opinion of his Attorney-General; and you should have time, in a questionable case, to consult with me before called upon to act. The office of Secretary of War is a civil office, as completely so as that of Secretary of State; and you as a military officer cannot, I think, be required to assume or exercise it. This may, if necessary, be a subject for further consideration. Such, however, will not, I think, be the case. The appeal is to the people, and it is better for the President to persist in the course he has for some time pursued--let the aggressions all come from the other side; and I think there is no doubt he will do so. Affectionately, T. EWING.

To--Lieutenant-General SHERMAN.

LIBRARY ROOM, WAR DEPARTMENT,
WASHINGTON, D. C., January 31, 1868.

To the President:

Since our interview of yesterday I have given the subject of our conversation all my thoughts, and I beg you will pardon my reducing the same to writing.

My personal preferences, as expressed, were to be allowed to return to St. Louis to resume my present command, because my command was important, large, suited to my rank and inclination, and because my family was well provided for there in house, facilities, schools, living, and agreeable society; while, on the other hand, Washington was for many (to me) good reasons highly objectionable, especially because it is the political capital of the country; and focus of intrigue, gossip, and slander. Your personal preferences were, as expressed, to make a new department East, adequate to my rank, with headquarters at Washington, and assign me to its command, to remove my family here, and to avail myself of its schools, etc.; to remove Mr. Stanton from his office as Secretary of War, and have me to discharge the duties.

To effect this removal two modes were indicated: to simply cause him to quit the War-Office Building, and notify the Treasury Department and the Army Staff Departments no longer to respect him as Secretary of War; or to remove him and submit my name to the Senate for confirmation.

Permit me to discuss these points a little, and I will premise by saying that I have spoken to no one on the subject, and have not even seen Mr. Ewing, Mr. Stanbery, or General Grant, since I was with you.

It has been the rule and custom of our army, since the organization of the government, that the second officer of the army should be at the second (in importance) command, and remote from general headquarters. To bring me to Washington would put three heads to an army, yourself, General Grant, and myself, and we would be more than human if we were not to differ. In my judgment it would ruin the army, and would be fatal to one or two of us.

Generals Scott and Taylor proved themselves soldiers and patriots in the field, but Washington was fatal to both. This city, and the influences that centre here, defeated every army that had its headquarters here from 1861 to 1864, and would have overwhelmed General Grant at Spottsylvania and Petersburg, had he not been fortified by a strong reputation, already hard-earned, and because no one then living coveted the place; whereas, in the West, we made progress from the start, because there was no political capital near enough to poison our minds, and kindle into life that craving, itching for fame which has killed more good men than bullets. I have been with General Grant in the midst of death and slaughter when the howls of people reached him after Shiloh; when messengers were speeding to and from his army to Washington, bearing slanders, to induce his removal before he took Vicksburg; in Chattanooga, when the soldiers were stealing the corn of the starving mules to satisfy their own hunger; at Nashville, when he was ordered to the "forlorn hope" to command the Army of the Potomac, so often defeated--and yet I never saw him more troubled than since he has been in Washington, and been compelled to read himself a "sneak and deceiver," based on reports of four of the Cabinet, and apparently with your knowledge. If this political atmosphere can disturb the equanimity of one so guarded and so prudent as he is, what will be the result with me, so careless, so outspoken as I am? Therefore, with my consent, Washington never.

As to the Secretary of War, his office is twofold. As a Cabinet officer he should not be there without your hearty, cheerful assent, and I believe that is the judgment and opinion of every fair-minded man. As the holder of a civil office, having the supervision of moneys appropriated by Congress and of contracts for army supplies, I do think Congress, or the Senate by delegation from Congress, has a lawful right to be consulted. At all events, I would not risk a suit or contest on that phase of the question. The law of Congress, of March 2, 1867, prescribing the manner in which orders and instructions relating to "military movements" shall reach the army, gives you as constitutional Commander-in-Chief the very power you want to exercise, and enables you to prevent the Secretary from making any such orders and instructions; and consequently he cannot control the army, but is limited and restricted to a duty that an Auditor of the Treasury could perform. You certainly can afford to await the result. The Executive power is not weakened, but rather strengthened. Surely he is not such an obstruction as would warrant violence, or even s show of force, which would produce the very reaction and clamor that he hopes for to save him from the absurdity of holding an empty office "for the safety of the country."

This is so much as I ought to say, and more too, but if it produces the result I will be more than satisfied, viz., that I be simply allowed to resume my proper post and duties in St. Louis. With great respect, yours truly,

W. T. SHERMAN, Lieutenant-General.

On the 1st of February, the board of which I was the president submitted to the adjutant-general our draft of the "Articles of War and Army Regulations," condensed to a small compass, the result of our war experience. But they did not suit the powers that were, and have ever since slept the sleep that knows no waking, to make room for the ponderous document now in vogue, which will not stand the strain of a week's campaign in real war.

I hurried back to St. Louis to escape the political storm I saw brewing. The President repeatedly said to me that he wanted me in Washington, and I as often answered that nothing could tempt me to live in that center of intrigue and excitement; but soon came the following:

HEADQUARTERS ARMY OF THE UNITED STATES,
WASHINGTON, February 10, 1868.

DEAR GENERAL: I have received at last the President's reply to my last, letter. He attempts to substantiate his statements by his Cabinet. In this view it is important that I should have a letter from you, if you are willing to give it, of what I said to you about the effect of the "Tenure-of-Office Bill," and my object in going to see the President on Saturday before the installment of Mr. Stanton. What occurred after the meeting of the Cabinet on the Tuesday following is not a subject under controversy now; therefore, if you choose to write down your recollection (and I would like to have it) on Wednesday, when you and I called on the President, and your conversation with him the last time you saw him, make that a separate communication.

Your order to come East was received several days ago, but the President withdrew it, I supposed to make some alteration, but it has not been returned. Yours truly,

U. S. GRANT.

[TELEGRAM.]

WASHINGTON, D. C., February 18, 1868.

Lieutenant-General W. T. SHERMAN, St. Louis.

The order is issued ordering you to Atlantic Division.

U. S. GRANT, General.

[TELEGRAM]

HEADQUARTERS MILITARY DIVISION OF THE MISSOURI, St. Louis, February 14, 1868.

General U. S. GRANT, Washington, D. C.

Your dispatch is received informing me that the order for the Atlantic Division has been issued, and that I am assigned to its command. I was in hopes I had escaped the danger, and now were I prepared I should resign on the spot, as it requires no foresight to predict such must be the inevitable result in the end. I will make one more desperate effort by mail, which please await.

W. T. SHERMAN, *Lieutenant-General.*

[TELEGRAM.]

WASHINGTON, February 14, 1868.
Lieutenant-General W. T. SHERMAN, St. Louis.

I think it due to you that your letter of January 31st to the President of the United States should be published, to correct misapprehension in the public mind about your willingness to come to Washington. It will not be published against your will.

(Sent in cipher.)

[TELEGRAM.]

HEADQUARTERS MILITARY DIVISION OF THE MISSOURI,
St. Louis, MISSOURI, February 14, 1868.

General U. S. GRANT, Washington, D. C.

Dispatch of to-day received. Please await a letter I address this day through you to the President, which will in due time reach the public, covering the very point you make.

I don't want to come to Washington at all.

W. T. SHERMAN, *Lieutenant-General.*

[TELEGRAM.]

HEADQUARTERS MILITARY DIVISION OF THE MISSOURI,
St. Louis, MISSOURI, February 14, 1868.

Hon. John SHERMAN, United States Senate, Washington, D. C.

Oppose confirmation of myself as brevet general, on ground that it is unprecedented, and that it is better not to extend the system of brevets above major-general. If I can't avoid coming to Washington, I may have to resign.

W. T. SHERMAN, *Lieutenant-General.*

HEADQUARTERS OF THE ARMY,
WASHINGTON, D. C., February 12, 1868.

The following orders are published for the information and guidance of all concerned:

U. S. GRANT, General.

EXECUTIVE MANSION,
WASHINGTON, D. C., February 12, 1868.

GENERAL: You will please issue an order creating a military division to be styled the Military Division of the Atlantic, to be composed of the Department of the Lakes, the Department of the East, and the Department of Washington, to be commanded by Lieutenant-General W. T. Sherman, with his headquarters at Washington. Until further orders from the President, you will assign no officer to the permanent command of the Military Division of the Missouri.

180

Respectfully yours,

ANDREW JOHNSON.

GENERAL U. S. GRANT,
Commanding Armies of The United States, Washington, D. C.

Major-General P. H. Sheridan, the senior officer in the Military Division of the Missouri, will temporarily perform the duties of commander of the Military Division of the Missouri in addition to his duties of department commander. By command of General Grant:

E. D. TOWNSEND, Assistant Adjutant-General.

This order, if carried into effect, would have grouped in Washington:
1. The President, constitutional Commander-in-Chief.
2. The Secretary of War, congressional Commander-in-Chief.
3. The General of the Armies of the United States.
4. The Lieutenant-General of the Army.
5. The Commanding General of the Department of Washington.
6. The commander of the post-of Washington.

At that date the garrison of Washington was a brigade of infantry and a battery of artillery. I never doubted Mr. Johnson's sincerity in wishing to befriend me, but this was the broadest kind of a farce, or meant mischief. I therefore appealed to him by letter to allow me to remain where I was, and where I could do service, real service, and received his most satisfactory answer.

HEADQUARTERS MILITARY DIVISION OF THE MISSOURI,
St. Louis, MISSOURI, February 14, 1868.

General U. S. GRANT, Washington, D. C.

DEAR GENERAL: Last evening, just before leaving my office, I received your note of the 10th, and had intended answering it according to your request; but, after I got home, I got your dispatch of yesterday, announcing that the order I dreaded so much was issued. I never felt so troubled in my life. Were it an order to go to Sitka, to the devil, to battle with rebels or Indians, I think you would not hear a whimper from me, but it comes in such a questionable form that, like Hamlet's ghost, it curdles my blood and mars my judgment. My first thoughts were of resignation, and I had almost made up my mind to ask Dodge for some place on the Pacific road, or on one of the Iowa roads, and then again various colleges ran through my memory, but hard times and an expensive family have brought me back to staring the proposition square in the face, and I have just written a letter to the President, which I herewith transmit through you, on which I will hang a hope of respite till you telegraph me its effect. The uncertainties ahead are too great to warrant my incurring the expense of breaking up my house and family here, and therefore in no event will I do this till I can be assured of some permanence elsewhere. If it were at all certain that you would accept the nomination of President in May, I would try and kill the intervening time, and then judge of the chances, but I do not want you to reveal your plans to me till you choose to do so.

I have telegraphed to John Sherman to oppose the nomination which the papers announce has been made of me for brevet general.

I have this minute received your cipher dispatch of to-day, which I have just answered and sent down to the telegraph-office, and the clerk is just engaged in copying my letter to the President to go with this. If the President or his friends pretend that I seek to go to Washington, it will be fully rebutted by letters I have written to the President, to you, to John Sherman, to Mr. Ewing, and to Mr. Stanbery. You remember that in our last talk you suggested I should write again to the President. I thought of it, and concluded my letter of January 31st, already delivered, was full and emphatic. Still, I did write again to Mr. Stanbery, asking him as a friend to interpose in my behalf. There are plenty of people who know my wishes, and I would avoid, if possible, the publication of a letter so confidential as that of January 31st, in which I notice I allude to the President's purpose of removing Mr. Stanton by force, a fact that ought not to be drawn out through me if it be possible to avoid it. In the letter herewith I confine myself to purely private matters, and will not object if it reaches the public in any proper way. My opinion is, the President thinks Mrs. Sherman would like to come to Washington by reason of her father and brothers being there. This is true, for Mrs. Sherman has an idea that St. Louis is unhealthy for our children, and because most of the Catholics here are tainted with the old secesh feeling. But I know better what is to our common interest, and prefer to judge of the proprieties myself. What I do object to is the false position I would occupy as between you and the President. Were there an actual army at or near Washington, I could be withdrawn from the most unpleasant attitude of a "go-between," but there is no army there, nor any military duties which you with a host of subordinates can not perform. Therefore I would be there with naked, informal, and sinecure duties, and utterly out of place. This you understand well enough, and the army too, but the President and the politicians, who flatter themselves they are saving the country, cannot and will not understand. My opinion is, the country is doctored to death, and if President and Congress would go to sleep like Rip Van Winkle, the country would go on under natural influences, and recover far faster than under their joint and several treatment. This doctrine would be accounted by Congress, and by the President too, as high treason, and therefore I don't care about saying so to either of them, but I know you can hear anything, and give it just what thought or action it merits.

Excuse this long letter, and telegraph me the result of my letter to the President as early as you can. If he holds my letter so long as to make it improper for me to await his answer, also telegraph me.

The order, when received, will, I suppose, direct me as to whom and how I am to turn over this command, which should, in my judgment, not be broken up, as the three departments composing the division should be under one head.

I expect my staff-officers to be making for me within the hour to learn their fate, so advise me all you can as quick as possible.

With great respect, yours truly,

W. T. SHERMAN, Lieutenant-General.

To the President.

DEAR SIR: It is hard for me to conceive you would purposely do me an unkindness unless under the pressure of a sense of public duty, or because you do not believe me sincere. I was in hopes, since my letter to you of the 31st of January, that you had concluded to pass over that purpose of yours expressed more than once in conversation--to organize a new command for me in the East, with headquarters in Washington; but a telegram from General Grant of yesterday says that "the order was issued ordering you" (me) "to Atlantic Division"; and the newspapers of this morning contain the same information, with the addition that I have been nominated as brevet general. I have telegraphed my own brother in the Senate to oppose my confirmation, on the ground that the two higher grades in the army ought not to be complicated with brevets, and I trust you will conceive my motives aright. If I could see my way clear to maintain my family, I should not hesitate a moment to resign my present commission, and seek some business wherein I would be free from these unhappy complications that seem to be closing about me, spite of my earnest efforts to avoid them; but necessity ties my hands, and I must submit with the best grace I can till I make other arrangements.

In Washington are already the headquarters of a department, and of the army itself, and it is hard for me to see wherein I can render military service there. Any staff-officer with the rank of major could surely fill any gap left between these two military officers; and, by being placed in Washington, I will be universally construed as a rival to the General-in-Chief, a position damaging to me in the highest degree. Our relations have always been most confidential and friendly, and if, unhappily, any cloud of differences should arise between us, my sense of personal dignity and duty would leave me no alternative but resignation. For this I am not yet prepared, but I shall proceed to arrange for it as rapidly as possible, so that when the time does come (as it surely will if this plan is carried into effect) I may act promptly.

Inasmuch as the order is now issued, I cannot expect a full revocation of it, but I beg the privilege of taking post at New York, or any point you may name within the new military division other than Washington. This privilege is generally granted to all military commanders, and I see no good reason why I too may not ask for it, and this simple concession, involving no public interest, will much soften the blow, which, right or wrong, I construe as one of the hardest I have sustained in a life somewhat checkered with adversity. With great respects yours truly,

W. T. SHERMAN, Lieutenant-General.

WASHINGTON, D. C., 2 p.m., February 19, 1888.
Lieutenant-General W. T. SHERMAN, St. Louis, Missouri:

I have just received, with General Grant's indorsement of reference, your letter to me of the fourteenth (14th) inst.

The order to which you refer was made in good faith, and with a view to the best interests of the country and the service; as, however, your assignment to a new military division seems so objectionable, you will retain your present command.

On that same 19th of February he appointed Adjutant, General Lorenzo Thomas to be Secretary of War ad interim, which finally resulted in the articles of impeachment and trial of President Johnson before the Senate. I was a witness on that trial, but of course the lawyers would not allow me to express any opinion of the President's motives or intentions, and restricted me to the facts set forth in the articles of impeachment, of which I was glad to know nothing. The final test vote revealed less than two thirds, and the President was consequently acquitted. Mr. Stanton resigned. General Schofield, previously nominated, was confirmed as Secretary of War, thus putting an end to what ought never to have happened at all.

INDIAN PEACE COMMISSION.

On the 20th of July, 1867, President Johnson approved an act to establish peace with certain hostile Indian tribes, the first section of which reads as follows: "Be it enacted, etc., that the President of the United States be and is hereby authorized to appoint a commission to consist of three (3) officers of the army not below the rank of brigadier-general, who, together with N. G. Taylor, Commissioner of Indian Affairs, John B. Henderson, chairman of the Committee of Indian Affairs of the Senate, S. F. Tappan, and John B. Sanborn, shall have power and authority to call together the chiefs and head men of such bands or tribes of Indians as are now waging war against the United States, or committing depredations on the people thereof, to ascertain the alleged reasons for their acts of hostility, and in their discretion, under the direction of the President, to make and conclude with said bands or tribes such treaty stipulations, subject to the action of the Senate, as may remove all just causes of complaint on their part, and at the same time establish security for person and property along the lines of railroad now being constructed to the Pacific and other thoroughfares of travel to the Western Territories, and such as will most likely insure civilization for the Indians, and peace and safety for the whites."

The President named as the military members Lieutenant-General Sherman, Brigadier-Generals A. H. Terry and W. S. Harney. Subsequently, to insure a full attendance, Brigadier-General C. C. Augur was added to the commission, and his name will be found on most of the treaties. The commissioners met at St. Louis and elected N. G. Taylor, the Commissioner of Indian Affairs, president; J. B. Sanborn, treasurer; and A. S. H. White, Esq., of Washington, D. C., secretary. The year 1867 was too far advanced to complete the task assigned during that season, and it was agreed that a steamboat (St. John's) should be chartered to convey the commission up the Missouri River, and we adjourned to meet at Omaha. In the St. John's the commission proceeded up the Missouri River, holding informal "talks" with the Santees at their agency near the Niobrara, the Yanktonnais at Fort Thompson, and the Ogallallas, Minneconjous, Sans Arcs, etc., at Fort Sully. From this point runners were sent out to the Sioux occupying the country west of the Missouri River, to meet us in council at the Forks of the Platte that fall, and to Sitting Bull's band of outlaw Sioux, and the Crows on the upper Yellowstone, to meet us in May, 1868, at Fort Laramie. We proceeded up the river to the mouth of the Cheyenne and turned back to Omaha, having ample time on this steamboat to discuss and deliberate on the problems submitted to our charge.

We all agreed that the nomad Indians should be removed from the vicinity of the two great railroads then in rapid construction, and be localized on one or other of the two great reservations south of Kansas and north of Nebraska; that agreements not treaties, should be made for their liberal maintenance as to food, clothing, schools, and farming implements for ten years, during which time we believed that these Indians should become self-supporting. To the north we proposed to remove the various bands of Sioux, with such others as could be induced to locate near them; and to the south, on the Indian Territory already established, we proposed to remove the Cheyennes, Arapahoes, Kiowas, Comanches, and such others as we could prevail on to move thither.

At that date the Union Pacific construction had reached the Rocky Mountains at Cheyenne, and the Kansas Pacific to about Fort Wallace. We held council with the Ogallallas at the Forks of the Platte, and arranged to meet them all the next spring, 1868. In the spring of 1868 we met the Crows in council at Fort Laramie, the Sioux at the North Platte, the Shoshones or Snakes at Fort Hall, the Navajos at Fort Sumner, on the Pecos, and the Cheyennes and Arapahoes at Medicine Lodge. To accomplish these results the commission divided up into committees, General Augur going to the Shoshones, Mr. Tappan and I to the Navajos, and the remainder to Medicine Lodge. In that year we made treaties or arrangements with all the tribes which before had followed the buffalo in their annual migrations, and which brought them into constant conflict with the whites.

Mr. Tappan and I found it impossible to prevail on the Navajos to remove to the Indian Territory, and had to consent to their return to their former home, restricted to a limited reservation west of Santa Fe, about old Fort Defiance, and there they continue unto this day, rich in the possession of herds of sheep and goats, with some cattle and horses; and they have remained at peace ever since.

A part of our general plan was to organize the two great reservations into regular Territorial governments, with Governor, Council, courts, and civil officers. General Harney was temporarily assigned to that of the Sioux at the north, and General Hazen to that of the Kiowas, Comanches, Cheyennes, Arapahoes, etc., etc., at the south, but the patronage of the Indian Bureau was too strong for us, and that part of our labor failed. Still, the Indian Peace Commission of 1867-'68 did prepare the way for the great Pacific Railroads, which, for better or worse, have settled the fate of the buffalo and Indian forever. There have been wars and conflicts since with these Indians up to a recent period too numerous and complicated in their detail for me to unravel and record, but they have been the dying struggles of a singular race of brave men fighting against destiny, each less and less violent, till now the wild game is gone, the whites too numerous and powerful; so that the Indian question has become one of sentiment and charity, but not of war.

The peace, or "Quaker" policy, of which so much has been said, originated about thus: By the act of Congress, approved March 3,1869, the forty-five regiments of infantry were reduced to twenty-five, and provision was made for the "muster out" of many of the surplus officers, and for retaining others to be absorbed by the usual promotions and casualties. On the 7th of May of that year, by authority of an act of Congress approved June 30, 1834, nine field-officers and fifty-nine captains and subalterns were detached and ordered to report to the Commissioner of Indian Affairs, to serve as Indian superintendents and agents. Thus by an old law surplus army officers were made to displace the usual civil appointees, undoubtedly a change for the better, but most distasteful to members of Congress, who looked to these appointments as part of their proper patronage. The consequence was the law of July 15, 1870, which vacated the military commission of any officer who accepted or exercised the functions of a civil officer. I was then told that certain politicians called on President Grant, informing him that this law was chiefly designed to prevent his using army officers for Indian agents, "civil offices," which he believed to be both judicious and wise; army officers, as a rule, being better qualified to deal with Indians than the average political appointees. The President then quietly replied: "Gentlemen, you have defeated my plan of Indian management; but you shall not succeed in your purpose, for I will divide these appointments up among the religious churches, with which you dare not contend." The army officers were consequently relieved of their "civil offices," and the Indian agencies were apportioned to the several religious churches in about the proportion of their--supposed strength--some to the Quakers, some to the Methodists, to the Catholics, Episcopalians, Presbyterians, etc., etc.--and thus it remains to the present time, these religious communities selecting the agents to be appointed by the Secretary of the Interior. The Quakers, being first named, gave name to the policy, and it is called the "Quaker" policy to-day. Meantime railroads and settlements by hardy, bold pioneers have made the character of Indian agents of small concern, and it matters little who are the beneficiaries.

As was clearly foreseen, General U. S. Grant was duly nominated, and on the 7th of November, 1868, was elected President of the United States for the four years beginning with March 4, 1869.

On the 15th and 16th of December, 1868, the four societies of the Armies of the Cumberland, Tennessee, Ohio, and Georgia, held a joint reunion at Chicago, at which were present over two thousand of the surviving officers and soldiers of the war. The ceremonies consisted of the joint meeting in Crosby's magnificent opera-house, at which General George H. Thomas presided. General W. W. Belknap was the orator for the Army of the Tennessee, General Charles Cruft for the Army of the Cumberland, General J. D. Cox for the Army of the Ohio, and General William Cogswell for the Army of Georgia. The banquet was held in the vast Chamber of Commerce, at which I presided. General Grant, President-elect, General J. M. Schofield, Secretary of War, General H. W. Slocum, and nearly every general officer of note was present except General Sheridan, who at the moment was fighting the Cheyennes in Southern Kansas and the Indian country.

At that time we discussed the army changes which would necessarily occur in the following March, and it was generally understood that I was to succeed General Grant as general-in-chief, but as to my successor, Meade, Thomas, and Sheridan were candidates. And here I will remark that General Grant, afterward famous as the "silent man," used to be very gossipy, and no one was ever more fond than he of telling anecdotes of our West Point and early army life. At the Chicago reunion he told me that I would have to come to Washington, that he wanted me to effect a change as to the general staff, which he had long contemplated, and which was outlined in his letter to Mr. Stanton of January 29,1866, given hereafter, which had been repeatedly published, and was well known to the military world; that on being inaugurated President on the 4th of March he would retain General Schofield as his Secretary of War until the change had become habitual; that the modern custom of the Secretary of War giving military orders to the adjutant-general and other staff officers was positively wrong and should be stopped. Speaking of General Grant's personal characteristics at that period of his life, I recall a conversation in his carriage, when, riding down Pennsylvania Avenue, he, inquired of me in a humorous way, "Sherman, what special hobby do you intend to adopt?" I inquired what he meant, and he explained that all men had their special weakness or vanity, and that it was wiser to choose one's own than to leave the newspapers to affix one less acceptable, and that for his part he had chosen the "horse," so that when anyone tried to pump him he would turn the conversation to his "horse." I answered that I would stick to the "theatre

184

and balls," for I was always fond of seeing young people happy, and did actually acquire a reputation for "dancing," though I had not attempted the waltz, or anything more than the ordinary cotillon, since the war.

On the 24th of February, 1869, I was summoned to Washington, arriving on the 26th, taking along my aides, Lieutenant-Colonels Dayton and Audenried.

On the 4th of March General Grant was duly inaugurated President of the United States, and I was nominated and confirmed as General of the Army.

Major-General P. H. Sheridan was at the same time nominated and confirmed as lieutenant-general, with orders to command the Military Division of the Missouri, which he did, moving the headquarters from St. Louis to Chicago; and General Meade was assigned to command the Military Division of the Atlantic, with headquarters at Philadelphia.

At that moment General Meade was in Atlanta, Georgia, commanding the Third Military District under the "Reconstruction Act;" and General Thomas, whose post was in Nashville, was in Washington on a court of inquiry investigating certain allegations against General A. B. Dyer, Chief of Ordnance. He occupied the room of the second floor in the building on the corner of H and Fifteenth Streets, since become Wormley's Hotel. I at the time was staying with my brother, Senator Sherman, at his residence, 1321 K Street, and it was my habit each morning to stop at Thomas's room on my way to the office in the War Department to tell him the military news, and to talk over matters of common interest. We had been intimately associated as "man and boy" for thirty-odd years, and I profess to have had better opportunities to know him than any man then living. His fame as the "Rock of Chickamauga" was perfect, and by the world at large he was considered as the embodiment of strength, calmness, and imperturbability. Yet of all my acquaintances Thomas worried and fretted over what he construed neglects or acts of favoritism more than any other.

At that time he was much worried by what he supposed was injustice in the promotion of General Sheridan, and still more that General Meade should have an Eastern station, which compelled him to remain at Nashville or go to the Pacific. General Thomas claimed that all his life he had been stationed in the South or remote West, and had not had a fair share of Eastern posts, whereas that General Meade had always been there. I tried to get him to go with me to see President Grant and talk the matter over frankly, but he would not, and I had to act as a friendly mediator. General Grant assured me at the time that he not only admired and respected General Thomas, but actually loved him as a man, and he authorized me in making up commands for the general officers to do anything and everything to favor him, only he could not recede from his former action in respect to Generals Sheridan and Meade.

Prior to General Grant's inauguration the army register showed as major-generals Halleck, Meade, Sheridan, Thomas, and Hancock. Therefore, the promotion of General Sheridan to be lieutenant-general did not "overslaugh" Thomas, but it did Meade and Halleck. The latter did not expect promotion; General Meade did, but was partially, not wholly, reconciled by being stationed at Philadelphia, the home of his family; and President Grant assured me that he knew of his own knowledge that General Sheridan had been nominated major-general before General Meade, but had waived dates out of respect for his age and longer service, and that he had nominated him as lieutenant-general by reason of his special fitness to command the Military Division of the Missouri, embracing all the wild Indians, at that very moment in a state of hostility. I gave General Thomas the choice of every other command in the army, and of his own choice he went to San Francisco, California, where he died, March 28, 1870. The truth is, Congress should have provided by law for three lieutenant-generals for these three pre-eminent soldiers, and should have dated their commissions with "Gettysburg," "Winchester," and "Nashville." It would have been a graceful act, and might have prolonged the lives of two most popular officers, who died soon after, feeling that they had experienced ingratitude and neglect.

Soon after General Grant's inauguration as President, and, as I supposed, in fulfilment of his plan divulged in Chicago the previous December, were made the following:

HEADQUARTERS OF THE ARMY,
WASHINGTON, March 8, 1869.

General Orders No. 11:

The following orders of the President of the United States are published for the information and government of all concerned:

WAR DEPARTMENT,
WASHINGTON CITY, March 5, 1869.

By direction of the President, General William T. Sherman will assume command of the Army of the United States.

The chiefs of staff corps, departments, and bureaus will report to and act under the immediate orders of the general commanding the army.

Any official business which by law or regulation requires the action of the President or Secretary of War will be submitted by the General of the Army to the Secretary of War, and in general all orders from the President or Secretary of War to any portion of the army, line or staff, will be transmitted through the General of the Army.

J. M. SCHOFIELD, Secretary of War.

By command of the General of the Army.

E. D. TOWNSEND, Assistant Adjutant-General.

On the same day I issued my General Orders No. 12, assuming command and naming all the heads of staff departments and bureaus as members of my staff, adding to my then three aides, Colonels McCoy, Dayton, and Audenried, the names of Colonels Comstock, Horace Porter, and Dent, agreeing with President Grant that the two latter could remain with him till I should need their personal services or ask their resignations.

I was soon made aware that the heads of several of the staff corps were restive under this new order of things, for by long usage they had grown to believe themselves not officers of the army in a technical sense, but a part of the War Department, the civil branch of the Government which connects the army with the President and Congress.

In a short time General John A. Rawlins, General Grant's former chief of staff, was nominated and confirmed as Secretary of War; and soon appeared this order:

HEADQUARTERS OF THE ARMY,

ADJUTANT-GENERAL'S OFFICE, WASHINGTON, March 27, 1869.

General Orders No. 28:

The following orders received for the War Department are published for the government of all concerned:

WAR DEPARTMENT,

WASHINGTON CITY, March 26, 1869.

By direction of the President, the order of the Secretary of War, dated War Department, March 5, 1869, and published in General Orders No. 11, headquarters of the army, Adjutant-General's Office, dated March 8, 1869, except so much as directs General W. T. Sherman to assume command of the Army of the United States, is hereby rescinded.

All official business which by law or regulations requires the action of the President or Secretary of War will be submitted by the chiefs of staff corps, departments, and bureaus to the Secretary of War.

All orders and instructions relating to military operations issued by the President or Secretary of War will be issued through the General of the Army.

JOHN A. RAWLINS, Secretary of War.

By command of General SHERMAN:

E. D. TOWNSEND, Assistant Adjutant-General.

Thus we were thrown back on the old method in having a double--if not a treble-headed machine. Each head of a bureau in daily consultation with the Secretary of War, and the general to command without an adjutant, quartermaster, commissary, or any staff except his own aides, often reading in the newspapers of military events and orders before he could be consulted or informed. This was the very reverse of what General Grant, after four years' experience in Washington as general-in-chief, seemed to want, different from what he had explained to me in Chicago, and totally different from the demand he had made on Secretary of War

Stanton in his complete letter of January 29, 1866. I went to him to know the cause: He said he had been informed by members of Congress that his action, as defined by his order of March 5th, was regarded as a violation of laws making provision for the bureaus of the War Department; that he had repealed his own orders, but not mine, and that he had no doubt that General Rawlins and I could draw the line of separation satisfactorily to us both. General Rawlins was very conscientious, but a very sick man when appointed Secretary of War. Several times he made orders through the adjutant-general to individuals of the army without notifying me, but always when his attention was called to it he apologized, and repeatedly said to me that he understood from his experience on General Grant's staff how almost insulting it was for orders to go to individuals of a regiment, brigade, division, or an army of any kind without the commanding officer being consulted or even advised. This habit is more common at Washington than any place on earth, unless it be in London, where nearly the same condition of facts exists. Members of Congress daily appeal to the Secretary of War for the discharge of some soldier on the application of a mother, or some young officer has to be dry-nursed, withdrawn from his company on the plains to be stationed near home. The Secretary of War, sometimes moved by private reasons, or more likely to oblige the member of Congress, grants the order, of which the commanding general knows nothing till he reads it in the newspapers. Also, an Indian tribe, goaded by the pressure of white neighbors, breaks out in revolt. The general-in-chief must reenforce the local garrisons not only with men, but horses, wagons, ammunition, and food. All the necessary information is in the staff bureaus in Washington, but the general has no right to call for it, and generally finds it more practicable to ask by telegraph of the distant division or department commanders for the information before making the formal orders. The general in actual command of the army should have a full staff, subject to his own command. If not, he cannot be held responsible for results.

General Rawlins sank away visibly, rapidly, and died in Washington, September 6,1869, and I was appointed to perform the duties of his office till a successor could be selected. I realized how much easier and better it was to have both offices conjoined.

The army then had one constitutional commander-in-chief of both army and navy, and one actual commanding general, bringing all parts into real harmony. An army to be useful must be a unit, and out of this has grown the saying, attributed to Napoleon, but doubtless spoken before the days of Alexander, that an army with an inefficient commander was better than one with two able heads. Our political system and methods, however, demanded a separate Secretary of War, and in October President Grant asked me to scan the list of the volunteer generals of good record who had served in the civil war, preferably from the "West." I did so, and submitted to him in writing the names of W. W. Belknap, of Iowa; G. M. Dodge, the Chief Engineer of the Union Pacific Railroad; and Lucius Fairchild, of Madison, Wisconsin. I also named General John W. Sprague, then employed by the Northern Pacific Railroad in Washington Territory. General Grant knew them all personally, and said if General Dodge were not connected with the Union Pacific Railroad, with which the Secretary of War must necessarily have large transactions, he would choose him, but as the case stood, and remembering the very excellent speech made by General Belknap at the Chicago reunion of December, 1868, he authorized me to communicate with him to ascertain if he were willing to come to Washington as Secretary of War. General Belknap was then the collector of internal revenue at Keokuk, Iowa. I telegraphed him and received a prompt and favorable answer. His name was sent to the Senate, promptly confirmed, and he entered on his duties October 25,1869. General Belknap surely had at that date as fair a fame as any officer of volunteers of my personal acquaintance. He took up the business where it was left off, and gradually fell into the current which led to the command of the army itself as of the legal and financial matters which properly pertain to the War Department. Orders granting leaves of absence to officers, transfers, discharges of soldiers for favor, and all the old abuses, which had embittered the life of General Scott in the days of Secretaries of War Marcy and Davis, were renewed. I called his attention to these facts, but without sensible effect. My office was under his in the old War Department, and one day I sent my aide-de-camp, Colonel Audenried, up to him with some message, and when he returned red as a beet, very much agitated, he asked me as a personal favor never again to send him to General Belknap. I inquired his reason, and he explained that he had been treated with a rudeness and discourtesy he had never seen displayed by any officer to a soldier. Colonel Audenried was one of the most polished gentlemen in the army, noted for his personal bearing and deportment, and I had some trouble to impress on him the patience necessary for the occasion, but I promised on future occasions to send some other or go myself. Things went on from bad to worse, till in 1870 I received from Mr. Hugh Campbell, of St. Louis, a personal friend and an honorable gentleman, a telegraphic message complaining that I had removed from his position Mr. Ward, post trader at Fort Laramie, with only a month in which to dispose of his large stock of goods, to make room for his successor.

It so happened that we of the Indian Peace Commission had been much indebted to this same trader, Ward, for advances of flour, sugar, and coffee, to provide for the Crow Indians, who had come down from their reservation on the Yellowstone to meet us in 1868, before our own supplies had been received. For a time I could not comprehend the nature of Mr. Campbell's complaint, so I telegraphed to the department commander, General C. C. Augur, at Omaha, to know if any such occurrence had happened, and the reasons therefor. I received a prompt answer that it was substantially true, and had been ordered by The Secretary of War. It so happened that during General Grant's command of the army Congress had given to the general of the army the appointment of "post-traders." He had naturally devolved it on the subordinate division and department commanders, but the legal power remained with the general of the army. I went up to the Secretary of War, showed him the telegraphic correspondence, and pointed out the existing law in the Revised Statutes. General Belknap was visibly taken aback, and explained that he had supposed the right of appointment rested with him, that Ward was an old rebel Democrat, etc.; whereas Ward had been in fact the sutler of Fort Laramie, a United States military post, throughout the civil war. I told him that I should revoke his orders, and leave the matter where it belonged, to the local council of administration and commanding officers. Ward was unanimously reelected and reinstated. He remained the trader of the post until Congress repealed the law, and gave back the power of appointment to the Secretary of War, when of course he had to go. But meantime he was able to make the necessary business arrangements which saved him and his partners the sacrifice which would have been necessary in the first instance. I never had any knowledge whatever of General Belknap's transactions with the traders at Fort Sill and Fort Lincoln which resulted in his downfall. I have never sought to ascertain his motives for breaking with me, because he knew I had always befriended him while under my military command, and in securing him his office of Secretary of War. I spoke frequently to President Grant of the growing tendency of his Secretary of War to usurp all the powers of the commanding general, which would surely result in driving me away. He as frequently promised to bring us together to agree upon a just line of separation of our respective offices, but never did.

Determined to bring the matter to an issue, I wrote the following letter:

HEADQUARTERS ARMY OF THE UNITED STATES,
WASHINGTON, D. C., August 17, 1870.

General W. W. BELKNAP, Secretary of War.

GENERAL: I must urgently and respectfully invite your attention when at leisure to a matter of deep interest to future commanding generals of the army more than to myself, of the imperative necessity of fixing and clearly defining the limits of the powers and duties of the general of the army or of whomsoever may succeed to the place of commander-in-chief.

The case is well stated by General Grant in his letter of January 29, 1866, to the Secretary of War, Mr. Stanton, hereto appended, and though I find no official answer recorded, I remember that General Grant told me that the Secretary of War had promptly assured him in conversation that he fully approved of his views as expressed in this letter.

At that time the subject was much discussed, and soon after Congress enacted the bill reviving the grade of general, which bill was approved July 25, 1866, and provided that the general, when commissioned, may be authorized under the direction and during the pleasure of the President to command the armies of the United States; and a few days after, viz., July 28, 1866, was enacted the law which defined the military peace establishment. The enacting clause reads: "That the military peace establishment of the United States shall hereafter consist of five regiments of artillery, ten regiments of cavalry, forty-five regiments of infantry, the professors and Corps of Cadets of the United States Military Academy, and such other forces as shall be provided for by this act, to be known as the army of the United States."

The act then recites in great detail all the parts of the army, making no distinction between the line and staff, but clearly makes each and every part an element of the whole.

Section 37 provides for a board to revise the army regulations and report; and declares that the regulations then in force, viz., those of 1863, should remain until Congress "shall act on said report;" and section 38 and last enacts that all laws and parts of laws inconsistent with the provisions of this act be and the same are hereby repealed.

Under the provisions of this law my predecessor, General Grant, did not hesitate to command and make orders to all parts of the army, the Military Academy, and staff, and it was under his advice that the new regulations were compiled in 1868 that drew the line more clearly between the high and responsible duties of the Secretary of War and the general of the army. He assured me many a time before I was called here to succeed him that he wanted me to perfect the distinction, and it was by his express orders that on assuming the command of the army I specifically placed the heads of the staff corps here in Washington in the exact relation to the army which they would bear to an army in the field.

I am aware that subsequently, in his orders of March 26th, he modified his former orders of March 5th, but only as to the heads of bureaus in Washington, who have, he told me, certain functions of office imposed on them by special laws of Congress, which laws, of course, override all orders and regulations, but I did not either understand from him in person, or from General Rawlins, at whose instance this order was made, that it was designed in any way to modify, alter, or change his purposes that division and department commanders, as well as the general of the army, should exercise the same command of the staff as they did of the line of the army.

I need not remind the Secretary that orders and reports are made to and from the Military Academy which the general does not even see, though the Military Academy is specifically named as a part of that army which he is required to command. Leaves of absence are granted, the stations of officers are changed, and other orders are now made directly to the army, not through the general, but direct through other officials and the adjutant-general.

So long as this is the case I surely do not command the army of the United States, and am not responsible for it.

I am aware that the confusion results from the fact that the thirty-seventh section of the act of July 28, 1866, clothes the army regulations of 1863 with the sanction of law, but the next section repeals all laws and parts of laws inconsistent with the provisions of this act. The regulations of 1863 are but a compilation of orders made prior to the war, when such men as Davis and Floyd took pleasure in stripping General Scott of even the semblance of power, and purposely reduced him to a cipher in the command of the army.

Not one word can be found in those regulations speaking of the duties of the lieutenant-general commanding the army, or defining a single act of authority rightfully devolving on him. Not a single mention is made of the rights and duties of a commander-in-chief of the army. He is ignored, and purposely, too, as a part of the programme resulting in the rebellion, that the army without a legitimate head should pass into the anarchy which these men were shaping for the whole country.

I invite your attention to the army regulations of 1847, when our best soldiers lived, among whom was your own father, and see paragraphs 48 and 49, page 8, and they are so important that I quote them entire:

"48. The military establishment is placed under the orders of the major-general commanding in chief in all that regards its discipline and military control. Its fiscal arrangements properly belong to the administrative departments of the staff and to the Treasury Department under the direction of the Secretary of War.

"49. The general of the army will watch over the economy of the service in all that relates to the expenditure of money, supply of arms, ordnance and ordnance stores, clothing, equipments, camp-equipage, medical and hospital stores, barracks, quarters, transportation, Military Academy, pay, and subsistence: in short, everything which enters into the expenses of the military establishment, whether personal or material. He will also see that the estimates for the military service are based on proper data, and made for the objects contemplated by law, and necessary to the due support and useful employment of the army. In carrying into effect these important duties, he will call to his counsel and assistance the staff, and those officers proper, in his opinion, to be employed in verifying and inspecting all the objects which may require attention. The rules and regulations established for the government of the army, and the laws relating to the military establishment, are the guides to the commanding general in the performance of his duties."

Why was this, or why was all mention of any field of duty for the head of the army left out of the army regulations? Simply because Jefferson Davis had a purpose, and absorbed to himself, as Secretary of War, as General Grant well says, all the powers of commander-in-chief. Floyd succeeded him, and the last regulations of 1863 were but a new compilation of their orders, hastily collected and published to supply a vast army with a new edition.

I contend that all parts of these regulations inconsistent with the law of July 28, 1866, are repealed.

I surely do not ask for any power myself, but I hope and trust, now when we have a military President and a military Secretary of War, that in the new regulations to be laid before Congress next session the functions and duties of the commander-in-chief will be so clearly marked out and defined that they may be understood by himself and the army at large.

I am, with great respect, your obedient servant,

W. T. SHERMAN, General.

[Inclosure.]

WASHINGTON, January 29, 1866.

Hon. E. M. STANTON, Secretary of War:

From the period of the difficulties between Major-General (now Lieutenant-General) Scott with Secretary Marcy, during the administration of President Polk, the command of the army virtually passed into the hands of the Secretary of War.

From that day to the breaking out of the rebellion the general-in-chief never kept his headquarters in Washington, and could not, consequently, with propriety resume his proper functions. To administer the affairs of the army properly, headquarters and the adjutant-general's office must be in the same place.

During the war, while in the field, my functions as commander of all the armies was never impaired, but were facilitated in all essential matters by the Administration and by the War Department. Now, however, that the war is over, and I have brought my head-quarters to the city, I find my present position embarrassing and, I think, out of place. I have been intending, or did intend, to make the beginning of the New Year the time to bring this matter before you, with the view of asking to have the old condition of affairs restored, but from diffidence about mentioning the matter have delayed. In a few words I will state what I conceive to be my duties and my place, and ask respectfully to be restored to them and it.

The entire adjutant-general's office should be under the entire control of the general-in-chief of the army. No orders should go to the army, or the adjutant-general, except through the general-in-chief. Such as require the action of the President would be laid before the Secretary of War, whose actions would be regarded as those of the President. In short, in my opinion, the general-in-chief stands between the President and the army in all official matters, and the Secretary of War is between the army (through the general-in-chief) and the President.

I can very well conceive that a rule so long disregarded could not, or would not, be restored without the subject being presented, and I now do so respectfully for your consideration.

U. S. GRANT, Lieutenant-General.

General Belknap never answered that letter.

In August, 1870, was held at Des Moines, Iowa, an encampment of old soldiers which I attended, en route to the Pacific, and at Omaha received this letter:

LONG BRANCH, New Jersey, August 18,1870.

General W. T. SHERMAN.

DEAR GENERAL: Your letter of the 7th inst. did not reach Long Branch until after I had left for St. Louis, and consequently is just before me for the first time. I do not know what changes recent laws, particularly the last army bill passed, make in the relations between the general of the army and the Secretary of War.

Not having this law or other statutes here, I cannot examine the subject now, nor would I want to without consultation with the Secretary of War. On our return to Washington I have no doubt but that the relations between the Secretary and yourself can be made pleasant, and the duties of each be so clearly defined as to leave no doubt where the authority of one leaves off and the other commences.

My own views, when commanding the army, were that orders to the army should go through the general. No changes should be made, however, either of the location of troops or officers, without the knowledge of the Secretary of War.

In peace, the general commanded them without reporting to the Secretary farther than he chose the specific orders he gave from time to time, but subjected himself to orders from the Secretary, the latter deriving his authority to give orders from the President. As Congress has the right, however, to make rules and regulations for the government of the army, rules made by them whether they are as they should be or not, will have to govern. As before stated, I have not examined the recent law.

Yours truly,

U. S. GRANT.

To which I replied:

OMAHA, NEBRASKA, September 2,1870.

General U. S. GRANT, Washington, D. C.

DEAR GENERAL: I have received your most acceptable letter of August 18th, and assure you that I am perfectly willing to abide by any decision you may make. We had a most enthusiastic meeting at Des Moines, and General Bellknap gave us a fine, finished address. I have concluded to go over to San Francisco to attend the annual celebration of the Pioneers, to be held on the 9th instant; from there I will make a short tour, aiming to get back to St. Louis by the 1st of October, and so on to Washington without unnecessary delay.

Conscious of the heavy burdens already on you, I should refrain from adding one ounce to your load of care, but it seems to me now is the time to fix clearly and plainly the field of duty for the Secretary of War and the commanding general of the army, so that we may escape the unpleasant controversy that gave so much scandal in General Scott's time, and leave to our successors a clear field.

No matter what the result, I promise to submit to whatever decision you may make. I also feel certain that General Belknap thinks he is simply executing the law as it now stands, but I am equally certain that he does not interpret the law reviving the grade of general, and that fixing the "peace establishment" of 1868, as I construe them.

For instance, I am supposed to control the discipline of the Military Academy as a part of the army, whereas General Belknap ordered a court of inquiry in the case of the colored cadet, made the detail, reviewed the proceedings, and made his order, without my knowing a word of it, except through the newspapers; and more recently, when I went to Chicago to attend to some division business, I found the inspector-general (Hardie) under orders from the Secretary of War to go to Montana on some claim business.

All I ask is that such orders should go through me. If all the staff-officers are subject to receive orders direct from the Secretary of War it will surely clash with the orders they may be in the act of executing from me, or from their immediate commanders.

I ask that General Belknap draw up some clear, well-defined rules for my action, that he show them to me before publication, that I make on them my remarks, and then that you make a final decision. I promise faithfully to abide by it, or give up my commission.

Please show this to General Belknap, and I will be back early in October. With great respect, your friend,

W. T. SHERMAN

I did return about October 15th, saw President Grant, who said nothing had been done in the premises, but that he would bring General Belknap and me together and settle this matter. Matters went along pretty much as usual till the month of August, 1871, when I dined at the Arlington with Admiral Alder and General Belknap. The former said he had been promoted to rear-admiral and appointed to command the European squadron, then at Villa Franca, near Nice, and that he was going out in the frigate Wabash, inviting me to go along. I had never been to Europe, and the opportunity was too tempting to refuse. After some preliminaries I agreed to go along, taking with me as aides-de-camp Colonel Audenried and Lieutenant Fred Grant. The Wabash was being overhauled at the Navy-Yard at Boston, and was not ready to sail till November, when she came to New-York, where we all embarked Saturday, November 11th.

I have very full notes of the whole trip, and here need only state that we went out to the Island of Madeira, and thence to Cadiz and Gibraltar. Here my party landed, and the Wabash went on to Villa Franca. From Gibraltar we made the general tour of Spain to Bordeaux, through the south of France to Marseilles, Toulon, etc., to Nice, from which place we rejoined the Wabash and brought ashore our baggage.

From Nice we went to Genoa, Turin, the Mont Cenis Tunnel, Milan, Venice, etc., to Rome. Thence to Naples, Messina, and Syracuse, where we took a steamer to Malta. From Malta to Egypt and Constantinople, to Sebastopol, Poti, and Tiflis. At Constantinople and Sebastopol my party was increased by Governor Curtin, his son, and Mr. McGahan.

It was my purpose to have reached the Caspian, and taken boats to the Volga, and up that river as far as navigation would permit, but we were dissuaded by the Grand-Duke Michael, Governor-General of the Caucasas, and took carriages six hundred miles to Taganrog, on the Sea of Azof, to which point the railroad system of Russia was completed. From Taganrog we took cars to Moscow and St. Petersburg. Here Mr. Curtin and party remained, he being our Minister at that court; also Fred Grant left us to visit his aunt at Copenhagen. Colonel Audenried and I then completed the tour of interior Europe, taking in Warsaw, Berlin, Vienna, Switzerland, France, England, Scotland, and Ireland, embarking for home in the good steamer Baltic, Saturday, September 7, 1872, reaching Washington, D. C., September 22d. I refrain from dwelling on this trip, because it would swell this chapter beyond my purpose.

When I regained my office I found matters unchanged since my departure, the Secretary of War exercising all the functions of commander-in-chief, and I determined to allow things to run to their necessary conclusion. In 1873 my daughter Minnie also made a trip to Europe, and I resolved as soon as she returned that I would simply move back to St. Louis to execute my office there as best I could. But I was embarrassed by being the possessor of a large piece of property in Washington on I Street, near the corner of Third, which I could at the time neither sell nor give away. It came into my possession as a gift from friends in New York and Boston, who had purchased it of General Grant and transferred to me at the price of $65,000.

The house was very large, costly to light, heat, and maintain, and Congress had reduced my pay four or five thousand dollars a year, so that I was gradually being impoverished. Taxes, too, grew annually, from about four hundred dollars a year to fifteen hundred, besides all sorts of special taxes.

Finding myself caught in a dilemma, I added a new hall, and made out of it two houses, one of which I occupied, and the other I rented, and thus matters stood in 1873-'74. By the agency of Mr. Hall, a neighbor and broker, I effected a sale of the property to the present owner, Mr. Emory, at a fair price, accepting about half payment in notes, and the other half in a piece of property on E Street, which I afterward exchanged for a place in Cite Brilliante, a suburb of St. Louis, which I still own. Being thus foot-loose, and having repeatedly notified President Grant of my purpose, I wrote the Secretary of War on the 8th day of May, 1874, asking the authority of the President and the War Department to remove my headquarters to St. Louis.

On the 11th day of May General Belknap replied that I had the assent of the President and himself, inclosing the rough draft of an order to accomplish this result, which I answered on the 15th, expressing my entire satisfaction, only requesting delay in the publication of the orders till August or September, as I preferred to make the changes in the month of October.

On the 3d of September these orders were made:

WAR DEPARTMENT, ADJUTANT-GENERAL'S OFFICE, WASHINGTON, September 8, 1874.

General Orders No. 108.

With the assent of the President, and at the request of the General, the headquarters of the armies of the United States will be established at St. Louis, Missouri, in the month of October next.

The regulations and orders now governing the functions of the General of the Army, and those in relation to transactions of business with the War Department and its bureaus, will continue in force.

By order of the Secretary of War:

E. D. TOWNSEND, Adjutant-General.

Our daughter Minnie was married October 1, 1874, to Thomas W. Fitch, United States Navy, and we all forthwith packed up and regained our own house at St. Louis, taking an office on the corner of Tenth and Locust Streets. The only staff I brought with me were the aides allowed by law, and, though we went through the forms of "command," I realized that it was a farce, and it did not need a prophet to foretell it would end in a tragedy. We made ourselves very comfortable, made many pleasant excursions into the interior, had a large correspondence, and escaped the mortification of being slighted by men in Washington who were using their temporary power for selfish ends.

Early in March, 1676, appeared in all the newspapers of the day the sensational report from Washington that Secretary of War Belknap had been detected in selling sutlerships in the army; that he had confessed it to Representative Blackburn, of Kentucky; that he had tendered his resignation, which had been accepted by the President; and that he was still subject to impeachment,--would be impeached and tried by the Senate. I was surprised to learn that General Belknap was dishonest in money matters, for I believed him a brave soldier, and I sorely thought him honest; but the truth was soon revealed from Washington, and very soon after I received from Judge Alphonso Taft, of Cincinnati, a letter informing me that he had been appointed Secretary of War, and should insist on my immediate return to Washington. I answered that I was ready to go to Washington, or anywhere, if assured of decent treatment.

I proceeded to Washington, when, on the 6th of April, were published these orders:

General Orders No. 28.

The following orders of the President of the United States are hereby promulgated for the information and guidance of all concerned:

The headquarters of the army are hereby reestablished at Washington City, and all orders and instructions relative to military operations or affecting the military control and discipline of the army issued by the President through the Secretary of War, shall be promulgated through the General of the Army, and the departments of the Adjutant-General and the Inspector-General shall report to him, and be under his control in all matters relating thereto.

By order of the Secretary of War:

This was all I had ever asked; accordingly my personal staff were brought back to Washington, where we resumed our old places; only I did not, for some time, bring back the family, and then only to a rented house on Fifteenth Street, which we occupied till we left Washington for good. During the period from 1876 to 1884 we had as Secretaries of War in succession, the Hon's. Alphonso Taft, J. D. Cameron, George W. McCrary, Alexander Ramsey, and R. T. Lincoln, with each and all of whom I was on terms of the most intimate and friendly relations.

And here I will record of Washington that I saw it, under the magic hand of Alexander R. Shepherd, grow from a straggling, ill-paved city, to one of the cleanest, most beautiful, and attractive cities of the whole world. Its climate is salubrious, with as much sunshine as any city of America. The country immediately about it is naturally beautiful and romantic, especially up the Potomac, in the region of the Great Falls; and, though the soil be poor as compared with that of my present home, it is susceptible of easy improvement and embellishment. The social advantages cannot be surpassed even in London, Paris, or Vienna; and among the resident population, the members of the Supreme Court, Senate, House of Representatives, army, navy, and the several executive departments, may be found an intellectual class one cannot encounter in our commercial and manufacturing cities. The student may, without tax and without price, have access, in the libraries of Congress and of the several departments, to books of every nature and kind; and the museums of natural history are rapidly approaching a standard of comparison with the best of the world. Yet it is the usual and proper center of political intrigue, from which the army especially should keep aloof, because the army must be true and faithful to the powers that be, and not be subjected to a temptation to favor one or other of the great parties into which our people have divided, and will continue to divide, it may be, with advantage to the whole.

It would be a labor of love for me, in this connection, to pay a tribute of respect, by name, to the many able and most patriotic officers with whom I was so long associated as the commanding generals of military divisions and departments, as well as staff-officers; but I must forego the temptation, because of the magnitude of the subject, certain that each and all of them will find biographers better posted and more capable than myself; and I would also like to make recognition of the hundreds of acts of most graceful hospitality on the part of the officers and families at our remote military posts in the days, of the "adobe," the "jacal," and "dug-out," when a board floor and a shingle roof were luxuries expected by none except the commanding officer. I can see, in memory, a beautiful young city-bred lady, who had married a poor second-lieutenant, and followed him to his post on the plains, whose quarters were in a "dug-out" ten feet by about fifteen, seven feet high, with a dirt roof; four feet of the walls were the natural earth, the other three of sod, with holes for windows and corn-sacks for curtains. This little lady had her Saratoga trunk, which was the chief article of furniture; yet, by means of a rug on the ground-floor, a few candle-boxes covered with red cotton calico for seats, a table improvised out of a barrel-head, and a fireplace and chimney excavated in the back wall or bank, she had transformed her "hole in the ground" into a most attractive home for her young warrior husband; and she entertained me with a supper consisting of the best of coffee, fried ham, cakes, and jellies from the commissary, which made on my mind an impression more lasting than have any one of the hundreds of magnificent banquets I have since attended in the palaces and mansions of our own and foreign lands.

Still more would I like to go over again the many magnificent trips made across the interior plains, mountains, and deserts before the days of the completed Pacific Railroad, with regular "Doughertys" drawn by four smart mules, one soldier with carbine or loaded musket in hand seated alongside the driver; two in the back seat with loaded rifles swung in the loops made for them; the lightest kind of baggage, and generally a bag of oats to supplement the grass, and to attach the mules to their camp. With an outfit of two, three, or four of such, I have made journeys of as much as eighteen hundred miles in a single season, usually from post to post, averaging in distance about two hundred miles a week, with as much regularity as is done today by the steam-car its five hundred miles a day; but those days are gone, and, though I recognize the great national advantages of the more rapid locomotion, I cannot help occasionally regretting the change. One instance in 1866 rises in my memory, which I must record: Returning eastward from Fort Garland, we ascended the Rocky Mountains to the Sangre-de-Cristo Pass. The road descending the mountain was very rough and sidling. I got out with my rifle, and walked ahead about four miles, where I awaited my "Dougherty." After an hour or so I saw, coming down the road, a wagon; and did not recognize it as my own till quite near. It had been upset, the top all mashed in, and no means at hand for repairs. I consequently turned aside from the main road to a camp of cavalry near the Spanish Peaks, where we were most hospitably received by Major A——and his accomplished wife. They occupied a large hospital-tent, which about a dozen beautiful greyhounds were free to enter at will. The ambulance was repaired, and the next morning we renewed our journey, escorted by the major and his wife on their fine saddle-horses.

They accompanied us about ten miles of the way; and, though age has since begun to tell on them, I shall ever remember them in their pride and strength as they galloped alongside our wagons down the long slopes of the Spanish Peaks in a driving snow-storm.

And yet again would it be a pleasant task to recall the many banquets and feasts of the various associations of officers and soldiers, who had fought the good battles of the civil war, in which I shared as a guest or host, when we could indulge in a reasonable amount of glorification at deeds done and recorded, with wit, humor, and song; these when memory was fresh, and when the old soldiers were made welcome to the best of cheer and applause in every city and town of the land. But no! I must hurry to my conclusion, for this journey has already been sufficiently prolonged.

I had always intended to divide time with my natural successor, General P. H. Sheridan, and early, notified him that I should about the year 1884 retire from the command of the army, leaving him about an equal period of time for the highest office in the army. It so happened that Congress had meantime by successive "enactments" cut down the army to twenty-five thousand men, the usual strength of a corps d'armee, the legitimate command of a lieutenant-general. Up to 1882 officers not disabled by wounds or sickness could only avail themselves of the privileges of retirement on application, after thirty years of service, at sixty-two years of age; but on the 30th of June, 1882, a bill was passed which, by operation of the law itself, compulsorily retired all army officers, regardless of rank, at the age of sixty-four years. At the time this law was debated in Congress, I was consulted by Senators and others in the most friendly manner, representing that, if I wanted it, an exception could justly and easily be made in favor of the general and lieutenant-general, whose commissions expired with their lives; but I invariably replied that I did not ask or expect an exception in my case, because no one could know or realize when his own mental and physical powers began to decline. I remembered well the experience of Gil Blas with the Bishop of Granada, and favored the passage of the law fixing a positive period for retirement, to obviate in the future special cases of injustice such as I had seen in the recent past. The law was passed, and every officer then knew the very day on which he must retire, and could make his preparations accordingly. In my own case the law was liberal in the extreme, being "without reduction in his current pay and allowances."

I would be sixty-four years old on the 8th of February, 1884, a date inconvenient to move, and not suited to other incidents; so I resolved to retire on the 1st day of November, 1883, to resume my former home at St. Louis, and give my successor ample time to meet the incoming Congress, But, preliminary thereto, I concluded to make one more tour of the continent, going out to the Pacific by the Northern route, and returning by that of the thirty-fifth parallel. This we accomplished, beginning at Buffalo, June 21st, and ending at St. Louis, Missouri, September 30, 1883, a full and most excellent account of which can be found in Colonel Tidball's "Diary," which forms part of the report of the General of the Army for the year 1883.

Before retiring also, as was my duty, I desired that my aides-de-camp who had been so faithful and true to me should not suffer by my act. All were to retain the rank of colonels of cavalry till the last day, February 8, 1884; but meantime each secured places, as follows:

Colonel O. M. Poe was lieutenant-colonel of the Engineer Corps United States Army, and was by his own choice assigned to Detroit in charge of the engineering works on the Upper Lakes, which duty was most congenial to him.

Colonel J. C. Tidball was assigned to command the Artillery School at Fort Monroe, by virtue of his commission as lieutenant-colonel, Third Artillery, a station for which he was specially qualified.

Colonel John E. Tourtelotte was then entitled to promotion to major of the Seventh Cavalry, a rank in which he could be certain of an honorable command.

The only remaining aide-de-camp was Colonel John M. Bacon, who utterly ignored self in his personal attachment to me. He was then a captain of the Ninth Cavalry, but with almost a certainty of promotion to be major of the Seventh before the date of my official retirement, which actually resulted. The last two accompanied me to St. Louis, and remained with me to the end. Having previously accomplished the removal of my family to St. Louis, and having completed my last journey to the Pacific, I wrote the following letter:

HEADQUARTERS ARMY UNITED STATES,
WASHINGTON, D. C., October 8, 1883.

Hon. R. T. LINCOLN, Secretary of War.

SIR: By the act of Congress, approved June 30, 1882, all army-officers are retired on reaching the age of sixty-four years. If living, I will attain that age on the 8th day of February, 1884; but as that period of the year is not suited for the changes necessary on my retirement, I have contemplated anticipating the event by several months, to enable the President to meet these changes at a more convenient season of the year, and also to enable my successor to be in office before the assembling of the next Congress.

I therefore request authority to turn over the command of the army to Lieutenant-General Sheridan on the 1st day of November, 1883, and that I be ordered to my home at St. Louis, Missouri, there to await the date of my legal retirement; and inasmuch as for

194

a long time I must have much correspondence about war and official matters, I also ask the favor to have with me for a time my two present aides-de-camp, Colonels J. E. Tourtelotte and J. M. Bacon.

The others of my personal staff, viz., Colonels O. M. Poe and J. C. Tidball, have already been assigned to appropriate duties in their own branches of the military service, the engineers and artillery. All should retain the rank and pay as aides-de-camp until February 8,1884. By or before the 1st day of November I can complete all official reports, and believe I can surrender the army to my successor in good shape and condition, well provided in all respects, and distributed for the best interests of the country.

I am grateful that my physical and mental-strength remain unimpaired by years, and am thankful for the liberal provision made by Congress for my remaining years, which will enable me to respond promptly to any call the President may make for my military service or judgment as long as I live. I have the honor to be your obedient servant,

W. T. SHERMAN, General.

The answer was:

WAR DEPARTMENT,
WASHINGTON CITY, October 10, 1888.

General W. T. SHERMAN, Washington, D. C.

GENERAL: I have submitted to the President your letter of the 8th instant, requesting that you be relieved of the command of the army on the 1st of November next, as a more convenient time for making the changes in military commands which must follow your retirement from active service, than would be the date of your retirement under the law.

In signifying his approval of your request, the President directs me to express to you his earnest hope that there may be given you many years of health and happiness in which to enjoy the gratitude of your fellow-citizens, well earned by your most distinguished public services.

It will give me pleasure to comply with your wishes respecting your aides-de-camp, and the necessary orders will be duly issued.

I have the honor to be, General, your obedient servant,

ROBERT T. LINCOLN, Secretary of War.

On the 27th day of October I submitted to the Secretary of War, the Hon. R. T. Lincoln, my last annual report, embracing among other valuable matters the most interesting and condensed report of Colonel O. M. Poe, A. D. C., of the "original conception, progress, and completion" of the four great transcontinental railways, which have in my judgment done more for the subjugation and civilization of the Indians than all other causes combined, and have made possible the utilization of the vast area of pasture lands and mineral regions which before were almost inaccessible, for my agency in which I feel as much pride as for my share in any of the battles in which I took part.

Promptly on the 1st of November were made the following general orders, and the command of the Army of the United States passed from me to Lieutenant-General P. H. Sheridan, with as little ceremony as would attend the succession of the lieutenant-colonel of a regiment to his colonel about to take a leave of absence:

HEADQUARTERS OF THE ARMY
WASHINGTON, November 1, 1885.

General Orders No. 77:

By and with the consent of the President, as contained in General Orders No. 71, of October 13, 1883, the undersigned relinquishes command of the Army of the United States.

In thus severing relations which have hitherto existed between us, he thanks all officers and men for their fidelity to the high trust imposed on them during his official life, and will, in his retirement, watch with parental solicitude their progress upward in the noble profession to which they have devoted their lives.

W. T. SHERMAN, General.

Official: R. C. DRUM, Adjutant-General.

HEADQUARTERS OF THE ARMY
WASHINGTON, November 1, 1885.

General Orders No. 78:

In obedience to orders of the President, promulgated in General Orders No. 71, October 13, 1883, from these headquarters, the undersigned hereby assumes command of the Army of the United States....

P. H. SHERIDAN, Lieutenant-General.

Official: R. C. DRUM, adjutant-General.

After a few days in which to complete my social visits, and after a short visit to my daughter, Mrs. A. M. Thackara, at Philadelphia, I quietly departed for St. Louis; and, as I hope, for "good and all," the family was again reunited in the same place from which we were driven by a cruel, unnecessary civil war initiated in Charleston Harbor in April, 1861.

On the 8th day of February, 1884; I was sixty-four years of age, and therefore retired by the operation of the act of Congress, approved June 30, 1882; but the fact was gracefully noticed by President Arthur in the following general orders:

WAR DEPARTMENT, ADJUTANT GENERAL'S OFFICE,
WASHINGTON, February 8, 1984.

The following order of the President is published to the army:

EXECUTIVE MANSION, February 8, 1884.

General William T. Sherman, General of the Army, having this day reached the age of sixty-four years, is, in accordance with the law, placed upon the retired list of the army, without reduction in his current pay and allowances.

The announcement of the severance from the command of the army of one who has been for so many years its distinguished chief, can but awaken in the minds, not only of the army, but of the people of the United States, mingled emotions of regret and gratitude-- regret at the withdrawal from active military service of an officer whose lofty sense of duty has been a model for all soldiers since he first entered the army in July, 1840; and gratitude, freshly awakened, for the services of incalculable value rendered by him in the war for the Union, which his great military genius and daring did so much to end.

The President deems this a fitting occasion to give expression, in this manner, to the gratitude felt toward General Sherman by his fellow-citizens, and to the hope that Providence may grant him many years of health and happiness in the relief from the active duties of his profession.

By order of the Secretary of War:

CHESTER A. ARTHUR.

R. C. DRUM, Adjutant-General.

To which I replied:

St. Louis, February 9, 1884.

His Excellency CHESTER A. ARTHUR, President of the United States.

DEAR SIR: Permit me with a soldier's frankness to thank you personally for the handsome compliment bestowed in general orders of yesterday, which are reported in the journals of the day. To me it was a surprise and a most agreeable one. I had supposed the actual date of my retirement would form a short paragraph in the common series of special orders of the War Department; but as the honored Executive of our country has made it the occasion for his own hand to pen a tribute of respect and affection to an officer passing from the active stage of life to one of ease and rest, I can only say I feel highly honored, and congratulate myself in thus rounding out my record of service in a manner most gratifying to my family and friends. Not only this, but I feel sure, when the orders of yesterday are read on parade to the regiments and garrisons of the United States, many a young hero will tighten his belt, and resolve anew to be brave and true to the starry flag, which we of our day have carried safely through one epoch of danger, but which may yet be subjected to other trials, which may demand similar sacrifices, equal fidelity and courage, and a larger measure of intelligence. Again thanking you for so marked a compliment, and reciprocating the kind wishes for the future,

I am, with profound respect, your friend and servant,

W. T. SHERMAN, General.

      This I construe as the end of my military career. In looking back upon the past I can only say, with millions of others, that I have done many things I should not have done, and have left undone still more which ought to have been done; that I can see where hundreds of opportunities have been neglected, but on the whole am content; and feel sure that I can travel this broad country of ours, and be each night the welcome guest in palace or cabin; and, as

    "all the world's stage,
    And all the men and women merely players,"
I claim the privilege to ring down the curtain.
W. T. SHERMAN, General.